The (

The (

The Charged Void: Architecture

Alison and Peter Smithson

THE MONACELLI PRESS

Editorial coordination and design: Sze Tsung Leong and Chuihua Judy Chung

First published in the United States of America in 2001 by

The Monacelli Press, Inc.

10 East 92nd Street, New York, New York 10128.

Library of Congress Cataloging-in-Publication Data

Smithson, Alison Margaret.

The charged void—architecture / Alison and Peter Smithson.

p. cm.

ISBN 1-58093-050-6

1. Smithson, Alison Margaret—Themes, motives. 2. Smithson, Peter—Themes,
motives. 3. Architecture, Modern—20th century. 4. Modern movement
(Architecture)—Influence. I. Smithson, Peter. II. Title.

NA997.S57 A4 2000

720'.92'2—dc21   00-033962

Production assistance: Eleanor Chung, Jeannie Kim, Hunter Tura, Christopher Chew

Printed in China

opposite: Alison and Peter Smithson in the workroom of their Chelsea house
at 46 Limerston Street, London.

Contents

Intention 10

Evolution 12

Observation 14

1 Simple Inheritors
1947...

Town Planning Studies *(1946–48)* 20

Crematorium at Gosforth Park *(1947)* 21

Royal Academy *(1949)* 24

Fitzwilliam Museum *(1948–49)* 28

Vertical Feature and Restaurant, Festival of Britain *(1949)* 33

2 Transmissions and Connections
extending the polemic of the Heroic period, 1950...

Hunstanton Secondary Modern School *(1949–54)* 40

Coventry Cathedral *(1950–51)* 68

Limerston Street *(1953–61)* 81

3 Graphics of Movement
*the comprehension of the city's structure
through its patterns of movement, 1952...*

Golden Lane *(1952)* 86

Colville Place *(1952)* 96

Offices for the Electricity Board, Kampala *(1952–53)* 98

House Extension, Alderbury *(1953)* 102

One-Thousand-Square-Foot House *(1952–53)* 103

Cheddar House of Cheese *(1955)* 104

Doha Hospital *(1953)* 105

Sheffield University *(1953)* 108

4 Structuring of Spaces
*the interaction between the existing
and the added, 1953...*

'Parallel of Life and Art' Exhibition *(1953)* 118

Bates' Burrows Lea Farm *(1953–55)* 124

Five Projects for 'Housing Appropriate to the Valley Section' *(1954–56)*: 130

Isolate: Bates' Burrows Lea Farm 131

Hamlet: Galleon Cottages 134

Village: Fold Houses 135

Town: Close Houses 136

City: Terraced Crescent Housing 138

Chance Glass Flat and Mammoth Terrace House Conversion/Renewal *(1953–56)* 140

Crematorium at Kirkcaldy *(1954)* 142

Caro House *(1954–91)* 143

Rumble Villa *(1954)* 144

Bark Place Mews *(1954–56)* 146

Monument on the Goodwin Sands and a Church Sort of Place *(1955)* 148

Pierced Wall Structure *(1955)* 149

Sugden House *(1955–56)* 150

Hot Springs *(1955)* 157

5   Conglomerate Ordering

a sensed naturalness in an ordering of a built fabric . . .

House of the Future *(1955–56)* 162
Patio and Pavilion, 'This Is Tomorrow' Exhibition *(1956)* 178
Sydney Opera House *(1956)* 188

Appliance Houses *(1956–58)*: 190
Snowball House 192
Bread House 193
Cubicle House or Cupboard House 193
Portico Row and the 'Wareite' or White 'Formica' House 194
The Strip House 195
Provençal House 196

Cordell Studio House *(1957)* 197
English Climate House *(1957)* 198
Berlin Hauptstadt *(1957)* 200
Wokingham Infants School *(1958)* 206
Langside College of Further Education *(1958)* 212
Paolozzi Studio House *(1959)* 216
Retirement House *(1959)* 218

6   Pavilion and Route

the architectural implications of this
theme of our urban structuring . . .

Wayland Young Pavilion, Bayswater *(1959–82)* 224
Churchill College *(1959)* 230
Folly . . . A 'Solar' Pavilion, Upper Lawn *(1959–82)* 238
The Economist Building *(1959–64)* 248
Losey House *(1959–61)* 280
Cliff House *(1959–61)* 281
Redington Road *(1960)* 282
Seafront Flats *(1960)* 283
Iraqi House *(1960–61)* 284
Steilshoop *(1961)* 288
Priory Walk *(1961–71)* 289
Mehringplatz *(1962)* 292
Robin Hood Gardens *(1966–72)* 296
Occupational Health Clinic *(1962–64)* 314
'Painting and Sculpture of a Decade, 1954–1964' Exhibition *(1963–64)* 316

7   Layers of Fabric, Layers of Meaning

these reflective meanings, most dear to the
European architect, are seemingly more private
to architects than ever intended or ever before . . .

'Extensions of Man' Exhibition *(1962)* 326
British Embassy, Brasilia *(1964–68)* 328
Burleigh Lane Houses *(1965–66)* 336
Crispin Hall *(1965–66)* 338
Garden Building, St. Hilda's College, Oxford *(1967–70)* 340
Wedding in the City *(1968)* 352
Government Offices, Kuwait *(1970)* 356
New Model House *(1971)* 366
Married Graduate Flats and Squash Courts, Queen's College, Oxford *(1971)* 367
Gilston Road, South Kensington *(1971–)* 368
Cherry Garden Pier *(1972–76, 1983)* 369
Battlebridge Basin *(1972–74)* 372

8   The Treillage'd Space   Lucas Headquarters *(1973–74)*   380
    something of a return to our first   'A Line of Trees . . . A Steel Structure' Exhibition *(1975, 1976)*   386
    interest in the steel structure . . .   Magdalen College, Oxford *(1974)*   388
    the wood structure, the built grove,   Adalbergstrasse *(1975)*   392
    the grown line of trees . . .   'Sticks and Stones' Exhibition *(1976)*   393
                                              The Yellow House at an Intersection *(1976)*   394
                                            Solar-Energy-Collecting Pyramid, Giza *(1976)*   396
                                                                Landwehrkanal *(1976)*   397
                                             Riverside Apartments, Millbank *(1976–77)*   398
                                    Anil Avenue Commercial Offices, Khartoum *(1976–77)*   402

9   Variable-Density Plans, Variable-Density Sections   Cubitt Houses *(1977)*   408
    were it achievable, a radical break with the   Llangennith Cluster Housing *(1977)*   409
    all-over density inherited from the Heroic period . . .

                                                             Landscape into Art *(1977)*:   410
                                                                  Swinging Elland   411
                                                               Kingsbury Lookouts   412
                                                                      Tees Pudding   414
                                         The Slaggie Eleven of the Spenymoor Slag Heaps   415
                                                             Skateboard Junction   416
                                       Kelvingrove Art Gallery and Museum Approach   417

                                       Leafy Arbours over the Verbindungskanal *(1977)*   418
                                                              Cookies' Nook *(1977)*   419
                                            A House with Two Gantries *(1977)*   420

10 The Harnessing of Light   Pahlavi National Library *(1977–78)*   426
    the visits most people make   Walk in the Dry Passages and New West End to Worcester Cathedral *(1977–78)*   432
    to places of hot sun and shadow   Colleges' Gate, Colleges' Path, and Distance Stones, Urbino *(1979–83)*   436
    have, over thirty years,   Amenity Building, University of Bath *(1978–80, 1984–85)*   438
    changed attitudes to light,   Melbourne's Magic Mountains *(1979–80)*   444
    to reflective qualities . . .   Damascus Gate *(1979–81)*   446
    maybe ultimately to the pleasures of the underlit . . .   'Twenty-Four Doors to Christmas' Exhibition *(1979)*   448

11 Interval   Second Arts Building, University of Bath *(1979–81)*   456
    to do with rightful spheres of influence,   Der Berlinerbaum *(1980)*   468
    space for each to be its own thing . . .   Christmas ☥ Hogmanay *(1980–81)*   471
    ultimately the sense of territory,
    respect for another's sense of territory,
    which is not only the ground but also spatial,
    to do with sense of overlooking,
    of unbreathed air, blocking of sunlight,
    and so, shade and shadow . . .

12 Sun Acceptance/Energy Containment   Arts Barn, University of Bath *(1980–81, 1990)*   476
    and the signals of response . . .   Lützowstrasse Housing *(1980)*   484
                                                       Lützowstrasse Apartments for the Elderly *(1980)*   490
                                                                  Lützowstrasse Youth Centre *(1980)*   491
                                                             Lützowstrasse Child-Care Centre *(1980)*   492
                                                                            National Gallery *(1982)*   496
                                                                       Parc de la Villette *(1982)*   502

13 Sensibility to Car Movement   Communal Houses on Two Sites, Urban and Rural, Delft *(1982–83)*   514
    car movement has changed   Second Polytechnic, Hong Kong *(1982)*   516
    our inherited view   Porta Camollia, Siena *(1983)*   517
    of the landscapes and   School of Architecture and Building Engineering, University of Bath *(1982–88)*   518
    cities of Europe . . .   Twenty-First-Century Tenement, Maryhill *(1984)*   536

14 Roofs and Ways   Animal House, University of Bath *(1981)*   544
    two characteristics of 'conglomerate ordering',   Area di Pré, Genova *(1981)*   545
    a phrase invented in 1983 to describe formulations   Come Deck the Hall *(1981)*   546
    that were coming into being in our work . . .   Porch to University Hall, University of Bath *(1983)*   547
                                                                         Bath as a Fringed Mat *(1983)*   548
                                                                     Agitation of Surface, Siena *(1985)*   550
                                                               Restoration of Territory, Rackève *(1985)*   551
                                                                                Axel's Porch *(1986)*   552

15 Outside Inside   The Toilet Tree, Tecta *(1986–90)*   560
    paying attention, outside inside . . .   Triangle Workshop *(1987)*   562
                                                                                Janus, Siena *(1987)*   563
                                                                     Bibliotheca Alexandrina *(1989)*   564
                                                                                 Tecta Paths *(1990)*   571
                                                                            Riverbank Window *(1990)*   572
                                                                             Hexenhaus Holes *(1990)*   573
                                                                         Tecta Canteen Porch *(1990)*   574
                                                                              Acropolis Place *(1990)*   576
                                                                         Hexenbesenraum *(1990–96)*   584
                                                                             Beverungen Roof *(1990)*   588
                                                                             Brodia Road *(1990–95)*   589
                                                                            Deodar Road *(1991–99)*   590
                                                                     Tischleindeckdich *(1992–93)*   592
                                                                            Tecta Yard Gates *(1992)*   594
                                                                           Porter House *(1993–95)*   595

                                                                                          Attributions   596
                                                                                                 Index   598

Intention

In calling our collected works *The Charged Void: Architecture*, we are thinking of architecture's capacity to charge the space around it with an energy which can join up with other energies, influence the nature of things that might come . . . a capacity we can feel and act upon, but cannot necessarily describe or record.

—PS, 1992

Our intention has always been—consciously since the Doorn Manifesto in 1954—to turn architecture towards particularity . . . of place, person, activity: the form to arise from these.

That is why there has been so much effort . . . projects, histories, novels, films, essays, furniture, exhibitions.

To use a military analogy, the realised buildings are objectives we have taken; they are not the intention of the war.

It has been a big effort because buildings, as objects to be copied from books, have been with us since printing, since the 1400s.

550 years, say twenty-two generations . . . the flywheel effect of all those years!

1954 to now is only two generations to set against those twenty-two.

—PS, 1997

Evolution

We write—and publish—in an attempt to help architects who intend to build to make another 'jump' themselves. After the architect is dead, one receives another sort of 'catalogue', with every scrap of paper interpreted by historians. But building architects ask of the detritus of a working, thinking life completely different kinds of questions that wish to receive totally different kinds of answers.

—AS, 1992

In this volume, small essays introduce each theme as it begins its run: the works are illustrated in date order where a few paragraphs describe the essence of each.

—AS, 1982

The 'essence' is usually taken from the texts of the projects when they were made, so that afterthoughts as to intention are eliminated.

The first typescript is dated 1974. The texts were assembled and the introductory small essays written by Alison Smithson until her death in 1993.

This date has been taken as the cut-off point, although the completion of some of the projects occurred later.

—PS, 1999

Observation

During the process of final selection of the images for *The Charged Void: Architecture,* one became conscious that the special natures of the architectural works are somewhat incomprehensible without some understanding of the urban ideas that sustain them. But, surely, these can be deduced.

—PS, 1997

A+PS in the backyard at 32 Doughty Street, Bloomsbury, at the time of
working at the London County Council. Theo Crosby, September 1949.

1 Simple Inheritors

1947 . . .

Town Planning Studies *(1946–48)*   20

Crematorium at Gosforth Park *(1947)*   21

Royal Academy *(1949)*   24

Fitzwilliam Museum *(1948–49)*   28

Vertical Feature and Restaurant, Festival of Britain *(1949)*   33

from a fresco by Mantegna

As students—respectively, 1944 to 1949 and 1939 to 1948—we were the conscious inheritors of three European architectural languages:

. . . the Swedish—and related, war-interrupted, Danish—social architecture, whose character is equable, contributory: a message principally received through Gunnar Asplund;*

. . . Le Corbusier, up to his African years (obviously, then not yet known about), which included his first conch-shell museum studies;

. . . the first works of Mies van der Rohe at the Illinois Institute of Technology in Chicago, supported by the timely publication of his European works.

These sources are self-evident in the respective architecture school theses and in the final project by PS at the Royal Academy Schools, 1947 . . .

* *Gunnar Asplund, Arkitekt 1885–1940* (Stockholm: AB Tidskriften Byggmastaren, 1943).

opposite: Detail after painting by Mantegna. Copied as a day-sketch design: its chimneys will influence Golden Lane; its transient decoration—by the daily use of space—sets the theme for the 1950s. AS, 1947.

Study by PS undertaken in Department of Town Planning, University of Durham in Newcastle, academic years 1946–48.

All the studies towards the final examination of the Town Planning Institute were heavily influenced by 1940s Swedish town extensions, then the only new places in Europe to be experienced on the ground. Considered retrospectively, it must have been in Sweden where the change of grouping characteristics of squarish towers effected by knocking off the corners came to be observed . . . to appear later in the Hauptstadt, in the Economist Building, and so on . . . to become the 'charged void', not the street or any other urban-form that already had a name.

General plan. PS, 1948.

Crematorium at Gosforth Park, Newcastle

Thesis by PS, Department of Architecture, University of Durham in Newcastle, academic year ending summer 1947.

The technology has to be muted; the space must be liberating and nondenominational, yet capable of chameleon-like change for acquisition by a particular religious group, perhaps for barely an hour. The fabric has, therefore, to be in a language without direct connections: this is a first attempt at an anonymous, calm group, so placed within a park that the natural scene predominates.

Heavily influenced by Gunnar Asplund's crematorium in the South Cemetery, Stockholm.

Site plan: Again the Swedish influence, particularly the work of Asplund, is obvious even in the draughting technique. PS, 1947.

A CREMATORIUM IN GOSFORTH PARK

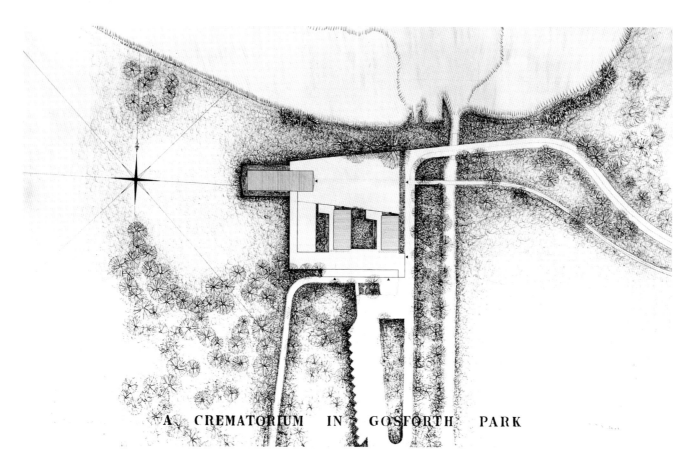

A CREMATORIUM IN GOSFORTH PARK

Detail layout plan. PS, 1947.

Plan of basement. PS, 1947.

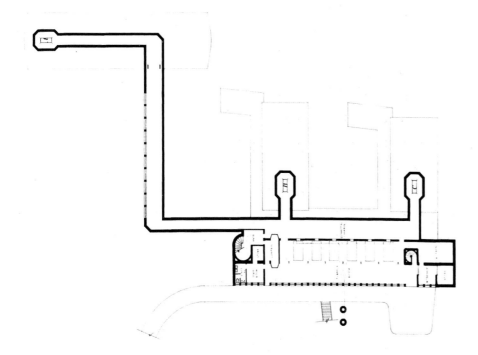

A CREMATORIUM IN GOSFORTH PARK

South elevation. PS, 1947.

Perspective view across lake. PS, 1947.

A CREMATORIUM IN GOSFORTH PARK

View from North across Lake

Thesis by AS, Department of Architecture, University of Durham in Newcastle, academic year ending summer 1949.

Already the impulse to hollow out the site to allow the various flows of visitors, staff, exhibits, service to sweetly interweave: this use of different levels gives autonomy to the parts.

To assuage fatigue—visual, mental, physical—the flow pattern allows divergence to different qualities of place . . . a covered walkway round the part-open, part-covered sculpture garden . . . places to sit with a view of the river . . . the reserve collection . . . refreshment . . . and so on.

Site plan. AS, 1949.

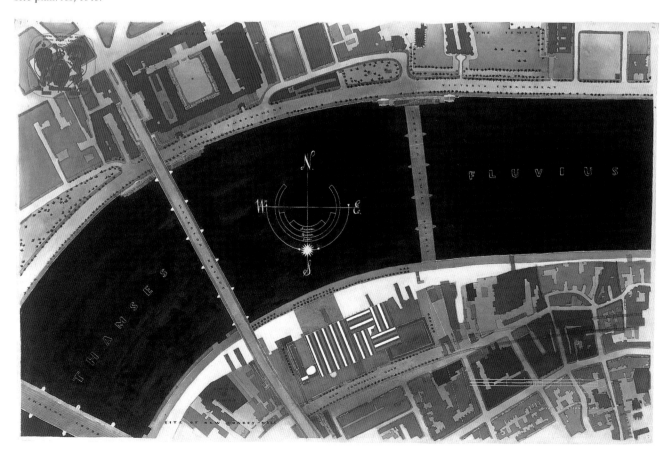

Photomontage of project from north bank of the River Thames, looking downstream. Model by E. Gill.

Model photograph: The site was taken from the Abercrombie 'envelope' plan. Leslie Martin, then working on the festival hall on the site, was external examiner.

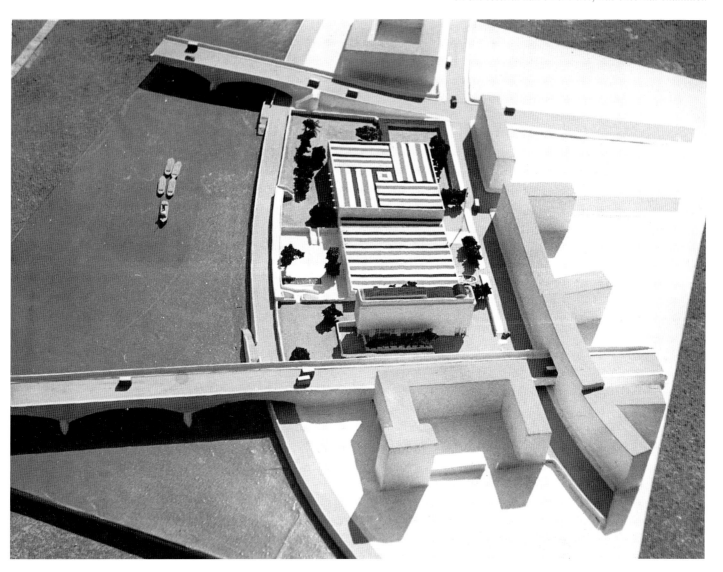

View across the River Thames from the north bank. AS, 1949.

opposite top: Elevation facing the river. AS, 1949.
opposite bottom: North-south section: An attempt to make
the sections of Le Corbusier's art gallery constructable
without losing the idea of the visitor being able to see the
sky and read the mood of the weather. AS, 1949.

LONG ELEVATION TO THE RIVER.

CROSS SECTION THRO' BANQUETING HALL.

Fitzwilliam Museum, Cambridge

Final project by PS, Royal Academy Schools, academic year ending summer 1949.

An attempt, using English rolled-steel sections and the English scale, to extend the steel-frame and glass language of Mies van der Rohe: an exercise that was to bear fruit in Hunstanton.

The Backs elevation. PS, 1948–49.

Site plan: The influence of Mies van der Rohe is clear in the structure and the aesthetic. PS, 1948–49.

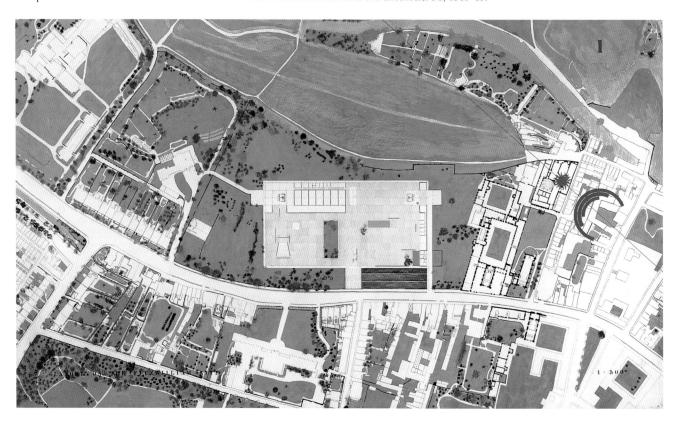

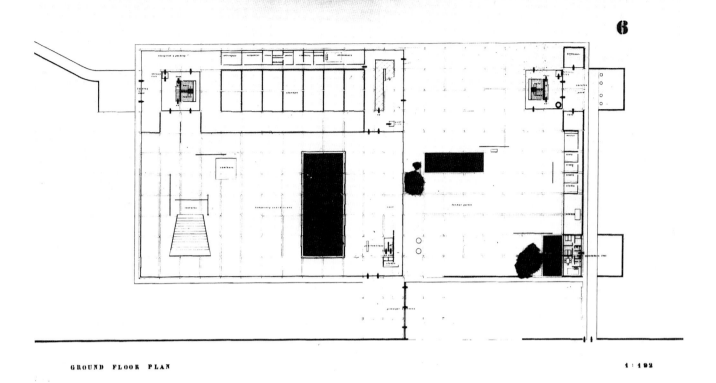

GROUND FLOOR PLAN   1 : 192

Ground-floor plan. PS, 1948–49.

Second-floor plan. First-floor plan similar. PS, 1948–49.

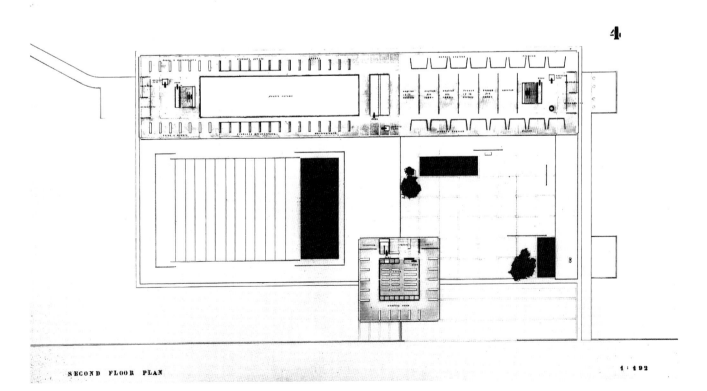

SECOND FLOOR PLAN   1 : 192

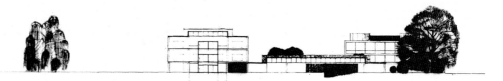

CROSS SECTION   1 : 192

Cross section. PS, 1948–49.

Long section. PS, 1948–49.

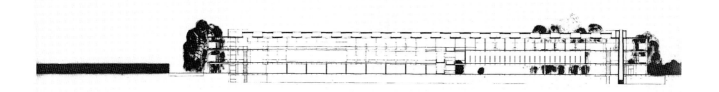

LONGITUDINAL SECTION   1 : 192

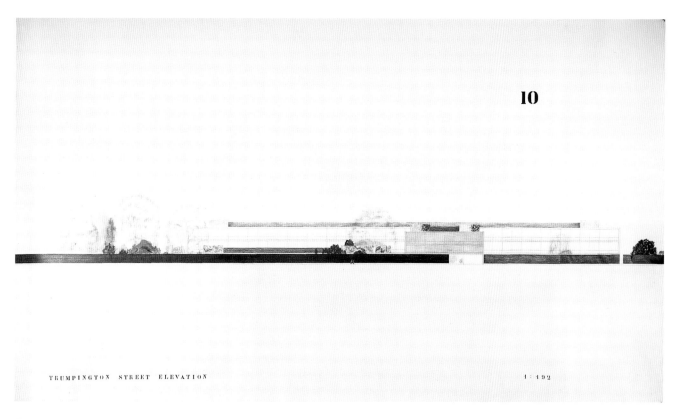

Trumpington Street elevation. PS, 1948–49.

Section through the library block. PS, 1948–49.

Perspective drawing of the formal garden from the pool. PS, 1948–49.

Perspective drawing of the temporary exhibition gallery. PS, 1948–49.

Vertical Feature and Restaurant, Festival of Britain

Autumn 1949

Restaurant in association with Theo Crosby

The Vertical Feature was intended as a traceried, poised structure introducing the 1950s; to be read—the Thames water's treillage between them—with the Pugin tracery on the tower of the Houses of Parliament.

The restaurant was an exercise in the temporary pavilion; an attempt at an aesthetic that rests lightly on its site, a sort of 'visiting' building that, in this case, appropriately speaks of its transient nature. (Drawings cannot be located.)

An English structure, carrying searchlights whose beams extend the structure at night. Ronald Simpson, 1949.

A+PS at the time of winning the Hunstanton School competition. Anne Fischer, 1950.

2 Transmissions and Connections

extending the polemic of the Heroic period, 1950 . . .

Hunstanton Secondary Modern School *(1949–54)*   40

Coventry Cathedral *(1950–51)*   68

Limerston Street *(1953–61)*   81

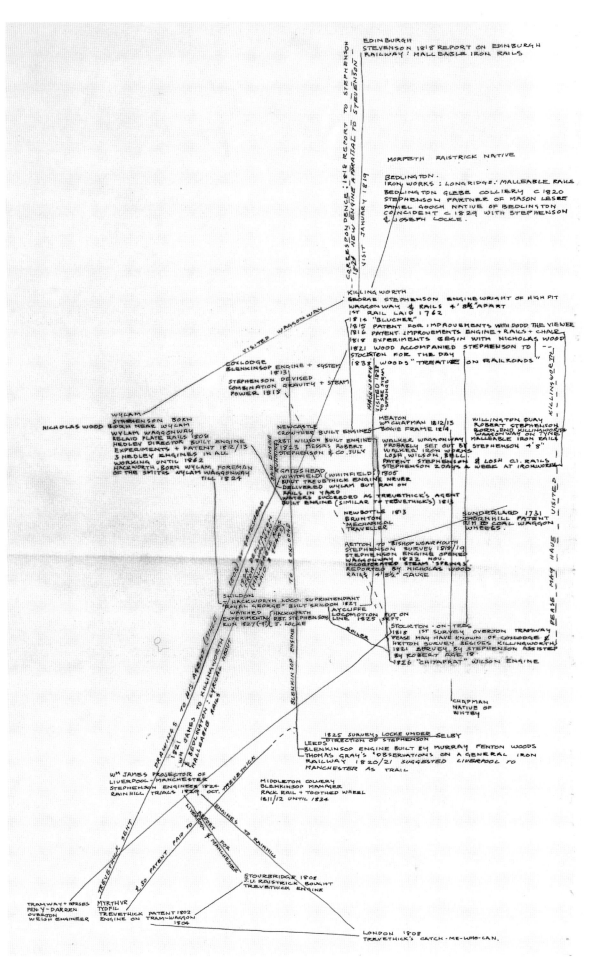

EDINBURGH
STEVENSON 1818 REPORT ON EDINBURGH
RAILWAY: MALLEABLE IRON RAILS

CORRESPONDENCE 1818 REPORT TO STEPHENSON
1829 NEW ENGINE A PRAISAL TO STEVENSON
VISIT JANUARY 1819

MORPETH RAISTRICK NATIVE

BEDLINGTON.
IRON WORKS: LONGRIDGE: MALLEABLE RAILS
BEDLINGTON GLEBE COLLIERY C 1820
STEPHENSON PARTNER OF MASON LESEE
DANIEL GOOCH NATIVE OF BEDLINGTON
CONCIDENT C 1829 WITH STEPHENSON
& JOSEPH LOCKE.

KILLINGWORTH
GEORGE STEPHENSON ENGINE WRIGHT OF HIGH PIT
WAGGON WAY & RAILS 4' 8½" APART
1ST RAIL LAID 1762
1814 "BLUCHER"
1815 PATENT FOR IMPROVEMENTS WITH DODD THE VIEWER
1816 PATENT IMPROVEMENTS ENGINE + RAILS + CHAIR
1818 EXPERIMENTS BEGIN WITH NICHOLAS WOOD
1821 WOOD ACCOMPANIED STEPHENSON TO
STOCKTON FOR THE DAY
1838 WOODS "TREATISE ON RAILROADS"

VISITED WAGGON WAY

COXLODGE
BLENKINSOP ENGINE + SYSTEM
1813
STEPHENSON DEVISED
COMBINATION GRAVITY + STEAM
POWER 1818

HACKWORTH
VISITED 1823
TO SEE STEAM
SPRINGS

WYLAM
STEPHENSON BORN
NICHOLAS WOOD BORN NEAR WYLAM
WYLAM WAGGONWAY
RELAID PLATE RAILS 1808
HEDLEY DIRECTOR BUILT ENGINE
EXPERIMENTS + PATENT 1812/13
3 HEDLEY ENGINES IN ALL
WORKING UNTIL 1862
HACKWORTH, BORN WYLAM FOREMAN
OF THE SMITHS WYLAM WAGGONWAY
TILL 1824

NEWCASTLE
CROWTHER BUILT ENGINES
RBT WILSON BUILT ENGINE
1823 MESSRS ROBERT
STEPHENSON & CO. JULY

HEATON
WM CHAPMAN 1812/13
BOGIE FRAME 1814

WALKER WAGGONWAY
PROBABLY SET OUT BY STEPHENSON 4'8"
WALKER IRON WORKS
LOSH, WILSON, BELL
PATENT STEPHENSON & LOSH CI. RAILS
STEPHENSON 2 DAYS A WEEK AT IRONWORKS

WILLINGTON QUAY
ROBERT STEPHENSON
BORN. END KILLINGWORTH
WAGGONWAY ON TYNE
MALLEABLE IRON RAILS
4'8"

KILLINGWORTH

PEASE MAY HAVE VISITED

GATESHEAD
WHITFIELD (WHINFIELD)
BUILT TREVETHICK ENGINE NEVER
DELIVERED WYLAM BUT RAN ON
RAILS IN YARD
WATERS SUCCEEDED AS TREVETHICK'S AGENT
BUILT ENGINE (SIMILAR TO TREVETHICK'S) 1813

NEWBOTTLE 1813
BRUNTON
MECHANICAL
TRAVELLER

SUNDERLAND 1731
THORNHILL PATENT
RIM TO COAL WAGGON
WHEELS.

HETTON TO BISHOP WEARMOUTH
STEPHENSON SURVEY 1818/19
STEPHENSON ENGINE OPENED
WAGGONWAY 1822 NOV.
INCORPORATED STEAM SPRINGS
REPORTED BY NICHOLAS WOOD
RAILS 4' 8½" GAUGE

SHILDON
HACKWORTH LOCO. SUPERINTENDANT
"ROYAL GEORGE" BUILT SHILDON 1827
WATCHED HACKWORTH
EXPERIMENTAL RBT. STEPHENSON
RUN 1827 (-9) J. LOCKE

AYCLIFFE
LOCOMOTION PUT ON
LINE 1825 SEPT.

STOCKTON-ON-TEES
1818 1ST SURVEY OVERTON TRAMWAY
PEASE MAY HAVE KNOWN OF COXLODGE &
HETTON SURVEY BESIDES KILLINGWORTH
1821 SURVEY BY STEPHENSON ASSISTED
BY ROBERT AGE 18
1826 "CHITAPRAT" WILSON ENGINE

CHAPMAN
NATIVE OF
WHITBY

1821 DRAWINGS TO HIS AGENT (SINCE
WM JAMES TO KILLINGWORTH)
BEDLINGTON EXTREME ABOUT
MALLEABLE RAILS

BLENKINSOP ENGINE

TO COXLODGE

BOILER

1825 SURVEY, LOCKE UNDER
DIRECTION OF STEPHENSON
SELBY
LEEDS
BLENKINSOP ENGINE BUILT BY MURRAY FENTON WOODS
THOMAS GRAY'S "OBSERVATIONS ON A GENERAL IRON
RAILWAY 1820/21 SUGGESTED LIVERPOOL TO
MANCHESTER AS TRAIL

WM JAMES PROJECTOR OF
LIVERPOOL - MANCHESTER
STEPHENSON ENGINEER 1824
RAINHILL TRIALS 1829 OCT.

MIDDLETON COLLIERY
BLENKINSOP MANAGER
RACK RAIL + TOOTHED WHEEL
1811/12 UNTIL 1834

TREVETHICK SENT
ENGINES TO RAINHILL

£50 PATENT PAID TO
REPORT TO LIVERPOOL & MANCHESTER

STOURBRIDGE 1808
J.U. RAISTRICK BOUGHT
TREVETHICK ENGINE

TRAMWAY + HORSES
PEN Y-DARREN
OVERTON
WELSH ENGINEER

MYRTHVR
TYDFIL
TREVETHICK PATENT 1802
ENGINE ON TRAM-WAGGON
1804

LONDON 1808
TREVETHICK'S CATCH-ME-WHO-CAN.

Evolution in form-giving proceeds from an incomplete thought; the invention completes and gives body to the thought. In this sense, a book about architectural ideas does not have to be completely logical to produce in some happy recipient a design impulse.

A diagram showing contacts between early railway engineers represents a probable transmission of inventive-energy, idea-energy. The diagram was an afterthought on *The Arch Criminals of the Euston Arch.** The creative impulse often springs from a sense of connection, such as that recognised by the diagram. Idea-energies are sparked off one another; a well-timed sighting can be a recognition of something capable of bearing idea-seeds, or an informed word can initiate quite other ideas.

Transmission can happen without there needing to be an obvious connection; so the sense of fellowship spans history, since the creative artist feeds off whatever he needs. Transmission of ideated energy has at certain times in the past been inseparable from the reuse of the inspirational forms: as in the manner of the successive, beneficial inspirations with which the Palladian style touched English architecture, in ways recognisably different from those influencing other cultures.

In the second half of this century, such obvious, direct transference seems inappropriate. More apposite today is an architect's receptivity to the spirit and the inventive-energy that the Modern movement transmits.

* A+PS, *The Arch Criminals of the Euston Arch* (London: Thames and Hudson, 1968).

opposite: Engineer's Contact Diagram (post–*Euston Arch*), to do with the transmission of energy and the connections of ideas: Showing the known contacts of those visits by one engineer to another or a connection by the visit of a third party to both, also the known movements of skilled workmen and orders for parts to be made . . . all these connections are indicated by lines joining places of work at the time of the 'contact'. AS, 1968.

The heroic struggle of the first period of Modern architecture, followed immediately by the prolonged fight for other truths, had so closely passed before us, which gave a sense of moral responsibility to invent for ourselves forms appropriate to the postwar period; forms equal in power—but of a different order of strength—to those in 'Purism', 'Constructivism', 'de Stijl', and 'Futurism': forms responding to the more complicated, even confused, needs of our time. The achievements of the Heroic period of Modern architecture are certain; against these certainties, offered in the spirit of hope, today's achievements can be measured for their appropriateness, their furtherance of hopeful ideals, their quality of invention.

Le Corbusier's polemic for Modern architecture used the building of antiquity, of Gothic times, and of the Renaissance accomplishment to be matched with new reason and hope.

The key buildings of preceding styles still sit in formal judgment as to the internal consistency of a language. The integrity of all architecture relies on this consistency.

The essence of the Heroic period was invention.

Invention in the sense that Doric architecture apparently sprang fully formed; invented despite the seemingly insubstantial, crude qualities of the preceding dark ages. The sense of connection with the Heroic period, the beginning as with the Doric, is an energiser; that a message is received implies a capability in the receiver, which in turn instils the confidence that encourages the receiver to be his own man: even in adversity.

The sense of connection within Modern architecture is achieved in the act of extending the polemic. The sense of continuity resides in the transmission of the energy of the spirit; that is, in the pitch of the achievement.

Out of this deep sense of connection grew such concepts as cluster, identity, patterns of association.* These became translated into a new kind of aesthetic.†

"If a building or an element of city is to give intellectual access to its occupants, access to their affections and their skills, access to their sensibilities, the fabric must have special formal characteristics. Layering has such characteristics, for between the layers there is room for illusion as well as activity. Layering is an idea unfolded from within the formal usages of the existing language of modern architecture . . ."

A layering of intellectual meaning, a density of thought.

---

* Fully explored in *Urban Structuring* (London: Studio Vista, 1967) and *Ordinariness and Light* (London: Faber and Faber, 1970; Tokyo: Shokokusha, 1979).
† The ephemera that show our hands translating our attitudes in formation and change are in *The Shift*, Architectural Monographs (London: Academy Editions, 1982).

Hunstanton Secondary Modern School

In the report submitted with the competition we wrote:*"This school is an attempt to carry beyond the diagrammatic stage into a work of architecture, and its form is dictated by a close study of educational needs and purely formal requirements rather than by precedent. The core of the school is the assembly hall, which flows freely into the dining areas and entrance areas, carrying into the school the planes of the forecourt, the green courts, and the playing fields. This grouping allows the circulations of the hall, the dining areas, and the school generally to be superimposed, resulting in a compact and economical plan: on the first floor it is impossible to be more than twenty-five feet from a stair escape. No doors open onto the greencourts, only hopper windows for ventilation, as no children's movement is to be there; the green courts are light areas, quite free from noise."*

During the construction of Hunstanton, we saw layering of structure at the naked stage, layering of reflection at the glazed stage.

Perspective of exterior looking towards Braithwaite
water tank up-ended in steel frame. PS, 1950.

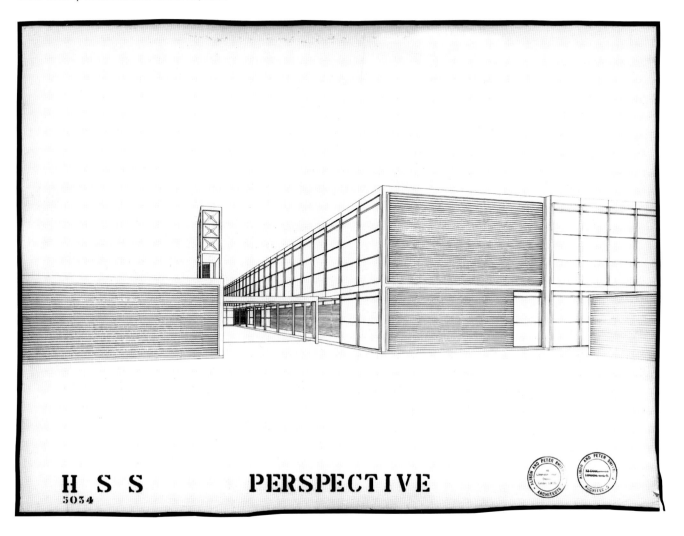

H S S   **PERSPECTIVE**
5034

After its three-year building period (due to steel rationing at the time of the Korean War), we wrote: *"The idea behind this school was to try and prove that in every programme there exists an inherent order which once discovered appears static, immutable, and entirely lucid. In other words, we were determined that we would, from the requirements of the client and the recommendations of the educationists, create architecture."*

A footnote to this text stated: *"Only a person familiar with the pathetic figure of English functionalism supported since the war on a crutch of pseudo-science can understand why it was necessary to make such an obvious statement and design such a didactic building."*

And indeed, already by February 1953, referring to prefabrication in England, we had written: *"Hertfordshire County Council has explored the field of pre-fabricated large module design with the limited success that one would expect in a system where only approximations are possible and plastic necessity is discounted as a first principle. To counteract this tendency the Hunstanton School tries to re-establish the finite order which is architecture.*

Perspective of interior looking across hall to doors out to playing fields. PS, 1950.

H S S
5033
PERSPECTIVE

Technically it rejects the inflexible system of large standard elements and instead assembles existing components from families-of-components already available in industry—steel sections, bricks, etc.—into architecturally finite elements, each part being indispensable structurally and architecturally. For example the mullions and transoms of the windows are supporting and at the same time eliminate the glazing sub-frames. In this way there are established modules and harmonies for this job and this time.

Functionally it provides a raised teaching floor with interrelated practical and theoretical rooms looking onto green courts all centred round the hall—the core and expression of the whole school community and its connection to the town.

Plastically it achieves its ends through finite, locked, symmetrical relationships, a complex on a raised podium whose ancestor is the Sunion Temenos."

On 7 September 1954, under the title 'Reflections on Hunstanton Becoming a School,' PS wrote: *"In the Golden Age, the humblest swineherd between his doorposts was the image of all humanity: deliberate, noble, and even elegant. The dream takes positive shape—a built domain where our everyday life will seem heroic.*

Radiant Cities:* A regenerated countryside.† By what means?

Through architecture; by an acceptance of our full responsibilities as builders.

We must answer the functional requirements of the moment in such a way that the resulting built form has a permanent validity.

Tomorrow will inherit only space.

Our ultimate responsibility is therefore the creation of noble space.

Consider, therefore, the Hunstanton School as having two lives: an everyday life of teaching children, noise, furniture, and chalk dust, as equals with the building elements, all of which add up to the word 'School'.

And a secret life of pure space, the permanent built Form which will persist when School has given way to Museum or Warehouse, and which will continue to exist as idea even when the Built Form has long disappeared. It is through BUILT FORM that the inherent nobility of man finds release."

Thus, the ground and the seed of New Brutalism are already prepared.

* From Le Corbusier.
† We had already written the UR—Urban Re-Identification—Document and it was in mock-up with a cover horizontally striped in Neapolitan ice colours: see *Ordinariness and Light* (London: Faber and Faber, 1970; Tokyo: Shokokusha, 1979).

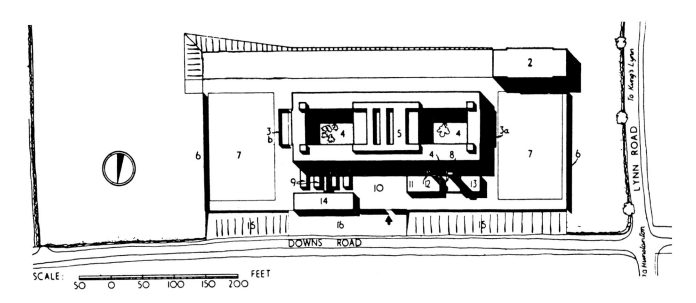

below: Site plan (publication drawing). Numbers 1, 8, and 12 are not indicated: 2. Gymnasium and changing rooms; 3a. Caretaker's garden; 3b. School garden; 4. Green court; 5. Main block; 6. Wall, 7 feet high; 7. Pitch, 100 feet by 160 feet; 9. Cycle sheds; 10. Forecourt; 11. Kitchen; 13. Adult housecraft; 14. Workshops; 15. Revetment, 3 feet 6 inches high; 16. Car-park.

below and pages 44–46: Hunstanton working drawings. A+PS, 1950.

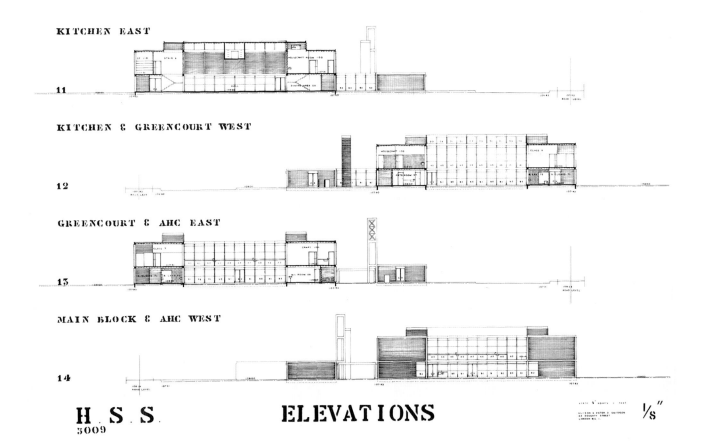

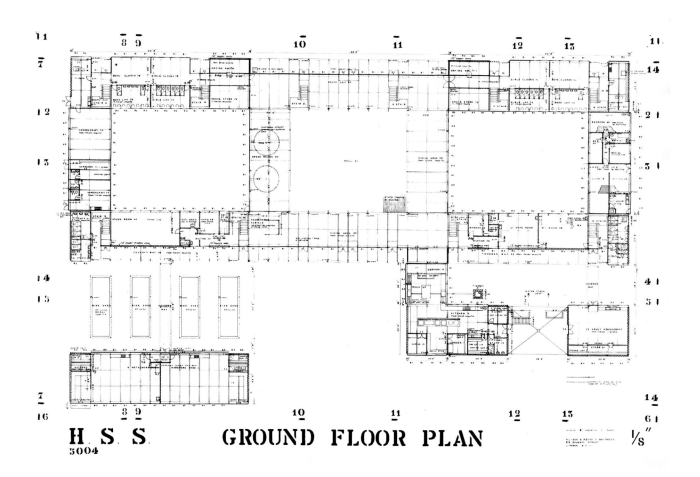

H. S. S.   GROUND FLOOR PLAN   ⅛"
5004

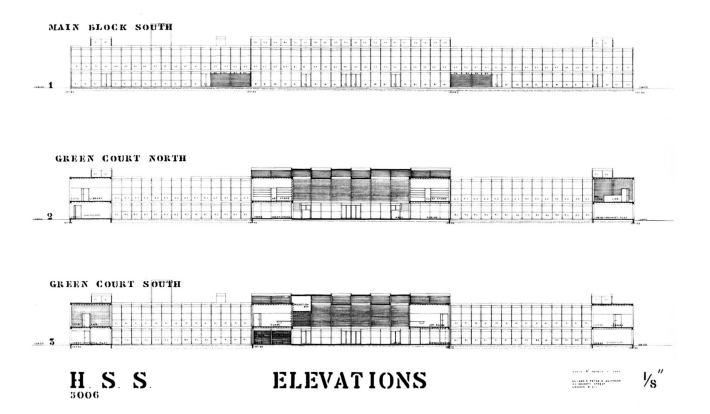

MAIN BLOCK SOUTH

GREEN COURT NORTH

GREEN COURT SOUTH

H. S. S.   ELEVATIONS   ⅛"
5006

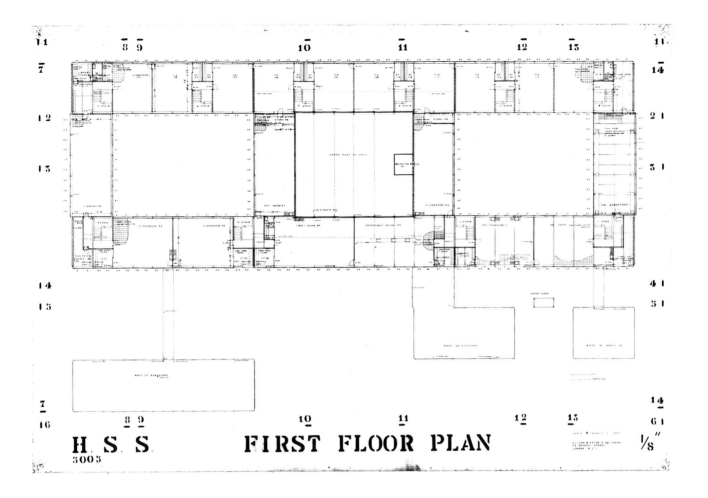

H. S. S.
5005

FIRST FLOOR PLAN

⅛"

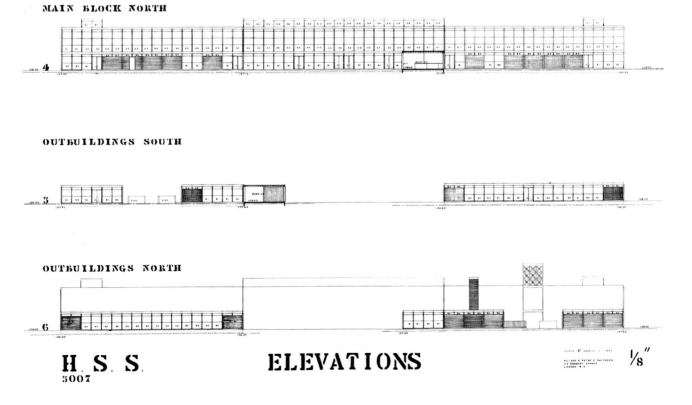

MAIN BLOCK NORTH

OUTBUILDINGS SOUTH

OUTBUILDINGS NORTH

H. S. S.
5007

ELEVATIONS

⅛"

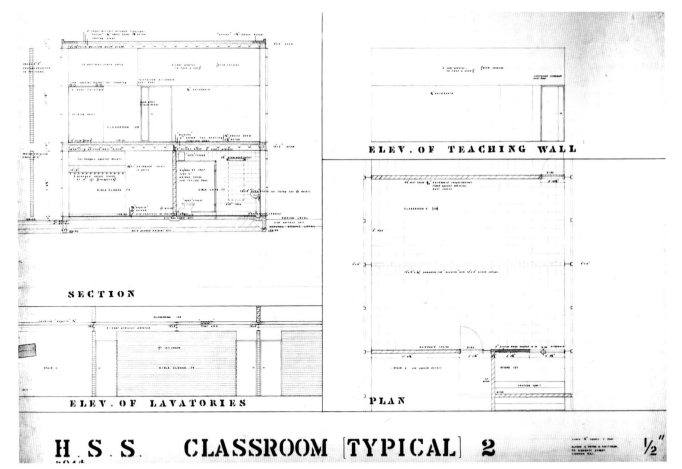

SECTION

ELEV. OF LAVATORIES

ELEV. OF TEACHING WALL

PLAN

H. S. S.   CLASSROOM [TYPICAL] 2   ½"

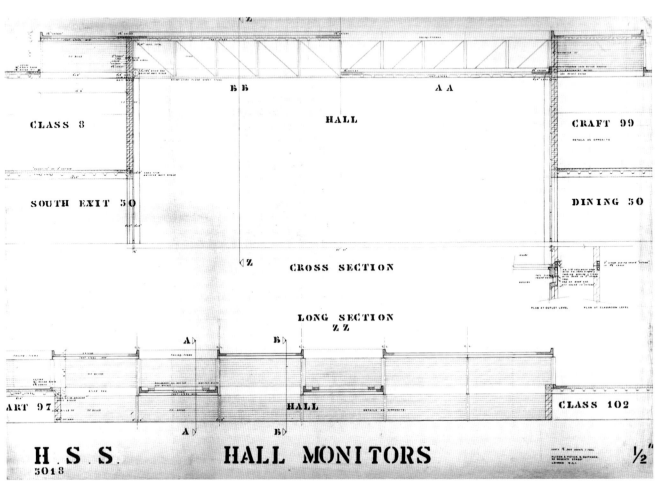

CLASS 8

HALL

CRAFT 99

SOUTH EXIT 50

DINING 50

BB   AA

Z

CROSS SECTION

LONG SECTION
ZZ

ART 97

HALL

CLASS 102

A   B

A   B

H. S. S.   HALL MONITORS   ½"
5018

In the original competition programme there was a requirement for a headmaster's house.

This was given the format of a central top-lit general-use space enclosed by subsidiary closed spaces. That is, it had, in miniature, the same spatial organisation as the school itself. As was said at that time . . . the 'microcosm of the macrocosm'.

Plan: A 'microcosm of the macrocosm'. A late requirement that seemed to us undesirable.
A+PS, 1950.

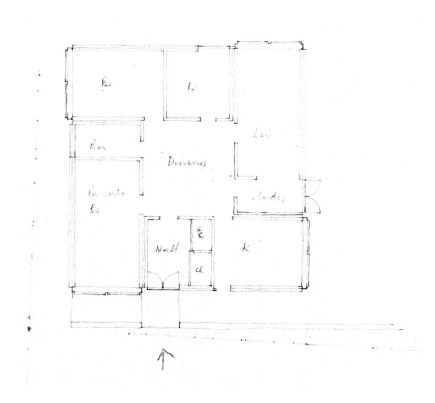

Elevation: All were similar. Unbuilt.
A+PS, 1950.

Record of early building works. PS, 1 September 1952.

Record of steel erection. Smith of Boulton and Paul, 1952.

Courtyard corner under construction. Nigel Henderson.

Interior of hall under construction. Nigel Henderson.

Series of four photographs of painters and windows. Nigel Henderson.

top left: Painters in west green court, water tower beyond.
above left: West green court with snagging party.

top right: Painters in green court through rainy panes.
above right: Painter in west green court.

Series of four photographs of construction details: The anglicisation of the Mies influence of the Fitzwilliam is complete.
Nigel Henderson.

top left: First-floor level: Staircase steelwork in; classroom store walls and heavier walls between classrooms in construction.
above left: Interior of classroom under construction. Heating being installed on slabs through which a proportion of heat passes to ground-floor cloaks.

top right: In construction: AS in field-side porch.
above right: The hall with its clerestory. First-floor classroom walls begun. The clerk of works, Mr. Mantelli, speaks with a workman.

Series of four photographs of steel details. The extended building period was due to steel rationing; the school took the county's quota for that time. Nigel Henderson.

top left: Green court with ladders.
above left: West green court from top of stairs on the south side.

top right: Gymnasium and reflected gymnasium.
above right: Kitchen yard.

top: PS with jeep. Nigel Henderson.
above: Checking party, 1953: Clerk of works (Mantelli),
PS, and contractor (Crown). Nigel Henderson.

above: Interior of changing room in gymnasium. De Burgh Galwey.
opposite: Wash basins. John Maltby.

Coventry Cathedral

October 1950 – 20 July 1951

A+PS

With engineer Ronald Jenkins

It is an unnoticed art-historical fact that in the 1950s, among the inheritors of the Modern movement, there was a fascination with centristic geometries . . . squares, circles, diagonals. The difference between these architectures lay in the different ways that their inventors blunted the 'carrying' geometric perfections. In the architecture of that generation, the symmetry appears as a convenience, akin to the string on a neatly tied parcel . . . a straightforward, sound, and sensible way to wrap something up.*

In our work, the use of squares, squares subdivided, axes born of the locating, generating, and anchoring geometries, is conscious because simple geometries are so generally understandable as to be unobtrusive and, therefore, can be used as neutral structuring, yet devices potent enough for re-energising the area around.

By these traditional architectonic means of axis and visual connection, our first conscious essay in layering of function and meaning is tied into what remained of the bombed historic city of Coventry. In our competition report, we wrote: "*In Coventry, the general lack of order and the size and scale of adjacent buildings seem to point to the cathedral being conceived as one large simple volume containing all the cathedral functions, rather than a series of small related volumes whose tension would be slackened and confused by the existing chaos. This large simple volume has been placed on the site in such a manner as to bring discipline and cohesion to the neighbourhood and city; the axis joining the city centre with the old tower has been taken as site-dominant and the base line on which the geometric harmonies of the cathedral have been built up.*"

By this means we fixed in place the new within the existing.

The cathedral floor is an island with limited access that floats free of the ground of the city of Coventry, connected, axially, by its bridge to the western approach and on a subsidiary but parallel axis by a ramped bridge which spears through the surviving spire of the destroyed mediaeval church. The device of separation is that of the moat before the castle's bulk. Those that use the bridges that span the moat are given the sense of having to 'leave' the city and 'enter' a place apart.

In a document of the period, 'Will Our Cathedral Be White?', PS questioned '. . . the likelihood of a new cathedral being a success unless it is based on a fundamental idea'. We stated: "*Builders since the Reformation have been unable to translate the changes that have taken place in the Anglican Church into architectural terms. The only attempts that have been made borrowed their ideas from an entirely foreign tradition—the classical centralised plan of a universal order rather than a place of communal worship. In this project, to resolve the Anglican programme, the congregation is disposed equidistant from the altar rather than progressively from it. The plan is a 'square on the diagonal'. The directional placing of the square and the need to emphasise the west-to-east axis and subdue the north-to-south suggest that the space should be vaulted by an anti-clastic shell, which seen internally is concave on the west-to-east axis and convex on the north-to-south . . . a 'pulling-out' of the space above the altar and a 'drawing-in', wing-like motion, over the Chapter House and Unity Chapel. And in order to provide an unmistakable symbol for the cathedral of our time, this shell has been tilted, up in the east and down in the west. Seen from the city, the great square area of the roof would be visible: its polished marble-aggregate surface would shine out white like the top of the Florence Baptistry.*"

---

*   One of our earliest contacts with architecture was Seaton Delaval, Northumberland, where the work of Vanbrugh and Hawksmoor was a discovery, even obsession, shared with certain contemporaries in Newcastle. In London we dropped, without conscious choice, into that small circle of architects around Sam Stevens who knew about Rudolph Wittkower. In 1949 Wittkower's *Architectural Principles in the Age of Humanism* was published by the Warburg Institute; it confirmed a direction already taken.

Photomontage of cathedral axonometric set in aerial photograph of
the period, showing extent of the bombed area. 1951.

The site is modelled to reflect the disciplines of the cathedral. To achieve this, the tie-beam between the two principal points of support has been accepted in the undercroft as a north-to-south 'wall' which passes under the centre of the cathedral. To the east of this 'wall' the ground is retained at its natural level to be used as a garden by the laity. To the west of this 'wall' the ground has been excavated to some ten feet below the cathedral floor level to provide space for the cathedral ancillary buildings and to provide service access. The ground is thus withdrawn from the cathedral level; its glazing is able to descend to floor level: the cathedral floats as an island of calm in the chaos of everyday life . . ."

Working with our structural engineer, Ronald Jenkins, meeting virtually every day, we had a clear image of the building finished.

"The basic structure being concrete, an attempt has been made to make all the subsidiary parts in the same material; as stone was used in mediaeval times. Thought has been given as to how each part should be shuttered . . . texturing the work by grooving, by beading, and by lining."

Site plan. A+PS.

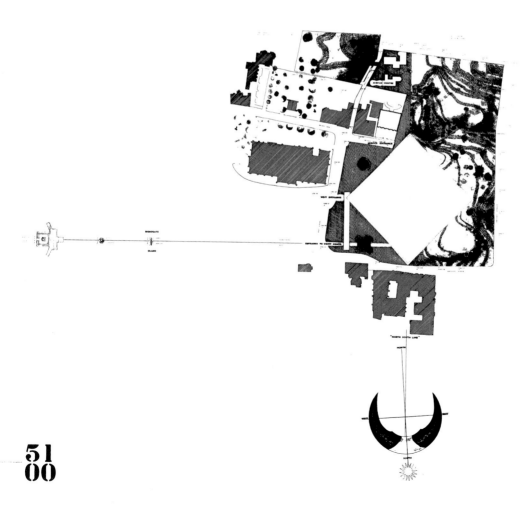

51
00

top: Model, looking south (note without vertical tension mullions). Model by A+PS, 1952. PS, 1954.

above: Model, looking west. Model by A+PS, 1952. PS, 1954.

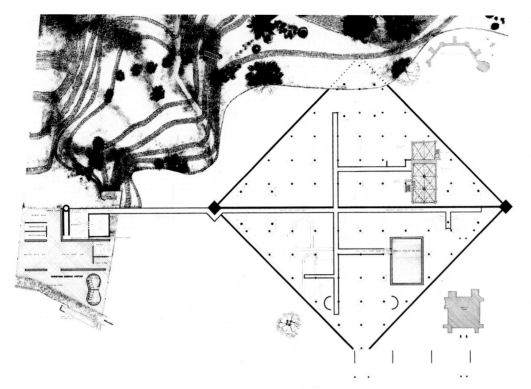

51
01

PLAN OF CHRISTIAN SERVICE CENTRE AT 273 LEVEL

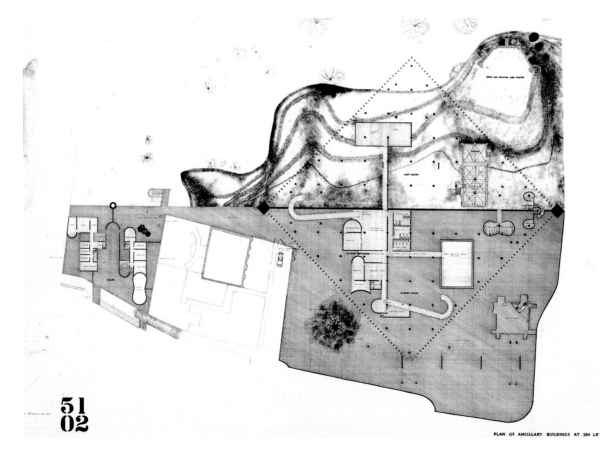

51
02

PLAN OF ANCILLARY BUILDINGS AT 284 LE'

opposite top: Plan at garden and mediaeval crypt level, below ancillary buildings and cathedral floor. The north-south wall joining the two foundations of the supports is a tie-beam perforated only by a door. The Christian Service Centre, with its access from the garden and mediaeval lane, is at left. A+PS.

opposite bottom: Plan of ancillary buildings at ground level. The major structural tie between the two springings of the 'legs' is a wall that divides the public area—where the garden flows up to the wall—and the clerical domain. A+PS.

below: Axonometric of undercroft of cathedral, with trees of 1951 shadowed and gravel hatched. The ground under the west entrance is excavated so that the ancillary accommodation of the cathedral stands in the open air, but sheltered under the great cathedral floor above. The old vaulted undercroft is excavated and can be accessed by the public. The structural tie-wall between supports separates public area from cathedral area. Amanda Marshall, AS, 1978.

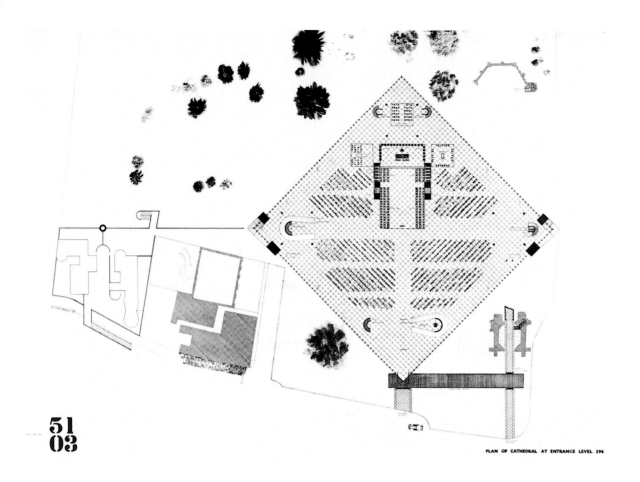

51
03

PLAN OF CATHEDRAL AT ENTRANCE LEVEL 294

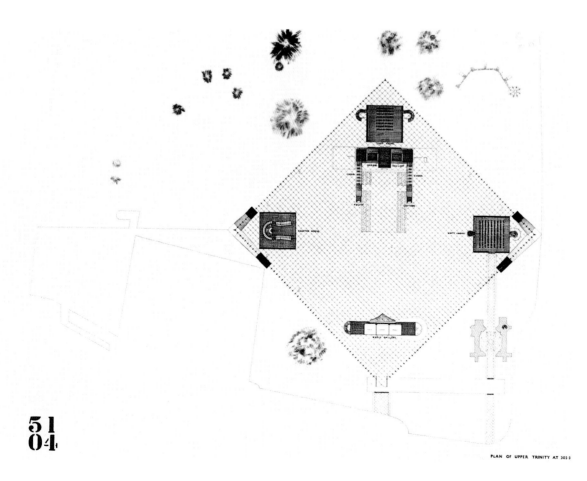

51
04

PLAN OF UPPER TRINITY AT 303-3

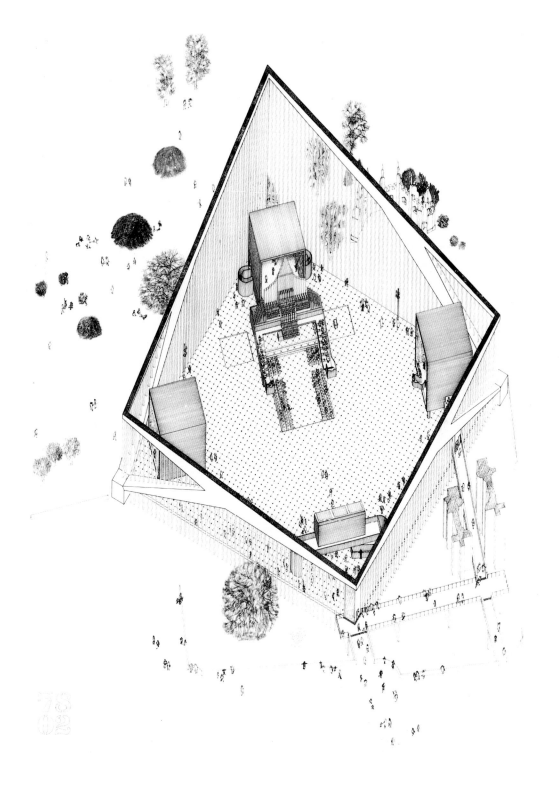

opposite top: Plan of cathedral at entrance level. The cathedral floor floats free of the surrounding space—the end towards the altar and stairs up to the Lady Chapel—as if sailing out over the garden. The approach is made by bridges over the excavated 'moat' onto which the undercroft opens. A+PS.

opposite bottom: Plan of upper 'trinity' level above the cathedral floor, the three chapels, and the organ gallery. A+PS.

above: Axonometric of the frame of the structure, inhabited and placed on site with trees of 1951.

Amanda Marshall, AS, 1978.

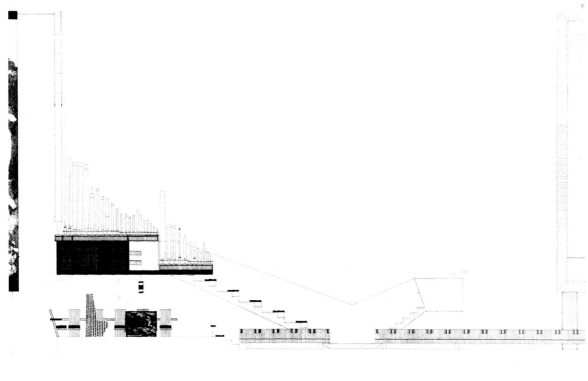

51
11

LONG SECTION THRO' ARK

above: Detail of long section through choir. The altar platform, raised three steps on the line of the communion rail, is fringed with the canon's seating. The ark—the Scuola Cantorum—is raised one step above the main cathedral floor. The organ, cantilevered over the altar by stepped ramps on which sit the choir, forms the climax to the whole. The westward upsweep (above the floor) of the counterbalances to these ramps provides pulpit and lectern. Vertical access from the undercroft to the main cathedral level is by means of two ramps: one for everyday use coming up under the Chapter House; the other bringing processions into position at the west door. A+PS.

opposite top: Section looking south. From left to right, the section shows: Lady Chapel (in its traditional position), the ark or Scuola Cantorum, the nave, the fanfare trumpets of the organ gallery, and the west entrance over the 'moat' that allows all the ancillary buildings in the undercroft to have windows to the open air. Note mediaeval basement excavated and exposed in the undercroft. A+PS.

opposite bottom: North-east 'true' elevation, that is, in the plane of a single facade. A+PS.

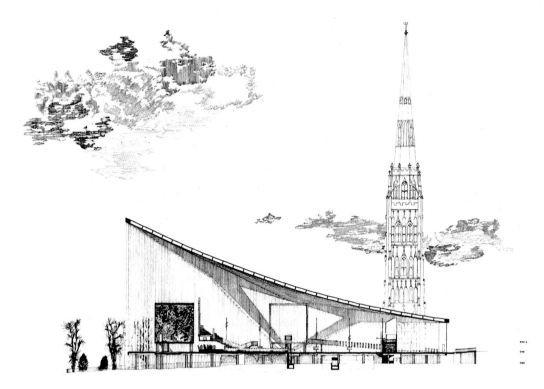

51
05

SECTION THRO' CATHEDRAL LOOKING SOUTH

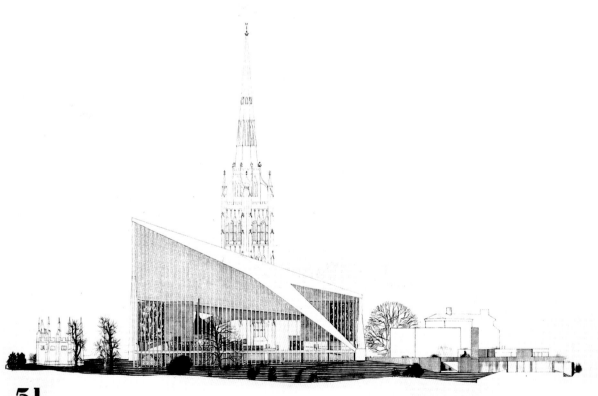

51
12

NORTH EAST "TRUE" ELEVATION

51
09

SOUTH ELEVATION OF CATHEDRAL

51
13

SOUTH WEST 'TRUE' ELEVATION

top: South elevation of cathedral showing ramps passing through tower—remains of the bombed cathedral—to the inside of the Unity Chapel. A+PS.
above: South-west 'true' elevation. A+PS.

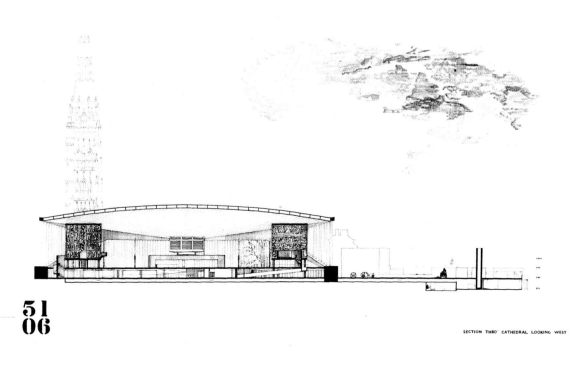

51
06

SECTION THRO' CATHEDRAL LOOKING WEST

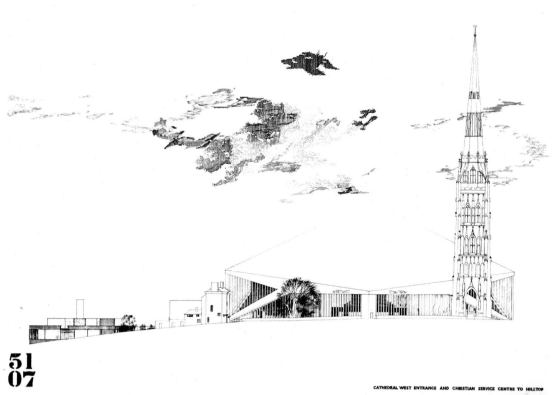

51
07

CATHEDRAL WEST ENTRANCE AND CHRISTIAN SERVICE CENTRE TO HILLTOP

top: Section looking west towards the entrance. The pedal organs with their well-boxes are located over the entrance. A fanfare of pipes speaks from the balcony front. A+PS.

above: Elevation showing west entrance, accessible by bridge over surrounding moat. At right, a bridge ramp rises to pass through the tower into the Unity Chapel. To the left is the Christian Service Centre with section through mediaeval lane. A+PS.

51
OS

EAST END AND CHRISTIAN SERVICE CENTRE TO GARDEN

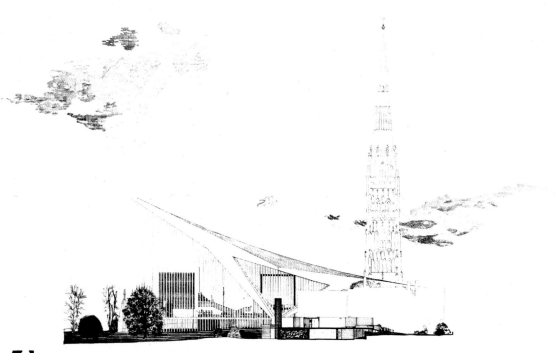

51
10

SECTION THRO' SERVICE CENTRE AND CATHEDRAL FROM THE NORTH

top: East elevation of the cathedral showing the roofline of the Christian Service Centre (right) at the level of the undercroft of the cathedral. A+PS.

above: Section through Christian Service Centre and cathedral from the north. Section is taken through ancillary accommodation, which are flats over the Christian Service Centre accessed from both the cathedral grounds and a mediaeval lane. Beyond is the red sandstone tower remaining from the bombed cathedral. A+PS.

Limerston Street, Chelsea

In 1953 we moved from rooms in Doughty Street in Bloomsbury to a small terrace house in Chelsea; we had the last short years of a twenty-one-year lease.

In this house the 'as-found' was celebrated: the bath stood naked on its four legs; the lavatory chain hung galvanised before Paolozzi wallpaper; in the backyard, new things, new plants sat against old sooty walls.

right: 'The famous photograph'. PS, Eduardo Paolozzi, AS, and Nigel Henderson sitting on chairs in the middle of Limerston Street at the time of the 'This Is Tomorrow' exhibition. Nigel Henderson, 1956.
below left: The backyard was up against the high old wall surrounding the workhouse. This was used as a backdrop to set plantings and objects.
below right: The decoration of the W.C. on the landing with wallpaper by Eduardo Paolozzi, in style later used by Nigel Henderson at Bethnal Green and Thorpe-le-Soken. A classic Brutalist image. PS, 1956.

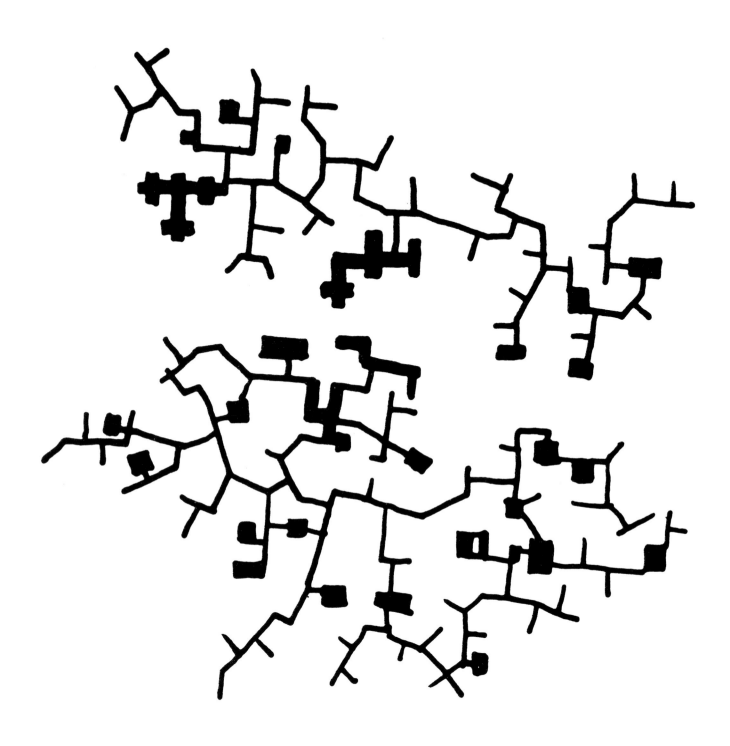

Cluster City, 1952–53: Diagrammatic plan of a small city. The diagram's development, out
of the Golden Lane idea, for the Urban Re-Identification Document of 1952 (see preface
of *Ordinariness and Light*), is one of a series that underpins our urbanism, which sprang into
realistic form with Berlin Hauptstadt (see *The Charged Void: Urbanism*). AS, 1953.

3 Graphics of Movement

the comprehension of the city's structure through its patterns of movement, 1952 . . .

Golden Lane *(1952)* 86

Colville Place *(1952)* 96

Offices for the Electricity Board, Kampala *(1952–53)* 98

House Extension, Alderbury *(1953)* 102

One-Thousand-Square-Foot House *(1952–53)* 103

Cheddar House of Cheese *(1955)* 104

Doha Hospital *(1953)* 105

Sheffield University *(1953)* 108

Intellectually indicative graphics might be said to have been invented by Paul Klee: extended as a teaching graphic to convey the ability of shapes to work together—as if in the manner of the rasping legs of a grasshopper—conveying a message that a new ordering of image-making, as a comprehensible language, was possible.

Klee invented the forms he disposed . . . and by judging their appropriate/necessary fields of magnetism, so ordered their disposal; their disposal taking possession of a void and thereby charging it with a potency responding to the new spirit of invention. Once the idea has entered the mind of an indicative graphics, which recognises patterns of association, of use, of identity, and of movement, it is possible to extend this to an idea that a building's ordering can be sufficiently comprehensible so as to indicate possible creative use and that it is open to change.

In our work of the early 1950s on the image of a new city—its clusters, its districts—one of the first is a diagram of city elements with an angular pedestrian linkage as 'streets-in-the-air' that built towards the association of dwellings at high densities in cities, allowing sweeter, more agreeably differentiated patterns of vehicle and leisure movement on the freed ground. Linkage built towards a new identity of districts, and these towards a new ordering of densities, acknowledged a differentiated place-quality for the parts of the city.* These links, as comprehensible images of a new ordering—indicative of and based on pedestrian movement—were the first offering of places where the pedestrian could walk in safety and feel himself or herself in calm surroundings.

Golden Lane is a piece of connective urban form of sufficient size to match in scale those last pieces of urban-form invention, the railway stations that followed directly on from Stephenson's invention of the railway engine. The immediate post-Stephenson-era building still visible in our cities indicates that the art of urbanism can be reenergised: urban nerve can be transmitted or created by the existence in a community of other forms of confidence.

* A start had been made towards the Urban Re-Identification Document when we received the invitation to take part in the preparation of the MARS Group presentation at CIAM 9 in Aix-en-Provence. The diagrams already prepared were photographically reproduced to the desired sizes for the CIAM GRILLE.

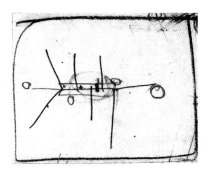

Originating ideogram of street-twig as a unit of the district. PS.

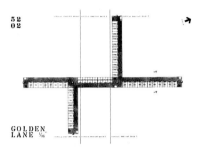

Typical deck plans. A+PS, 1952.

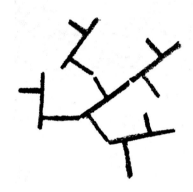

Cluster of street-twigs that becomes a district: A net of 'streets-in-the-air'. PS.

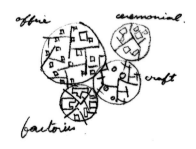

Cluster diagram, 1952–53: The Golden Lane idea becomes fully fledged as districts of a city whose form is generated by the coming together of like, mutually supportive activities. AS.

Stemming from Golden Lane, we have invented a family of connectively inclined buildings in which it is possible to make neighbourly contact in calm safety:

. . . outside the dwelling . . . Robin Hood Gardens;

. . . park/walk/shop/sit in café . . . Berlin Hauptstadt;

. . . walk-in-the-dry . . . Mehringplatz, Worcester;*

. . . park a vehicle/walk unseen/visit a patient . . . the hospital at Doha;

. . . connect easily/work in 'islands of calm' . . . Sheffield, Pahlavi;

. . . walk/pause/walk . . . Magdalen College;

. . . park in the shade/walk in the shade/ascend easily/visit . . . Kuwait.

* Fully explored in *The Charged Void: Urbanism*: 'Holes in Cities'.

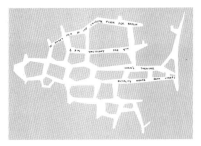

Berlin Hauptstadt, 1957: Cut-out of pedestrian network used as invitation to a film screening. AS.

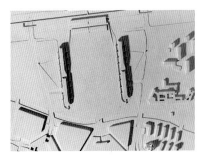

Mehringplatz, Berlin, 1962.
J. Stanton Abbott, 1962.

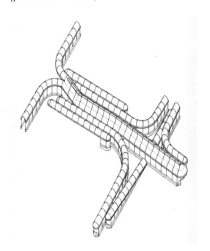

Pahlavi National Library, 1977–78: Axonometric of entrance court glass canopies. Wally Banks, 1977–78.

Government Offices, Kuwait, 1970: Axonometric of shaded garage. AS, 1980.

In the first note-text written at the time of designing, PS wrote: *"Our aim is to create a true street-in-the-air, each 'street' having a large number of people dependent on it for access, and in addition some streets are to be thoroughfares—that is, leading to places—so that they will each acquire special characteristics—be identified in fact. Each part of each street-in-the-air will have sufficient people accessed from it for it to become a social entity and be within reach of a much larger number at the same level.*

Streets will be places and not corridors or balconies.

Where a street is purely residential, the individual house and garden will provide the same lively pattern as a true street or square—nothing is lost and elevation is gained.

Thoroughfares can house small shops, post-boxes, telephone kiosks, etc.—the flat block disappears and vertical living becomes a reality. The refuse chute takes the place of the village pump."

In this text, repeatedly, the word 'street' has been altered to 'deck' and back again. The first ideograms are attached to this note-text, and these include the roof,* evidence of our determination both to give a 'hat' to the building and to make poetry out of the services.

We continued: *"The yard-gardens, being contiguous with the street, bring the extramural life of the home—gardening—bicycle cleaning—joinery—pigeon fancying—children's play—etc.—into the street, identifying man with his house and his street. Houses being*

---

* That chimneys, vents could have their own rich language of 'pooping into the air' was realised when a Mantegna painting was part copied by AS in 1947 as a student day-sketch design. (See 'Simple Inheritors'.)

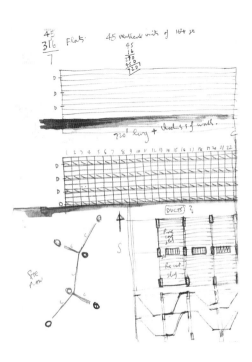

left: First ideogram of street-twig as a unit of the district. PS.
opposite top: Photomontage of street deck with a supposed Marilyn Monroe and Joe DiMaggio in foreground. PS, 1953.
opposite bottom: Photomontage of proposed decks on actual site, viewed through yard-gardens. PS, 1952.

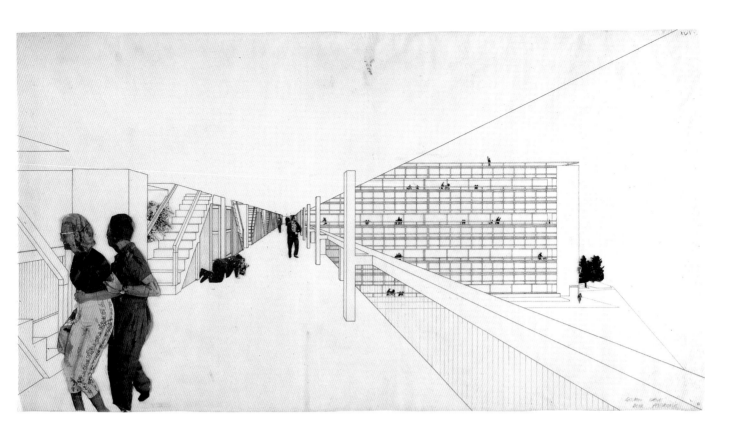

'detached', 'semi-detached', or 'terrace' (each deck differs) achieve the cottage scale in keeping with the scale of the accommodation and areas required. The passing stranger's view is enriched by glimpses through the open yard-gardens of the city and the River Thames.

The streets are safe play-spaces, for the only wheeled vehicles are the tradesmen's hand- and electrically propelled trollies."

As always, our concern with buildability shows in the competition report: *"The structural 'rack' is a reinforced-concrete box-frame with seven-inch bearing walls and six-inch floors. The site has been planned to use a mobile tower-crane to best advantage.**
The walls will be cast in large-panel, timber-faced, light steel-framed shutters which can be lifted vertically . . . erection finally taking place at all levels in a pyramidal fashion. Floors are lifted to the next level through the slot left for the pre-cast stairs.

Into this 'rack' are built the dwellings; standardised factory-fabricated, with the minimum of site work.

As there are no totally exposed end-walls it has been possible to leave all the concrete unfaced, with a designed shuttering pattern.
The remainder of the external walls is self-cleansing materials—glass and vitreous-enamelled steel-sheeting.†

Parapets are perforated pre-cast concrete panels; also pre-cast are the mullions and transoms.

All windows are in softwood, stained with wood preservative and unpainted."‡

In retrospect, we can see that in Golden Lane the screening layers are the parapet to the deck and rear wall of deck; then on the other facade the parapet of the yard-garden and penetrable facade of French windows. In many of the drawings there is the obvious and acknowledged debt to Le Corbusier's Unité d'Habitation in Marseilles, which was being designed and built from 1946 onwards.

* First seen in Genoa in 1950. In 1951 it had not yet been introduced in England.
† We were influenced by the imperviousness of vitreous-enamelled advertising panels to the industrial pollution of the north-east of England in the 1950s.
‡ Wood was then—1950s—not fashionable; metal windows were the most common practice; staining was unheard of.

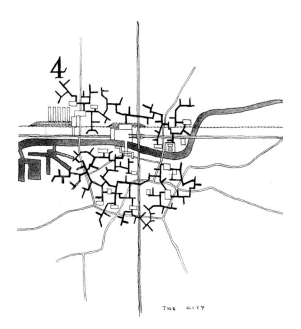

left: The idea elaborated into a city fabric. PS, 1953.
opposite top: Photomontage showing the planned construction process of Golden Lane. The project was designed to be erected using a tower-crane, not then used in the United Kingdom. AS, 1953.
opposite bottom: Axonometric drawing of construction. Ove Arup and Partners, 1952.

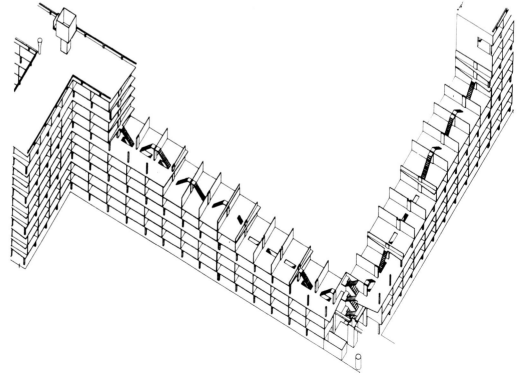

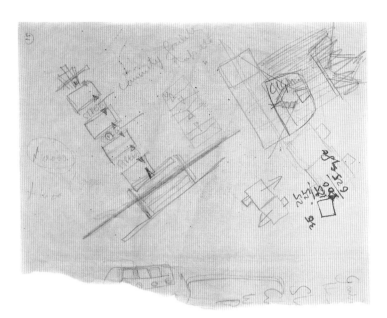

Original 'thinking' sketch of section of 'streets-in-the-air' and access to housing, among calculations. PS, 1952.

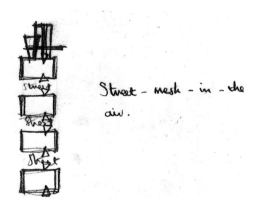

Diagrammatic section showing roofworks. PS, 1952.

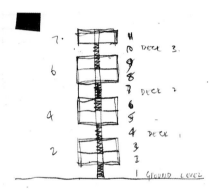

Diagrammatic section without roofworks. PS, 1952.

Final diagram for publication, showing access. PS, 1953.

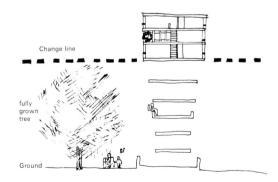

Final diagram for publication, showing how dwelling spaces should change in relation to their height above ground, particularly above the tree-top line, where the needs of people must be different when out of 'shouting' range of their children on the ground. PS, 1960.

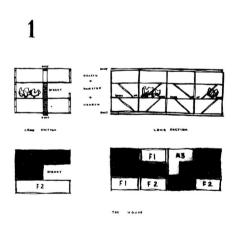

Explanatory diagrams: Cross and long sections with houses identified in both. PS, 1952.

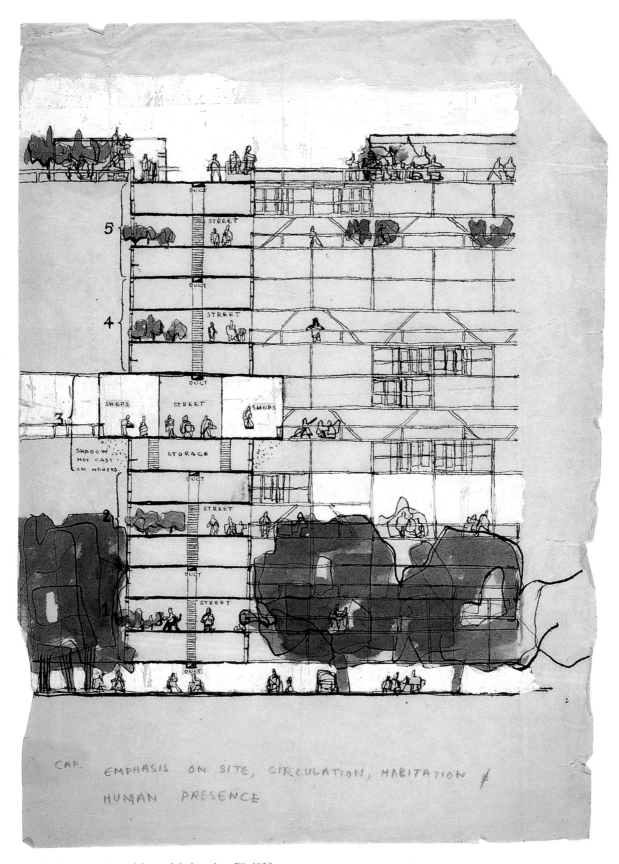

Elaborate section with partial elevation. PS, 1952.

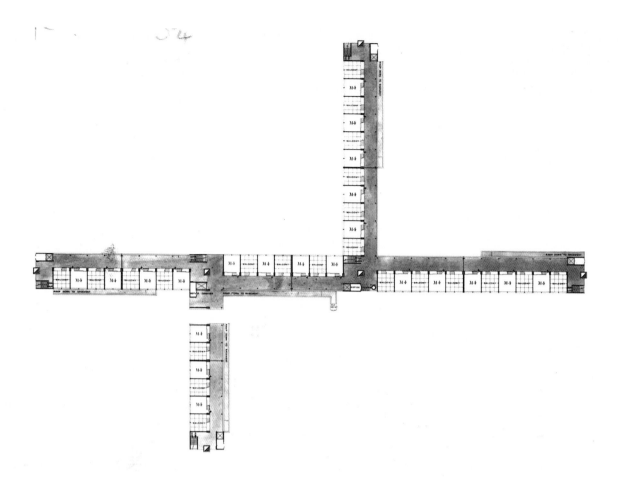

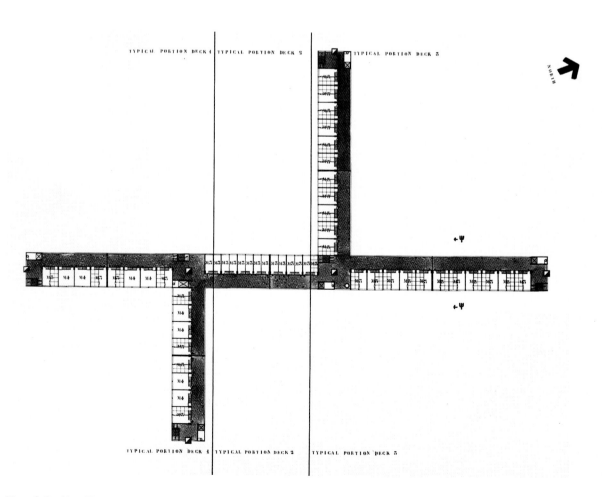

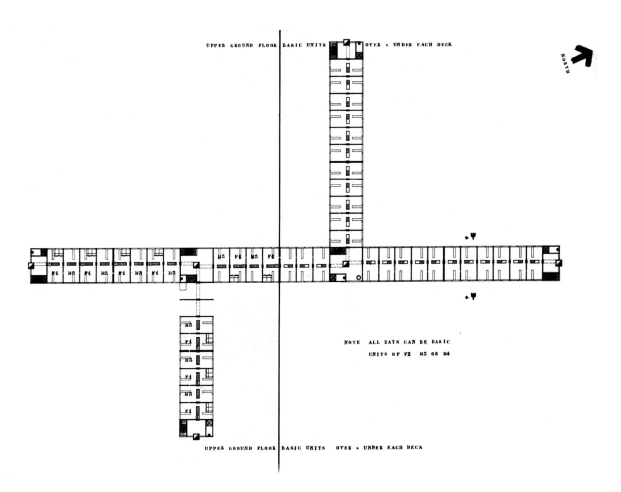

Three plans as submitted in competition. A+PS.

opposite top: Large yard-garden and kitchen level. 'Deck' or 'street' shaded.
opposite bottom: Composite of deck levels 1, 2, and 3.
above: Composite plan: Upper ground floor shown in detail (left);
the basic unit, over and under each deck (right).

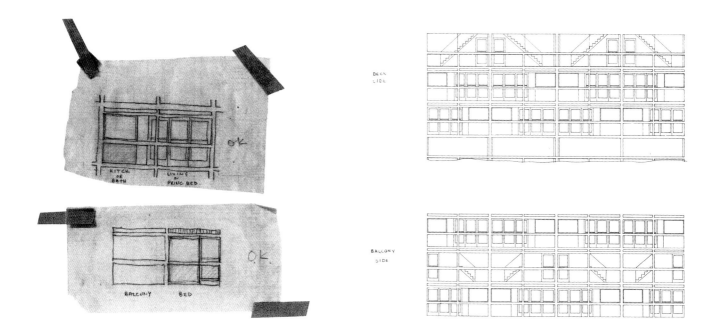

Initial sketches of facades. AS, 1952.

Preliminary elevation studies. PS, 1952.

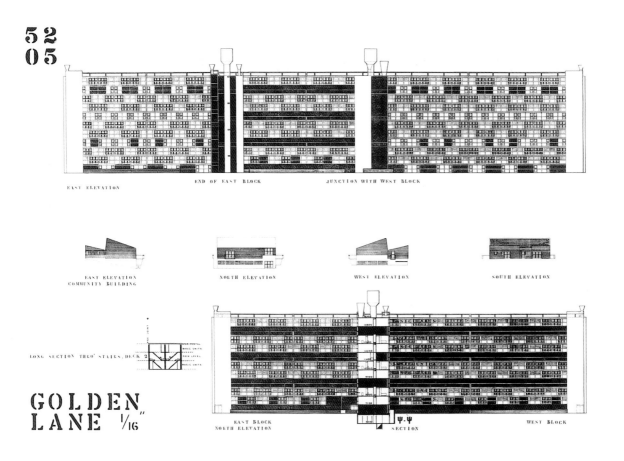

Elevations as submitted in competition. A+PS, 1952.

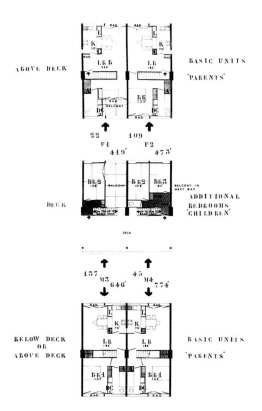

NOTE: ALL DWELLINGS CONSIST OF A STANDARD BASIC UNIT WITH ADDITIONAL BEDROOMS AT DECK LEVEL AS REQUIRED.

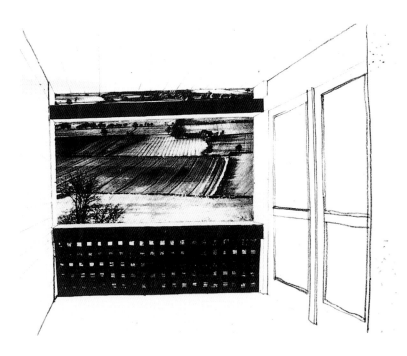

left: Three detail plans: Above deck, deck level, below deck. The 'basic unit' is that accommodation required by the couple: the bedroom, the bathroom, the kitchen, the living room.

above: Photomontage of yard-garden (measuring sixteen by eight feet) adjacent to kitchen. AS, 1952.

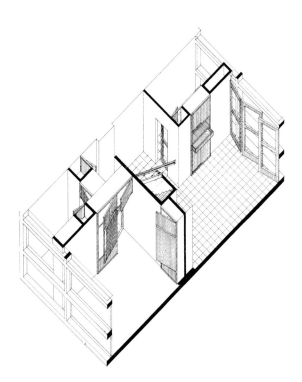

Axonometric of two-person flat accessed by stair from the deck. AS, 1952.

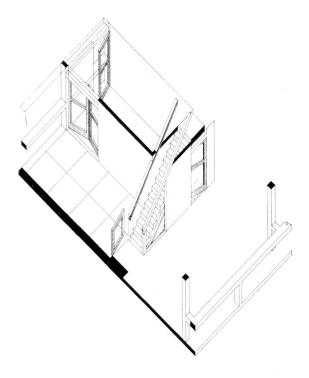

Axonometric of yard-garden, kitchen, and access deck. The stairs of the maisonette descend to the bedrooms, bathroom, and living room. The ascending stairs rise to a two-person flat above. AS, 1952.

Colville Place

With Colville Place, New Brutalism is announced.

A crystallisation of an attitude to purity of structure; services that speak of their own disciplines. The disposition of the rooms relates to the amount of light and sunlight desired, balanced by their need for access from the pedestrian way and their positions relative to each other according to pattern of use:

. . . bedroom to kitchen considering breakfast making and last things at night;

. . . studio to pedestrian way and to rear yard-garden functioning as a 'tokonoma' behind the wall-to-wall windows;

. . . living space at the top to enjoy the evening sun and to distance its leisure use from the public use of city in the evenings and at weekends;

. . . half the basement area as storage, so as not to have to live with all one's possessions;*

. . . a basement bathroom, to maintain an equable temperature and to receive machines;

. . . a poem of a stair to connect all levels.

This attempt at difference of character in the parts achieved by layering of functions is seen at its most primitive in Colville Place, a tiny site.

"The walls in common brick, the beams in ordinary concrete. An ambition not yet realised."

* Achieved in Priory Walk.

left: Ground-floor view out to tiny rear yard, with bench with glass brick providing secondary light to basement. AS, 1952.
opposite top: Location plan, plans, sections, elevations. A+PS, 1952.
opposite bottom: Working drawing sections and plan at first-floor level. A+PS, 1952.

ARCHITECTS HO.   24 COLVILLE PLACE W1

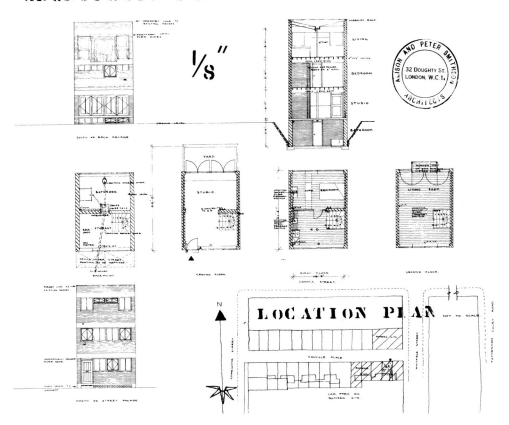

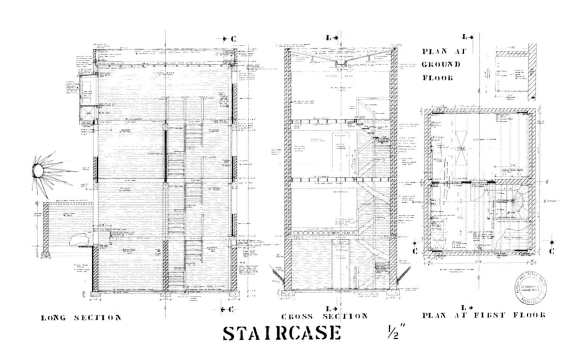

LONG SECTION   CROSS SECTION   PLAN AT FIRST FLOOR

STAIRCASE   ½"

Offices for the Electricity Board, Kampala

The first steps in developing a language of external surface for warm climates very different from England's are taken in Kampala; here, layers of roof, layers of facade screens and fins protect the office building against the worst effects of strong sunlight, allowing comfortable occupancy even when the air-conditioning breaks down.

In the report we wrote: *"A high sun tracking symmetrically over the site—to the north in summer, to the south in winter—seems to point to a symmetrically organised building with its principal facades facing north and south and presenting a blank face east and west . . . and upwards. The building is conceived as a sun-proof case with a breezeway between this case and its contained offices. This sun-proof case on the north and south keeps direct sun off window glass and the office floor surfaces, and although the vertical spacing of its shading membranes is the same as the floors, the membranes are slid downwards so that the enclosed volume is to the sun-proofing as the nun's head to her coif, apparently independent. Yet the dropped horizontal membrane penetrates the external screening of the enclosed volume, reflecting from its top surface into the depth of the interior. To facilitate the interchangeability of internal partitions and outer wall screening, the vertical membranes of the brise-soleil are set slightly to the west of the main column structure; this enables standard partition and outer wall screens to be used in all possible positions. This interchangeability further stresses the independence of the supporting, the sheltering, and the screening elements."*

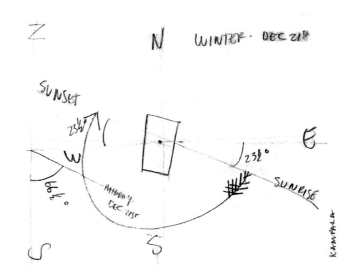

Sun-movement diagram: Winter. PS.

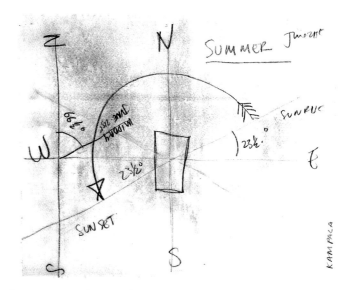

Sun-movement diagram: Summer. PS.

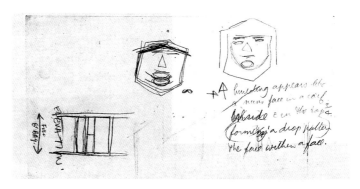

Facade ideogram: The building appears like a nun's face in a coif. AS.

The separation of means of access—a kind of layering—is described in the report: *"Vehicular and bicycle access is to the parking area under the podium, for there is a lower ground floor under the whole of the building proper and under the principal entrance. To this principal entrance for pedestrians a hooded path is taken over the grass to the heart of the building. A wide, cranked canopy forms both a covered forecourt and the main entrance foyer."*

The Kampala facades took as the start of their concrete membrane language the shifted egg-crate facade that Le Corbusier built in St. Dié: it was the shift that interested us:

. . . supporting, sheltering, and screening elements share a related dimensional geometry;

. . . the structure is coarse; twelve-inch-minimum thickness, on a sixteen-foot grid, with ten feet between floor slabs;

. . . the brise-soleil is a sturdy—six-inch minimum—framework whose basic eight-foot-by-ten-foot cells give measure to the units of internal organisation, and which, by means of horizontal and vertical displacements, key structure to screening;

. . . the internal partition and outer window screens are of light construction, two-inch nominal thickness, six feet eight inches high, with a four-foot horizontal measure externally and an eight-foot measure internally.

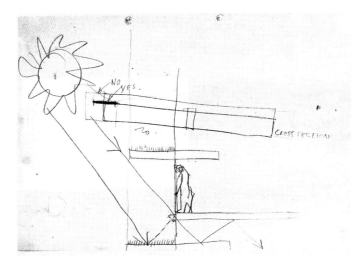

Sketch of cross section: Consideration of grass or other sympathetic-to-eyes surface on top surface of sun screens. Use of 'liveliness' of reflected light. PS.

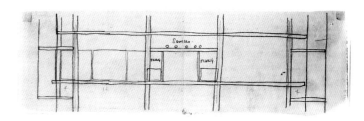

Cross section through one level of offices, central corridor, and displaced sun-shades. PS.

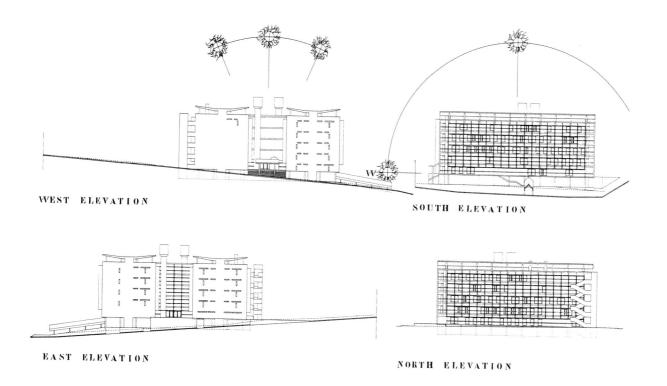

WEST ELEVATION

SOUTH ELEVATION

EAST ELEVATION

NORTH ELEVATION

U.E.B. KAMPALA

1/16″

Elevations as submitted in competition. A+PS, 1953.

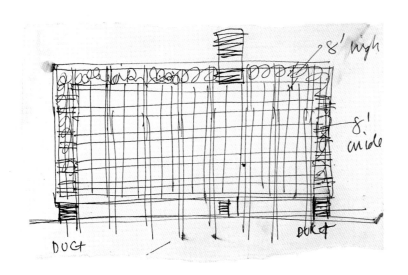

left: Elevation sketch of 'service duct' framing
brise-soleil. PS.
opposite top: Site plan and sections. A+PS, 1953.
opposite bottom: Plans. A+PS, 1953.

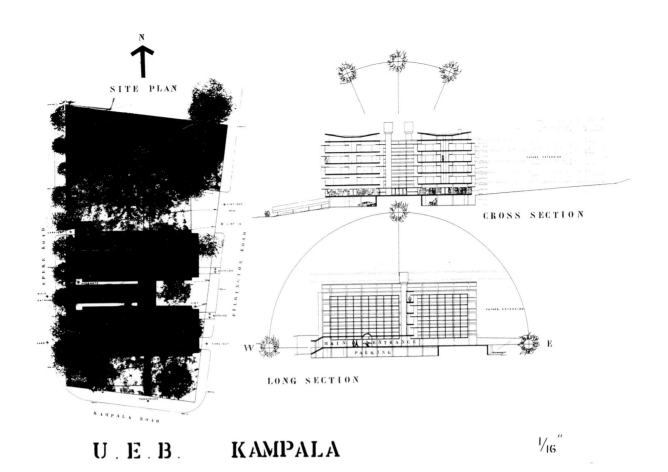

SITE PLAN

CROSS SECTION

LONG SECTION

U.E.B.   KAMPALA   ¹/₁₆"

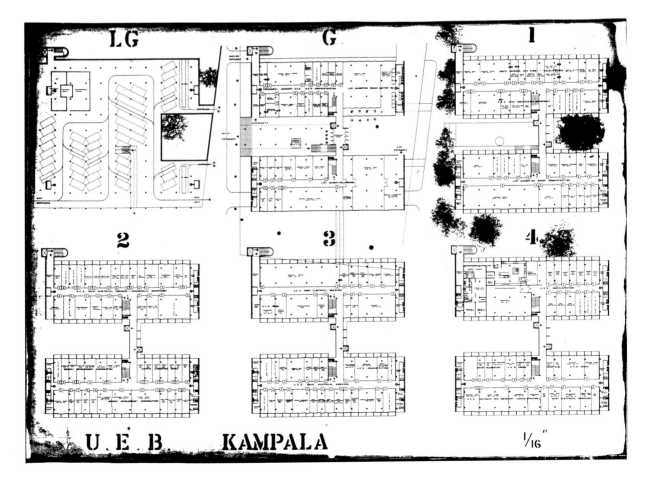

LG   G   1

2   3   4

U.E.B.   KAMPALA   ¹/₁₆"

House Extension, Alderbury, Wiltshire

The shoddy inter-war house in a wonderful setting called for an extension that would better appreciate the dimensions of site and provide interior spaces worthy of the contents: an exercise in stepping up the scale.

View from rear corner of the addition to the existing small house. AS, 1953.

View from above the old quarry. AS, 1953.

One-Thousand-Square-Foot House,
otherwise known as the 'Tea Tray' House*

This project harks back to our concern at Golden Lane with providing a 'hat'.

With one thousand square feet then permitted in house building, the idea was to dispose this all on one level, and make the roof as interesting to look at as a well-laid English tea tray. Each room has its informal 'cap' suitable to its space; its form made out of chicken wire on a simple frame/reinforcing, sprayed internally and externally to complete; the waterproofing a spray finish as renewable as paintwork; its maintenance made easy by containment within the deep edges of the 'tray'.

* We tried to buy a garden site in Fitzroy Park on which to build such a house.

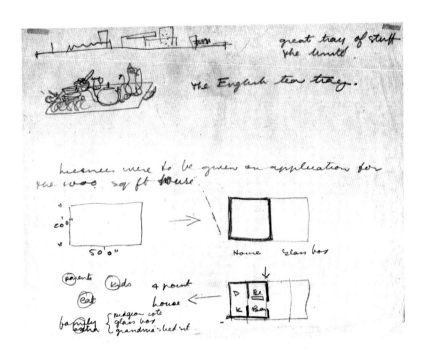

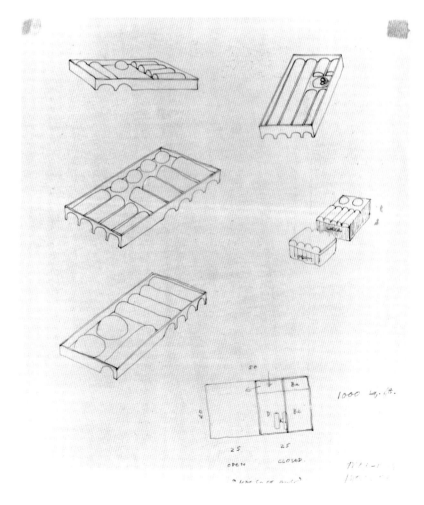

top: Ideogram of an 'arrangement roof' as offering to the sky. AS, 1953.
right: Sketches of roof that would identify the room cells: Domes intended to be sprayed concrete over mesh formers. AS, 1953.

Cheddar House of Cheese

January 1955

AS

Again the one-thousand-square-foot floor space providing for the basic couple:

. . . a house of simple construction;

. . . a house offering a variety of spaces by means of basic cells, basic space.

Provision of the 'basics' had not happened in England: a poor start in life was affecting a whole age group, unable to find homes of their own, new fabric they could make their own.

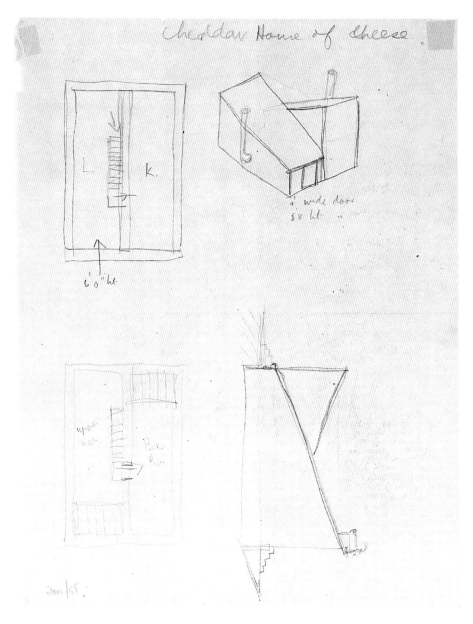

Composite sketch of plans, perspective, section. Again, the one-thousand-square-foot house (the standard permissible at that time) containing the basic cells, basic space for the young couple. AS, 1955.

The climate of Doha demands a structure—particularly for a hospital—that is eminently protective. In the layout, high walls for protection work inwards from the outer, general compound to contained compounds of single function.

We chose to utilise the insulating value of the local dense limestone masonry, thickly rendered and whitened, with all openings in their traditional balance of small apertures on the outer walls, fully shaded and openable onto shaded courtyards. Against the sun, the report describes: *"The roof is designed as two skins to allow the air to pass. In addition, roof loggias—for outdoor sleeping—are located to protect the building structure over the wards, treatment rooms, and operating theatres.*

The hospital building is sited so that the northern winds blow over its length and the west evening breeze passes across its courts and loggias."

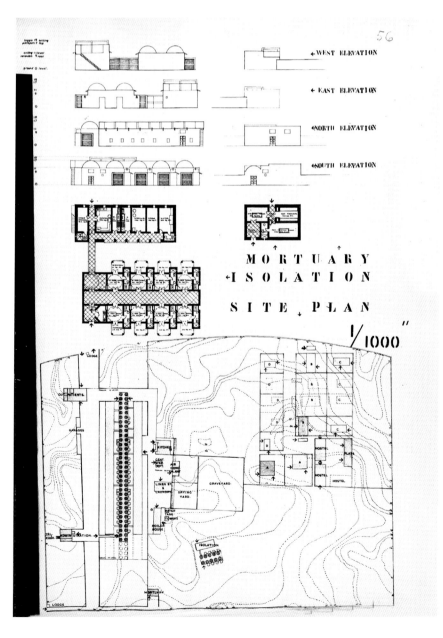

First attempt at a building tailored to the Gulf climate: An extendable mat within a compound. Elevations and plans (top and middle) represent the 'microcosm of the macrocosm', the isolation unit for contagious diseases; site plan (bottom) shows compound walls that prevent excessive dust movement. AS, 1953.

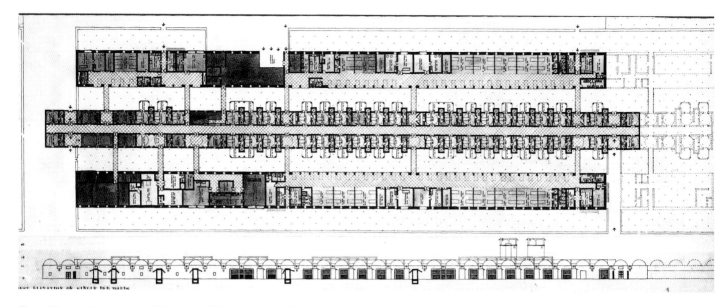

Plan of hospital as an extendable mat-building structured by its spine of domed private rooms with verandahs. AS.

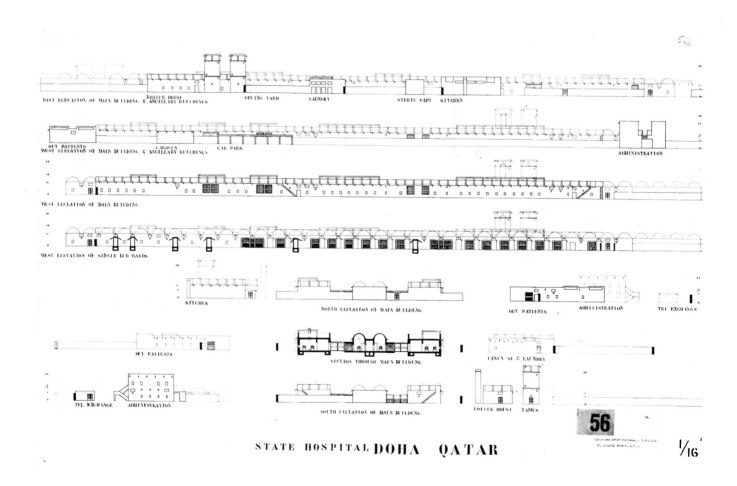

Complete elevations and sections of all buildings: East elevations of complex with compound walls in section (top); west elevation of complex (second from top); west elevation to access road on site (third from top); section through complex showing internal elevation of spine of domed private rooms and sections through departmental corridor (fourth from top); elevations and section of ancillary buildings within complex (fifth, sixth, and seventh from top). AS.

Overall, the domed private spaces and their verandahs, the wards and their verandahs stepping regularly along their organising internal streets, and the calmness of the anonymity of the structure together tried to achieve the equivalent to the healing qualities embodied in classical times in the Aesculapia.

We take as the generating impulse our awareness that when we are ill, we are in a state of heightened sensitivity, requiring a tangible privacy. At such times, the consciousness of glare is also heightened; therefore, veiling out glare has, in these circumstances, a healing power.

The private room is a domed eleven-foot cube; such individual rooms form the spine of the plan, and their measured tread is down the centre of the hospital. In the report we wrote: *"The general circulation throughout is superimposed on the ward verandah circulation; an economical plan-form in which distances between rooms are kept to a minimum.*

The hospital can extend either end, and each department can extend independently by units laid in parallel."

The traditional construction, the use of the dome form, seems some kind of failure of inventive energy . . . yet something else, hidden in embryo, resides in the plans. In 1974 came the realisation of its nature: in its response to the Arab inheritance of a different architectural ordering it is an embryo mat-building*

. . . compactly organised;
. . . well protected from the sun;
. . . rooms able to function for their occupants if the air-conditioning fails.

* 'How to Recognise and Read Mat Building', *Architectural Design*, September 1974, 573–90.

Exfoliated axonometric of domed private room. AS, 1980.

Axonometric of screened verandah off domed private room. AS, 1980.

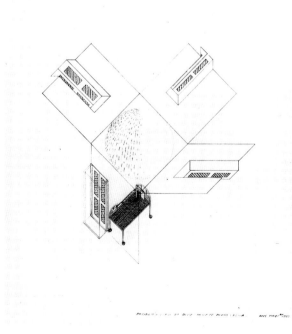

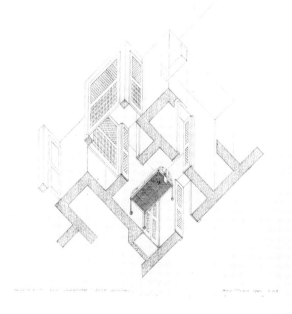

Sheffield University*

February – September 1953

A+PS

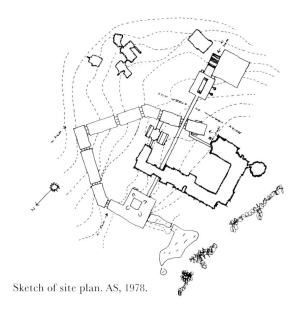

Sketch of site plan. AS, 1978.

Sheffield is the first of the 'encompassing' buildings whose slightly angled forms seemed at the time—and still seem—so much another invention from the twigs of Golden Lane that their relationship is in the deck idea only. For us the noises of occupation, the tempo of use of the decks in dwellings and those in a university, are fundamentally different.

"Connection is the generator of Sheffield. The straightforward horizontal layering above and below the pedestrian deck is so disposed on the site that the number of floors increases with the fall of the site to give a range of built volumes that indicate where are the large faculties, and where the small. The faculties with the greatest number of students are thus farthest from the union and library as these can be relied upon to keep the connective route of the pedestrian deck always busy.

The new entrances to the university, both occurring in the first phase, mean that the most important part of the'concept will be accomplished; for the north-to-south link joins the administration and arts directly to the library and architecture, and spearing through the existing main building enables the students here to reach the library, or the union over Western Bank, with equal facility.

Thus the north-to-south link—whose structure is its walkable duct—will function as a 'people-aqueduct' carrying both students and services to 'draw-off points'."†

This idea looks forward to the inevitable 'growth and change' of an expanding university: *"The ring‡ of high-level circulation and service in a continuous building complex makes it possible to satisfy the university's desire to extend horizontally rather than vertically, in spite of the huge volume of building. Furthermore, the technological intention of much of the university seems to point to buildings of the maximum flexibility—so that today's laboratory can be tomorrow's testing room or group of studies.*

This flexibility is most easily achieved in a simple, repetitive, continuous structure."

* Read with the University of Bath projects in the 1970s, 1980s, and 1990s.

† Here, for the first time, we get one of our favourite images of sweet servicing.

‡ In the report it was termed 'ring-main' . . . for constantly recharged movement.

Revised axonometric with trees. Wally Banks, AS, 1978.

Sheffield tries to take account of two paces of change: one responding to adjustment, the other to reorganisation.

"All the buildings of the new university have reinforced-concrete fixed construction and light steel flexible construction.* Two floors of flexible accommodation between main floors that are two and a half feet deep and twenty feet apart. The flexible accommodation is in lightweight construction—steel mullions, facias, a panel wall and window system, beams with steel decking for the intermediate floors. By this means, the accommodation can be large or small, single or double volume, or any combination which may suit functional requirements at any given time in a department's life. Floors and panel walls can be stripped out as desired without involving the permanent structure."

The report makes clear that the building's identity is given by patterns of use and not by 'design': *"The external and internal panel system can mesh in completely with the internal organisation of the building; when this organisation alters, the facade panel system is altered, thus continuing to give complete identity to the internal disposition."*

The growth and change of Sheffield can be seen—in retrospect—as layers of strengths; of permanence and transience.

Le Corbusier's earliest studies had the simplest regular concrete frame with free-form walls. This was so much his own language that we discovered in the undercroft of Coventry the need for another sort of language indicating possibilities of accretion or adaptability.

* Here entered the concept of the fixed and the changing; the permanent contrasting with the temporary.

Perspective of entrance from Western Bank Street connecting to the high-level student street-deck. Robinson, 1953.

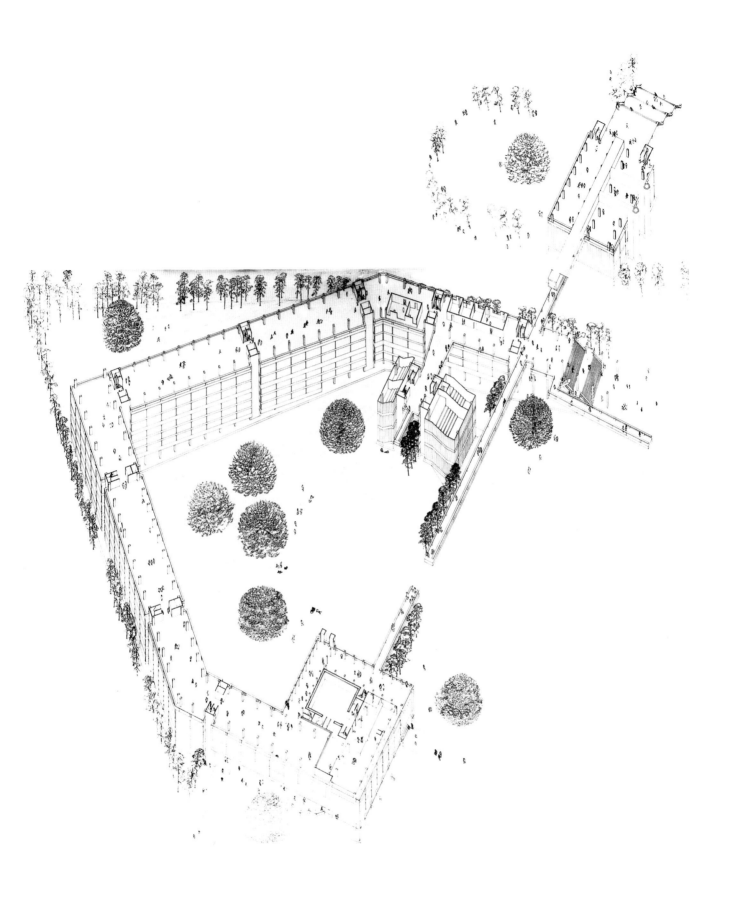

Axonometric at deck level and accommodation below, with trees as if twenty years on, and peopled with students passing to and from their classes and between library and union. The adjoining Weston Park flows into the enclosed areas of the old and new buildings as the calm green centre. Looked down on from the ring of high-level deck, the university's 'circulation' is 'stood off' to better appreciate the university's protected calm and location in the city. Wally Banks, AS, 1978.

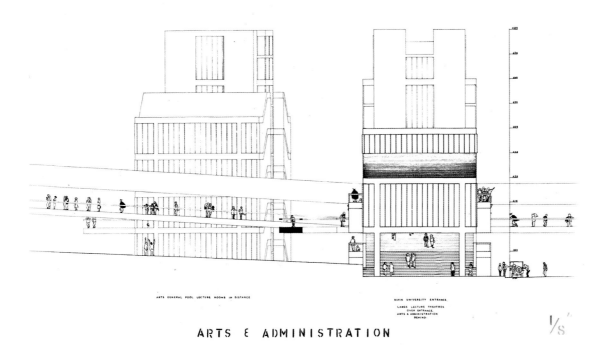

ARTS & ADMINISTRATION

Detail of arts entrance as submitted in competition. A+PS.

Competition drawing of library elevation coloured to record as visualised. A+PS.

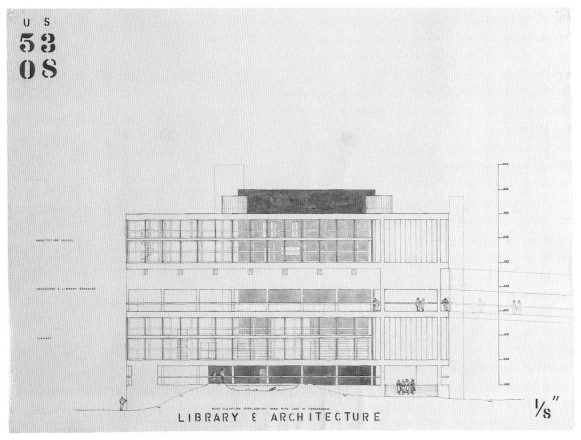

LIBRARY & ARCHITECTURE

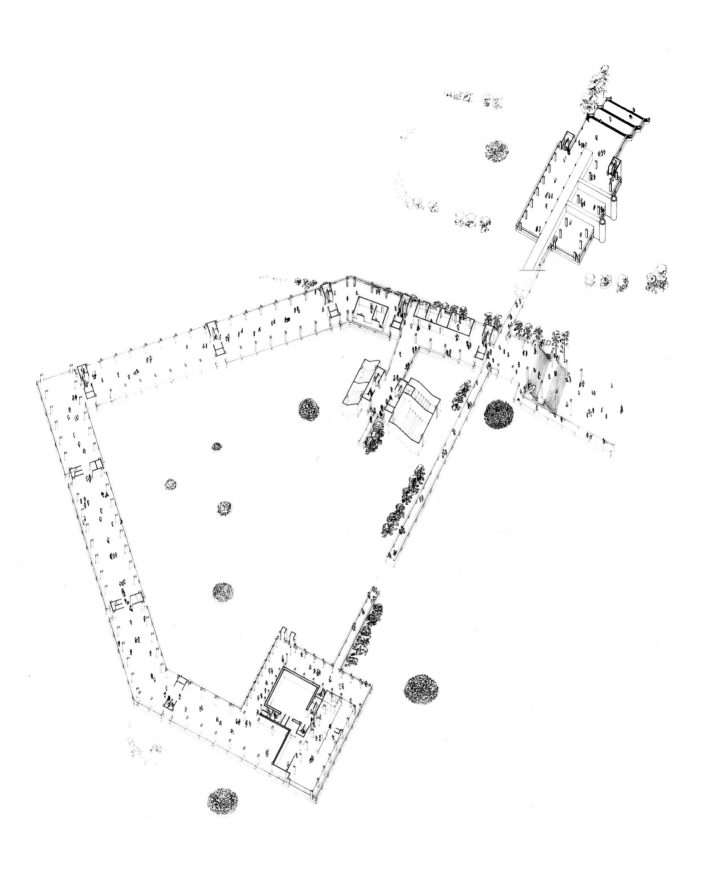

Axonometric of deck only. Wally Banks, AS, 1978.

The 'famous photograph' of PS, Eduardo Paolozzi, AS, and Nigel Henderson, taken in Limerston Street,
Chelsea, found in the catalogue of the 'This is Tomorrow' exhibition. Nigel Henderson, 1956.

4 Structuring of Spaces

the interaction between the existing and the added, 1953 . . .

'Parallel of Life and Art' Exhibition *(1953)*   118

Bates' Burrows Lea Farm *(1953–55)*   124

Five Projects for 'Housing Appropriate to the Valley Section' *(1954–56)*:   130

Isolate: Bates' Burrows Lea Farm   131

Hamlet: Galleon Cottages   134

Village: Fold Houses   135

Town: Close Houses   136

City: Terraced Crescent Housing   138

Chance Glass Flat and Mammoth Terrace House Conversion/Renewal *(1953–56)*   140

Crematorium at Kirkcaldy *(1954)*   142

Caro House *(1954–91)*   143

Rumble Villa *(1954)*   144

Bark Place Mews *(1954–56)*   146

Monument on the Goodwin Sands and a Church Sort of Place *(1955)*   148

Pierced Wall Structure *(1955)*   149

Sugden House *(1955–56)*   150

Hot Springs *(1955)*   157

Reviewing the whole body of our architectural work, it can be seen in retrospect how the spirit of the programme is advanced:

Hunstanton . . . Economist . . . Brasilia . . . Lucas . . . Bath . . . each building shows a family of sheltered spaces, where the elements of construction mark out spaces for the foreseeable patterns of use.

Yet the characteristics of these spaces are such that they can be tuned by the occupants to the changing values of their time without denaturing the architecture.

Each building has particular ways of possessing its spaces:

. . . Hunstanton . . . takes possession of the fields before it by its shape (with Palladian connotations);

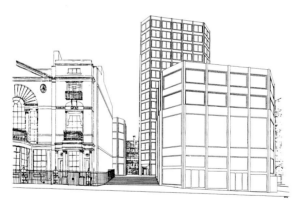

. . . the Economist . . . draws other, nearby city spaces into a field of reciprocity;

. . . Brasilia . . . offers a sense of security to the variously occupied spaces within an overall 'climate shell';

. . . Lucas . . . re-energises a field pattern at the fringe of the city;

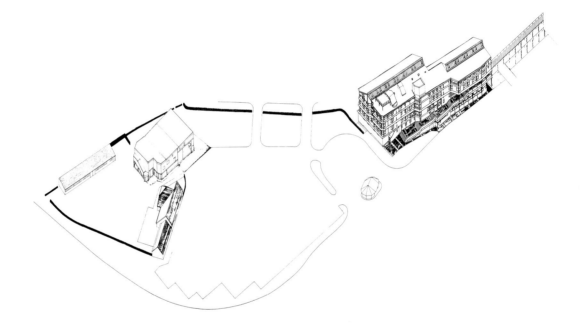

. . . Bath . . . takes possession of the car-park and bus-stop areas to give it a sense of being a generally useful assembly place like the old market squares.

The inside and the outside, the sheltered space and that open to the sky, intermingle within and without the structuring framework.

In all these cases the environment as found is re-energised, so that it is given the stamina to be receptive to the new buildings and the incoming people.

'Parallel of Life and Art' Exhibition, I.C.A., Dover Street, London

11 September – 18 October 1953

A+PS

With Nigel Henderson, Eduardo Paolozzi, and Ronald Jenkins

This exhibition—originally called 'Sources'—was to offer some evidence of a new attitude. It came about as a result of a manifesto under the title 'Documents 53', presented to the Institute of Contemporary Art in 1952.

A text of the time said: *"The purpose of this exhibition is to present material belonging intimately to the background of anyone trying to look at things today. An introduction of these visual by-products of our way of thinking will perhaps dispel the bewilderment most people feel when confronted with the most recent manifestations of man's activities."*

A later submission text explained: *"The method will be to juxtapose photo-enlargements of those images drawn from life, nature, industry, building, and the arts—of related phenomena that are parts of that New Landscape which experimental science has revealed and artists and theorists created.*

These images cannot be so arranged as to form a consecutive statement. Instead they will establish an intricate series of cross relationships between different fields of art and technics. Touching off a wide range of association and offering fruitful analogies . . . a kind of Rosetta stone.

In sum they will provide an outline, a fugitive delineation of the features of our time as they appeared to one particular group working together."

The exhibition's press handout expanded this joint statement: *"Technical inventions such as the photographic enlarger, aerial photography, and the high-speed flash have given us new tools with which to expand our field of vision beyond the limits imposed on previous generations.*

Their products feed our newspapers, our periodicals, and our films, being continually before our eyes; and thus we have become familiar with material, and aspects of material, hitherto inaccessible.

Today, the painter, for example, may find beneath the microscope a visual world that excites his senses far more than does the ordinary world of streets, trees, and faces; but his work will necessarily seem obscure to the observer who does not take into account the impact on him of these new visual discoveries."

The actuality became a first essay in free disposition, remaking the space of the gallery as a cave of images.

Images for a poster. Nigel Henderson, Eduardo Paolozzi, 1953.

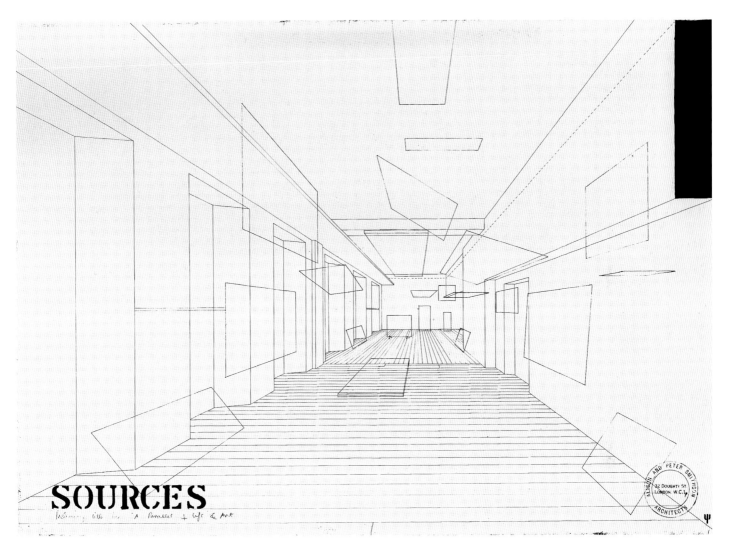

Perspective of proposed layout. PS, 1952.

Photograph of the exhibition. Nigel Henderson, 1953.

above: Photograph of the exhibition.

page 122: Photograph of the exhibition. Nigel Henderson, 1953.
page 123: Two general views of the exhibition.

Bates' Burrows Lea Farm, Shere

The Bates' Burrows Lea Farm—reached from a country lane—has to sit lightly in a market garden and use the minimal amount of territory, hardly interrupting the growing.

The new occupants are to be there to enjoy the panorama of the whole visible landscape within the circumference of the horizon. The 'floating form' of the Bates' Burrows Lea Farm 'possesses' this everyday landscape, compound of every age, in its own, new spirit—by a single bold act— extending its aesthetic of structuring of spaces into that landscape.

Appreciation of the English landscape requires any house's windows to have 'eyebrows' against the glare of our overcast skies . . . in the way that the Regency verandah came into being as soon as the house extended out into the garden as foreground to the greater landscape. Lattice screens appear for the first time in our work in the antiglare clerestory lights.

The house structure was to be the 1950s equivalent to the English half-timbered house: a light steel frame cantilevering off a fireproof concrete base. The frame is stiffened by an internal and external plywood skin using the scarfe-jointing techniques developed for boats during the war.

Of all the isolated houses we designed in the 1950s and 1960s this is the house we should most like to have built.

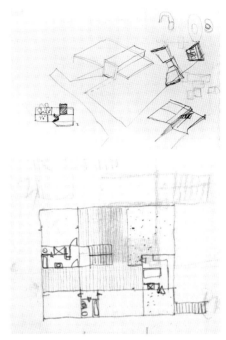

Analytical diagram showing entry as first proposed. 1953–55.

top: Sketch investigating possibility of changing location of garage to a place perpendicular to the road. PS, 1953.
second from top: Ideogram of plan disposition. AS, 1953–55.
above: Plan view of rough model. John Maltby, 1953–54.

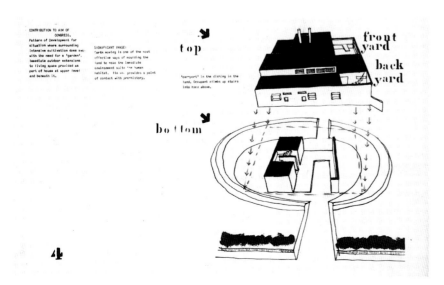

4

BURROWS LEA FARM 5401

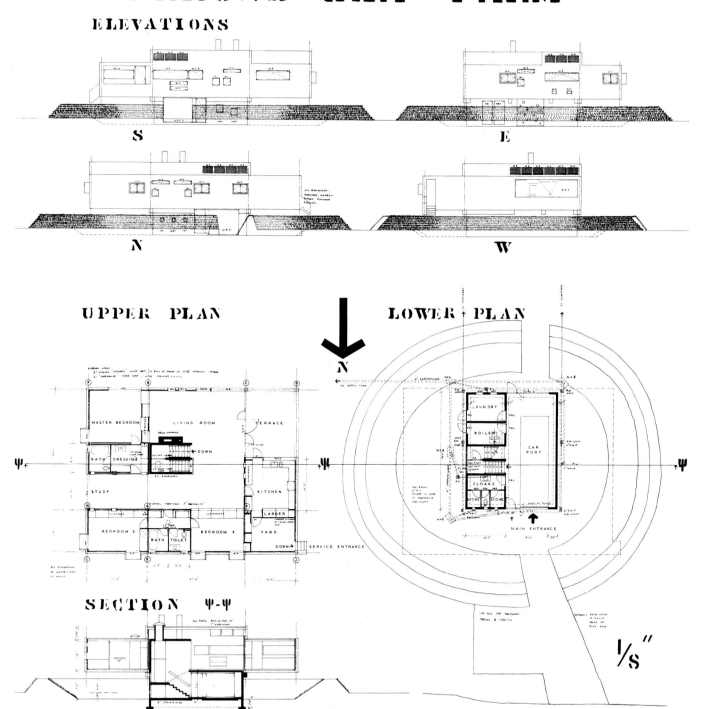

South, north, east, and west elevations (top);
upper and lower plans (middle); section (bottom).
A+PS, 1954.

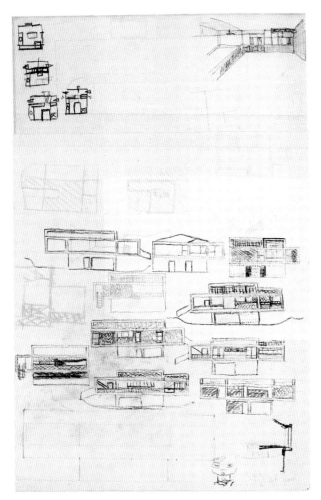

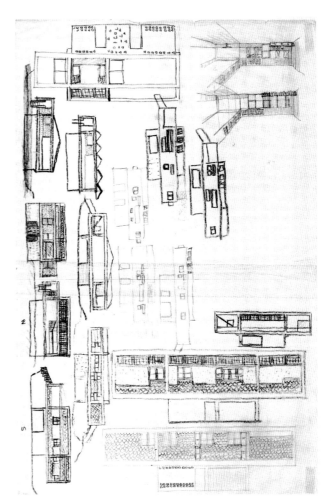

Sketches exploring cladding before investigation of scarfed waterproof plywood. AS, 1953.

Southwest view of rough model within the bund, showing
terrace onto which kitchen and living room open. Clerestory
windows allow west and south light to filter into living areas.
John Maltby, 1953–54.

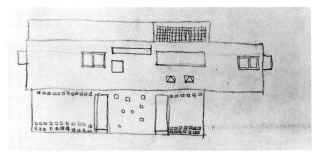

Ideomatic sketch elevation: Squares in concrete represent inset
glass bricks of different sizes and shapes. AS, 1953.

Sectional ideogram. A+PS, 1954.

North view of road side of rough model, with hooded windows
seen above bund. John Maltby, 1953–54.

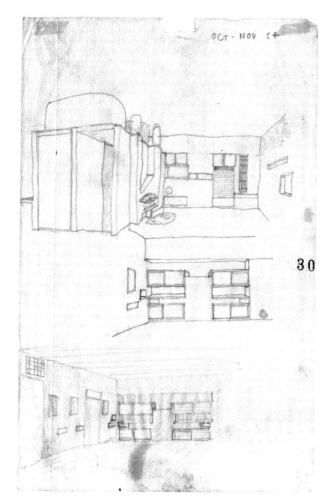

Interior sketches from notebook. AS, 1954.

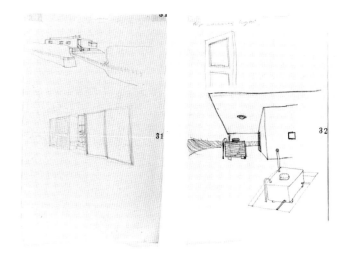

top: Sketch of view from lane and interior sketch of bedroom fittings
(left); sketch of oil tank under cover of overhang inside bund
(right). AS, 1954.

above: Sketch view of the nursery garden from proposed terrace at
piano nobile level. AS, 1953–55.

Axonometric of entire house. Luiz Breda Neto; shading, Mahasty Akavan Farshchi, 1981.

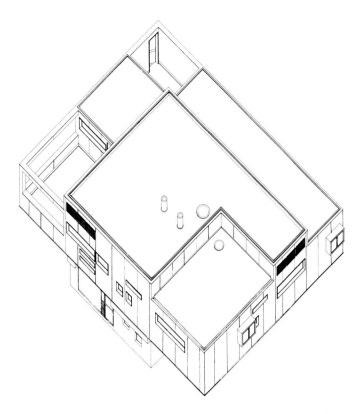

Axonometric of air view of roof. Luiz Breda Neto; final axonometric, Peter Salter.

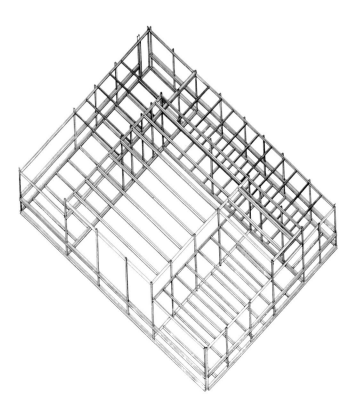

Axonometric of first-floor steel structure. Luiz Breda Neto; final axonometric, Peter Salter.

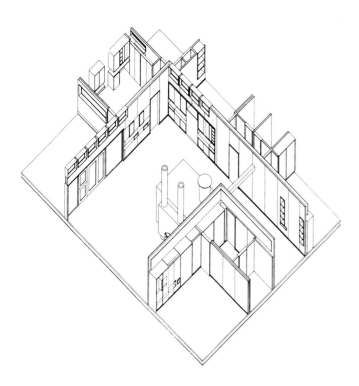

Axonometric of first-floor internal partitions. Luiz Breda Neto; final axonometric, Peter Salter.

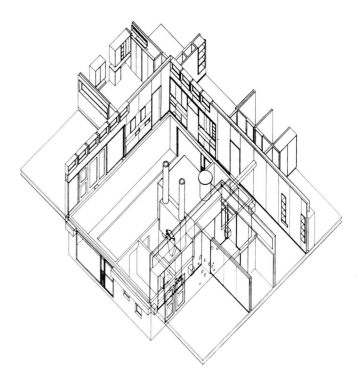

Axonometric of ground-floor and first-floor internal partitions. Luiz Breda Neto; final axonometric, Peter Salter.

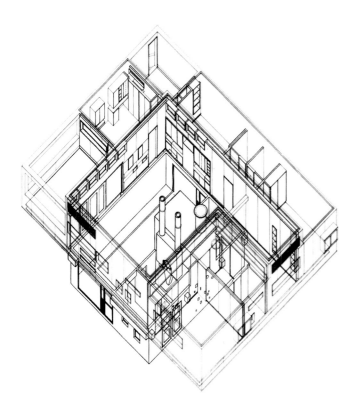

Composite axonometric of ground-floor concrete, first-floor internal steel structure, first-floor interior skins, and exterior skins. Luiz Breda Neto; final axonometric, Peter Salter.

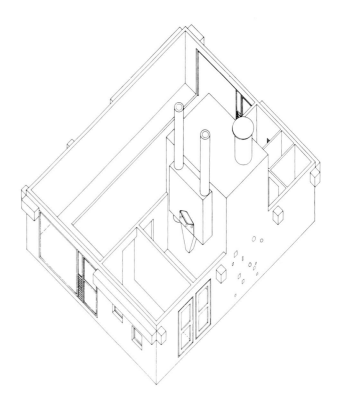

Axonometric of ground-floor concrete base. Luiz Breda Neto; final axonometric, Peter Salter.

Five Projects for 'Housing Appropriate to the Valley Section', CIAM 10, Dubrovnik

The name Team 10 originated in that designation being given to us by CIAM when we were made responsible for the CIAM 10 programme.

To explain what our generation felt about *specificity*, we (A+PS) made four projects specially to present in Dubrovnik, which, together with an existing project, were to show what we meant by being specific to *situation* (which is a word different from *location*).

We used the Valley Section because in our school time Patrick Geddes had been recently discovered by our teachers (as he, in turn, had found the Valley Section in Elisée Reclus/Le Play), so we assumed the older generation would be familiar with the concept.

The five situations: Isolate, Hamlet, Village, Town, City.

These fragmentarily published schemes were a slowly 'grown' language,* often starting with diagrams that were aids to thinking about the sort of movement likely to predominate in their locations; ideograms as steps towards form-invention.

Ideograms by which we also recognise that, both in their ordering and of their very nature, the forms to be invented needed to be connective. Connectors—bridging elements—links—transitional spaces—intermediary spaces—that are the stitch-up between one building and another, one district and another; in each case a space dedicated to the change of pace.

The pause-space in towns or villages may be almost nothing, only enough to require some small action-acknowledgement— as does the cottage gate—of transition that allows a person to sense where he is and what he is about.

* See Doorn Manifesto by Team 10, 1954; published in AS, ed., *Team 10 Meetings* (Delft: Delft University of Technology, Faculty of Architecture; New York: Rizzoli, 1991), 21.

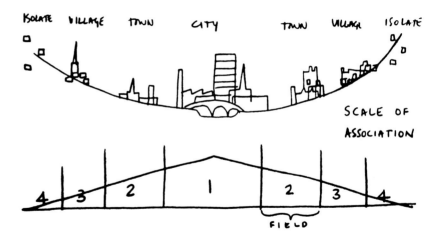

Diagram from the Doorn Manifesto, 1954.

Isolate: Bates' Burrows Lea Farm, 1953–55

From the unbuilt design, we reproduced four panels that were presented at Dubrovnik (for further details and text, see pages 124–29).

right: Grass study. Luiz Breda Neto, February 1981.

pages 132–33: Four presentation panels for CIAM 10 at Dubrovnik, 1956. A+PS.

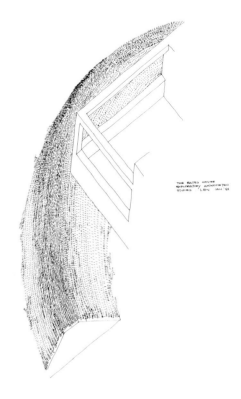

MARS GROUP
Alison and Peter Smithson,

London.

Parent Community:Shere,
Surrey.
Climate:Temperate.
Location:England.
Immediate parent community
Market Garden.
Population 15-20.

burrows
lea
farm

ISOLATE.

1

Peter de Hooch.

IDENTIFICATION IMAGE. The Dutch picture is significant because it portrays
two kinds of outdoor 'extension to the dwelling' , that for work and that
for recreation. It shows the life good- what is possible for every burger
family. Its equivalent is to be found in American advertising.
From the doorstep of the tent there is a view over the countryside.
The tent gives some indication of new possibilities of light manipulation.
Such effects are also typical of traditional Turkish architecture.
The project presented has turned away from simple glass walls into the
complexities of volume differentiation and pierced wall lighting in which
the varying use-zones of the dwelling are fully identified.

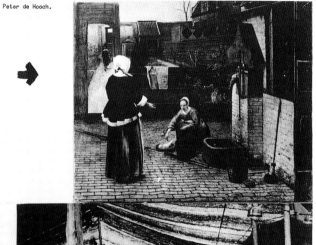

PROBLEM: TO DEVELOPE A SPECIAL FORM FOR A SINGLE

HOUSE WITH OUTDOOR LIVING SPACE SITED IN AN

INTENSLY CULTIVATED MARKET GARDEN.

Selim Bey's tent
Kara Darg in Hakkan Province.
photo P.H.Davis.

People Provided for:
    2 Parents
    2 grown up children
Extensions to Dwelling:
    front yard
    back yard
    covered drying area.
DEVELOPMENT PATTERN:
The area occupied by building
had to be as small as
possible so as not to
interfere with the market
garden surrounding it.
There is thus no need
for a private garden,
instead a dishing is
formed in the land and
the car comes straight
into the garage (an electric
eye operates garage doors)
like a yacht into its
moorings at the lower level
which is that of the lane.
The owner wanted to get
out of his car inside his
house. From the garage he
climbs the stairs into
the house which is
cantilevered over the
dishing,sufficiently
above the ground to get
the full benefit of the
excellent position and
views over the Surrey
Downs.

2

SITE PLAN   BURROWS LEA FARM.

HISTORICAL PARALLEL: A HOUSE ISOLATED BY A CIRCULAR EARTHWORK

(CASTLE RISING, NORFOLK, ENGLAND.)

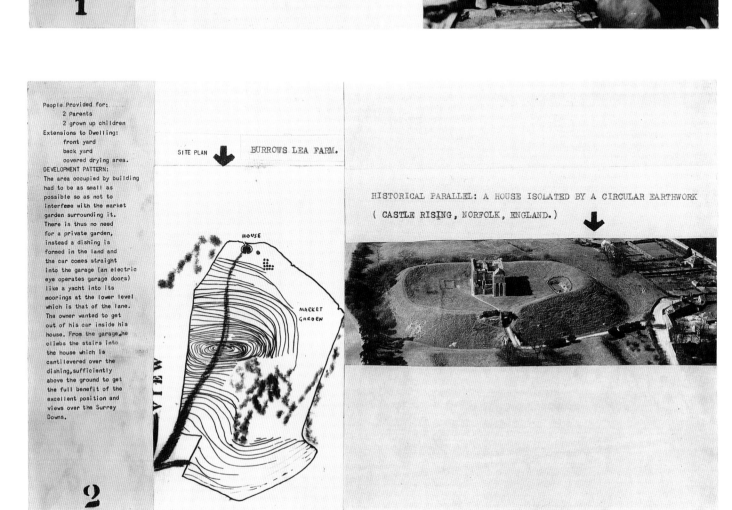

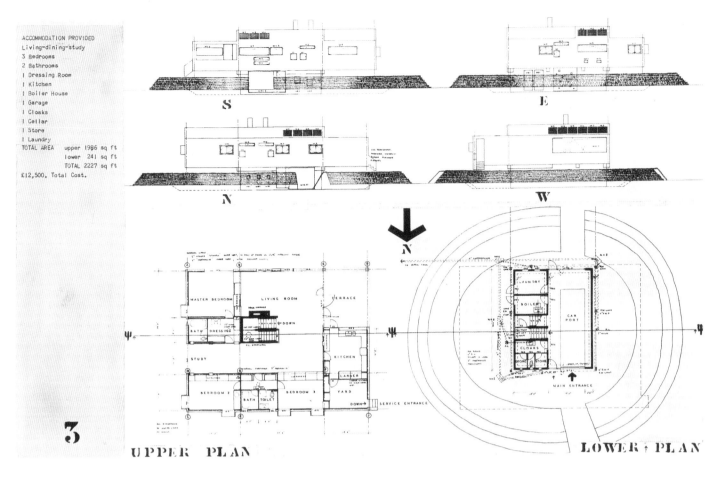

ACCOMMODATION PROVIDED
Living-dining-study
3 Bedrooms
2 Bathrooms
1 Dressing Room
1 Kitchen
1 Boiler House
1 Garage
1 Cloaks
1 Cellar
1 Store
1 Laundry
TOTAL AREA   upper 1986 sq ft
              lower 241 sq ft
              TOTAL 2227 sq ft
£12,500. Total Cost.

3

UPPER PLAN

LOWER PLAN

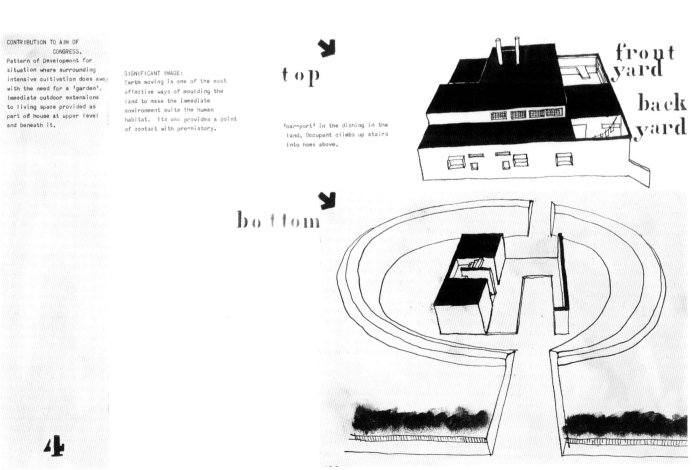

CONTRIBUTION TO AIM OF
                CONGRESS.
Pattern of Development for
situation where surrounding
intensive cultivation does away
with the need for a 'garden'.
Immediate outdoor extensions
to living space provided as
part of house at upper level
and beneath it.

SIGNIFICANT IMAGE:
Earth moving is one of the most
effective ways of moulding the
land to make the immediate
environment suite the human
habitat. Its use provides a point
of contact with pre-history.

top

'car-port' in the dishing in the
land. Occupant climbs up stairs
into home above.

front
yard

back
yard

bottom

4

Addition to the smallest village (such as the dales' hamlet of Bainbridge, North Riding) of the smallest social group of five houses.

Of Galleon Cottages we wrote: *"This is a new way of thinking about non-urban dwellings. This is a village 'Unité'; in such a small place the additional accommodation can easily be assessed—say two four-bedroom houses, one three-bedroom house, one two-bedroom house (the 'basic' unit), and one single old person's home: the idea is to put houses together so that they form an architectural unit which can be set against the backdrop of the fells; intensive cultivation— as is traditional for display—takes place in the front, sheltered garden."*

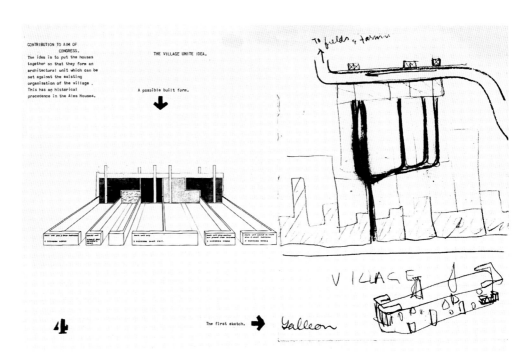

Occupancy diagram (left) and ideogram with sketch plan (right) of main green behind dwellings, with pedestrian access through an existing 'snicket', rear access by a field lane, and gardens to the west for the evening pattern of use. AS.

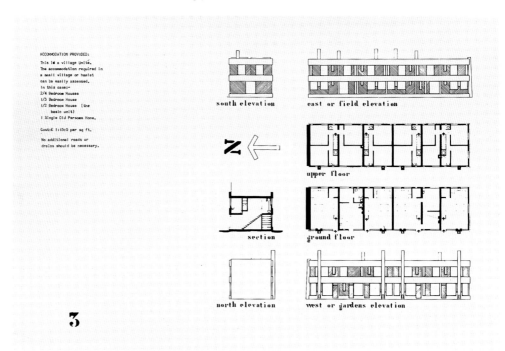

South elevation and eastern or field elevation (top); ground- and upper-floor plans and section (middle); north elevation and western or garden elevation (bottom). AS.

Village: Fold Houses, Dales' Village of West Burton, North Riding, Yorkshire, 1954, AS

Fold Houses for infill at the end of a 'lonnen' in the dales' village of West Burton, North Riding.

Of Fold Houses we wrote: *"Infill is all this type of dales' village can hold: like 'new fruits' on the old twigs of access and services. The fold is a wind-break; each house has its back to the prevailing wind so that each dales' village will accept these houses as its own."*

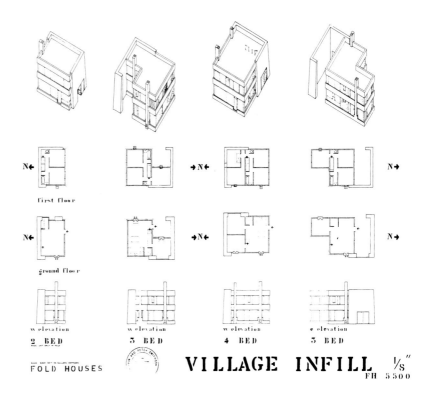

Four variations of Fold Houses (left to right): basic unit for a farm-labourer couple; unit for a couple with two children who need a living room and yard; four-bedroom house; three-bedroom house with a two-story yard. Drawings include axonometrics (first row); set of first- and ground-floor plans (second and third rows) showing expansion and variation possibilities; west and east elevations (fourth row) composed of half local material retrieved from derelict outhouses and half insulated timber panels. AS, 1954.

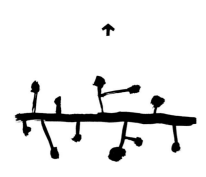

Ideogram showing the 'new fruits' on old twigs, areas where Fold Houses are additions to an existing village. One of a series of images made to match proposals in the Team 10 Doorn Manifesto. AS, 1954.

Plan of typical village, this one with a green showing positions where infill could occur, giving extra protection to the existing group and offering an amazing variety of new 'protected' relationships to the existing cluster and its setting.

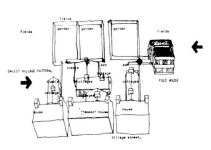

Aerial view sketch of a typical location with Fold House infill. 1954.

Town: Close Houses, 1955

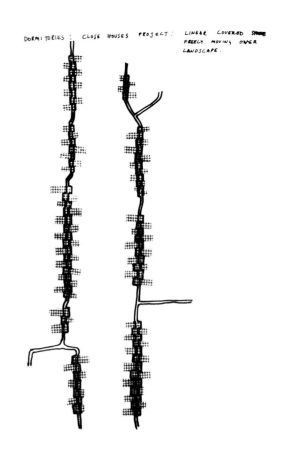

Close Houses ride the landscape for the renewal of small, northern, industrial towns, still compact in their landscape and still strong in a community sense, born of past travail.

The first invented of this series of housing studies (autumn 1954) in 'bottle diagrams' was the Close House, capable of response to place through its variable density possibilities. In the indicative graphics of these diagrams, the stalk represents walk-in-the-dry.

Of the developed Close Houses we wrote: *"The covered close, with individual access porticos off it, responds to new ways of living in a town. Every house can be different—to suit individual requirements—as were the early industrial, speculative houses for the middle classes—yet derived from the same organisational principle. Built from standard elements, they can economically form a continuous building operation.*

The 'split' section, admitting sunlight, permits new forms of internal planning and new sorts of spaces . . . together with a new sense of possession— even access to—the private air above one's head."

Diagram of linear pedestrian-way-accessed houses, arranged in a freely moving pattern which responds to topography and landscape features, such as mature trees. (Diagrams from the Dubrovnik Scroll.) AS, 1955.

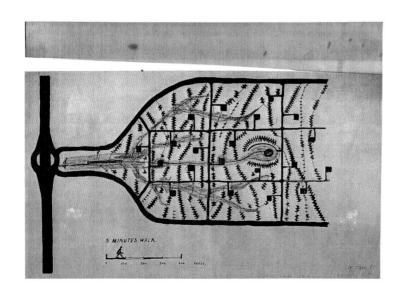

'Bottle diagram' of possible portion of a new town as a district of Close Houses. AS, 1954.

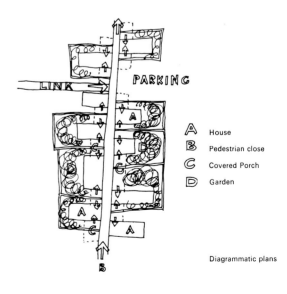

A House
B Pedestrian close
C Covered Porch
D Garden

Diagrammatic plans

Diagram of close layout. PS, 1955.

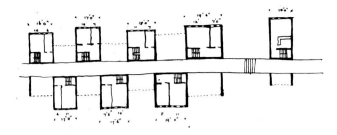

E   W

Diagram of different house sizes which correspond to different close conditions. AS.

First idea sketch of end elevation as the entrance to a close. PS, 1955.

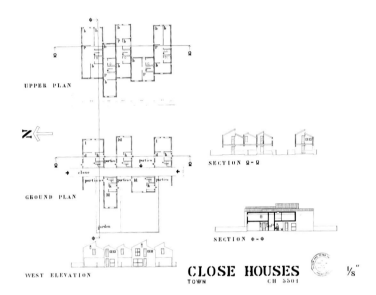

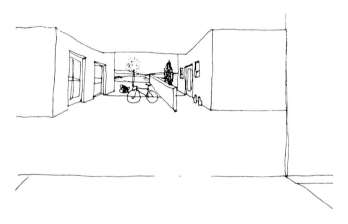

Ground- and upper-floor plans, cross section and long section, west elevation. PS.

First sketch of neighbouring adjoining houses and yard seen from a close. AS, 1955.

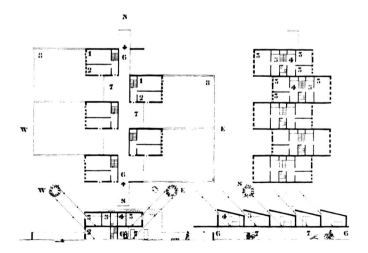

Diagrammatic ground- and first-floor plans of equal width houses, cross section showing sun penetration into all rooms, section taken the length of a close showing that all bedrooms benefit from the sun. PS.

City: Terraced Crescent Housing, London, 1955, PS

Faced as a 'scoop' to the sun; intended to be orientational 'sun signs', stepping through the collection of grown-together villages that comprise London; able to utilise a scatter of sites and cast a minimal shadow that could fall on intersections, railways, and roads.

Of this south-facing Terraced Crescent we wrote: *"All living accommodation faces the sun; the living areas open to porch-doorstep where every house has its own terrace. The crescent tapers as it rises . . . so we find families of children nearer the ground and couples and single people at a height."*

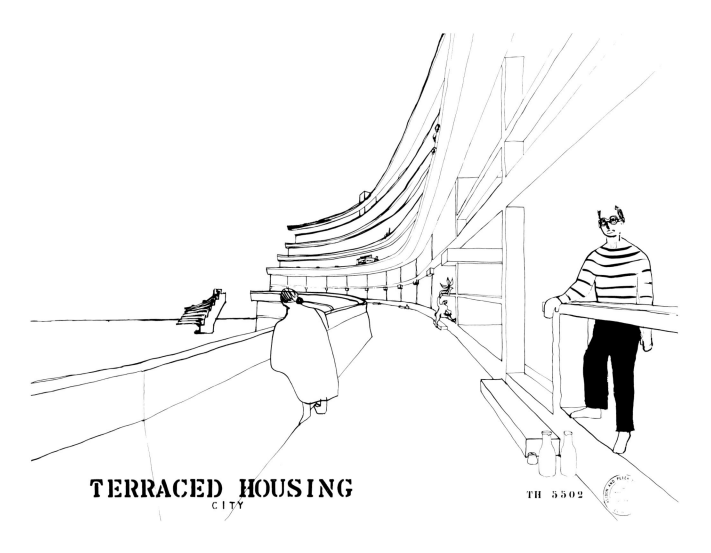

TERRACED HOUSING
CITY

TH 5502

Perspective along deck showing yard-terrace to maisonette. PS, 1955.

Terraced housing as a
unit of city: North
(rear) elevation; plan of
crescent; south (front)
elevation showing
stacked deck access and
yard-terraces. PS, 1955.

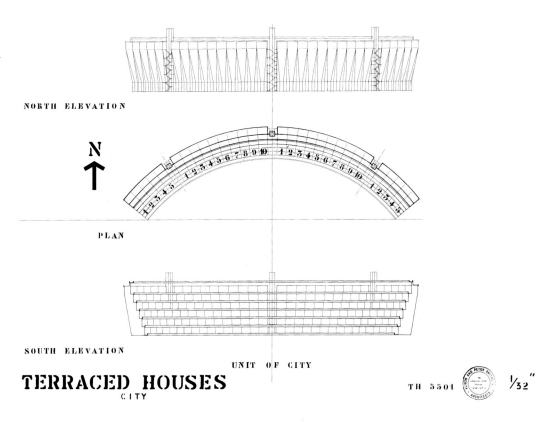

NORTH ELEVATION

PLAN

SOUTH ELEVATION

UNIT OF CITY

TERRACED HOUSES
CITY

TH 5501   1/32"

Plans of maisonette at
deck and upper levels;
portion of north (rear)
elevation; section
through sun-oriented
terraced housing
(for a worked example,
see the Hamburg
Steilshoop in *The
Charged Void: Urbanism*);
one-maisonette-wide
south (front) elevation.
PS, 1955.

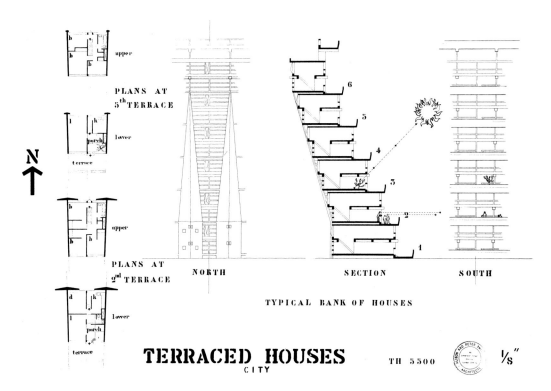

PLANS AT
5th TERRACE

PLANS AT
2nd TERRACE

NORTH   SECTION   SOUTH

TYPICAL BANK OF HOUSES

TERRACED HOUSES
CITY

TH 5500   1/8"

Chance Glass Flat
and Mammoth Terrace House Conversion/Renewal

Perspective sketch of proposed conversion: Detail of single floor. PS, 1953.

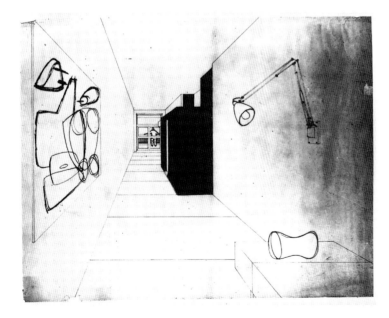

Perspective of typical interior. PS, 1954.

These are conversion projects for typical London speculator's terraces of the period of the Great Exhibition, 1851.

When we came to draw a perspective of the first project, it became clear that we would have to design our own furniture to inhabit our own architecture* . . . to draw, in a perspective, a Le Corbusier-period, French-made Thonet chair was evading our responsibility as form-givers.

In 1954, when the client Chance Glass approached us, we wrote: *"The good conversion has inherent the renewal of its immediate surroundings and, through these, of the wider environment of the community. The converter bears the same responsibility as someone building anew: to make an intervention of sufficient quality to play its part in realising the changing way of life. Should the site face a park, or river, the conversion should seek to respond to this and so revalue inherited 'place-capital'.*

In an existing square or good city space the responsibility is to contribute an idea about living in a city today as powerful as the original idea: only this way can we retain its value.

In the proposal for the conversation, all stairs in the terrace are removed to make two similar flats on each floor (which can be as many as seven, basement to second attic).

The back accretions are stripped away for access by new stairs and sitting-out galleries in the space regained at the back of the terrace.

Renewal internally is accomplished by the insertion of a precise, pre-fabricated cell containing the bathroom/kitchenette/central heating/ventilation."

* See A+PS, *The Shift* (London: Academy Editions, 1982).

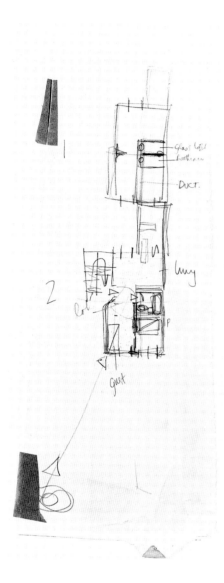

Sketch for proposed conversion. PS, 1953.

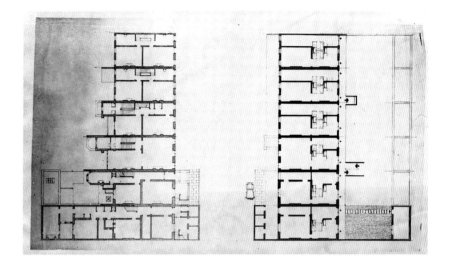

Plan of Mammoth Terrace at all levels
before conversion. PS.

Plan at all levels after conversion. PS.

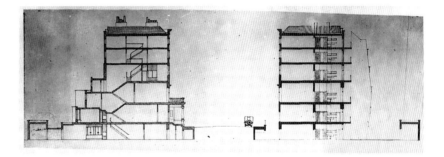

Section before conversion. PS.

Section after conversion. PS.

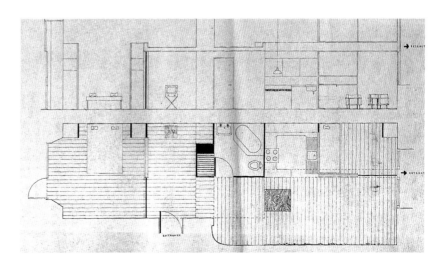

Detail plan and elevation after conversion. PS.

Crematorium at Kirkcaldy, Fife

The building is straightforward, even severe; its character is deliberately non-ecclesiastical, non-domestic, north of the Border. An architecture of stone, limewash, and untreated wood. On the south and east roof slopes are two long windows of alabaster slabs that distribute a subdued, yet warm light over the completely white, square room.

In the language of its architecture is that sense of privacy explored in Doha: screens as 'veils' are first found at Kirkcaldy in a trellis that speaks of a sense of garden seclusion.

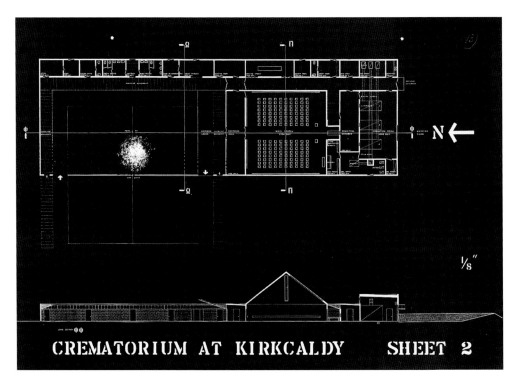

Ground plan and long section. AS, 1954.

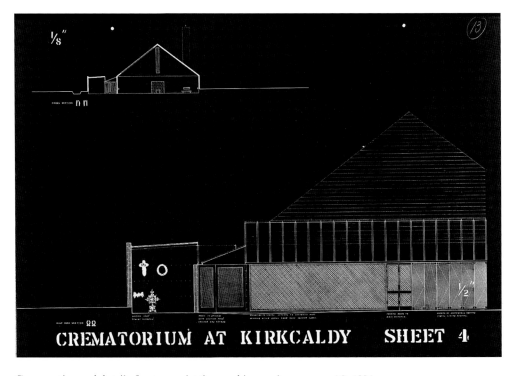

Cross section and detail of entrance lattices and inner-glass screen. AS, 1954.

Caro House, Frognal

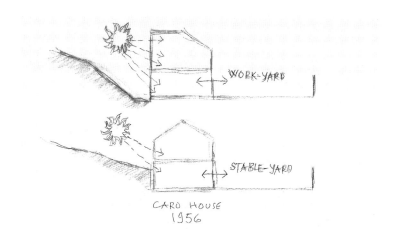

The sculptor Anthony Caro bought the 'stable range and cobbled yard' of the house called Frognal Grove, Hampstead, built by Henry Flitcroft for himself circa 1745. This stable range was converted to make a small house with studio and work yard in 1954 by cutting away the earth previously up to more or less first-floor level on the garden side, thus giving two-sided light to all rooms.

In 1960 the north end of the house was enlarged, and in 1990–91 the upper studio at the south end was made into a bathroom, the true work studios having moved elsewhere.

The resulting assembly is a true interaction between the existing and the added, reflecting the changes in a family work-life.

top: Cross sections to show how the house was opened to the garden. PS, March 1999.
above: West elevation as altered in 1956. PS, 1956.

far left: View out to the work yard from the old downstairs studio. PS, May 1992.
left: View of the work yard through south-end bathroom with marble floor and glass inset. PS, May 1992.

Rumble Villa, St. Albans

The house is to use—and to demonstrate—a shuttering system of the clients; the way the shuttering moves after casting dictates the contiguity and the range of volumes available.

The architect's principal aim is to break through the domination of the English semi-detached house and its devaluation of the rectangle and the pitched roof.

Allied to this is an interest in the grouping characteristics of a house holding potential for new patterns for both the small cluster and the district. Towards this end the house can accept a variety of orientations, be capable of enjoying prospects offered by a site, and be able to hold within its embrace some private outdoor space.

The grouping of the rooms around a core—that is both overlaid circulation and a greater family space than most small houses can have—harks back to the project for the headmaster's house, Hunstanton.

Sketch of house on site. AS.

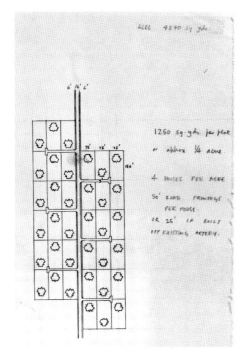

Proposal for layout of three villas deep at four to an acre. PS, 1954.

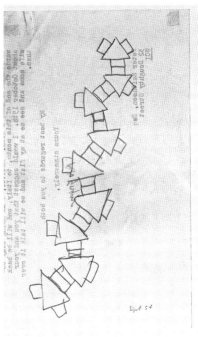

Layout sketch of a linked chain of villas. AS, 1954.

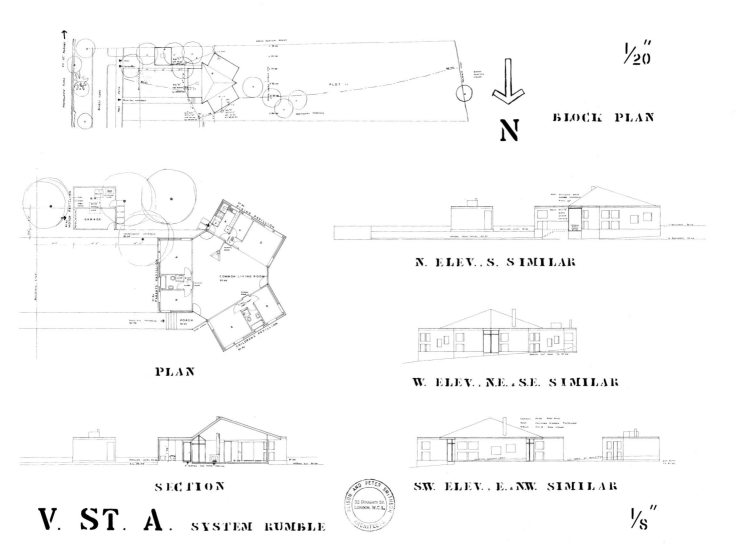

BLOCK PLAN

PLAN

N. ELEV., S. SIMILAR

W. ELEV., N.E., S.E. SIMILAR

SECTION

SW. ELEV., E., NW. SIMILAR

V. ST. A. SYSTEM RUMBLE

Site plan, floor plan, section (left); north, west, south-west elevations (right). PS, 1954.

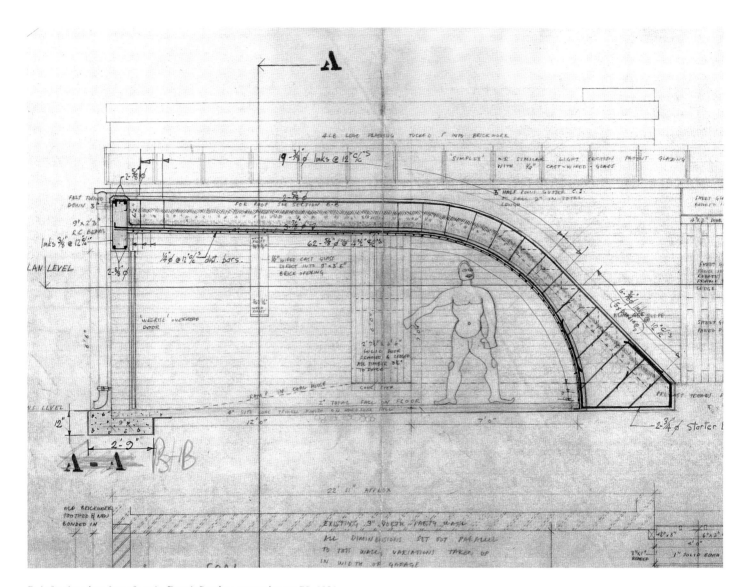

Reinforcing drawing of vault. Derek Sugden, overprint on PS, 1954.

Reconstruction of a garage to include specialised storage and—as our own objectives—to extend the actual area of the small garden (the slope was made into a rockery as soon as the surface stabilised that autumn) and to visually possess, for the occupants of the house, the airspace over the single-sided mews beyond the screen of trees.

Brush and green diagrams of intention. AS, 1954–56.

View of external storage as extension to garden. Sam Lambert, 1956.

Diagram of idea. AS.

Monument on the Goodwin Sands and
a Church Sort of Place (or Scatter Ideogram)

An aesthetic beginning . . . (see the Cordell Studio House, 1957).

The second image was used as a scatter ideogram in *Architectural Design* in April 1959.*

A number of household items were painted with this aesthetic, namely, coal scuttle at the 'Solar' Pavilion at Upper Lawn (in same colours as in 'Wallpaper'); child's play house, Priory Walk garden (in silver and vermilion).

* See also PS, 'Wallpaper: Sample of Design', *Architectural Design*, July 1959.

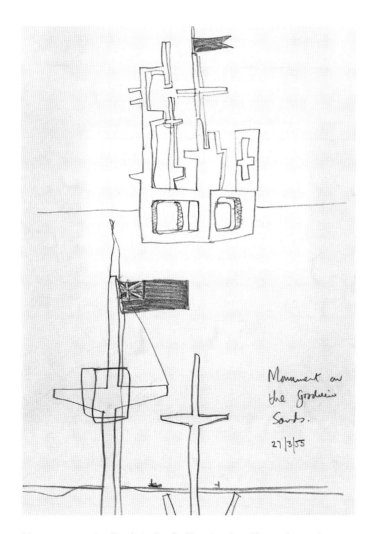

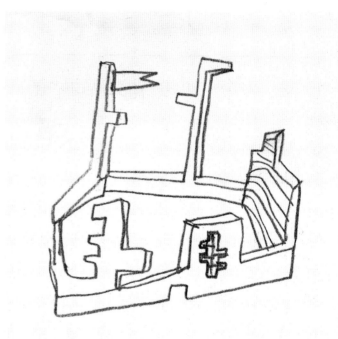

A Church Sort of Place: Scatter ideogram.

Monument on the Goodwin Sands: Top sketch as if seen from a boat;
lower detail with horizon and flag flying. PS, 27 March 1955.

Typical of ideas of this period . . .

You could say the realisation of this possibility only reentered with the infill urban grain of Worcester in 1977–78, to come to formal development in Damascus Gate, 1979–81.

Period image. PS, August 1955.

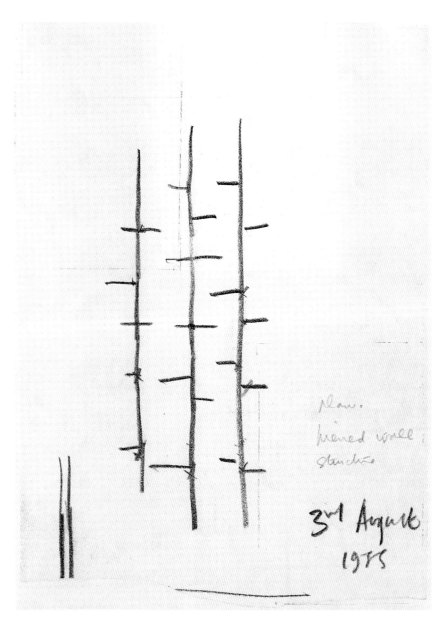

Sugden House, Watford

January 1955 – 1956

A+PS

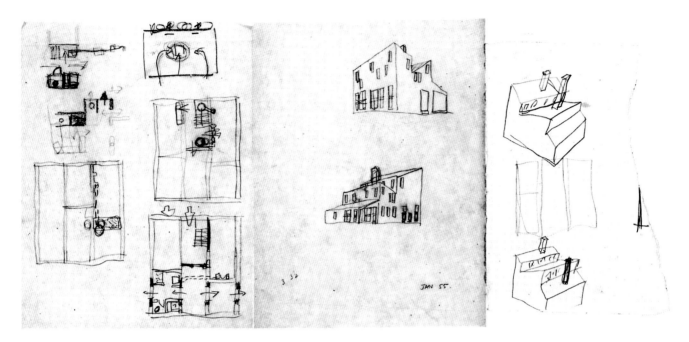

Sketch plans of first scheme using single standard windows for all purposes.

Sketch of house with opposing roof pitches which obtain views in three directions for bedrooms.

Sketch air view of roof profile. AS, 1955–56.

The use of the imposed materials—inexpensive bricks, tiles, standard metal windows—in an 'un-arty' manner we see as appropriate to the size of the dwelling, as seen in Dutch paintings. In like economic means the mass is tailored to the rooms.

The selection from a standard window range is, through repetition and grouping, made subservient to the aesthetic; the distribution of these windows allows the brickwork to flow and coalesce with the roof to form a solid mass, giving that appearance of all-round protection which was once characteristic of English popular architecture appropriate to our climate.

To 'manage' its piece of territory and to sit well in its surroundings, the house is given an earthwork apron, whose facets effect the transition between the natural dished contours and the squareness of the house.

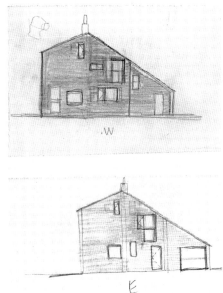

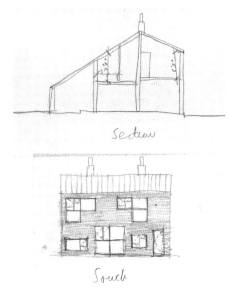

Studies to stress the scatter of the windows. AS, 1956.

West and east elevation sketches of final scheme.

Section and south elevation sketches of final scheme using Critall windows, stock bricks, Marley tiles, and PVC tiles. PS, 1956.

Plans of ground- and first-floors; section.

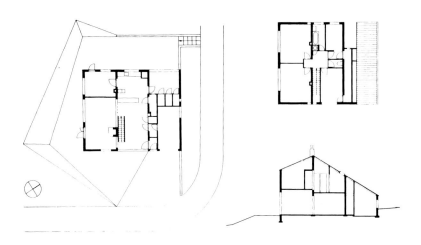

above: General view from the garden at the end of the construction period.

opposite top: Photograph of north and east sides of house.

opposite bottom: Photograph of south and west sides of house. William J. Toomey, 1955–56.

above: View of the dining room and garden from the kitchen. William J. Toomey, 1956.
opposite: Interior view of the 'open room' off the head of the stairs. William J. Toomey, 1955–56.

page 156, top: Forty years later: View into the dining room/kitchen from the outside. PS, August 1995.
page 156, bottom: Forty years later: View from the dining room into the kitchen. PS, August 1995.

Hot Springs, Ascot Water Heater Exhibition Stand, Olympia, London

"In Hot Springs the Ascot range of water heaters is grouped to make a display as impressive as a natural phenomenon. We aim to have as many 'live' as possible, to pick up the sound and amplify it to attract visitors to penetrate the white lattice screens of the pavilion; to find these water heaters spraying into a shallow pool lined with 'Ascot blue' tiles under water, white tiles on the bench surround . . . overall a sky blue canopy, perforated to allow steam to rise into a cloud and allow spotlights to illuminate the water. Blue and white: the two colours are symbolic of freshness and contrast sharply with the jumble of colours and materials on other stands."

This is the first 'pavilion' in our architecture . . . as distinct from the small version of the 'mother' building—the 'microcosm of the macrocosm'—that continued from Hunstanton to Brasilia.

Again, the use of 'veiling' lattice to make mysterious the place and to connect the sound and effects of water to man's remembrance of the idyllic and the natural.

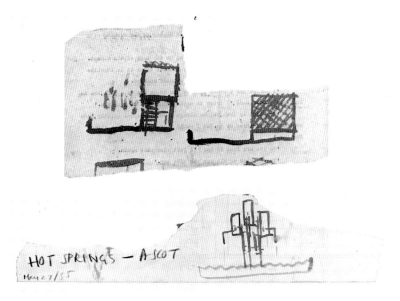

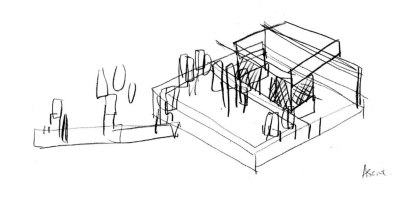

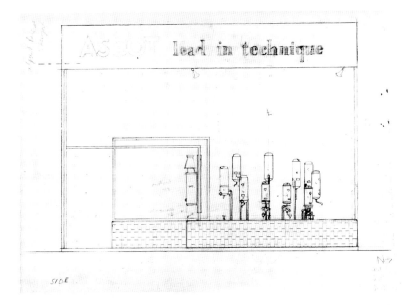

right top: First ideograms of Hot Springs idea: Use of lattices as 'built' water. AS, 27 May 1955.
right middle: Hot Springs idea in section, overlaid on diagram of stand contained within proposed lattices. PS, 1955.
right: Side elevation of tiled tank and freestanding heaters as hot-water fountain supported on service pipes; lattice screens not yet drawn in. AS, 1955.

Photograph of A+PS in the patio of Patio and Pavilion after return from Dubrovnik. Claimed by Richard Hamilton, September 1956.

5 Conglomerate Ordering

a sensed naturalness in an ordering of a built fabric . . .

House of the Future *(1955–56)*   162

Patio and Pavilion, 'This Is Tomorrow' Exhibition *(1956)*   178

Sydney Opera House *(1956)*   188

Appliance Houses *(1956–58)*:   190

Snowball House   192

Bread House   193

Cubicle House or Cupboard House   193

Portico Row and the 'Wareite' or White 'Formica' House   194

The Strip House   195

Provençal House   196

Cordell Studio House *(1957)*   197

English Climate House *(1957)*   198

Berlin Hauptstadt *(1957)*   200

Wokingham Infants School *(1958)*   206

Langside College of Further Education *(1958)*   212

Paolozzi Studio House *(1959)*   216

Retirement House *(1959)*   218

Two painting ideograms: Image typical of mid-1950s cluster and 'nuclear' thinking (above); cluster diagram (below). AS, 1955.

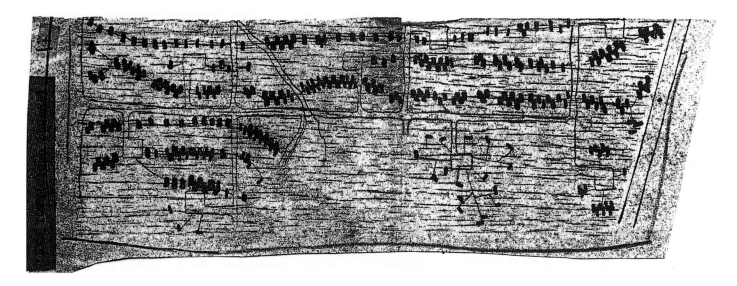

Conglomerate ordering harnesses all the senses. It can happily operate with a certain roughness; it can operate at night; it can offer, especially, pleasures beyond those of the eyes . . . they are perhaps the pleasures of territory that other animals feel so strongly. That is, we may not be able to see where we are, but can nevertheless navigate through our profound capacity to feel light and warmth and wind on our skins, somehow sense the density of a fabric, know that behind that wall are people, 'smell' who has been here, or where someone has gone.

House of the Future: Sections YY and RR with the holes in the walls and roof for exhibition viewing removed. The sections therefore show the house in its true volumetric condition. AS, 1955–56; LW and Pablo Olalquiaga, 1997.

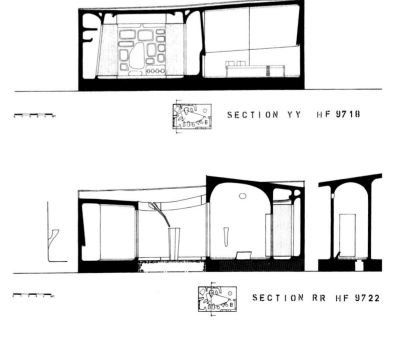

House of the Future, Ideal Home Exhibition, Olympia, London

In the original manuscript AS described the House of the Future thus: *"The House within the Community: The house of twenty-five years hence will be different not only in itself but also in the way in which it is arranged within the framework of the community.*

This particular house has been thought of as a town house; it is not set in its own garden but contains a garden within it. Such houses can be grouped together to form a compact community.* The tiny garden is obviously inadequate for the play of children so you must imagine this is the house of the couple, old or young, perhaps with a baby or toddler.

* A mat-cluster.

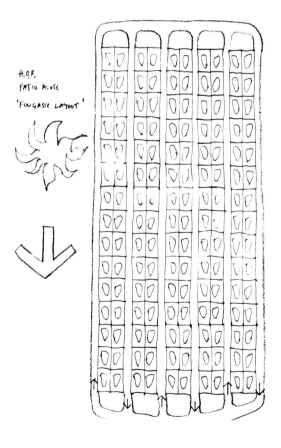

Fougasse Layout, designed to be built up into a 'mat' of a density of seventy to eighty houses to the acre. This aspect was perhaps overstated to counteract the accepted idea that the prefabricated house must mean a detached cottage centred in a garden plot. PS, 1955.

Axonometric of 1997 'crossover' layout with guest parking. Pablo Olalquiaga, September 1997.

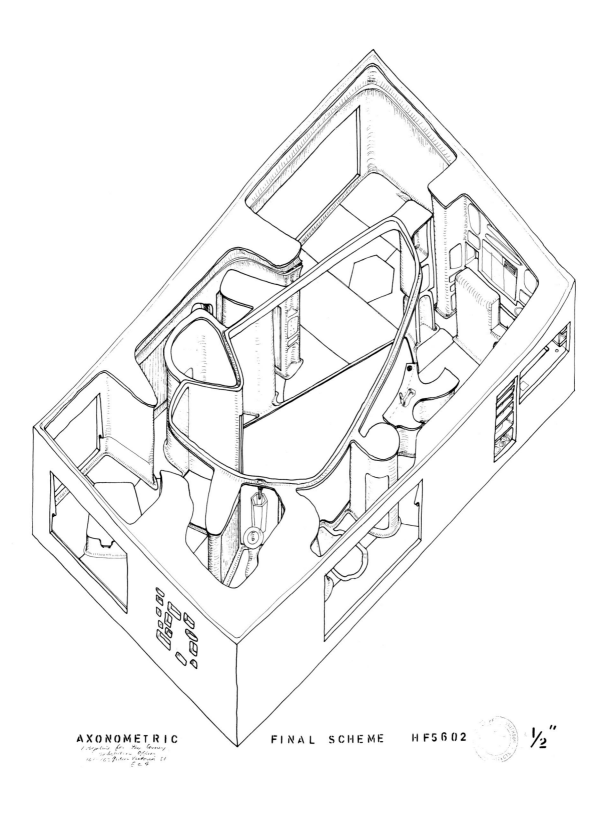

AXONOMETRIC   FINAL SCHEME   HF5602   ½"

Axonometric as built. AS, 1956.

The General Conception of the House: The rooms flow into one another like the compartments of a cave, and as in a cave, the skewed passage which joins one compartment with another effectively maintains privacy.

Each compartment is a different size—a different area and a different height—a totally differentiated shape to suit its purpose.

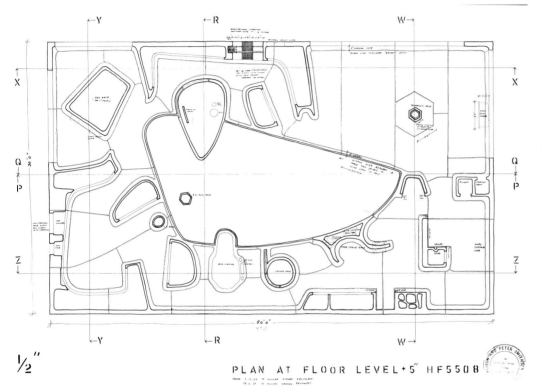

½"

PLAN AT FLOOR LEVEL+5" HF5508

Outline plan showing gasket joints: In this gasket aesthetic, the House of the Future was 'built' like a Citroën car, of specially formed pieces, for a limited role. This plan for construction shows the openings in the walls, so that visitors to the exhibition can look inside. AS, 1956.

Diagrammatic plan at middle level, with loose furniture shown.
1. Entrance
2. Cloaks
3. Toilet
4. Bedroom
5. Dressing room
6. Bathroom
7. Shower
8. Kitchen
9. Living room
0. Patio
AS, 1956; LW, 1992.

Five sections (all sections
show the holes in the
external walls which allow
visitors to the exhibition
to look inside). AS, 1956.

Through patio facing door.

Through bedroom.

Through kitchen,
laundry, bathroom,
and bedroom.

Facing into patio
from kitchen.

Through toilet and patio.

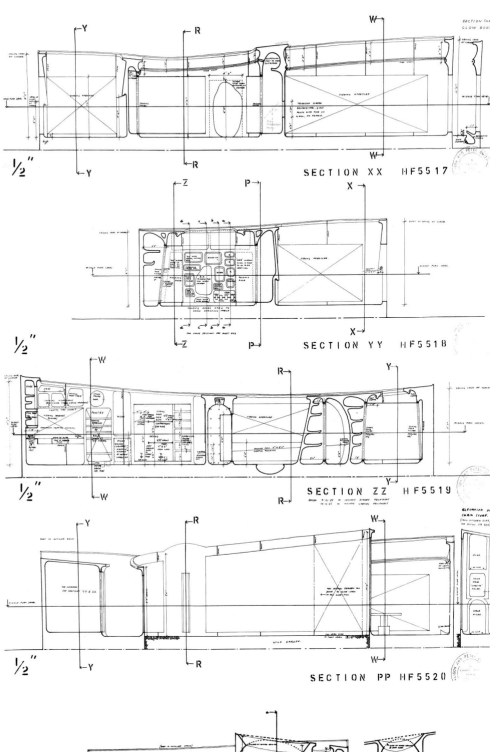

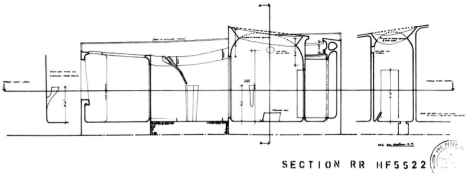

The Structure: The house is moulded in plastic-impregnated fibrous plaster, a kind of skin structure built up from separate parts with flexible joints to allow for thermal movement and to provide structural discontinuity. The joints break up the surface into parts in scale with the compartments in which they occur, the floor, wall, and ceiling being considered as a single entity. The lighting is integrated into this surface and is designed to give a different character to each part of the house.

The Outside Surfaces: The roof is doubly curved and dished to allow sunlight penetration, which dishing carries the rainwater to a single point from which it flows down a gargoyle into a container in the garden. To reflect the sun's rays the top surface is covered with aluminium foil."

There was preliminary discussion as to the feasibility of a mock-up of a winter-season closure—as a camera's shutter—over the patio.

below left: Construction photograph. Sam Lambert, 1956.
below right: Construction photograph. The forms were simulated in plywood on timber forms, the inside face later painted with the panel joints indicated in brown tape. Sam Lambert, 1956.
opposite: View into house from entrance door. Council of Industrial Design, 1956.

pages 168–69: Table down, flush with floor. John McCann, 1956.
pages 170–71: View from the patio into the kitchen. John McCann, 1956.
page 172: Wash-hand basin with rainwater holder and dipper outside in patio. John McCann, 1956.
page 173, top: Gaskets around bath in part of amorphous bathroom. Council of Industrial Design, 1956.
page 173, bottom: Photograph of kitchen: First exercise in the appliance way of life, showing the architectural consequences of the disintegration of the kitchen because of food packaging and treatment, mobile appliances (that would become more silent), etc. Council of Industrial Design, 1956.

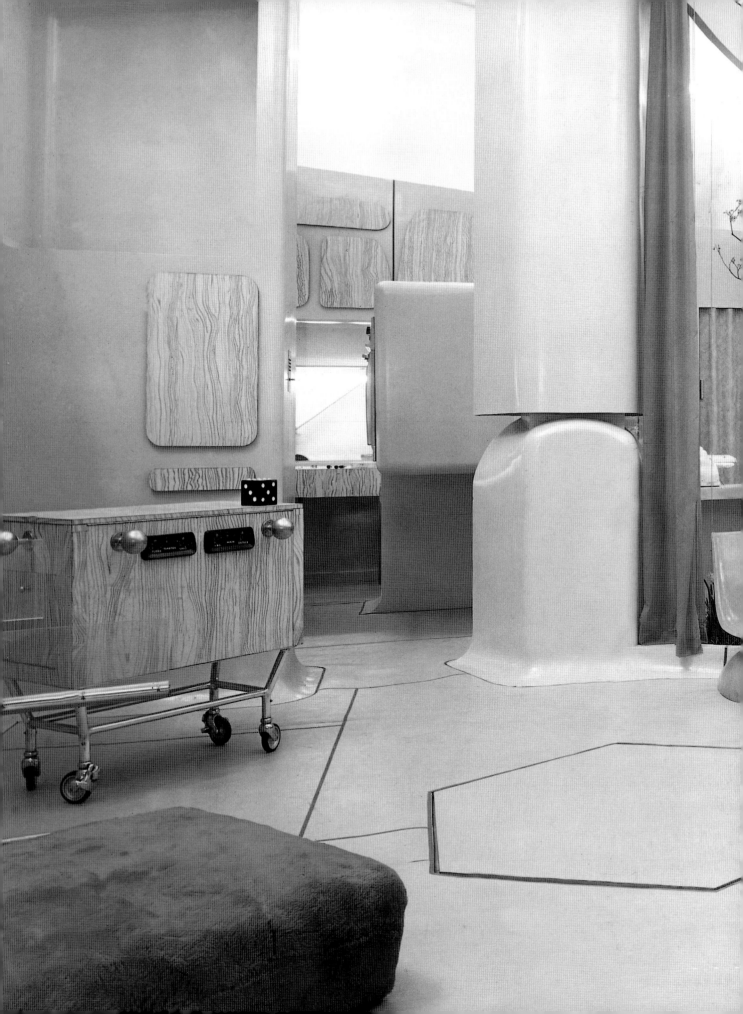

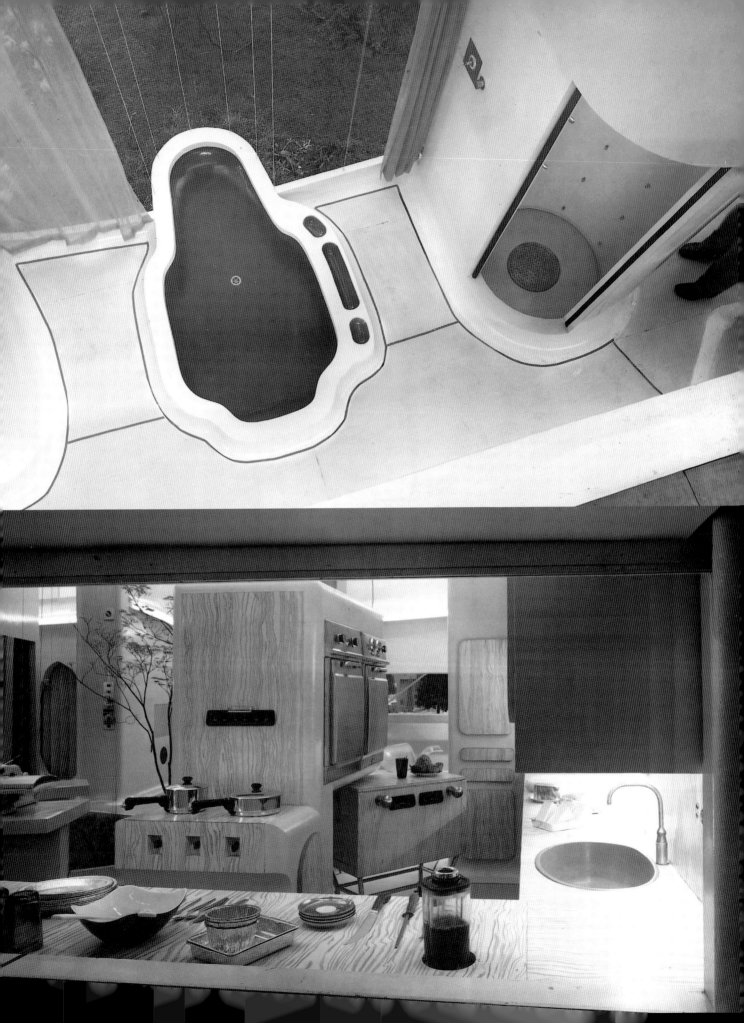

Of the furniture we wrote: "*The only mobile equipment in the whole house—if one discounts mobile mechanisms—is the chairs.*

One of these chairs—the POGO—is in a way a relic of the previous 'constructed' technology in that it is built up from standard tubing.

The remaining chairs are moulded and thus share the characteristics of the doubly curved modelling of the house itself . . . EGG chair, a low, television watching or reading chair; the TULIP chair, a showing-off chair for relaxing in; the SADDLE boudoir chair, reversible, its surface polished or nylon fur covered."

left: Detail of gaskets with TULIP and EGG chairs in the table place. Council of Industrial Design, 1956.
left below: EGG chair showing flexible gasket at joint of base to seat (as joints in houseshell). Council of Industrial Design, 1956.
opposite: Photograph of gasket joints around retractable table with table up. Council of Industrial Design, 1956.

As instructions to the designer of the clothes for the team of actor/occupiers we wrote: *"We must assume that it is a typical leisure period as both husband and wife are at home. As she circuits the house the wife will go through almost every type of movement from sitting down in low chairs to operating the sliding folding doors. There are no points in the house to catch garments, even controls are dial type.*

Each area is intended to appear controlled to individual temperatures: for example, the bathroom the highest; the bedroom at night to allow the occupants under a single sheet* all the year round; the kitchen to allow pleasant working conditions; the clothes therefore should recognise this atmosphere and the degree of change within the house itself.

Clothes for the woman for other occasions should be there when she slides back the folding doors on a section of her wardrobe.

The garments should not excite laughter, nor detract from the house or equipment the people are trying to demonstrate. The overall impression given to the public should be one of glamour."

* Fitted sheets were then unknown in England, and the clothes designer mocked-up these special shapes.

left: A scene in the dressing room with the SADDLE chair. Daily Mail, 1956.
opposite top: The two pairs of inhabitants in the bedroom. John McCann, 1956.
opposite bottom: One of the inhabitants in the kitchen explaining the features and processes of the house to viewers on the walkways above. 1956.

Patio and Pavilion, 'This Is Tomorrow' Exhibition, Whitechapel Art Gallery, London

August – September 1956*

A+PS

Our statement about the aim of the exhibition said: *"There will be introduced a new order of art manifestation; its object is the exploration of a new field: that of the large-scale art work; the borderline world between architecture and the plastic arts. Such an exploration is in the field of ideas. It is not a matter of the enlargement of existing objects, but the creation of a new visual world, of a more comprehensive imagery."*

We also wrote: *"Our own group interpret the general aim of the exhibition in a rather special way, for we believe that we are concerned in our separate disciplines with satisfying different aspects of man. We try in all our collaborations to establish contact between individuals at the level of ideas, not as a collaboration devoted to an aesthetic movement.*

In this instance, we have worked on a kind of symbolic 'Habitat', in which are found, in some form or other, the basic human needs—a piece of ground, a view of the sky, privacy, the presence of nature and animals—when we need them— and symbols of the basic human urges—to extend and control, to move.

The actual form is very simple; a patio, or enclosed space, in which sits a pavilion. The patio and pavilion are furnished with objects which are symbols for the things we need: for example a wheel, image for movement and machines.

The method of work has been for the group to agree on the general idea and for the architects to provide a framework and for the artists to provide the objects; for in this way, the architects' work of providing a context for the individual to realise himself in, and the artists' work of giving signs and images to the stages of this realisation, meet in a single act, full of those inconsistencies and apparent irrelevancies of every moment, but full of life."

* The idea of the 'This Is Tomorrow' exhibition was under discussion in Bill Scott's and other top-floor studios, Fitzroy Street, winter 1955 to 1956; pavilion designed by March 1956.

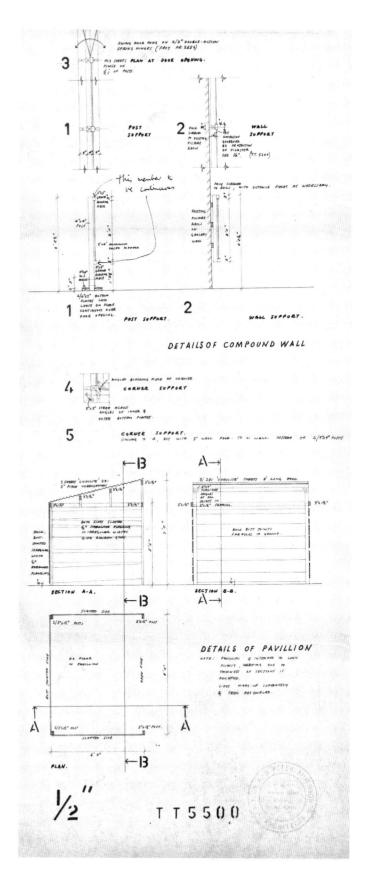

Working drawing of pavilion. PS.

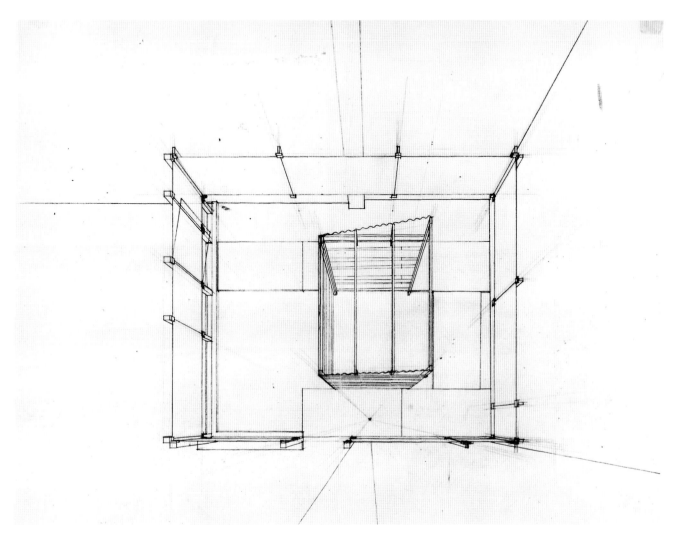

Base drawing for inhabitation collage. PS, 1956.

Inhabitation collage with photograph by Nigel
Henderson. Eduardo Paolozzi, PS.

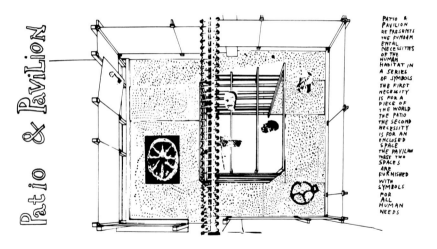

Top view of patio and pavilion.
Nigel Henderson, 1956.

opposite: The back of the pavilion. Nigel Henderson, 1956.
below: The front of the pavilion. John Maltby, 1956.

page 184, top: Scrutinising the floor. Nigel Henderson, 1956.
page 184, bottom: The floor. Nigel Henderson, 1956.
page 185, top: The path around the pavilion. Nigel Henderson, 1956.
page 185, bottom: Reflections resonate the contents. Nigel Henderson, 1956.

Exhibition as rebuilt, 1990: Reflections resonate the contents II. PS.

Exhibition as rebuilt, 1990: Reflections resonate the contents III. PS.

Sydney Opera House

February – November 1956

A+PS

Joint entry with W. and G. Howell, J. Killick, S. Meyrick, and R. S. Jenkins

Our interest is with the 'lining', the inner enclosing shell of the auditoriums. We wrote: *"Auditorium ceilings and walls are an overall jointed 'shell'—like a tortoise or armadillo inside out. No separate planes of walls and ceilings but the whole acoustically shaped and responding to the geometry of the seating. Each sector of the shell is contoured, convexly, in steps to diffuse the sound. Shell sections are lacquered scarlet in the large halls and crimson in the small. Between sectors are continuous cold cathode tubes located well behind the open joints to create the illusion of a trellised cage of light when lights go up. Seating tiers are faced with white marble; upholstered seats black velvet; grey carpets on the aisles.*

In 'Architectural Principles' *. . . the aesthetic is an architecture of facets—of irregular planes which envelop the whole building, outside and inside: the right-angle is treated as a precious thing.*

Response to the specific situation . . . The site is open on all sides and to the sky: the building is therefore developed like a flower on its peninsular ground of 'leaves'. The Sydney Harbour bridge is enormous and arched; the Opera House must be equally bold in scale and its form a contrast—a sort of combined suspension bridge and Chinese lantern.

The external surface and its colour . . . the exterior is covered in mosaic, white for the main volume with grey bands to emphasise change of direction or opening. The escape galleries and stair towers are grey all over to bring them out in profile against the white of the main bulk. The canopy of the small hall's entrance, blue glass in stainless-steel frame, allows the audience to look upwards at the belly of the auditorium it is entering." This banding of the facet's folds is used in the mosaic of the Banking Hall in the Economist Building.

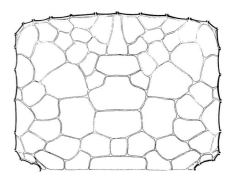

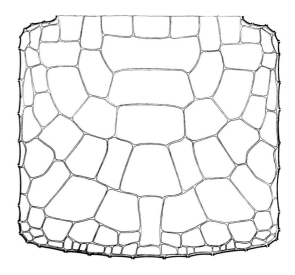

above: Pair of ceiling plans showing separately adjustable 'scales' in red lacquered plywood, in the manner of an armadillo's scales. PS.
opposite: Perspective view of underbelly. The margin aesthetic for the mosaic reappears in the bank interior in the Economist Building. PS.

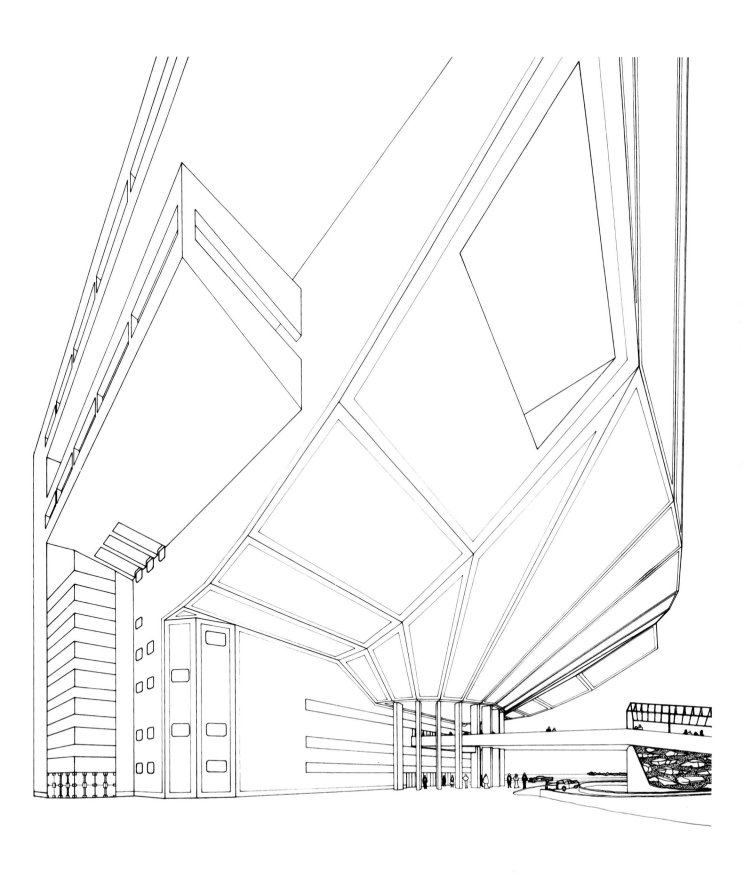

The programme for the Appliance House is:

. . . to be capable of mass production in today's technology;

. . . to be able to of group in any series of numbers;

. . . to take special account of the problem of electrical runs, etc.;

. . . to imply a new sort of garden;

. . . to have a high degree of privacy;

. . . to contain a 'glamour factor';

. . . to require little maintenance, i.e., to keep fresh looking with just cleaning down;

. . . to be highly insulated against cold weather and to respond quickly to climate variation.

Human factors considered are:

. . . covered access from car;

. . . access to all rooms without passing through others;

. . . a view of something decent;

. . . a choice of children's outdoor space included in the grouping;

. . . adolescents' space included in the larger grouping.

To regain as much as possible of the house as usable space, we assume that appliances do away with the need of the 'work space' in the old sense.

The appliance way of life suggests an entirely new sort of house that involves the put-away aesthetic in order not to have to live with the assorted styling of one's mechanisms.

This involves a change of orientation of the storage spaces and appliance spaces so that they hide themselves yet define the house space proper. Thus, the Appliance House consists of a system of appliance cubicles in which there are connections for appliances of preparation, sanitation, communication, storage, and maintenance.

The shells of these cubicles are the fixed things in the house and would define the architectural form. Their service connections would be the growth points of constantly changing appliances.

These projects also move towards a pattern of grouping for the favoured isolated house, or short row of houses of discreetly different floor areas; grouping that allows the garden spaces to flow together uninterruptedly so as to genuinely add up to a 'garden' suburb. However, one Appliance House was thought of as an isolated, square-form infill.

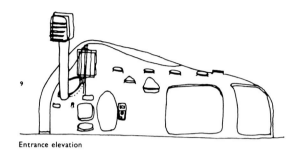

Entrance elevation

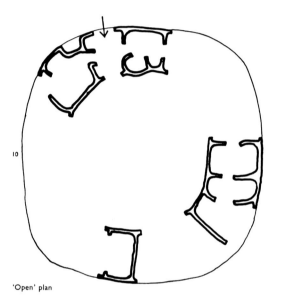

'Open' plan

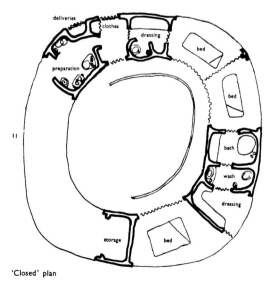

'Closed' plan

Elevation and plans of earliest Appliance House; in many ways, nearest to the House of the Future. AS.

Snowball House, 1956, AS

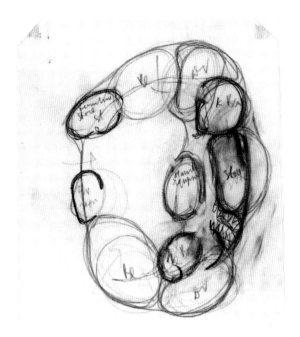

Overlaid thinking plans. AS.

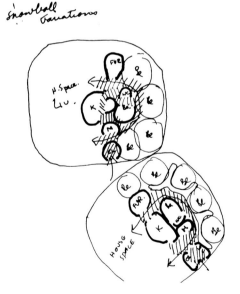

Plan variations. AS.

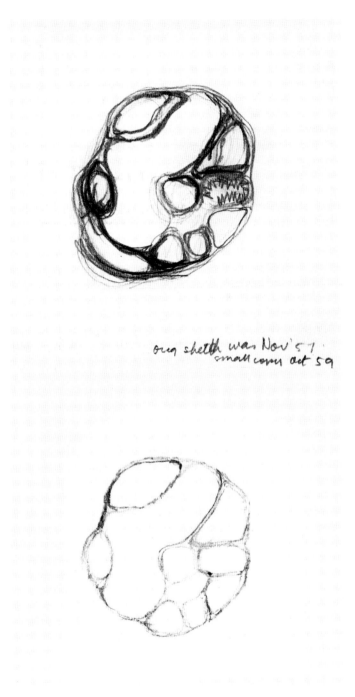

org shetth was Nov '57.
small corm act 59

Pair of roof plans. AS.

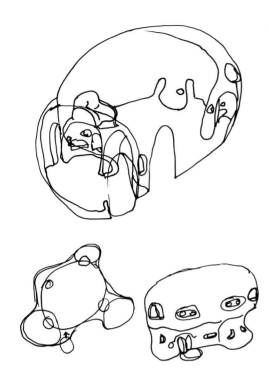

An idea for the standard house with extra ground-floor room with its own entrance and atmosphere:

studio
drawing room
study
surgery . . .

Sketches of the Bread House. AS.

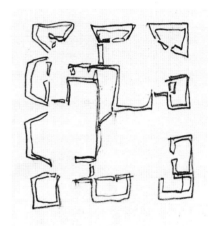

Cubicle House plan. AS.

Bread House village. AS.

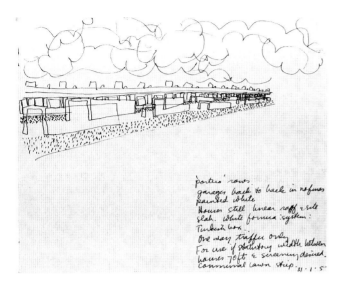

Sketch of portico rows from green centre. AS.

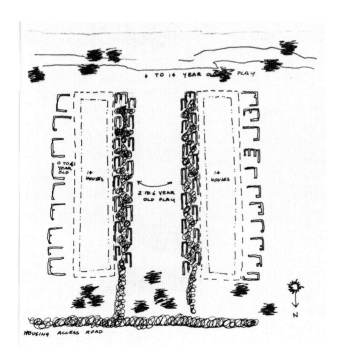

Plan and miniature layout that includes parking. AS.

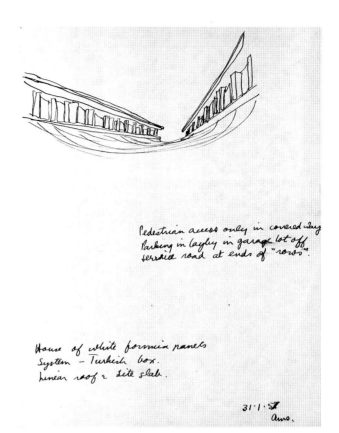

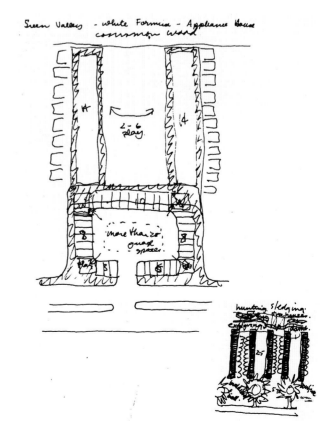

right top: Sketch of seated child's view of scooped-out 'vale' as green centre between two rows of the 'private' faces where no traffic can penetrate. AS.
right: Plan annotated for children's play. AS.

The Strip House, 1957–58, AS

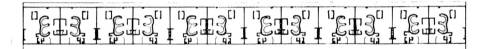

Plan of a terrace of Strip Houses.
AS, 1957–58.

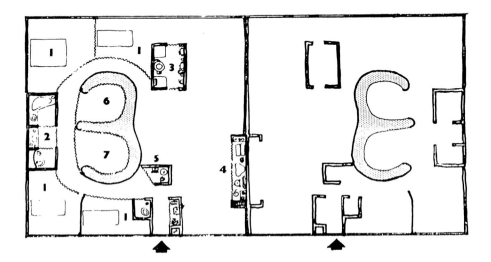

Detail plan of a Strip House.
AS, 1957–58.
1. Bedrooms
2. Bath cubicle
3. Preparations cubicle
4. Furniture storage cubicle
5. Maintenance cubicle
6. Female dressing room
7. Male dressing room

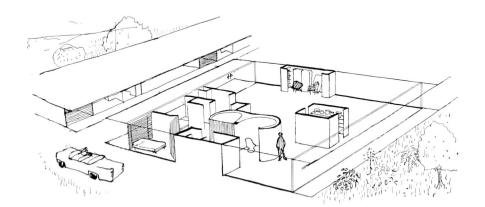

Perspective diagram. AS.

Technically, the Strip House attempts to take into account the economical layout of site slabs and the mechanisation of building processes.

The layout was further worked on in the following year.

Provençal House, 1957, PS

Ideas that contributed to the
Cordell Studio House.

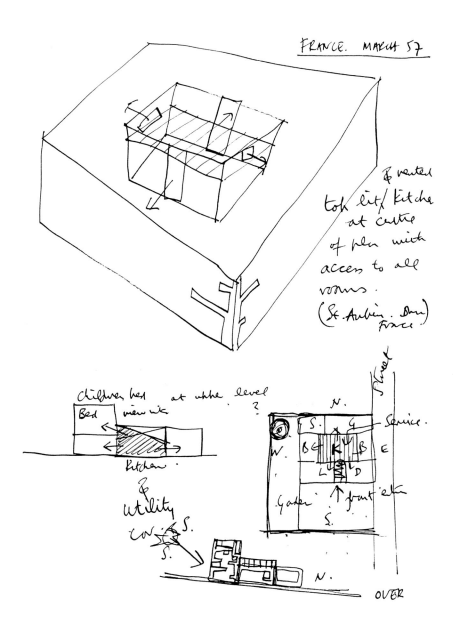

Plan and section: Kitchen as heart of
house. The section of this idea, its
aesthetic, became the Cordell Studio
House. PS.

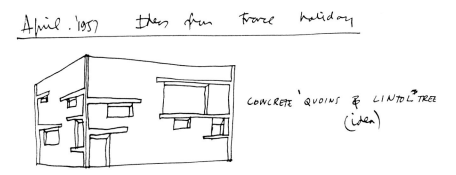

A new aesthetic utilised: The
'concrete' tree columns of the undercroft in La Villette have their roots
in Bramante. PS.

Cordell Studio House

Intended as a gift drawing—a thank you for the Hauptstadt film—something in the nature of what Nigel Henderson would call an 'Ideological Food Parcel'.

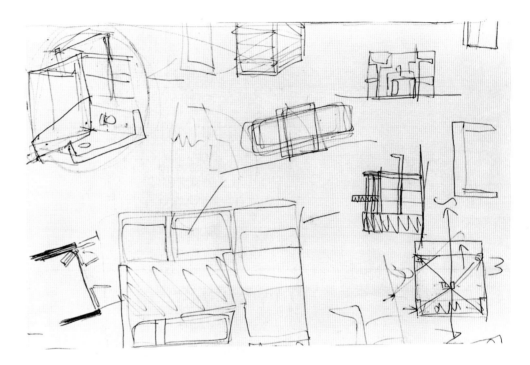

Thinking sketches.
PS, May 1957.

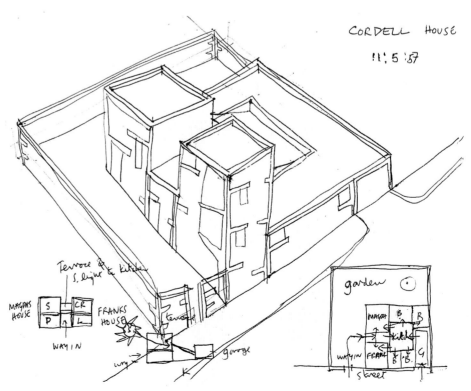

Composite sketch of overview
and idea. PS, May 1957.

English Climate House

An idea worked out at Redington Road in 1960.

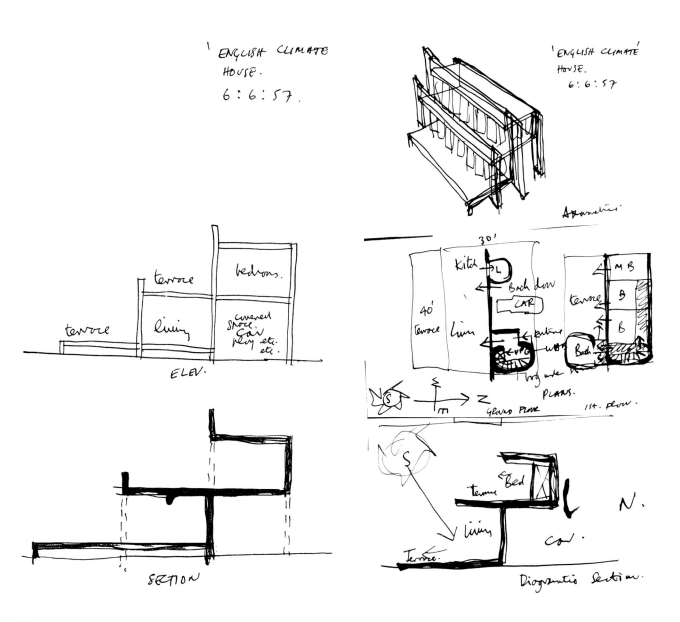

Jørn Utzon's housing at Skane in Lund, Sweden, with 'private terraces and common gardens', designed in 1953 and constructed in 1957, unknown of course to us at the time, established this mode, in his language, in an unbelievably radical and pure way.

opposite left: Pair of sections. PS, June 1957.
opposite right: Composite sketch: Volumetric sketch, ground- and first-floor plans with sun orientation, diagrammatic section. PS, June 1957.
left: Grouping and siting, showing aspect, prospect, and means of access. PS, June 1957.

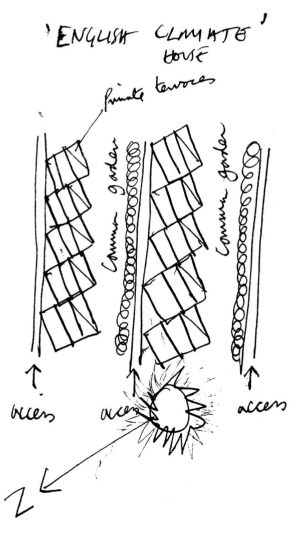

Berlin Hauptstadt

March – November 1957[*]

A+PS

With Peter Sigmonde

The form-invention of the urban framework[†] of Berlin Hauptstadt should naturally be looked at relative to the work that follows 1956.

[*] As regards dates, assessment appears to have been in June 1958 . . . possibly, there was a time extension on the competition.

[†] See *The Charged Void: Urbanism*.

right: Axonometric of the city centre. Peter Sigmonde, 1957.
below: Overview showing where platform net crosses Friedrichstrasse. Department stores and shopping arcades are located under the platform level, while office towers are attached to the pedestrian platform edge.

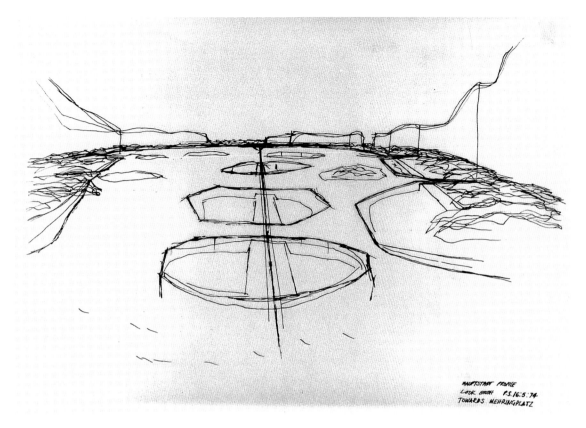

Ink sketch of Hauptstadt profile looking south towards Mehringplatz. PS, 1974.

Space contained within the wall of offices. AS, 1957.

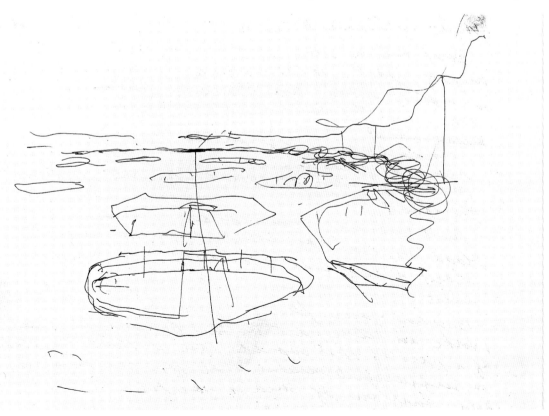

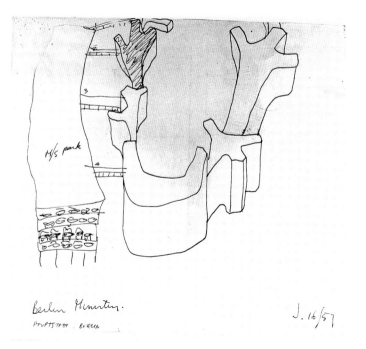

Ink sketch of the Berlin 'Antler' Ministry. AS, 1957.

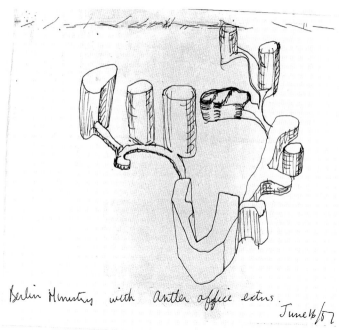

Ink sketch of office extensions for the 'Antler' Ministry. AS, 1957.

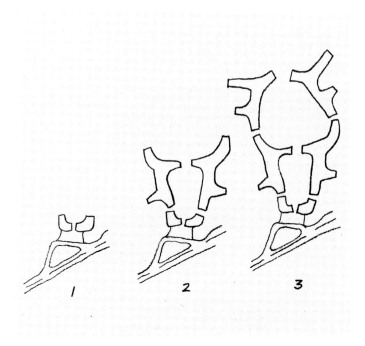

Pencil diagram of the 'Antler' Ministry growth. PS, 1957.

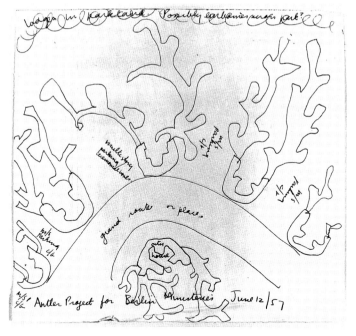

Ink sketch plan of the 'Antler' Ministry. AS, 1957.

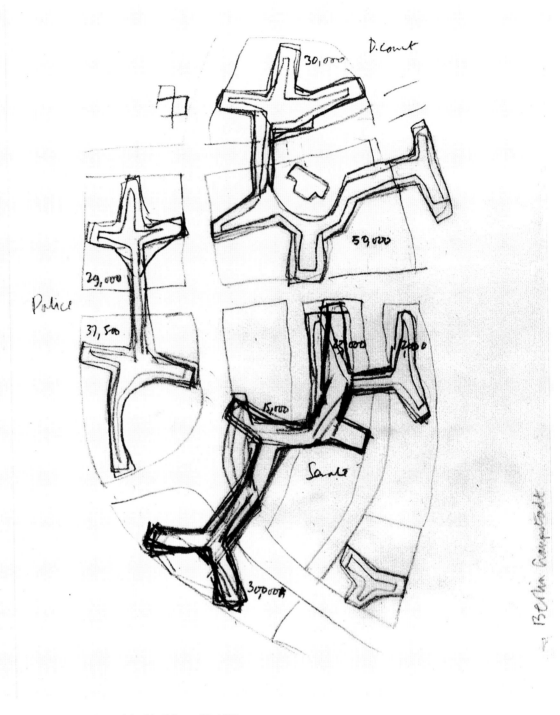

Pencil sketch plan of municipal buildings. PS, 1957.

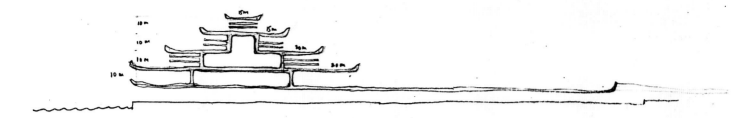

Six pencil sketches. PS, 1957.

Section through law courts building.

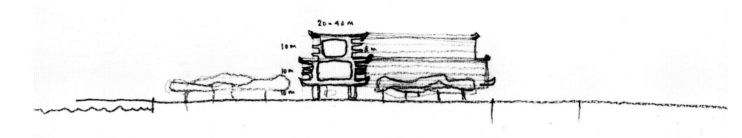

Section through civic administration building.

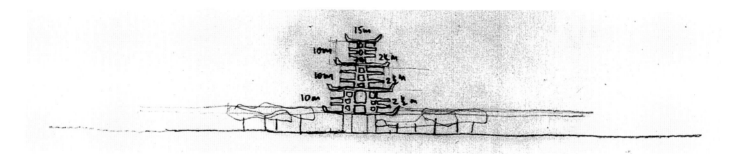

Section through a three-tier municipal building.

General section along the central street of the Hauptstadt showing the Museum of Technology in section.

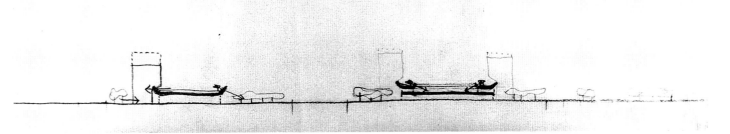

General section through pedestrian net with attached administrative 'towers'.

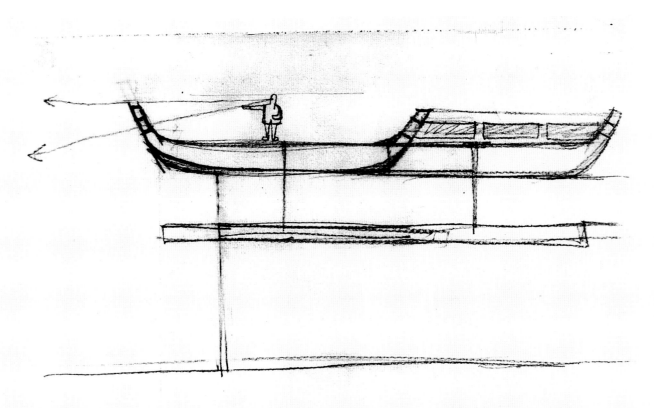

Typical detail section through pedestrian net platform.

Wokingham Infants School

Our personal programme, with which we bodied out the Ministry of Education Building Bulletins, listed that the school should be:

". . . easily identified as infants';

. . . small, very English in scale yet technological;

. . . capable of quick response to climate;

. . . have an absolute simplicity of day-to-day cleaning and building maintenance;*

. . . and—since surrounded by houses—not be a building enfolding a site."

A hierarchy of spaces comprehensible to small children is offered; the character of each part indicates clearly where to go, how to use, how long to stay, and so on.

* From about this time, maintenance increasingly interests us as part of the unwritten programme.

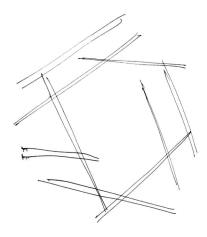

Ideogram of a building that makes an enclosure (instead of a building dumped on a site). AS.

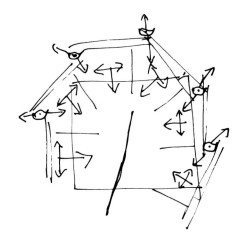

Diagram of views available to each class. Each class house is like a Japanese house, the attention of its occupants concentrated by means of screens on a private world of sky, changing seasons, weather, and growing plants. AS.

opposite top: Roof plan with shadows; section looking west through play area. AS.
opposite bottom: Ground plan. AS, 1958.

WOKINGHAM

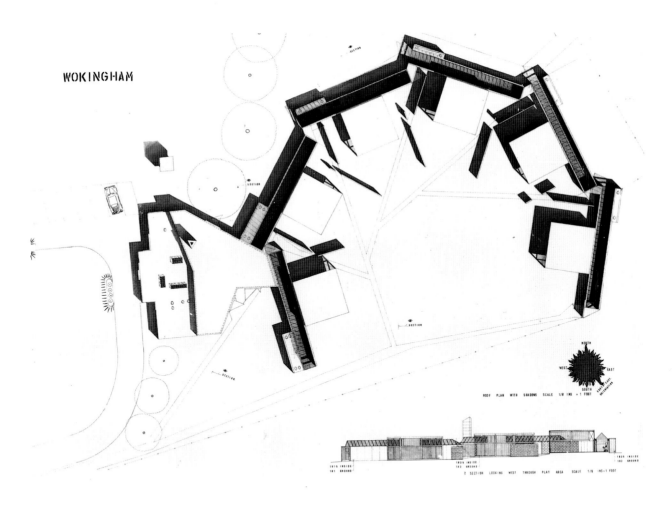

WOKINGHAM

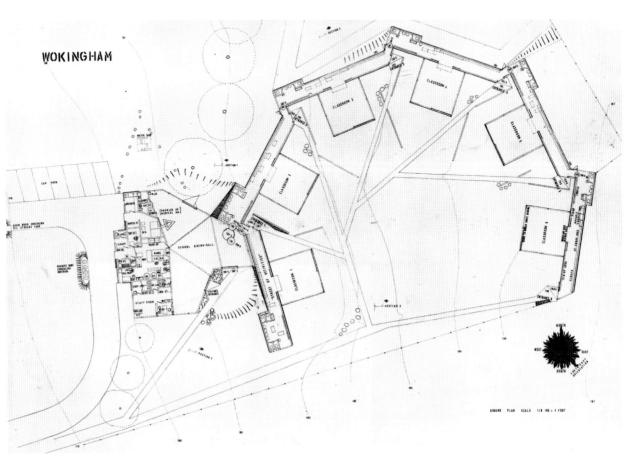

We wrote: *"In each class-world, two kinds of covering make two kinds of spaces. First, the walled 'street-activity-space', with the sky for ceiling; aeroplanes, birds, clouds, its diurnal decoration. 'Streets-of-activity', containing, as the day progresses, entering, messy, boisterous, parting activities; intended as a channel in the sun as much as being under the influence of the industrial back lane that was a place of secret escape from each house. Contrasting with this is the simple shelter of aluminium and glass: the class house-space. Inside the crystal cube the children can be snug and busy and yet in visual contact with the passing of time, the changes of weather and of season, in a way they cannot be in their own homes. The visual boundaries are the screen garden walls, strategically placed as sound and distraction barriers; in 'open' weather the children can use the space up to these 'solid' walls.*

The hall, as belonging to the whole school, might be used as a single space without it being frightening, or each limb might contain a different activity.

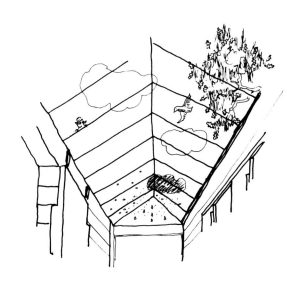

Sketch looking up through the glass roof of the 'street-activity-space'. AS.

Diagram of hall as generator space of communal life. AS.

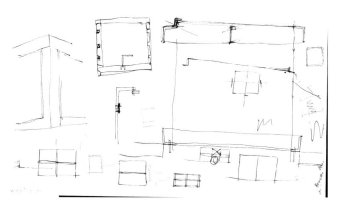

Sketches of working details. AS.

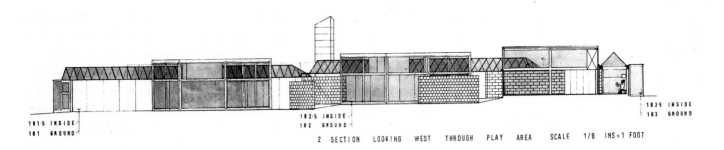

Section looking west through contained play area. AS.

South elevation of contained space with morning shadows. AS.

WOKINGHAM

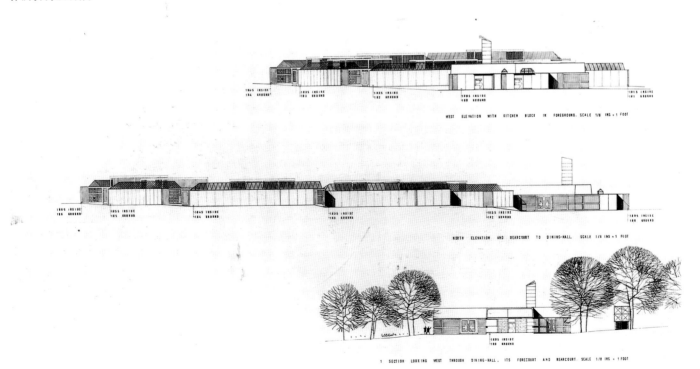

West elevation, protective north elevation, and section looking west through dining hall. AS, trees by Peter Sigmonde.

The glazed links between each street-space allow all children to connect to the hall. In these links children can look outwards to their home, inwards to their entrances via the garden. In this lobby-link will be shelves where first thing in the morning, and last thing at night, the child is able to see things he or she might have brought to school or is helping to grow there.

The children cross the heart of the playground to enter each lobby. A line of mature trees functions as an entrance screen before it passes between the rooms for the teaching staff, stepping over the limbs of the hall."

This relatedness, rootedness in the environment, managed by the incoming building's deference to the trees as place-memory markers growing out of the site, is a reemergence of the respect for the nature of place that allows layers of history to give a patina to the language of a building: a theme first explored in Wokingham.*

Again new, we find a change of palette, in contrast to the monotone to be used in Langside, to the rainbow that will reappear in Robin Hood Gardens: *"Colour is used as signal in the functioning: 'Class-world 1' will be all shades of green; the other 'class-worlds' follow: blue, purple, red, yellow, brown.*

The colours touch everything in each 'world', turning translucent when they are arrows on the glass of sliding doors."

* The notion of a spatial dialogue between existing lines of hedgerow trees and the configuration of the building becomes thematic in the Lucas Headquarters project of 1973–74.

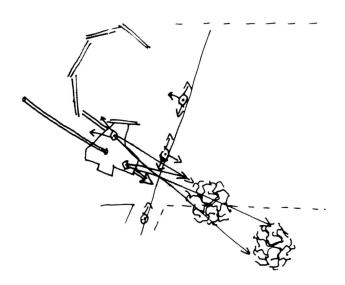

Diagram of view from hall. Those looking out from the staff room or the hall see the two best oak trees. The approaching visitor or child experiences a progression of spaces defined by trees. AS.

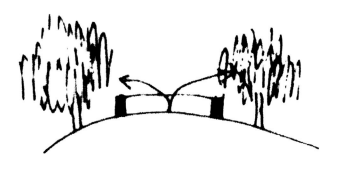

View of mature trees as second enclosure: A season-varied screen between infants and the outside world. AS.

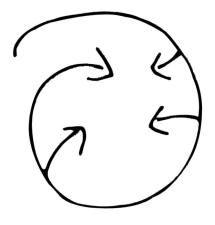

Ideogram of site. AS.

PROPOSED
COUNTY INFANTS SCHOOL
WOKINGHAM

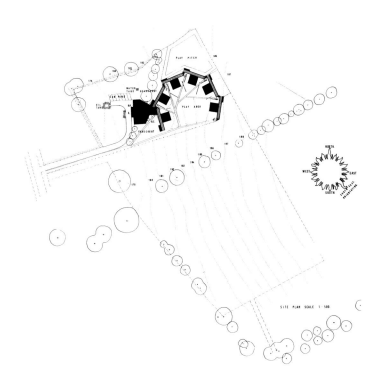

Site plan: Respect for trees 'as found' on-site. AS.

Axonometric with trees. AS, 1958; trees added 1983.

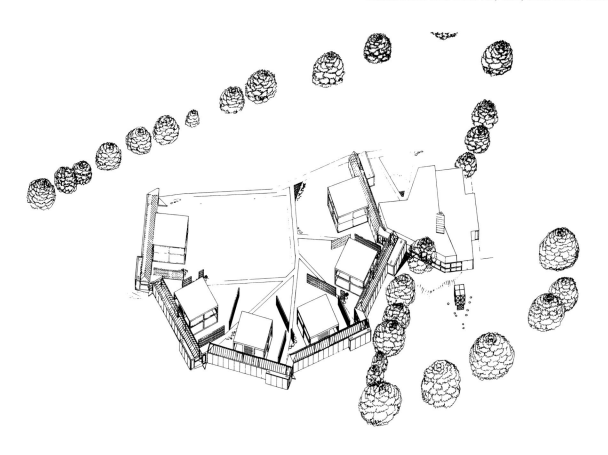

Langside College of Further Education

November – December 1958

A+PS

With Peter Sigmonde

"The main characteristic of this scheme is the use of levels bearing slipped layers of accommodation. The specialist teaching areas are grouped in two sandwiches of accommodation, each consisting of a circulation level serving areas above and below, each slid so that they lie on the natural slope of the ground. This virtual single-storey arrangement makes it easy to give top light supplemented by side light, with ventilation and service access to all areas." Thus we described a slid 'mat-building', structured through its 'running' staircases.

The colour of the building is that of its construction: *"Roof slabs of Z-section pre-cast concrete form roof lights. External walls are of cavity construction with a three-inch outer leaf of granite-aggregate concrete blocks. Internally the blockwork and soffits of floor slabs in corridors are fair-faced. To these greys of the exposed materials, other parts of the fabric respond: corridor floors are white terrazzo with four-inch grey strips at five-foot centres, running across the direction of route."* In this description of the fabric we get a sense of the grey and white 'tartan' of this mat-building. Then the colours of inhabitation: *"In the work areas blockwork is painted white. Small offices are lined with matte-surface white panels. Doors and fittings are faced in matte grey sheet. Metal windows are coated in brown bituminous paint, with opening lights and roller shutters in aluminium bituminous paint."*

This 'all-overness' was recognised in 1999 as one of the characteristics of the mat-building. The language of the mat-building in its pure state is the same all over, as if it were like a sand dune.

Composite plan showing all levels of stepped college. A+PS; trees by Peter Sigmonde.

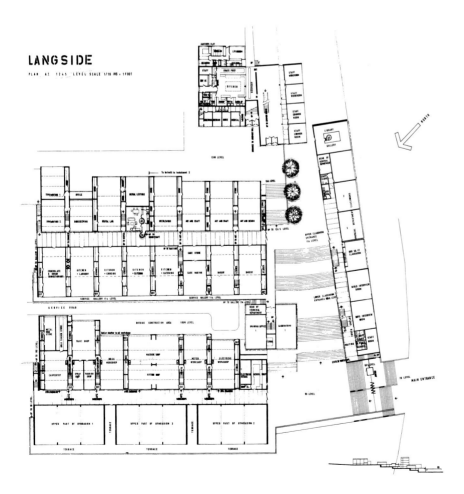

LANGSIDE

PLAN AT 1:245 LEVEL SCALE 1/16 INS = 1 FOOT

Three elevations.
Peter Sigmonde, 1958.

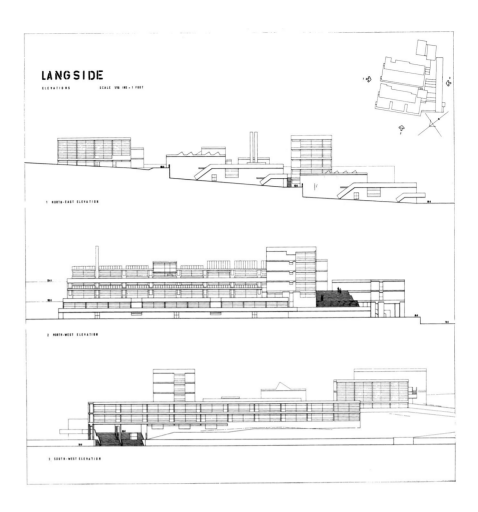

Three sections.
Peter Sigmonde, 1958.

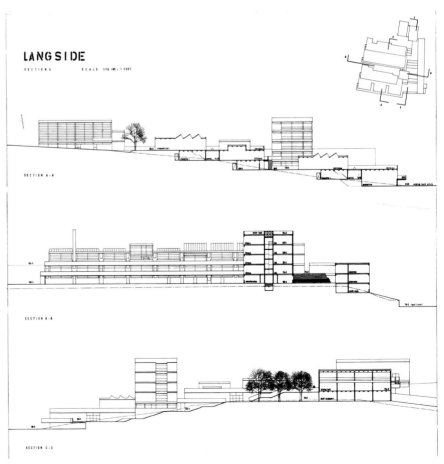

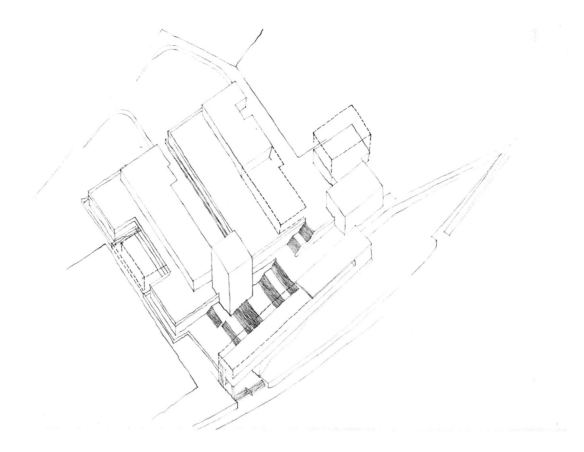

Axonometric diagram showing staging. Peter Sigmonde, 1958.

Diagram showing pedestrian, vehicle, and visitor flows. Peter Sigmonde, 1958.

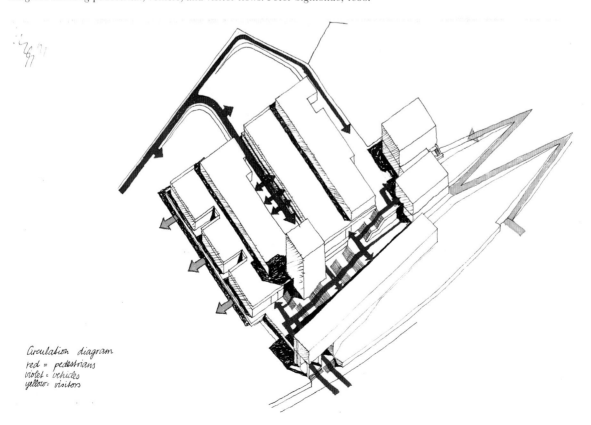

Circulation diagram
red = pedestrians
violet = vehicles
yellow = visitors

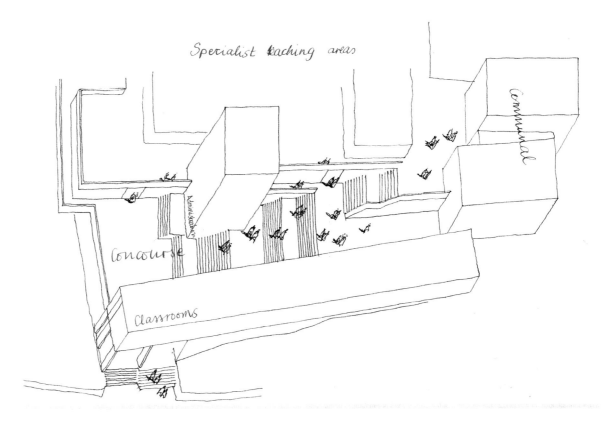

Diagrammatic axonometric of main approach. Peter Sigmonde, 1958.

Diagrammatic section with sun. Peter Sigmonde, 1958.

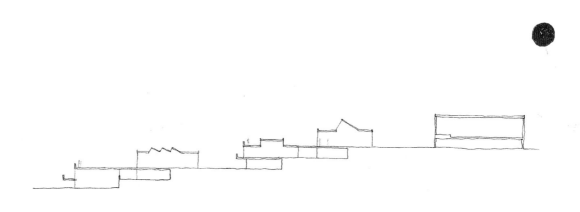

Paolozzi Studio House,
Lawson's Land, Hawkhurst, Kent

To visually 'possess' the site, this is a 'long house', which means the internal communications are linear; in response, the windows are formed so that the occupiers—in moving between studio and rooms—may appreciate views of the unspoiled field territory, fringed with pines.

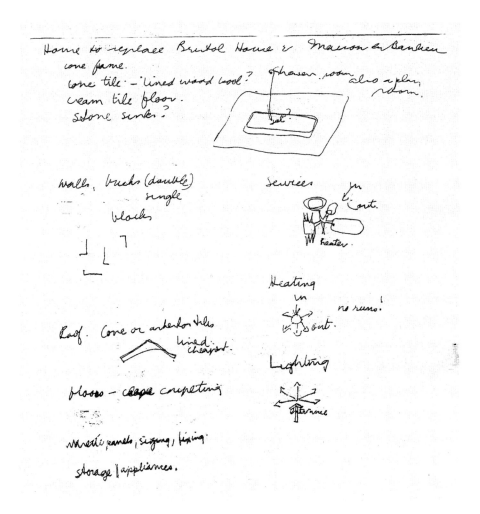

Programme agreed. AS.

opposite top: Plans, section, elevations, site plan. AS.
opposite bottom: Plans and elevations. AS.

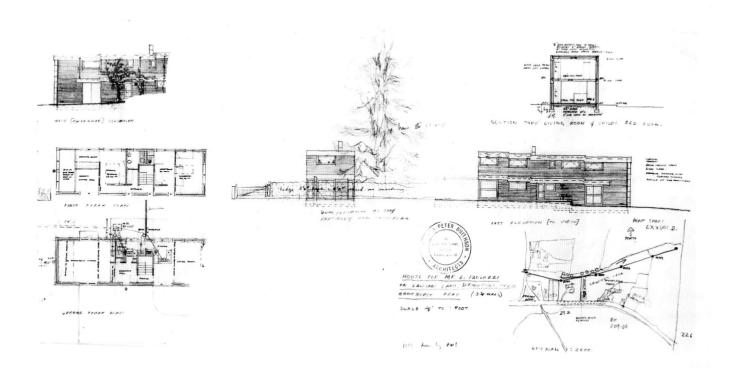

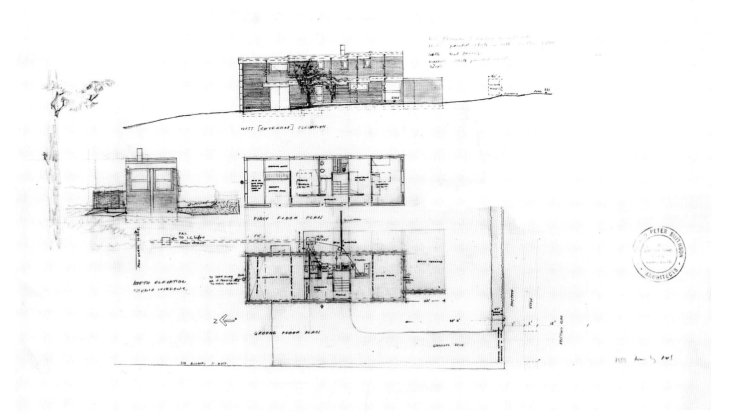

Retirement House,
The Homestead, Hawkhurst, Kent

The inexpensive Appliance House was to be fabricated out of off-the-peg components. As a retirement home, it was intended to have a 'built' garden as an outdoor room furnished with raised flower-beds. The situation at the crest of a diminutive wood on a slope allowed, in any sky condition, a screened overview of genuine country fields. The way the plan contained the service/storage cubicles, allowing a sitting position before every window, heralded the lodges of Churchill College.

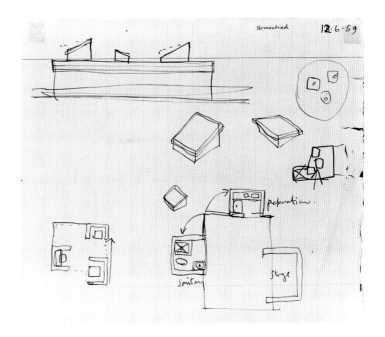

Ideogram. PS, June 1959.

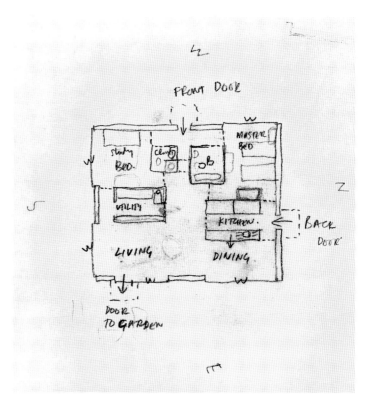

Structural diagram. PS, June 1959.

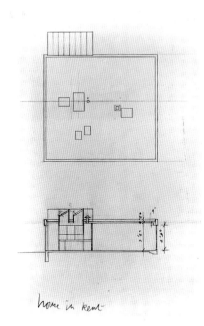

Roof plan and section. PS, June 1959.

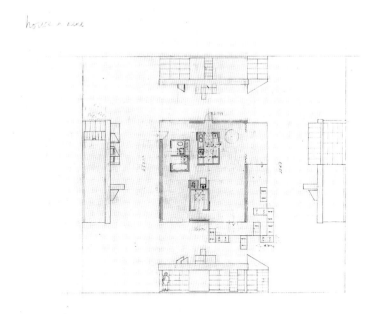

First drawing with facades disposed around plan. Elements of facade were to be industrial components. PS, June 1959.

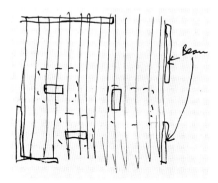

Structural diagram. PS, June 1959.

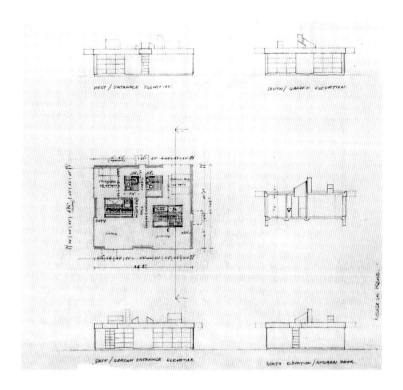

Second drawing with section showing sun-catching roof lights; insulated appliance cubicles freestanding within outer perimeter. PS, June 1959.

A+PS in Priory Walk, Kensington. Argent, 1969.

6 Pavilion and Route

the architectural implications of this theme of our urban structuring . . .

Wayland Young Pavilion, Bayswater *(1959–82)*   224

Churchill College *(1959)*   230

Folly . . . A 'Solar' Pavilion, Upper Lawn *(1959–82)*   238

The Economist Building *(1959–64)*   248

Losey House *(1959–61)*   280

Cliff House *(1959–61)*   281

Redington Road *(1960)*   282

Seafront Flats *(1960)*   283

Iraqi House *(1960–61)*   284

Steilshoop *(1961)*   288

Priory Walk *(1961–71)*   289

Mehringplatz *(1962)*   292

Robin Hood Gardens *(1966–72)*   296

Occupational Health Clinic *(1962–64)*   314

'Painting and Sculpture of a Decade, 1954–1964' Exhibition *(1963–64)*   316

Churchill College: Ground plan as an ideogram cut out of paper (becomes a camel-gram). PS, 1959.

Responses to themes we have identified weave in and out through our work; the idea of route can be said to be one such theme: starting in Golden Lane, generating the layers of Berlin Hauptstadt—where the towers may even be seen as urban pavilions perching at intervals on the edge of the network of routes. But the essay 'Pavilion and Route'* describes a post-Economist consciousness. How things come to be used with pleasure; offering opportunities for more appropriate patterns of light-touch inhabitation; the possibilities for stylish use . . . "*In Churchill College, the bicycle tracks are the student's connection to Cambridge. The bicycle's manoeuvrability is almost equal to that of the pedestrian; we can introduce small checks in the track system, which those 'in the know' will learn to manoeuvre with élan, but which will remind strangers who do not know that they are guests. Watching the flow of bicyclists, any sensitive observer would be able to decipher those subtle distinctions of speed between the residents and the guests.*"

* *Architectural Design*, March 1965, and *The Charged Void: Urbanism*.

Wayland Young Pavilion, Bayswater

Two appliance cubicles and a single mature tree give this garden pavilion its plan . . . an arrangement that has already successfully adapted itself to three generations of users.

As the appliance pavilion that got built, it connects to the blocks of 'sets' of Churchill College.

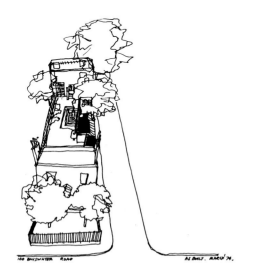

left: Sketch axonometric. PS, 1959.
below: Diagrammatic plan. PS, 1959.
opposite top: View of pavilion from the main house. William J. Toomey, 1959.
opposite bottom: View from garden. William J. Toomey, 1959.

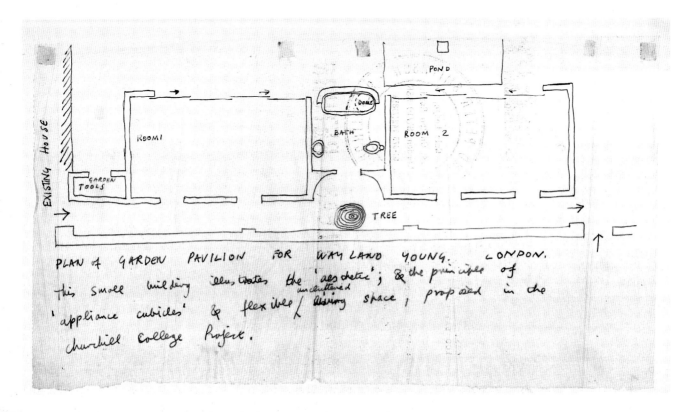

above: View of garden from pavilion. William J. Toomey, 1959.
left: View of the north side from the old coach house. PS, 1959.

above: View through pavilion out to old garden wall. William J. Toomey, 1959.
right: Bathroom alcove. William J. Toomey, 1959.

opposite: Corridor wall with tree 'as found'. William J. Toomey, 1959.
above: View down access passage with roof glass slid open. PS, 1983.

Here the blockwork left naked, as the old brick wall, helped to indicate route, by sound, feel, as well as by looks.

Rooms were plastered.

At Bath University's Second Arts Building (1 West North) the same arrangement was nullified by the client's careless plastering of the circulation spaces almost immediately after their occupation.

When an architect sees blockwork he thinks of cathedral cloisters; when a layman sees blockwork he thinks of dustbin enclosures.

Churchill College, Cambridge

The traditional college form dates from before the invention of the bicycle, which has been adopted by students of Cambridge—and Oxford—as the popular mode of transport: this college is 'structured' by bicycle tracks . . . a classic as-found.

The stair—one of the traditional arrangements of a college—is here updated by the addition of a lift: for the porterage of the yearly intake of student belongings and to aid the daily servicing. This vertical access is related to the bicycle tracks with their bicycle parking under the buildings among the piloti.

Each floor forms a small community of a size to invite several floor-friendship groups to emerge in each year's occupancy.

The traditional look of room-in-which-to-study is ensured by the layering of screens: nighttime and sun-control screens that slide behind the windows to each study bedroom . . . a choice of screens set well behind the sills, mullions, and window heads.

The window heads, to avoid glare, are one foot below ceiling level, and the sills are only one foot above floor level, so that the floor surface may be flooded with light to make for pleasant, relaxed reading conditions. The room orientations are east and west: the staggering in plan produces some view-out corners, and the stepping profile provides roof terraces and south orientation for the larger 'sets'. The overall aim of the stepping is to avoid the overshadowing of the forecourt by the afternoon sun. The staggering creates the half-open, half-closed space arrangement that suggests stage-by-stage building and future growth.

The structuring of the grounds is by wind-break thicket-hedges that provide release from the ever-present Cambridge winds . . . assure some measure of quiet by masking the sounds of road movement, garages, squash and tennis courts . . . provide seclusion by masking the sight of everything other than the college grounds fringed by the mature trees of suburban Cambridge and, up the slope to the west, the silver domes of the observatory.

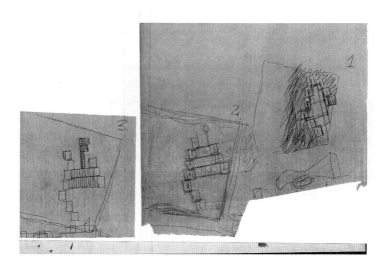

Sketches showing three stages of development. PS, 1959.

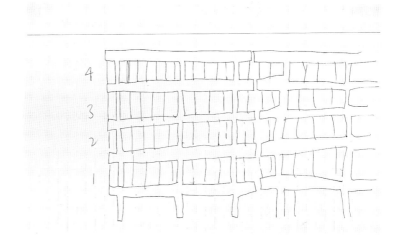

Development sketch showing elevations of range of rooms. PS, 1959.

Ideogram showing development of grounds. A+PS, 1959.

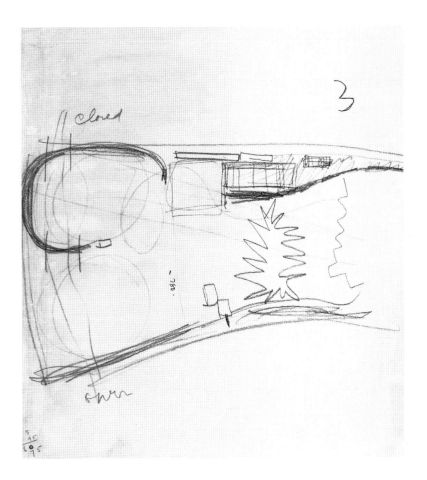

Sketch of grounds with high hedges. Here, at Churchill, begins the arabesque of hedge enclosures. AS, 1959.

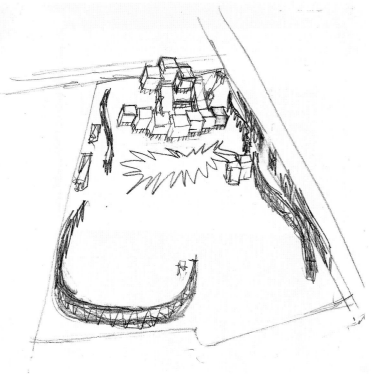

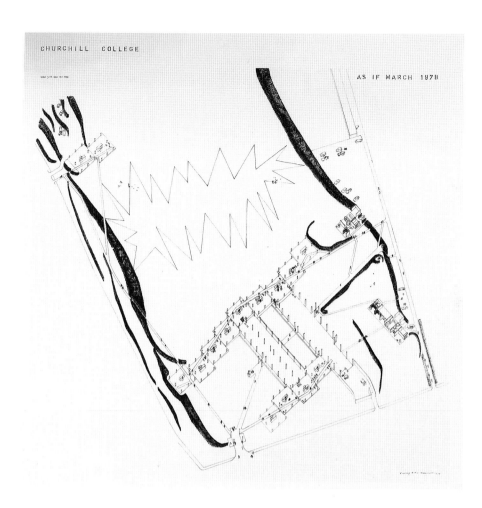

Axonometric twenty years on showing bicycle tracks. AS, 1978.

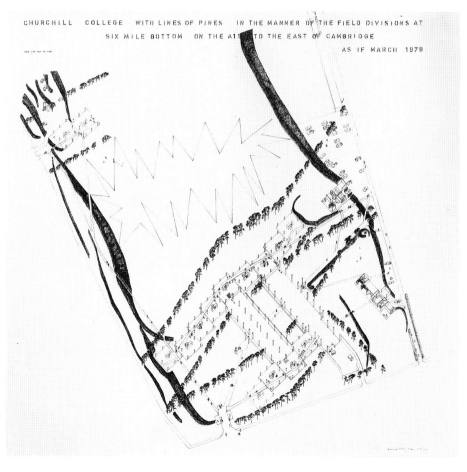

Axonometric twenty years on showing lines of pine trees in the manner of the field divisions at Six Mile Bottom on the A11 to the east of Cambridge. AS, 1978.

Axonometric twenty years on
showing gravelled roof of
new college surrounded by the
grounds containing lake.
AS, 1978.

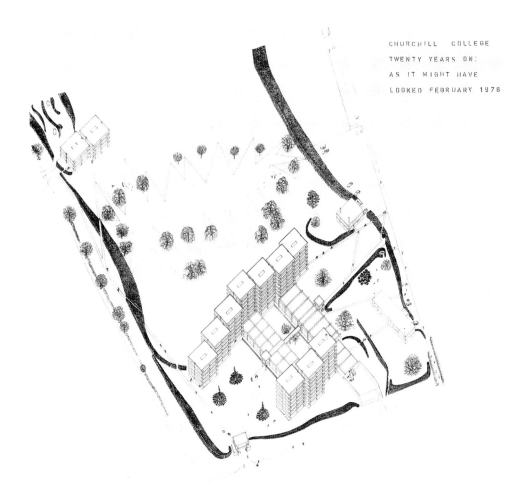

Axonometric twenty years on
showing roofs as planted terraces,
established grass, and mixed
deciduous trees. AS, 1978.

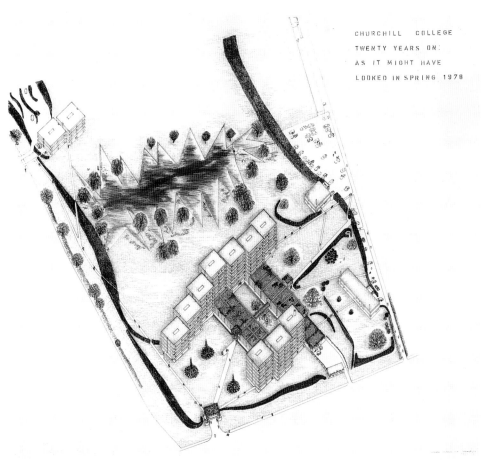

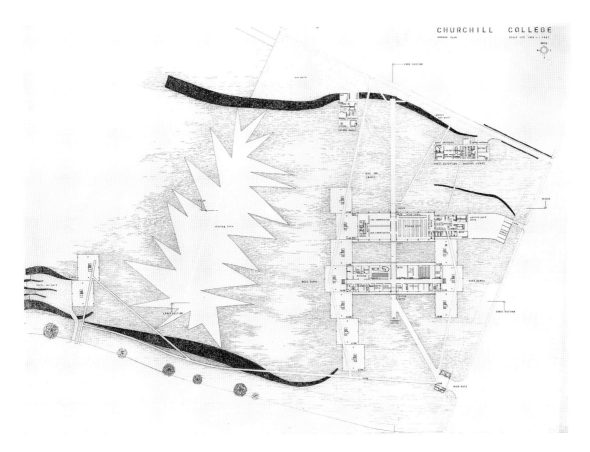

Ground-floor plan: Bicycle tracks are threaded through pilotis and weave between high hedges in the grounds.
A+PS, 1978.

First-floor plan showing rooms. Upper floors are similar. A+PS, 1959.

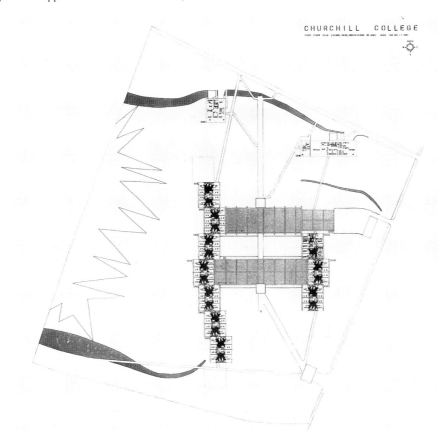

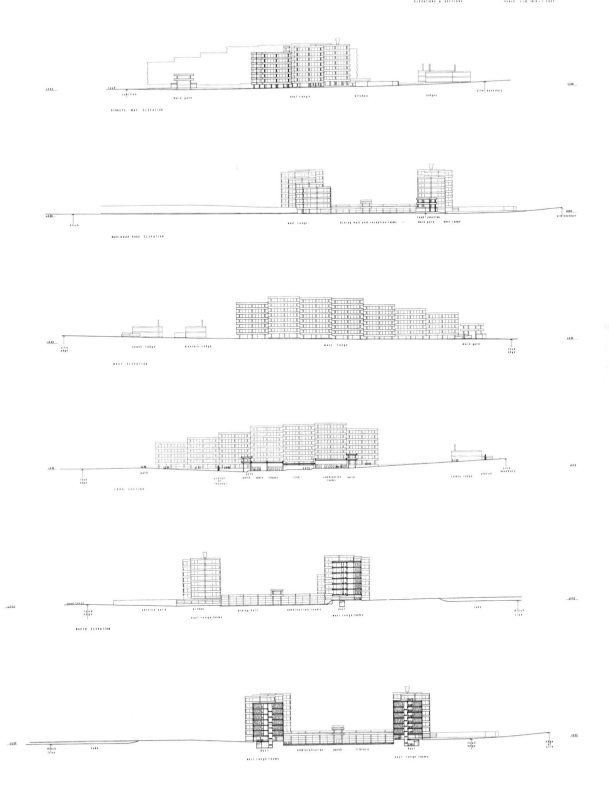

Storey's Way elevation (top); Madingley Road elevation with hall and portico between west and east ranges (second from top); west range elevation (third from top); long section through single-storey buildings between ranges (fourth from top); north elevation looking to Madingley Road with section through west range rooms (fifth from top); cross section through west range rooms with elevation of administration and library held between ranges (above). A+PS, 1959.

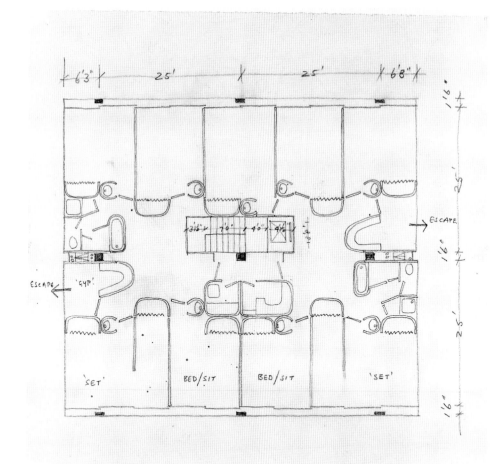

Typical floor plan of one block of rooms. AS, 1959.

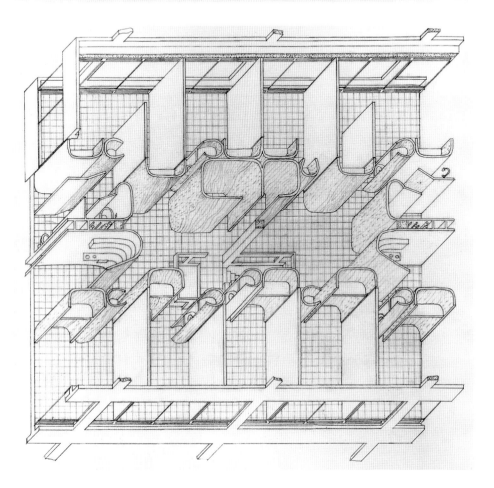

Axonometric of one floor of rooms. Staircase access is off centre, with a freestanding lift within a glass structural cage. Appliance cubicles cluster round this access space and form a layer of protection to the study-bedrooms and corner 'sets'. Windows and privacy screens slide in tracks behind the structure of the facade; the lintel thus becomes an 'eyebrow' against sky glare. AS, 1959.

In the lodges, doors link each room's walls to the enveloping skin of glass. If these doors are opened, the occupants of any room can enjoy long glancing views of the college grounds.

Lawn flows all around the building . . . and up to the lodges . . . grass even grows on the roofs of the bridging buildings—hall, library. Lawn is separated from the rougher grass of the playing fields by the very shallow skating lake: its splinter shape expresses its purpose (but is not, perhaps, natural to that purpose).

Ground-floor plans of master's house and bursar's lodge, with wind-break hedges and lawns crossed by bicycle paths.
A+PS, 1959.

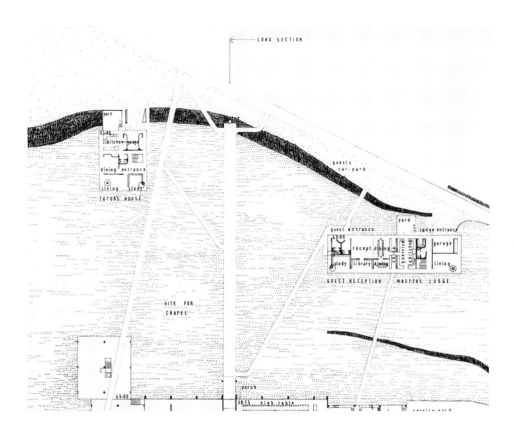

Axonometric of ground floor.
A+PS, 1959.

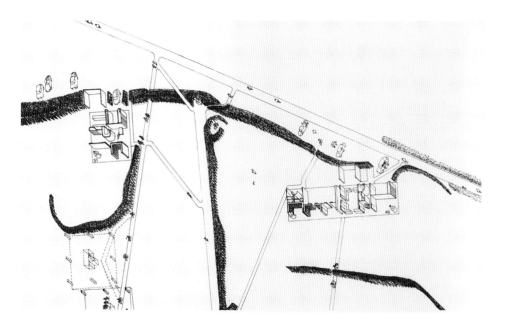

Folly . . . A 'Solar' Pavilion, Upper Lawn, Fonthill

A 'folly' implanted within the bounds of the original 'lawns' of Beckford's Folly at Fonthill.

Here, it is enough to say it is a pavilion in a compound, surfaced half by paving 'as found' and half by lawn; a pavilion in which to enjoy the seasons; a primitive solar-energy pavilion whose thin skin forms a new space against the thick masonry north walls of the original eighteenth-century and earlier farmstead cottages.

Diagram of assembly. AS.

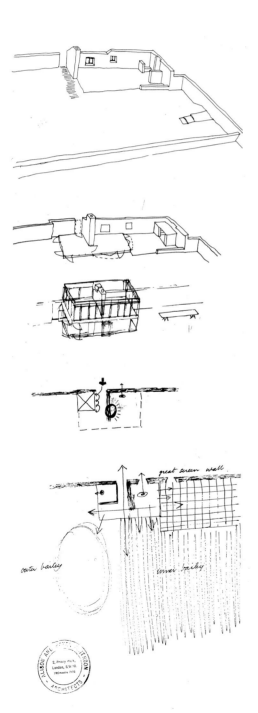

opposite top: View from the road side with Citroën ID 19. PS, 1962.
opposite bottom: Road side facade towards the Fonthill Woods. PS, June 1962.

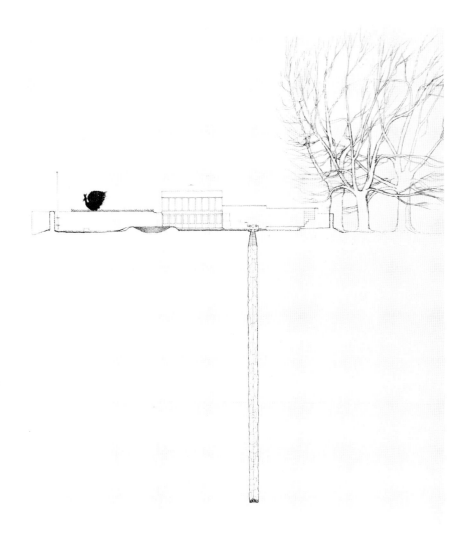

Garden front in its setting with section through the well. PS, 1975.

Sketches of arrangement in compound. AS, 1959.

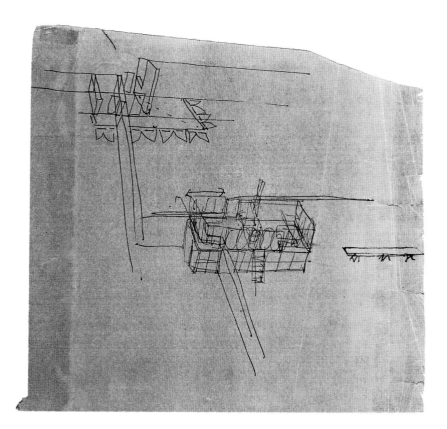

opposite top: Building and garden as one assembly. AS.
opposite bottom: Aerial view from south. Sky view, 1964.

pages 242–43: The 'Great Snow' of February 1978, with the Fonthill Woods beyond. PS, 1978.

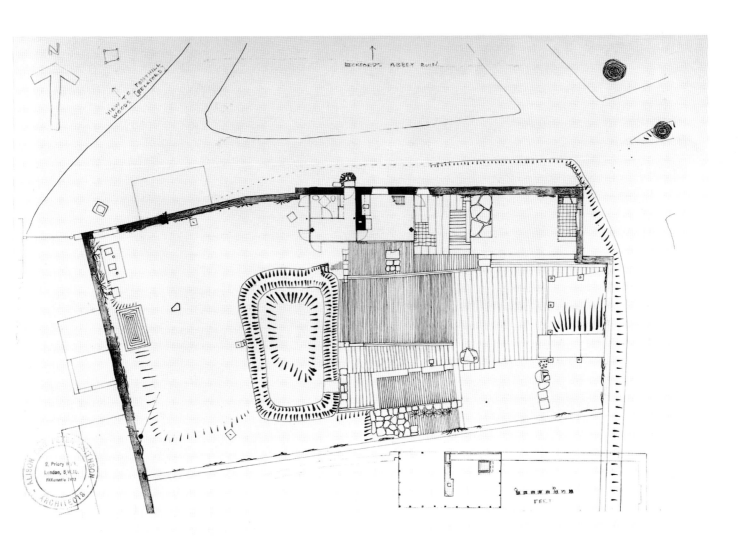

Folly . . . A 'Solar' Pavilion, Upper Lawn *(1959–82)* 241

View from the southeast with folding doors open for summer use. PS, 1963.

South face, folding doors closed, with AS cobbling in foreground. PS, 1962.

Timber frame under construction, summer 1960.
PS, 1960.

Detail view of stair lid and corner
(before lid reversal). PS.

Interior view of ground floor, east end.
De Burgh Galwey, 1962.

View of the yard, with window looking to the Fonthill Woods (photo taken after A+PS and family's occupation). Zürich, 1995.

The Economist Building, St. James's Street, London

A family of particularly English city scales is achieved in the Economist Building, stepping down from that of the bank fronting St. James's Street to the Economist Tower to the new bay on the side of Boodles' Club, finally to the Boodles' residential chambers. The plateau of the plaza raised above the surrounding streets offers a pedestrian pre-entry space in which there is time to rearrange sensibilities preparatory to entering the building to visit or work. The city is left outside the site boundary; another sort of intermediary place is contributed to the city; if—as in the past—many owners contribute these pauses, then other movement patterns are made possible: the man in the street can choose to find his 'secret' way about his city and can develop further urban sensibilities, evolving his own contribution to quality of use.

The articulation of the facing to the structure of the Economist Building—which solves many maintenance/aesthetic problems such as the control of run-off staining, and so on—has a wider, philosophical meaning: as in the components of ancient buildings, the modern components of the Economist Building indicate an architecture that has been first made in the mind.

* Entrance-hall refurbishment and security were revised at the twentieth anniversary, 1984. Later changes at this level and in the interior are not by A+PS.

First drawing: Elevation to St. James's Street. PS.

Child's impression of model. Simon Smithson, 1964.

opposite: Man on the Economist Plaza.
Michael Carapetian, 1964.

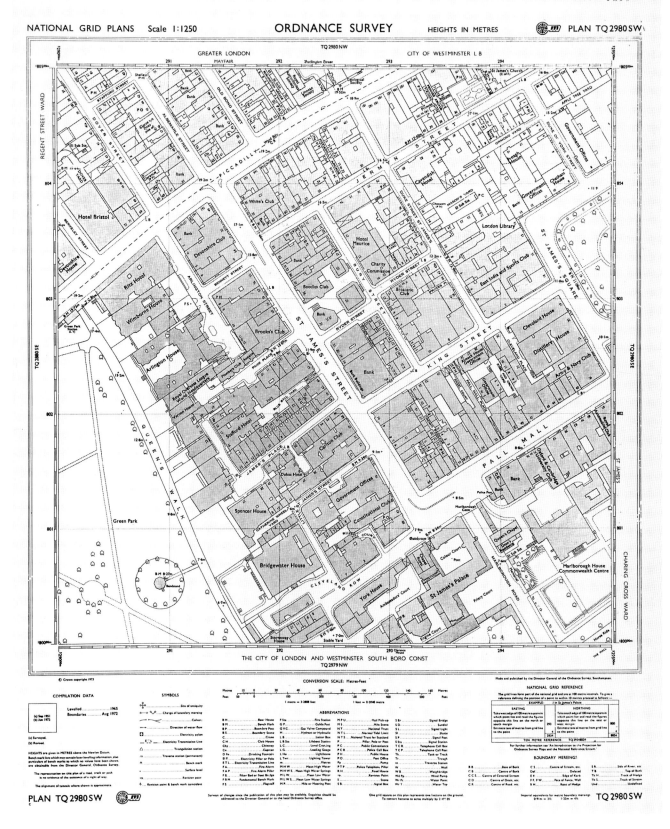

Plan in context of St. James's.

Typical plans at various levels.
Christopher Woodward for
Architectural Design, February 1965.

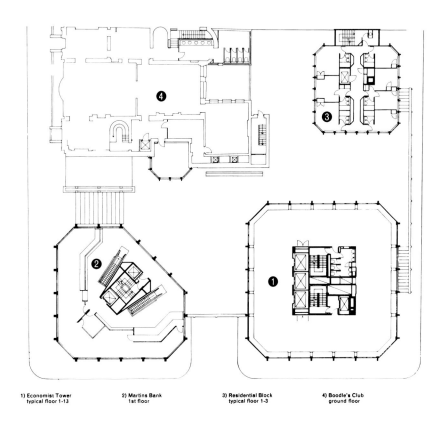

1) Economist Tower
typical floor 1-13

2) Martins Bank
1st floor

3) Residential Block
typical floor 1-3

4) Boodle's Club
ground floor

Plan at plaza level. Christopher
Woodward for *Architectural Design*,
February 1965.

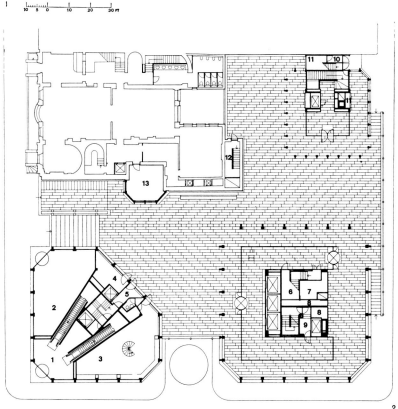

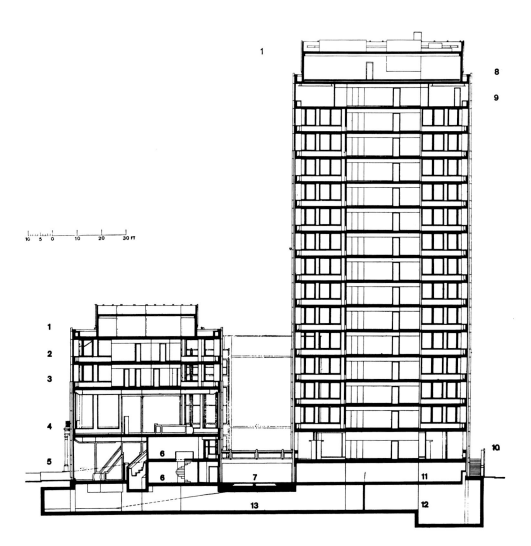

Section
1 bank plant room
2 lettable office floor
3 bank office floor
4 banking hall
5 bank entrance hall
6 shop 2
7 turntable and service entrance
8 tower plant room
9 fourteenth floor residential
10 plaza level and entrance halls
11 below plaza one level
12 tower boiler rooms
13 garage

Section.

Sketch scheme: Plan of corner with partial section and elevation. PS, 1960.

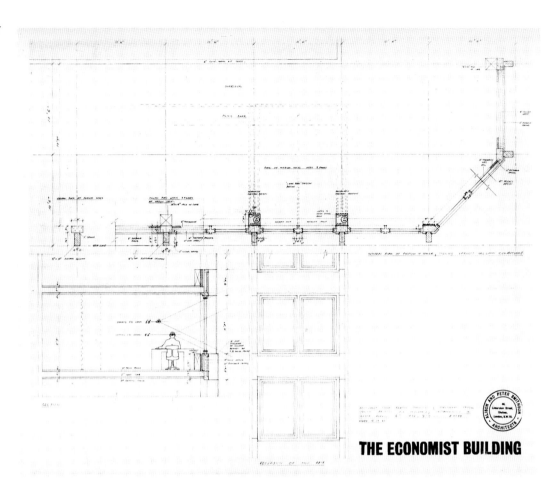

THE ECONOMIST BUILDING

right: Section detail of perimeter construction. Christopher Woodward, 1964.
far right: Plan detail of perimeter construction. Christopher Woodward, 1964.

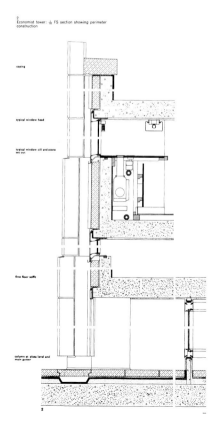

2
Economist tower; $\frac{1}{8}$ FS section showing perimeter construction

coping

typical window head

typical window cill and stone set out

first floor soffit

column at plate level and main gutter

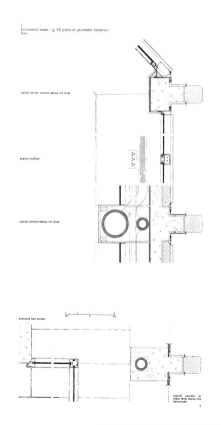

1
Economist tower; $\frac{1}{8}$ FS plans of perimeter construction

typical corner column above cill level

typical mullion

typical column below cill level

entrance hall screen

typical column at plate level above the balustrade

Drawing of interior view of bank's first floor. Gordon Cullen, 1964.

Collage of corner shop under the banking floor and beside the ramp up to the Economist Plaza. Studio Drawing, 1964.

top: Model of 1960, air view. All photographs of the model of 1960 show the
bank on St. James's Street in its preliminary plan profile. John Maltby, 1960.
above: Model of 1960, view from buildings in Bury Street. John Maltby, 1960.
above right: Model of 1960, view from St. James's Street. John Maltby, 1960.

Montage of air view of
model into air view
of St. James's. George
Kasabov, 1963.

Montage of several air
views of model into air
view of St. James's
(as office joke).
George Kasabov, 1963.

Detail of the residential building's skin during construction, showing roach-bed Portland-stone facings and stove-enamelled aluminium rain-run-off jointing elements. PS, 1964.

Roach-bed Portland-stone facing slabs and stove-enamelled aluminium rain-run-off jointing elements, stacked before assembly. '. . . What sticks and stones in their togetherness made' (see page 393). PS, 1964.

Roach-bed Portland-stone cappings to terminate the mullions at top coping level. PS, 1964.

opposite top: Collage of street-level view based on model. George Kasabov, 1963.
opposite bottom: View down St. James's Street as built. Michael Carapetian, 1964.

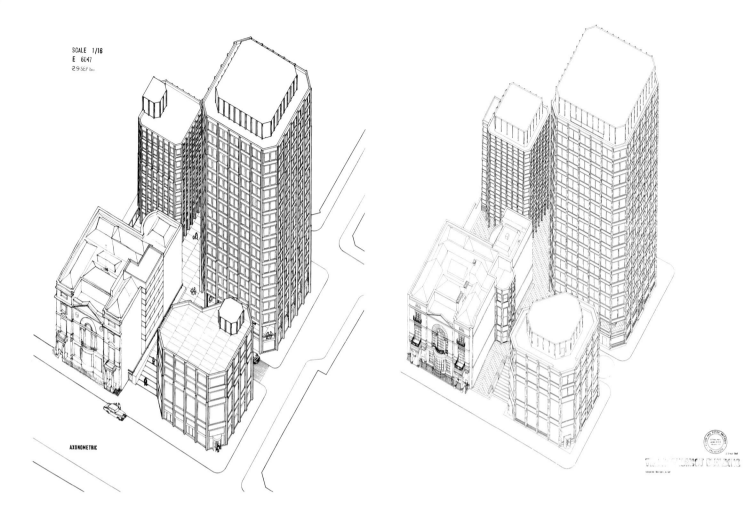

SCALE 1/16
E 6047
29 SEP 64

AXONOMETRIC

Second axonometric, preliminary design stage. George Kasabov.

Axonometric from the south-west, as built.
Christopher Woodward, November 1964.

Progress photograph, 24 September 1962. John Maltby.

Demolition at the corner of Ryder Street and Bury Street, 19 November 1962. John Maltby.

View from St. James's Street, 17 July 1963. John Maltby.

Progress photograph, 30 January 1964. John Maltby.

View from St. James's Street, 30 October 1964, almost at completion. The first issue of *The Economist* from 25 St. James's Street went out on 6 June 1964. John Maltby.

page 262: People standing on Bury Street. Michael Carapetian, 1964.

page 263: View up St. James's Street. Henk Snoek, 1964.

opposite: Night view of the plaza looking toward Brook's Club. Henk Snoek, 1964.

above: The plaza at night. Henk Snoek, 1964.

pages 266–67: The Economist buildings reflected in the banking-hall windows. Henk Snoek, 1964.

pages 268–69: Three men on the plaza, looking towards Brook's Club in St. James's Street. Michael Carapetian, 1964.

pages 270–71: Detail of the facades towards Bury Street. Brecht Einzig.

Interior of the first-floor banking hall
as originally occupied by Martins Bank.
Colin Westwood.

above: View of entrance hall to the bank, after passing through the revolving doors; the mosaic margin
at change of plane was first seen in the Sydney Opera House. Colin Westwood.
opposite: View of board room and meeting room. The balcony was to house bound back-numbers of
The Economist. William J. Toomey.

View of entrance hall to the Economist Building. The paving is the same as on the plaza outside;
the pattern of this paving is critical to the way one walks through the building group.

above: Typical 'half-corner' office at first occupation. William J. Toomey.
left: Typical office filing arrangements; air extract and ceiling lighting directly above; cupboard for personal things. William J. Toomey.

Twenty years on: Demonstrators resting on the Economist Building steps, up from St. James's Street. PS, 1983.

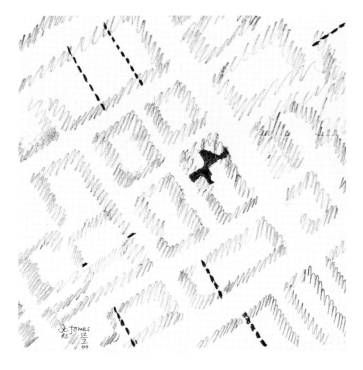

Plan of building blocks with vehicular streets in between as existing in 1959; footways are marked as dark broken lines. In 1964 a new footway was created at the Economist Building and is marked as a dark irregular shape in the centre of the drawing. It is a further contribution to a system of separated vehicular streets and walkways already established. PS, 1999.

New entrance hall collage: View across plaza, through corner of tower, to the balcony on the other side of Ryder Street.

New entrance hall collage: Detail of facade and stair to Bury Street; note, especially, balcony on other side of Ryder Street.

Plan of new entrance hall, 1985. One entry point in the new climate of security; scented plants; furniture still in the language of the building. LW, PS, 1985.

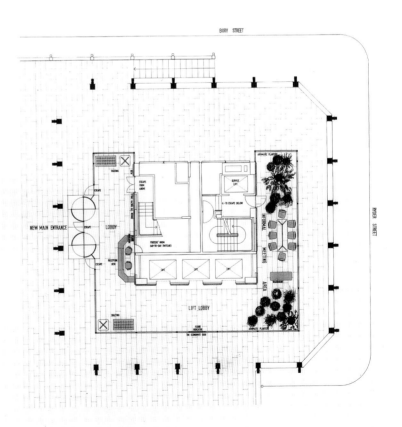

THE ECONOMIST BUILDING

NEW ENTRANCE-LOBBY ARRANGEMENT.
SCALE 1:50

Losey House, Snowdonia

At the height of the resurgence of consciousness about the English landscape, two clients chose very dramatic sites. We allowed the possibilities of a full appreciation of the place to give form to their requirements, intending to build with materials found on site and added to.

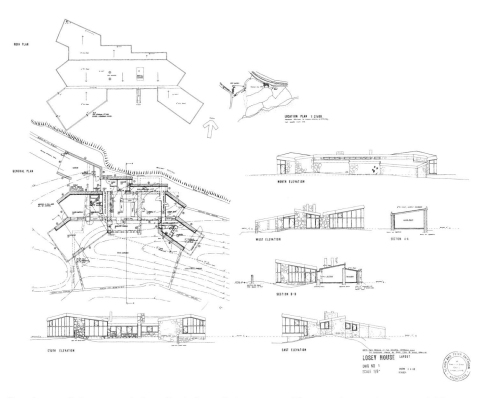

Site plan, roof plan, ground plan of existing ruin incorporated in new wings and entrance lobby, elevations, sections. PS, 1959–61.

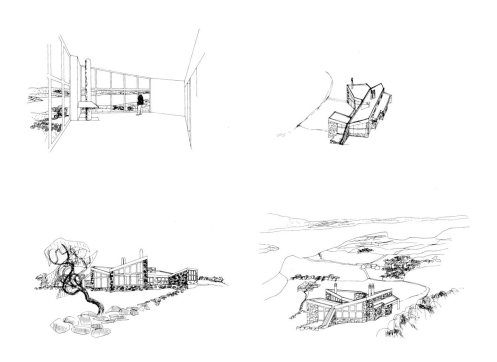

Perspective sketches: Air view from living room; house seen from immediate territory.
Ronald Simpson, 1960.

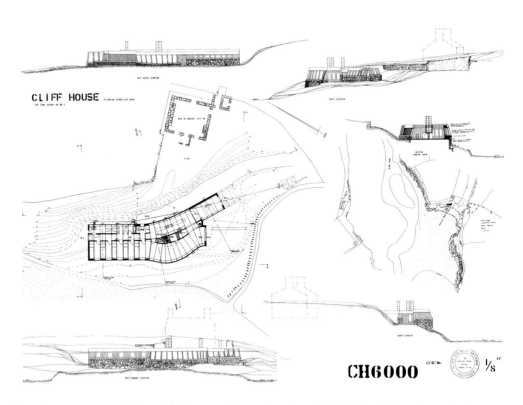

Elevation to sea, ground plan of single-storey house, elevation to land (left); end elevation to land, cross section, site plan, end elevation to estuary (right). AS, 1960.

Wonwell Beach, Devonshire. The Cliff House is sited next to the existing ruin, whose chimneys are visible. PS, 1960.

Redington Road, Hampstead

1960
PS

An application of the 'climate fit' ideas of the English Climate House as infill to the site in front of the Oliver Hill House.

Perspective of three rowhouses seen from the road with the
Oliver Hill House in the background. Ronald Simpson, 1960.

Seafront Flats, Western Lawns, Kings' Gardens, Hove

The 'tree' form of Hove derived from a reaction to the rudeness displayed on the seafront at Brighton and Hove by flat blocks completely obstructing the sense of the sea from those in the hinterland.

Considering the means of escape regulations in the light of a willingness to let the sense of the sea pass its flanks, we discovered that a 'tree' form could work to give economical vertical and horizontal access.

Flats in this 'tree' have the traditional Brighton and Hove glazed balcony/terraces for the all-year-round, all-weather experience of the English Channel. End flats are graced by terraces facing south-east and south-west, an open-hand response to location that reappears twenty years later in Lützowstrasse.

right: Four diagrams of ideas:
1. Aspect/prospect diagram of views out to sea
2. Circulation tree
3. Duplex section
4. Plan variants of type A flats.
PS, 1960.
far right, top: Site sketch: Ideogram of a fir tree stacking arrangement with stepped profile. AS, 1960.
far right, bottom: Elevation diagram. PS, 1960.

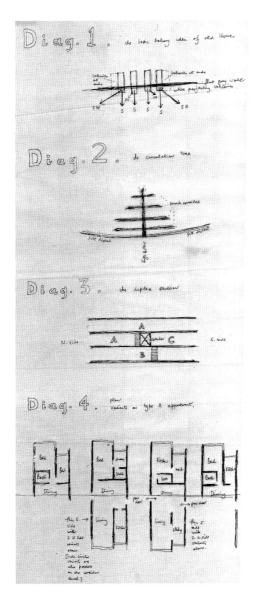

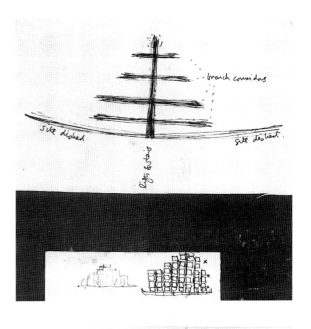

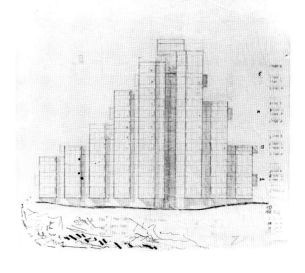

Iraqi House, Piccadilly

August 1960 – August 1961*

A+PS

Subsequently demolished

A new interior inside an Edwardian building . . . the new surfaces of the side walls in this long, narrow tunnel are sand finished and undulated; the carpet matched to the ceiling-wall sand colour; their textures mutating in relation to the light.

Inset into the walls are sand-coloured plaster casts of Assyrian reliefs from the British Museum workshops. To clear the view from Piccadilly into this spectacular tunnel—and to be sure of the passer-by seeing through the glass—the display case is dropped into the basement.

A circular parapet—to lean on—is a light well to the basement.

Tiles brought from Iraq differently surfaced the airline and bank counters.

The Iraqi House's curvaceous spaces, its simple pleasure of an ample bench on which to sit on a Zerb rug, hark back to the House of the Future, look ahead to Cookies' Nook.

* Period during construction of the Economist Building: first time two constructions on the same 1:1250 Ordnance Survey sheet (see page 250).

Passersby in Piccadilly look down into the sunken display case. Kerry Dundas, 1961.

opposite: Plans and section. Attributed to AS with Timothy Tinker.

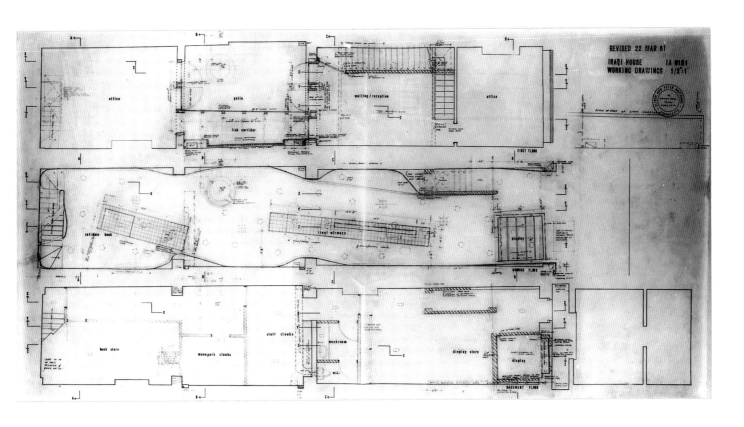

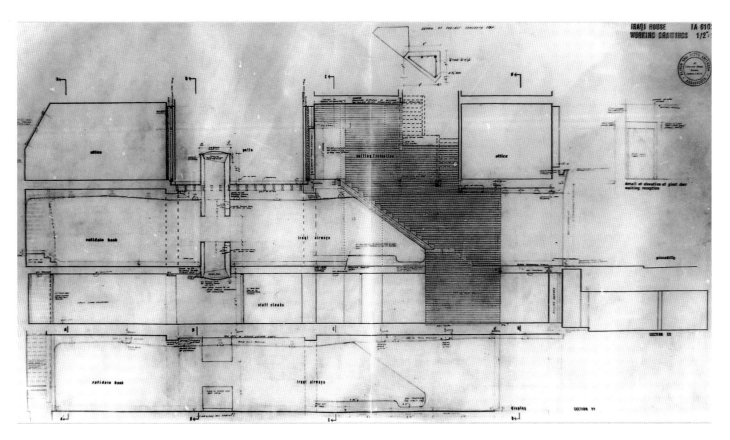

View of the light well to the basement lit by a dome light in the patio above. Kerry Dundas, 1961.

The bank counter at rear of the tunnel-like space. Kerry Dundas, 1961.

opposite: View from the entrance off Piccadilly. Kerry Dundas, 1961.

Steilshoop, Hamburg

The application of the already developed ideas of Close Houses, the addition of Terraced Crescent Housing, and the invention—for the 'palm' of this district of greater Hamburg—of the growable 'foci' central shopping were all themes considered in detail.*

Terraced Housing, answering Steilshoop programme requirements, appears in the 'Private Air' diagram, motivated by that sense of needing an escape from the intrusion felt by urban householders overshadowed, looked down upon, by office or hotel development.

* See *The Charged Void: Urbanism*.

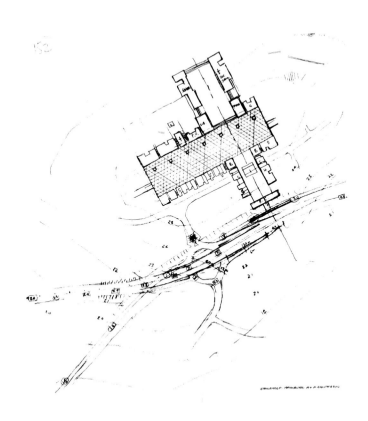

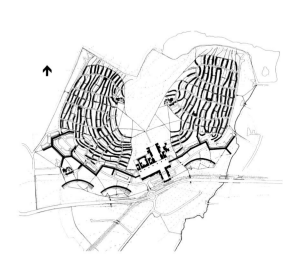

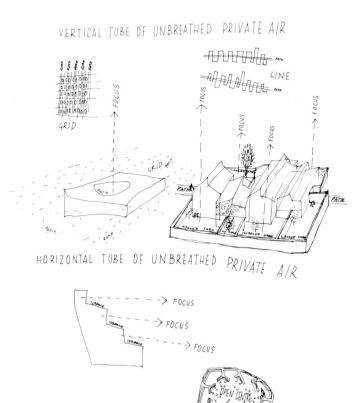

above: Diagrammatic plan.
right top: First sketch plan of the 'foci'. PS, 1961.
right: 'Private Air': Diagram of notion that one's territory encompasses the immediate air above and the view of the sky. For final version of diagram, see *The Shift*. PS, 1961.

Priory Walk, South Kensington

In 1961 we moved a few hundred metres, but across the borough boundary from Chelsea into South Kensington, into a bigger terrace house.

All terrace houses have their life around the staircase.

This house was spatially reorganised to give the main living area the top floor, with the sunlight and the views, in the space once occupied by the children's and maid's rooms. The workrooms were down below.

It was our first own-built experience of letting light in from the top, a notion maturing in the 1970s and 1980s.

The main works were carried out in 1961; later, a miniature pavilion with light from all sides was built at garden level.

All these works were subsequently destroyed by the incoming owners of the house.

Top-floor living room. Note House of the Future POGO chair (1956) still in use. PS, 1961.

View of the top-floor kitchen/living room. Djukanovic, 1964.

Ascending into the light. The kitchen equipment is visible from the stair. PS, 1961.

Soraya's shadow on the wall of the top-floor room. PS, 1968.

A+PS in their workroom. Topix.

View from above of a
child's room with its
own miniature storage
arrangement built out
into the garden over a
basement enlargement.
PS, 1967.

Poppies on the tiled kitchen benching.
PS, 1970.

Kitchen equipment in top-floor general living room.
PS, 1961.

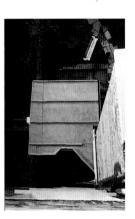

Mehringplatz, Berlin

Autumn 1962

A+PS

Collaboration with Gunter Nichke

A further exploration of horizontal layering appears in the progressively diminishing floors of the twin blocks of Mehringplatz. But it is principally their disposition and their length that manage the scale transition from motorway to individual office: the providing of adequate transitional spaces between journey undertaken and work arrived at is the main theme in Mehringplatz.*

The Roman symbol of portico is given a whole new graphic; the access system has its own notation of movement. The man or woman arrives at the workplace via several means . . . first by a mode of transport—the S-bahn, or the private car, or the delivery vehicle—to where they have to walk, then to a portico, and then by the gondola.

* See *The Charged Void: Urbanism.*

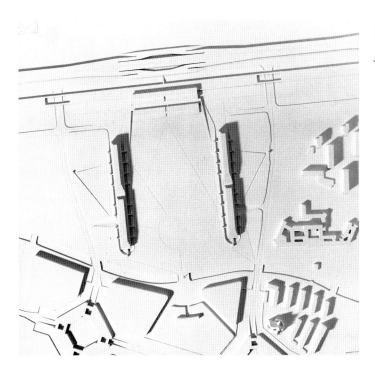

Air-view of model with the two parallel blocks hanging from their parking building alongside the motorway.
J. Stanton Abbott, 1962.

Initiatory sketches.
Previous to this, all work
had been on the urban
rationale (see *The
Charged Void: Urbanism*).
PS, October 1962.

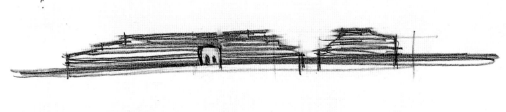

Elevation sketches.

Composite ideogram of
porches: Idea of portico
for buildings of
Mehringplatz; developed
idea for the elevation
with porticos; the section
in embryo.

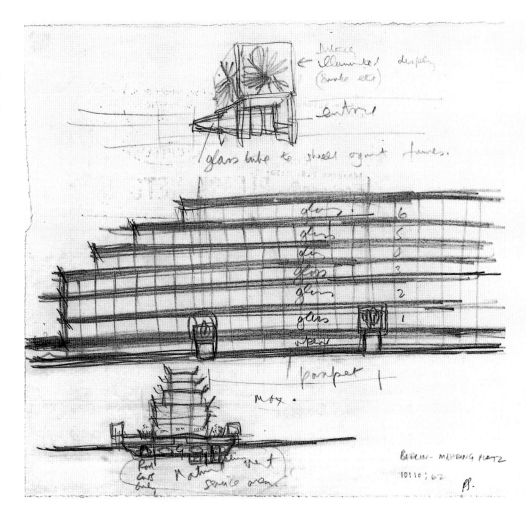

End elevation and
part-elevation of central
space. PS, 1962.

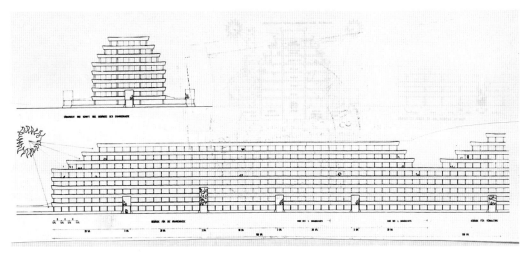

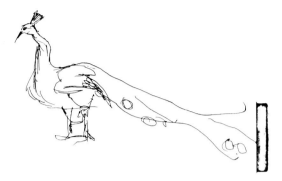

Peacock drawn for Mehringplatz perspective. PS, 1991.

View of model. J. Stanton Abbott, 1962.

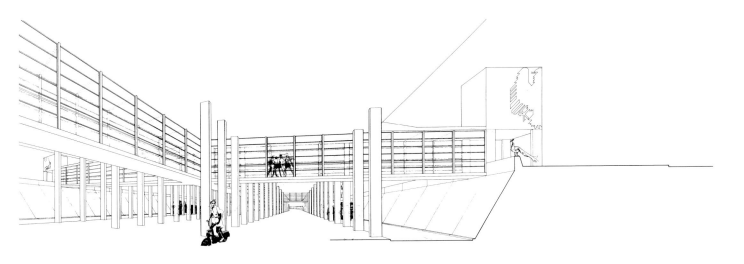

Perspective drawing at moat level—the level for vehicles—with 'gondola' walkways at natural ground level overhead. James McAdam, PS, 1991.

View of model. J. Stanton Abbott, 1962.

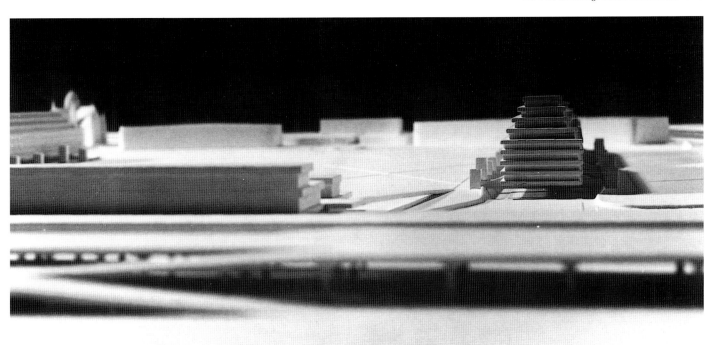

Robin Hood Gardens, London

1966 – 1972

A+PS

These buildings in Tower Hamlets started on three separate sites . . . as realised, the southern sites had coalesced into Robin Hood Gardens while the northern was still in 1994 semiderelict due to the vacillations of fashion in traffic management. By 1999 the sites along the northern edge have been redeveloped as brick-built housing.

The theme of Robin Hood Gardens is protection.

To achieve a calm centre, the pressures of the external world are held off by the buildings and outworks. This is effected, as near to the source of noise as possible, by the first layer of a boundary wall. Noises that penetrate this layer to the access decks along the outer facades are diffused by more domestic noises. The access decks are separated from the habitable rooms by the individual entrances and stairs so that this internal circulation acts as a further insulation to the bedrooms. These bedrooms have windows on the inner facade overlooking the quiet of the protected garden. On this quiet garden side, French windows open the rooms onto escape balconies, extending their usable space in 'expansive' weather.

This building for the socialist dream—which is something different from simply complying with a programme written by the socialist state—was for us a Roman activity and Roman at many levels:

. . . in that it was built for an elaborate system of government and one with its own permanent building bureaucracy;

. . . in that it takes its stand alongside the heroisms of what has been made before—the port and the roads;

. . . in that it is as heroic as supplying a Romanised city with water: whether one sees this service as dramatic and obvious as an aqueduct or as secret and craftsmanly as the underground conduit;

. . . in that one has to deal with the problem of repetition;

. . . in that it is a bold statement working with the land forms;

. . . in that it provides a place for the anonymous client;

. . . in that it wants to be universal, greater than our little state—related to a greater law.

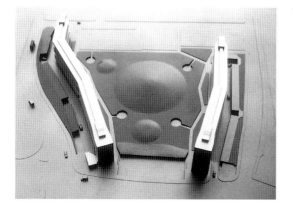

View from south of model made for the BBC television presentation. PS, 1970.

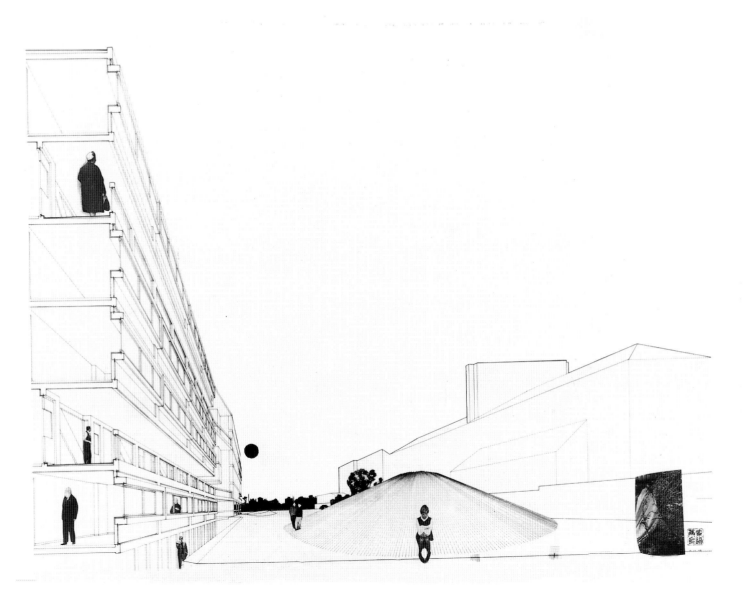

Collage of first scheme known as Manisty Street (1962–64), which became Robin Hood Gardens. The mound from the demolition 'spoil' is in foreground. This project was stopped by tenants in Manisty Street protesting their housing conditions. In the delay while the case was heard, the site was purchased by the Greater London Council; the whole site became Robin Hood Gardens. PS, 1963.

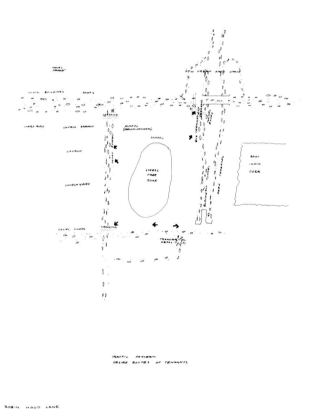

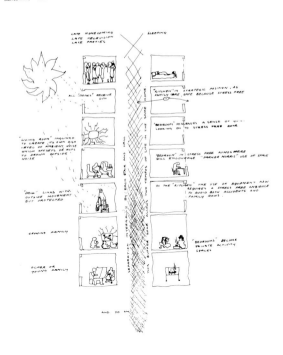

Diagram of traffic pattern and desire routes of tenants.

Diagrammatic section showing reasoning behind disposition of the required accommodation.

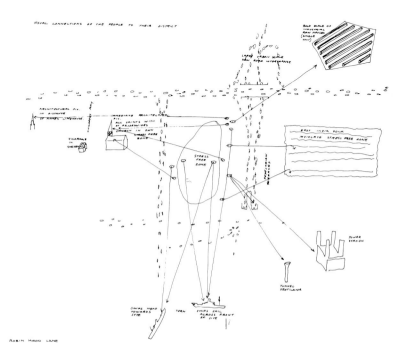

Diagram of visual connections of the people to their district. (The East India Dock basin, assumed to be inviolate, has subsequently been filled and built over . . . the higher building was placed on the East India Dock side, to overlook its stretch of water!) AS.

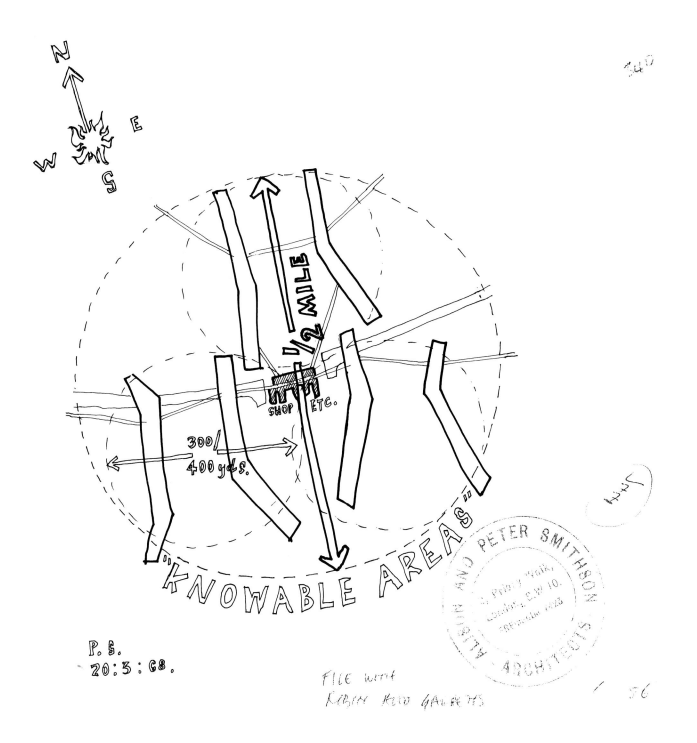

'Image of dimensions' for a group. PS, 1968.

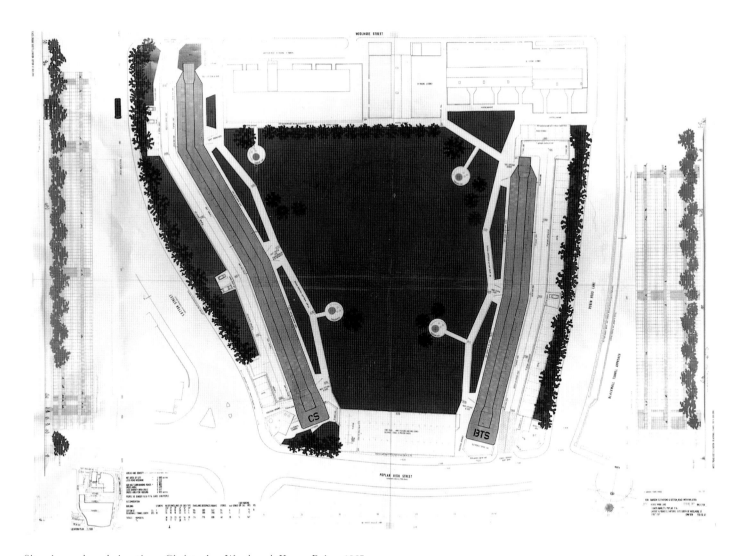

Site plan and road elevations. Christopher Woodward, Kenny Baker, 1967.

Plans of Cotton Street Block: Above deck level, at deck level, below deck level.

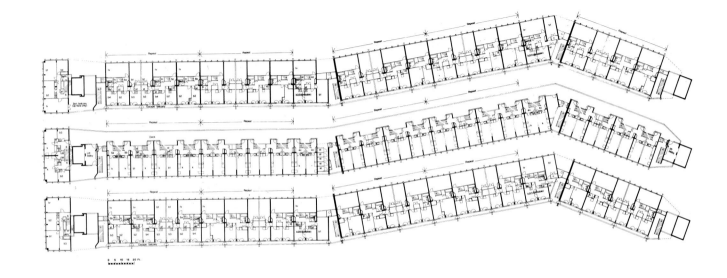

this page and page 303: Series of six axonometric collages (compare with Golden Lane). Drawings by Christopher Woodward, 1971. Collages by PS, 1972.

Blackwall Tunnel South Block, tenth floor, Type 6 up flat, deck level.

Blackwall Tunnel South Block, eleventh floor, Type 6 up flat, upper level.

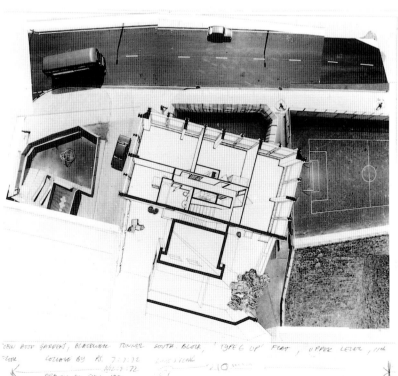

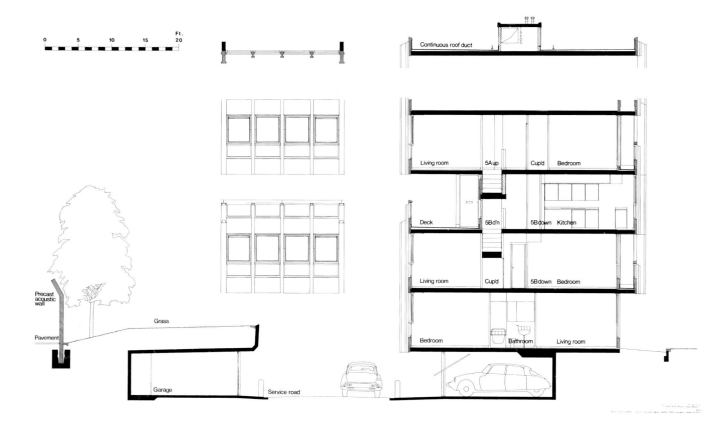

Section through Cotton Street Block with elevation elements. Kenny Baker.

Drawing of typical facade with projection
of mullions shown by pencil shading.
Kenny Baker.

Pre-cast skin components. PS, 1969.

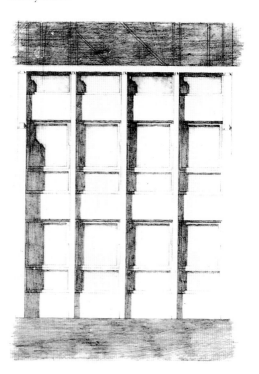

Cotton Street Block, sixth floor, outside flat 82 of Type 3 flat, looking north-west towards the spire of All Saints' with St. Frideswide's Church.

Cotton Street Block, sixth floor, outside maisonette 96 of Type 3 flat, looking south towards the River Thames.

Blackwall Tunnel South Block, ninth floor, outside maisonette 194 of Type 4B flat, looking south towards the River Thames.

Blackwall Tunnel South Block, ninth floor, outside maisonette 210 of Type 4B flat, looking south towards the River Thames.

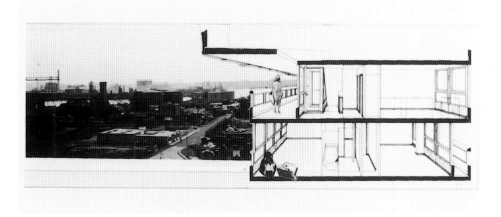

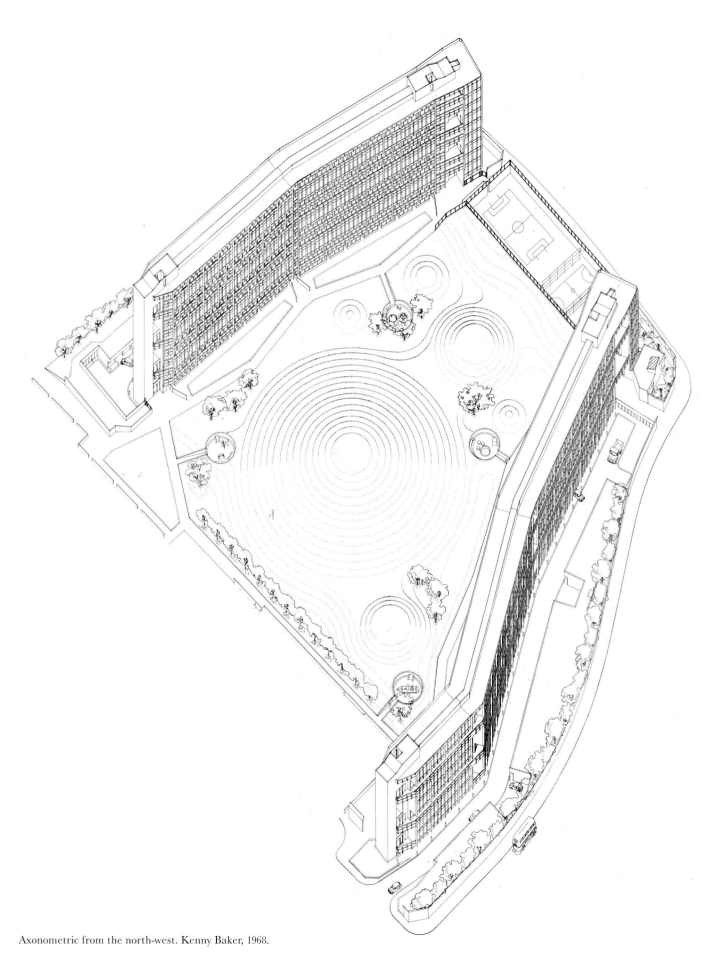

Axonometric from the north-west. Kenny Baker, 1968.

View from the north of the central open space seen over the East India Dock Road. Sandra Lousada, 1973.

pages 306–7: View of the largest mound in the central green space. Sandra Lousada, 1972.
page 308: Central garden space with St. Frideswide's beyond. *Building Design*, 1973.
page 309: Mound used as intended: Photograph taken during school holidays. *Building Design*, 1973.

The mound's core: Photograph during construction. PS, 1968.   A+PS on construction site of Robin Hood Gardens, 1970.

opposite: Cotton Street moat viewed from first deck level; St. Frideswide's beyond. *Building Design*, 1973.

right: View looking south towards the River Thames from a deck on the Blackwall Tunnel South Block. PS, 1971.

Older residents' ground-floor flats at foot of Cotton Street Block, seen from the central space. Sandra Lousada, 1972.

Circular play spaces for toddlers. Sandra Lousada, 1972.

pages 312–13: View from the north of the 'tail' of the Cotton Street Block. Sandra Lousada, 1972.

Occupational Health Clinic, Park Royal

Spring 1962 – 1964

AS

Subsequently demolished

This pavilion clinic is of the Bayswater/Upper Lawn family. It sits on given land at the foot of an unused Guinness Brewery embankment and faces—across a road—the canal. It is a centre for preventative medicine on an industrial estate.

The timber-and-glass pavilion is simplicity itself. The treatment rooms are almost secret adjuncts to the prime function of information giving—exhibitions as to the effects of smoking, machine-safety procedures, and so on—which is exposed in a see-through room that can be entered equally well from either side.

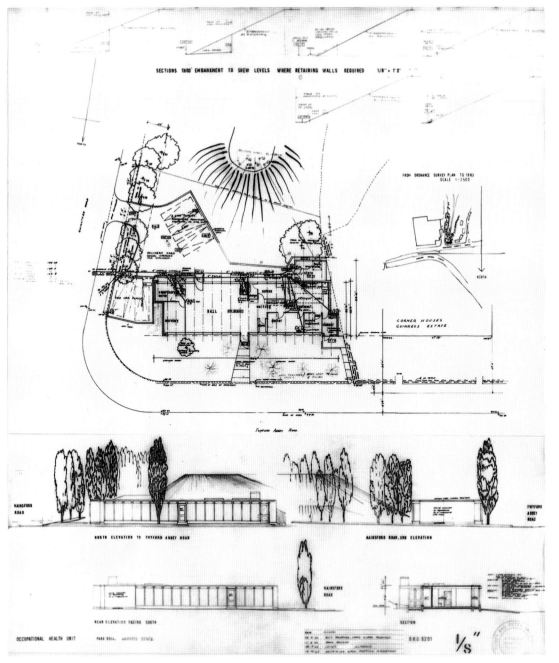

Site plan and plan; elevations. AS.

Elevation towards Guinness railway siding mound. Sam Lambert.

Two views from the road side. The view into the interior was an 'occupational' requirement. PS, 1963.

The brief was in the form of constellations of artists with a start point of Old Masters and an exit point where one left the Milky Way.

It was our intention to present the works in such a way as to make clear the relationships that governed their selection. The paintings and sculptures alone were intended to speak. No tricks of presentation were used, and nothing of the detailed architecture of the Tate allowed to obtrude.

To achieve this, the galleries were totally blacked-out, and a highly illuminated white screen was run around inside the existing walls, building up a pattern of spaces which served the groupings and the sizes and space needs of the individual paintings and sculptures. The brightness of the screens kept the eye at low level and allowed the mind to ignore the old spaces around and above.

The general schema was established in advance over a period of about a year and a half, from the known sizes and from photographs of the works brought to a common scale. Detailed adjustments to the screens, the lighting, and the painting and sculpture arrangements were made once the live material became available and the real spaces established.

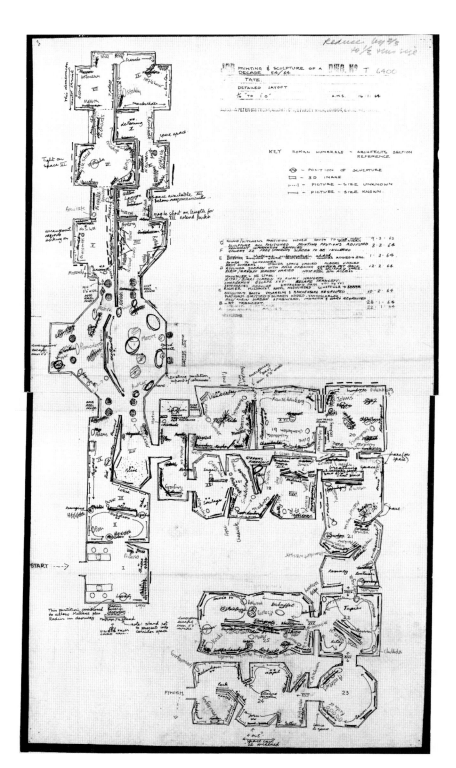

Plan of the galleries with the new spaces inserted, based on the groupings of the works. AS, 1964.

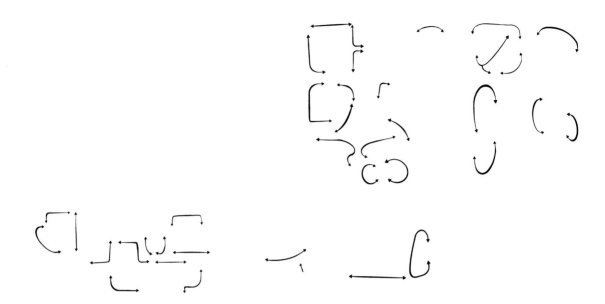

Diagram of the groupings of the works. Nuria Garcia de Duénas Geli, 1995.

Diagram of visitor movement. Nuria Garcia de Duénas Geli, 1995.

Three views of the spaces. Sandra Lousada.

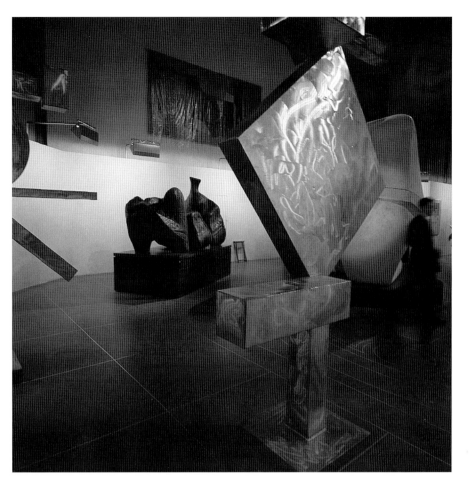

AS arranging the works within the new
spaces. Brian Heseltine.

7 Layers of Fabric, Layers of Meaning

these reflective meanings, most dear to the European architect, are seemingly more private to architects than ever intended or ever before . . .

'Extensions of Man' Exhibition *(1962)* 326

British Embassy, Brasilia *(1964–68)* 328

Burleigh Lane Houses *(1965–66)* 336

Crispin Hall *(1965–66)* 338

Garden Building, St. Hilda's College, Oxford *(1967–70)* 340

Wedding in the City *(1968)* 352

Government Offices, Kuwait *(1970)* 356

New Model House *(1971)* 366

Married Graduate Flats and Squash Courts, Queen's College, Oxford *(1971)* 367

Gilston Road, South Kensington *(1971–)* 368

Cherry Garden Pier *(1972–76, 1983)* 369

Battlebridge Basin *(1972–74)* 372

opposite: A+PS with celebratory flags. Jeremy Baker, 1965.

The Beach. PS, 1969.
Collection of Charles Howell.

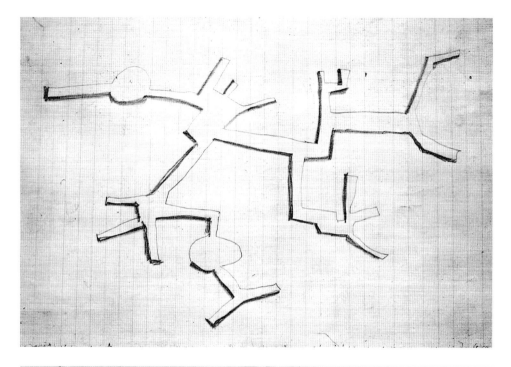

Five images made in parallel:
Animal of connection. PS.

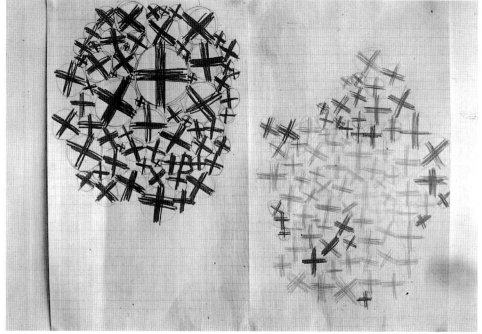

Clusters of crosses. PS, 1953.

Layers of fabric—external built or growing layers—are to do with privacy and protection, of capabilities of mutation in response to season and so on.*

The creeper grown on the wall offers such a seasonal transformation, clothing the surface, decorating, itself a series of layers: stalks, leaves, flowers if it has any; together, these are cover for another layer of inhabitation—even if it is only spiders. The nearest to this 'veiling' that the romantic period architect devised was treillage, what we call lattices. Perhaps something of a less obvious texture is an intermediate framework that belongs both to the outside and to the inside. The outside supports of an arcade are, for example, bridging elements, a plane of pause before the building enters the air.

Layers of reflective meaning carry responsibilities . . . towards those who have gone before . . . for those who will follow.

In the tradition of those-who-would-build, we deal with insights: the thoughts are there for when the need occurs. In the tradition of Vitruvius . . . Alberti, Francesco di Giorgio, Palladio, Serlio . . . Le Corbusier . . . our writings are directed at other building architects and their cast of mind. The themes of our earliest work were basic: identity, patterns of association, and so on, first documented in *Urban Structuring*.† The overall theme for the Hauptstadt period—connection—ran from 1957 to 1962, and all the sub-themes occur, at least in embryo, in Hauptstadt: education for town building; pavilion and route; order of movement; idea of mobility; inverted profile; growth and change;‡ green zones;§ connective linkage; open texture. In 1960s 'open texture' became identified as 'scatter', with the first ideogram that became the 'palm' of Steilshoop: it is a theme that still reoccurs.

Our overall theme post-Hauptstadt, 1959 to 1967, is given in *The Charged Void: Urbanism*, as 'cohesion', covering: contributions to a fragmentary utopia (Appliance Houses); building towards a community structure; roads and the community structure (Mehringplatz and the work for Street, Somerset); sensibility; density, interval, and measure. Dates of inception as to when these themes had been sufficiently identified—often recognised some time after their making—and sufficiently discussed, to be written down and published, can be interpolated from our bibliography.∂

*   See also A+PS, *The Shift* (London: Academy Editions, 1982).
†   *Urban Structuring: Studies of Alison & Peter Smithson* (London: Studio Vista, Reinhold, 1967).
‡   Shared with J. B. Bakema in Team 10.
§   Scharoun had this idea in the Hauptstadt period, more fully developed as a green supportive matrix.
∂   In the heroic period of *Architectural Design*, whose Bedford Row Chambers were pulled down in the spring of 1984.

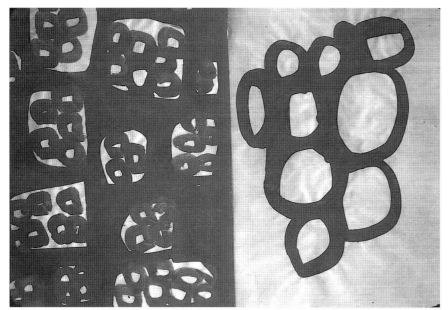

Painting of roundish cells. PS, 1950s.

Painting of squarish cells. PS, 1950s.

Painting of comb-like strips. PS.

The theme 'neutrality', which in architectural works can be a quality of anonymity, spans from 1968 to 1970.

Obviously, having to respond to the totally different nature of the old town of Kuwait—without anything of a fabric history in the Western sense and only traces, by 1968, of its original substance, yet with an inescapable ambience—brought about a change in our sensibilities.

The follow-on thematic group of urban projects is aptly termed 'holes in cities'. Under this collective heading, the individual themes are: nature of place (Cherry Garden and Battlebridge); metaphor for infill (Adalbergstrasse); acceptance of reality; catalytic gesture; connection (Verbindungskanal); holes in cities (Worcester, Urbino, Jerusalem). These ideas are intended to work their way into the remnants of the old fabric to encourage the inhabitants to regain their urban confidence.

Emergent themes have to do with sun acceptance, energy containment, and the signals of these new attitudes. The lead theme has returned to architecture—perhaps for the first time since Hunstanton and Coventry—although there has always been a back and forth between architecture and urbanism. But all these concerns do not cover the compost of meaning in our works; for at all times we have carried on our own dialogue with architects in history as we bounce energy off their abilities.

'Extensions of Man' Exhibition (or N.M.A. Exhibition)*

October 1962

A+PS

An exhibition intended to eliminate the bad taste the Festival of Britain exhibition had left.

Our response to the programme analysis provided by Reyner Banham† was on two pages: one page of ideograms, one page of text with diagram.

The open aesthetic: 'open' as opposite of 'closed' in that it can develop casual, 'informal art', net of human relations, as we now see them.

The *non-obvious structure* corresponding to 'Play Brubeck': cluster city implying cluster components of a region, new sorts of I.V.T.C. (Banham's abbreviation for *i*ndividual house, *v*illage, *t*own, *c*ity).

---

* After a meeting in the living room of Roland Penrose, held to discuss the exhibition, one of those attending commented on the 'largesse' of a Picasso in the toilet.
† Banham's programme seemed a breakthrough at the time in that it contained the concepts of pause, change of pace, diversions, escape, necessary to 'walking', looking.

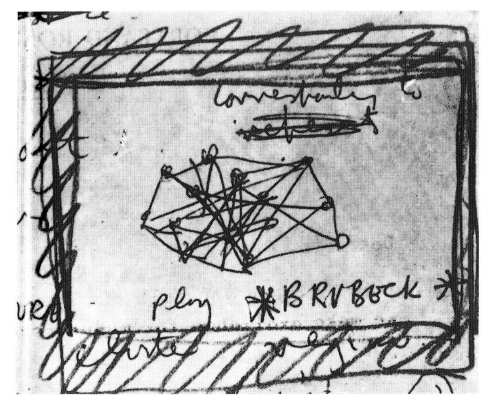

'Play Brubeck' image: Diagram part of response paper to Banham's programme notes for 'Extensions of Man' exhibition; discussed at house of Roland Penrose. PS, 1962.

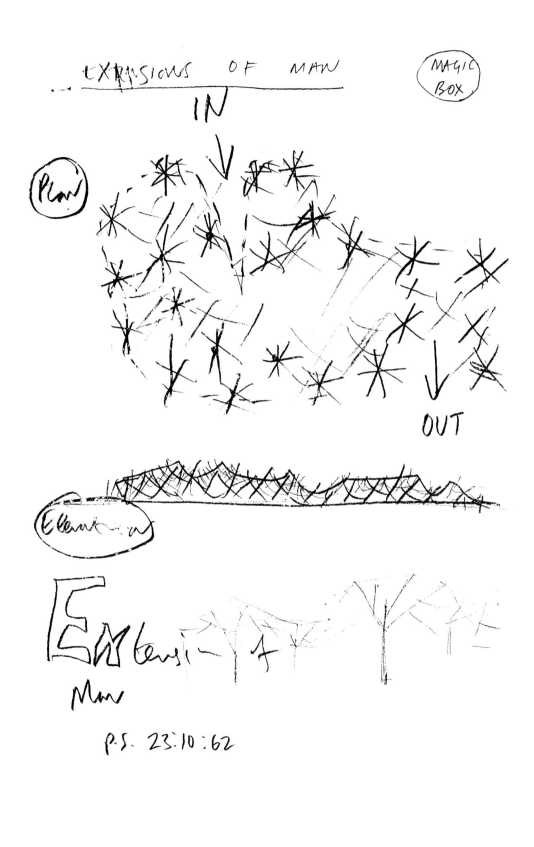

Ideograms of possible form of exhibition: Plan, elevation, interior. PS, 1962.

British Embassy, Brasilia

The use in our architectural language of slipped, connective layering reached its apogee in Brasilia, where the slight half-flights of stairs ease spatial and physical transmission from one level to another.

The curved interior partitions form rooms as freely as if they were decorative containers on a shelf: under the long beams between stair towers, the room layout can be reordered as necessary in the life of the building. And as at Sheffield University, the external screens can be rearranged to match; here, continuous screens of French windows of 'pau ferro' hardwood withstand the climate and the insects.

Detailing of the heads of all windows, doors, and internal partitions takes account of the deflection of the beams in use and in thermal movement.

Brasilia's layers of protection for the occupants begin with the two planes of the roof. An upper roof shelters the structural roof which carries all the services on its top surface. An angled overhang* protects the top levels of the building, followed in succession by the overhang incorporated in the parapet of each level of connective balcony. Protective layers also work from the ground upwards in the deep plinths of coloured concrete that protect the building from staining by splash-up.

The garden at Brasilia—intended for easy use for large open-air parties—extends the language of Churchill College's wind-breaks as layers of screens for privacy. Many of these screens were to be maintained at chest height, allowing a view out but not a view in from the surrounding roads, for the garden rides above the surrounding land as a many-levelled podium. The ha-ha of Hunstanton becomes in Brasilia, through its height above the in-cut moat, a genuine security barrier.

The garden colonnade and the two lodges—one serving as a gate portico—were miniatures of the embassy building: these with the garden itself take full possession of the site.

* The antiglare eyebrow, Moghul 'chujja', here occurs for the first time in our work: see Second Arts Building, University of Bath, 1979–81.

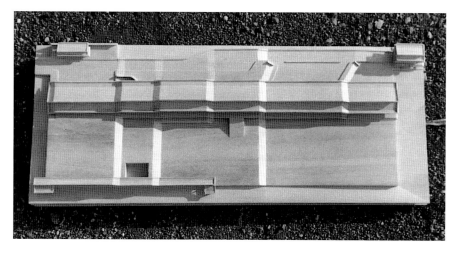

Preliminary model, photographed on site in Brasilia. PS, 1964.

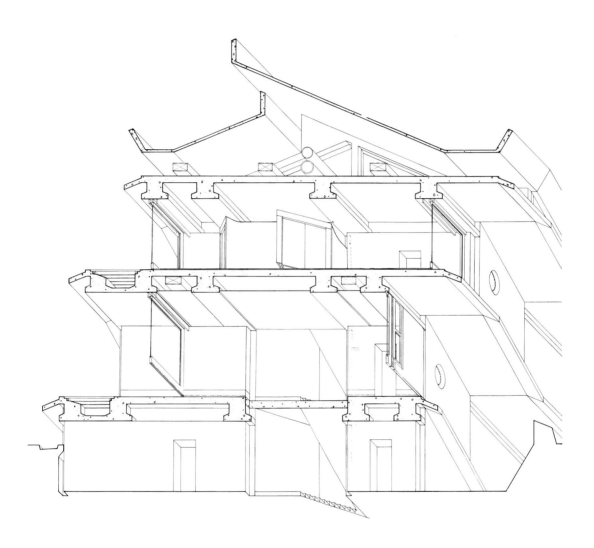

Axonometric section. Henry Bryce-Smith, 1984.

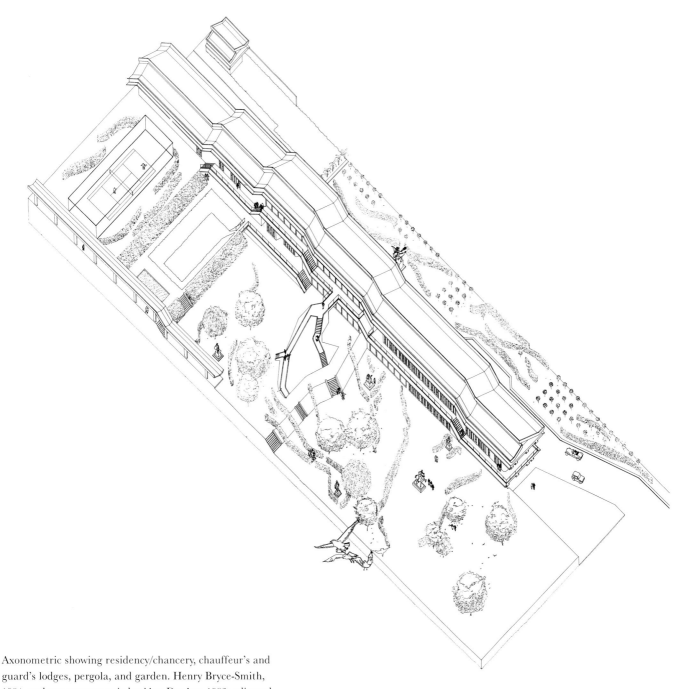

Axonometric showing residency/chancery, chauffeur's and
guard's lodges, pergola, and garden. Henry Bryce-Smith,
1984, on base axonometric by Alan Dunlop, 1983; adjusted
by Diego Varela, 1997.

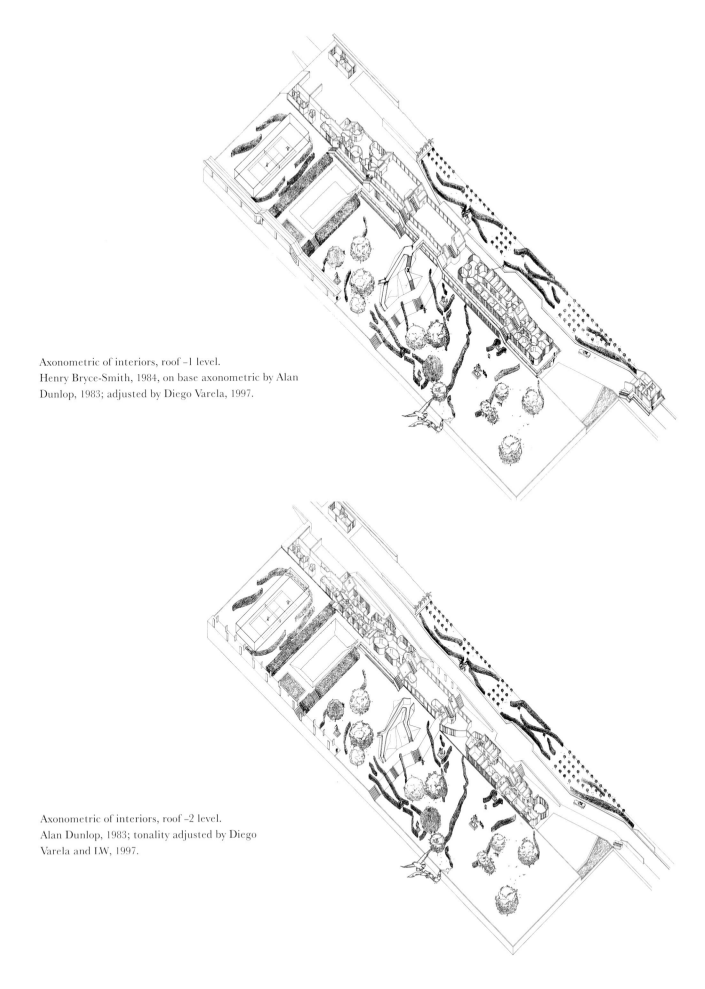

Axonometric of interiors, roof –1 level.
Henry Bryce-Smith, 1984, on base axonometric by Alan
Dunlop, 1983; adjusted by Diego Varela, 1997.

Axonometric of interiors, roof –2 level.
Alan Dunlop, 1983; tonality adjusted by Diego
Varela and IW, 1997.

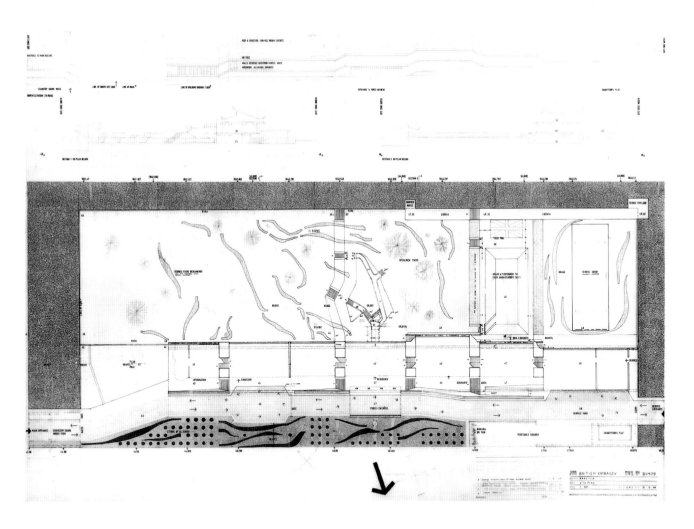

Site plan showing garden layout, long elevation, cross sections.

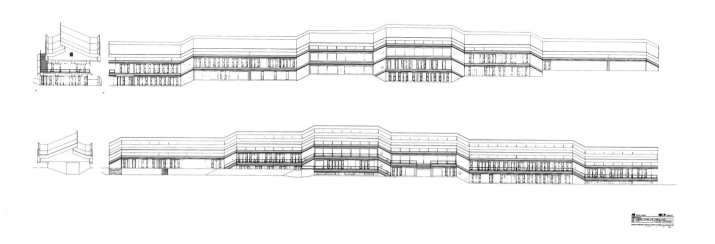

Elevations to principal access road from government centre (top left); to private access road (top right); to secondary access road in city plan (bottom right); to the garden (bottom left). Christopher Woodward, 1965.

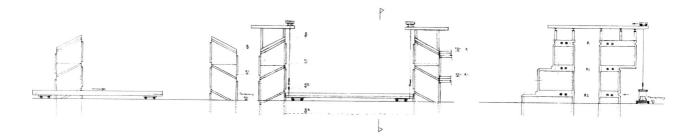

Diagram of the process of erection of the long floor beams between the stair towers. At the time of this project there were no cranes in Brasilia, so the building had to be self-erecting. Ove Arup & Partners.

Four elevations of the entrance lodge.

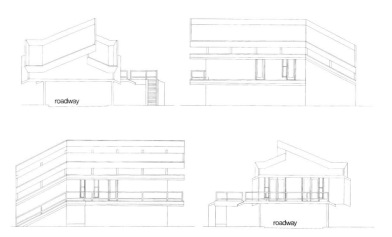

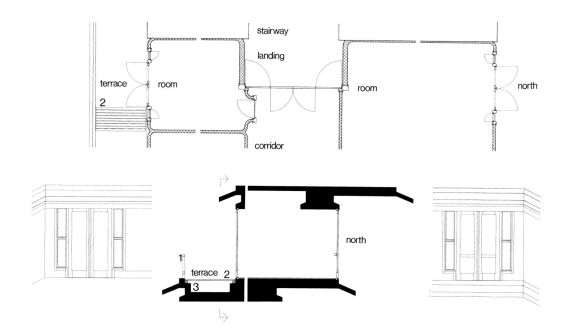

Details of room and facade arrangements.

Exploratory details for partitions and window screens under the long spans. Christopher Woodward, 1965.

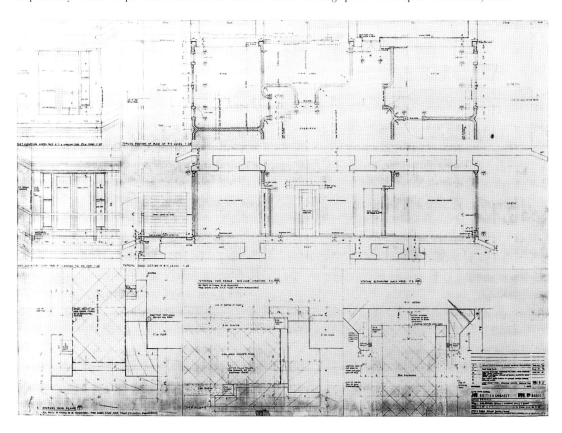

The fish-eye lens series. John Cook at Whitecross Studio.

Embassy viewed from private entrance. Garages are on the right, chauffeur's lodge on the left.

Embassy viewed from garden side of chancery lawn. Levels above are reception lawn, swimming pool, and tennis court.

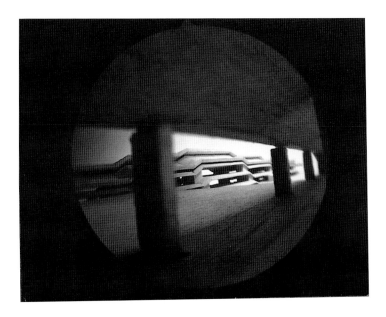

View towards the residency from the garden loggia, that gives privacy from the secondary road which descends past the German Embassy by Hans Scharoun, whose programme tripled in size as ours diminished . . . to nothing.

Burleigh Lane Houses, Street*

The general thought behind the houses is explored in the text called 'The New Model House':† the six houses also relate to the town structure studies undertaken in Street, from 1964 onwards.‡

The language of the houses responds to the material and colour as used traditionally in Street; the size of the masonry unit is in accord with the town's best nineteenth-century buildings.

There is locally an unusual abundance of round windows.

* A small town in Somerset, England.

† A+PS unpublished essay, since unable to be satisfactorily illustrated by built work. Its gist is incorporated in 'Thirty Years of Thought About Housing', an essay in *Architecture in an Age of Scepticism* (London: Heinemann, 1984).

‡ See *Urban Structuring: Studies of Alison & Peter Smithson* (London: Studio Vista, Reinhold, 1967) and *The Charged Void: Urbanism*.

Ground- and first-floor plans. PS.

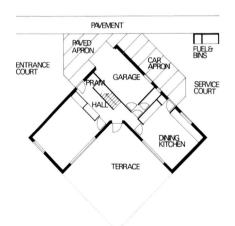

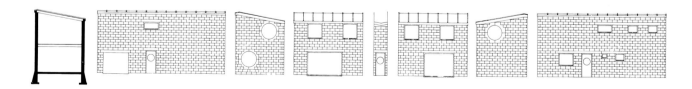

Section and seven elevations laid out as unfolding strip. PS.

Perspective of rear of detached house. Jeremy Dixon, A+PS.

Overview of part of group of detached houses. Jeremy Dixon, A+PS.

Crispin Hall, Street

The original Crispin Hall, opened in 1885, was a place for meetings, performances, and lectures for the people of Street. In 1965 it had fallen somewhat into disuse as its functions had been taken over by other institutions.

The site adjoins the high street, and as through traffic has been reduced by a town service road,* vehicular access to a service yard can be taken off the high street. The shops (which were seen as 'needed' in Street) are serviced from their enfolded, unseen rear and face away from the high street towards car-parks. In the car-parks, planted fingers of walkways make them like car-orchards. The walkways lead people safely to the colonnade around the shop-cluster and from that to the existing library and to the other shops of the high street. The colonnade is one of the classic forms of 'layering'.

Crispin Hall's enfolding of its service area parallels Sheffield University's enfolding of its 'calm green', both works concealing their 'private lives'.

* See A+PS, *Urban Structuring: Studies of Alison & Peter Smithson* (London: Studio Vista, Reinhold, 1967) and *The Charged Void: Urbanism*.

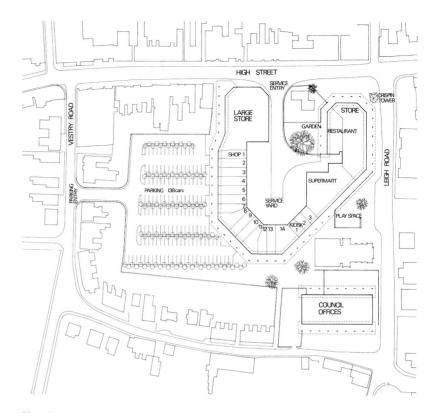

Site plan.

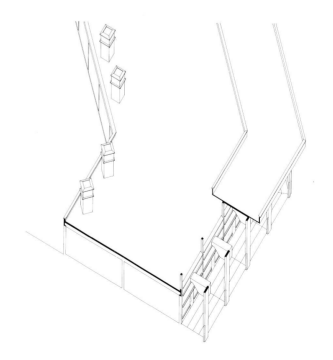

Detail axonometric of colonnade which encircles the shops and in turn encircles and conceals the off-loading bays both from the high street and from the shop car-park. The car-park is made to resemble a cherry orchard by the planted finger-ways which lead pedestrians to the colonnade.

Detail of colonnade encircling shops, which in turn encircle the service yard. Jeremy Dixon.

Integration into the fabric of a small town. The roof profile of the shopping precinct, curling up on the slight slope, can be seen from the high street.

Crispin Hall Tower retained as a marker to the corner of the high street.

View of Georgian house and garden retained as a remembrance of past quality on the high street.

Garden Building, St. Hilda's College, Oxford

In the text published in 1968* as a prebuilding explanation we wrote: *"Starting from the fundamental English problem of needing a lot of light, we have provided big windows. But to prevent the girls being too 'exposed' (their psyche as well as their person is exposed with much glass) there is a separate external screen of timber members, which we hope will cut down the glare, obviate any sense of insecurity, and prevent the casual eye from breaking too easily the 'skin' of the building. The timber screen is a kind of 'yashmak'. The glare and over-exposure will also be reduced by an existing tree—a beautiful, pale copper-beech. The timber screen is in untreated oak (pale grey when dry, brown when wet)."*

This lattice, protective of personal sensibilities at St. Hilda's, permits the occupants to modestly appreciate Christ Church Meadow and the mature trees of their own grounds. The covered ways to adjacent buildings, covered ways fabricated out of the same family of oak sections, and the porch to Old Hall have the same feeling of protection and openness.

* *Architectural Design*, October 1968.

above: View from the garden side. PS, 1971.
right: Site plan. Christopher Woodward, 1968.

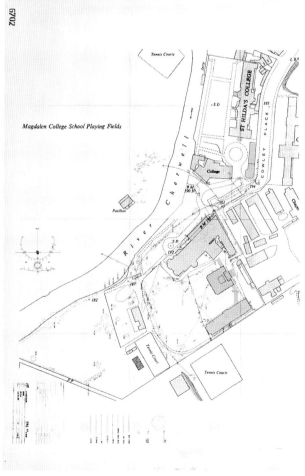

Aerial axonometric
showing roof.
Christopher Woodward,
AS, 1970; added to by
LW, 1977.

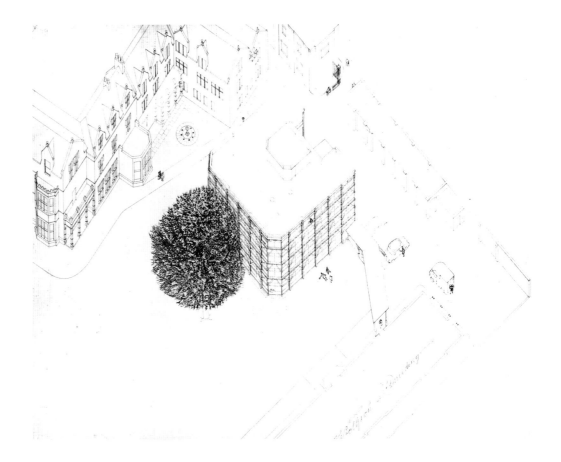

Aerial axonometric with
roof removed, showing
rooms occupied.
Christopher Woodward,
AS, 1970; added to by
LW, 1977.

Plans.

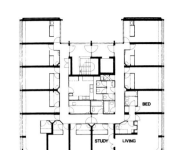

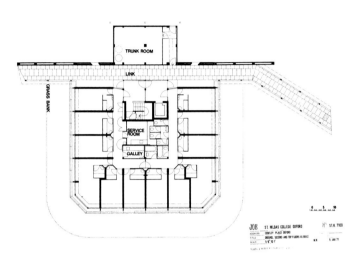

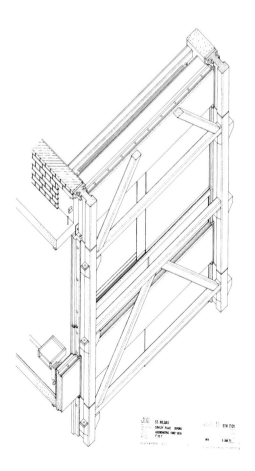

left: Axonometric of facade.
opposite top: Elevations and section. Christopher Woodward, 1968.
opposite bottom: Working drawing of long section. Christopher Woodward, 1968.

pages 344–45: Northwest corner. Michael Carapetian.
pages 346–47: West facade looking from garden. Michael Carapetian.

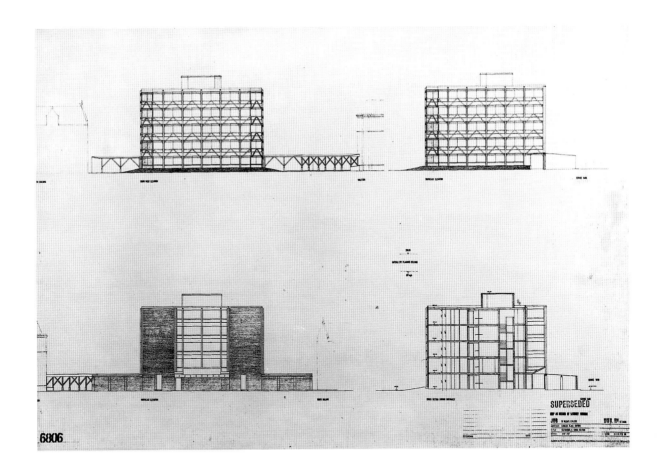

6806

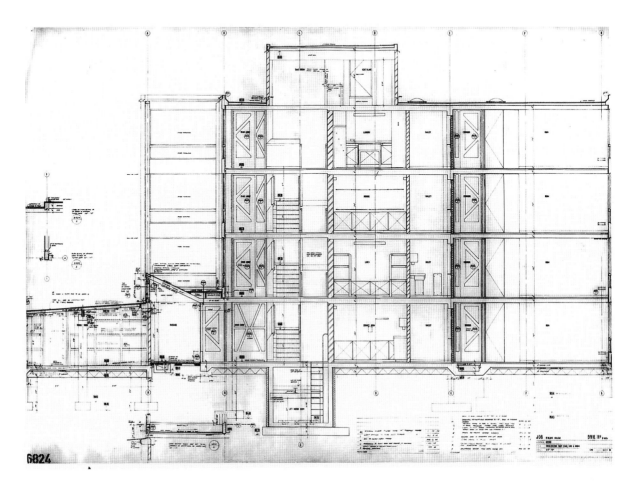

6824

Facade detail from the interior. Michael Carapetian.

Detail of 'yashmak' and 'moat' within grass 'skirt'. Michael Carapetian.

opposite: South-west corner with copper-beech. Michael Carapetian.

Dressing-room interior. Michael Carapetian.

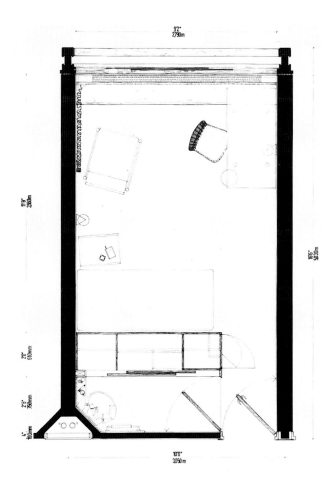

Typical plan of undergraduate room.

Covered walk to Wolfson Building. PS, 1971.

St. Hilda's College music room over the
bicycle shed (clockwise from bottom left):
Typical cross section; section through garden
building, service yard, and music room; plan
at ground level; two elevations to service yard;
plan at upper music-room level. Christopher
Woodward, 1970.

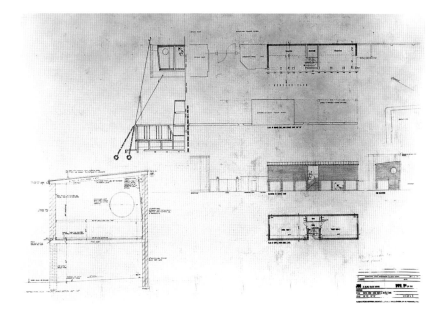

Porch to Old Hall, St. Hilda's College.
PS, 1969.

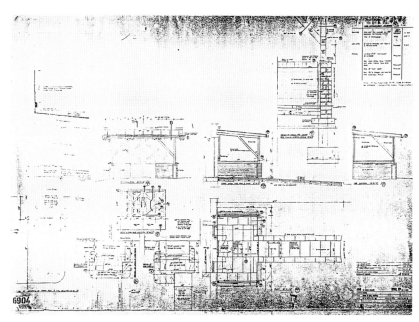

View from inside porch towards the lodge.
A fragment of the new Garden Building is,
as it were, implanted into the nineteenth-
century Old Hall, a manoeuvre equivalent to
that at Cambridge where a classical fragment
is embedded, as a bonding device, in the
side of the mediaeval hall opposite Wren's
new library. PS, May–June 1970.

Wedding in the City,* Fourteenth Triennale, Milan

Air view of Florence hangs as a cloud over the garden city Florence. Publiphoto.

In response to the invitation† to make the urban Decoration Salon exhibit, we pursued one of our most constant themes . . . that of interplay between the permanent, the built fabric, and the transient, the decoration of the built fabric by events within it.

The visitor was positioned . . . as if at a window sill, at a balustrade, in an arcade, as if in a Florentine roof gazebo . . . indicating that the positioning of the observer within the layers of the city also contributes to the pleasures of the decoration of the city.

* See A+PS, *The Shift* (London: Academy Editions, 1982).
† Giancarlo De Carlo was executive architect for the Fourteenth Triennale.

The Royal College of Art students of Janey Ironside
working on the wedding clothes they designed. PS, 1968.

Wedding flag cluster over the wedding group. PS, 1968.

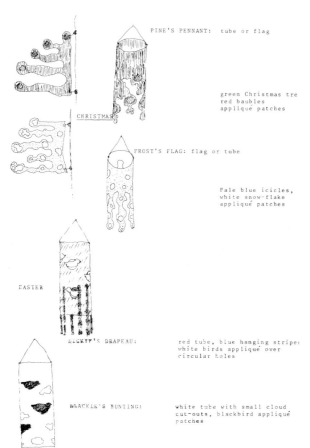

PINE'S PENNANT: tube or flag

green Christmas tre
red baubles
appliqué patches

CHRISTMAS

FROST'S FLAG: flag or tube

Pale blue icicles,
white snow-flake
appliqué patches

EASTER

DICKIE'S DRAPEAU: red tube, blue hanging stripe;
white birds appliqué over
circular holes

BLACKIE'S BUNTING: white tube with small cloud
cut-outs, blackbird appliqué
patches

All tubes cotton poplin; to be hung as wind decorations in windows,
in passageways, nurseries or outside.

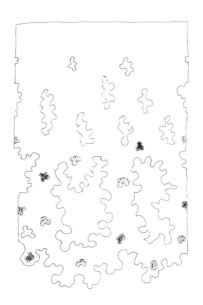

Cut flag prior to
seaming into a tube

BLOSSOM'S BUNTING: white tube, flower cut-outs
from pink tube and cerise
flowers sewn on by green
centre stitching

BRIDE'S BLOSSOM: pink tube, flower cut-outs
from white tube and cerise
flowers sewn on by green
centre stitching

Decorations.

above: General view of 'Transformations of the City' project. Publiphoto.
opposite: Axonometric of salon in the 'never seen' Triennale. AS, Christopher Woodward.

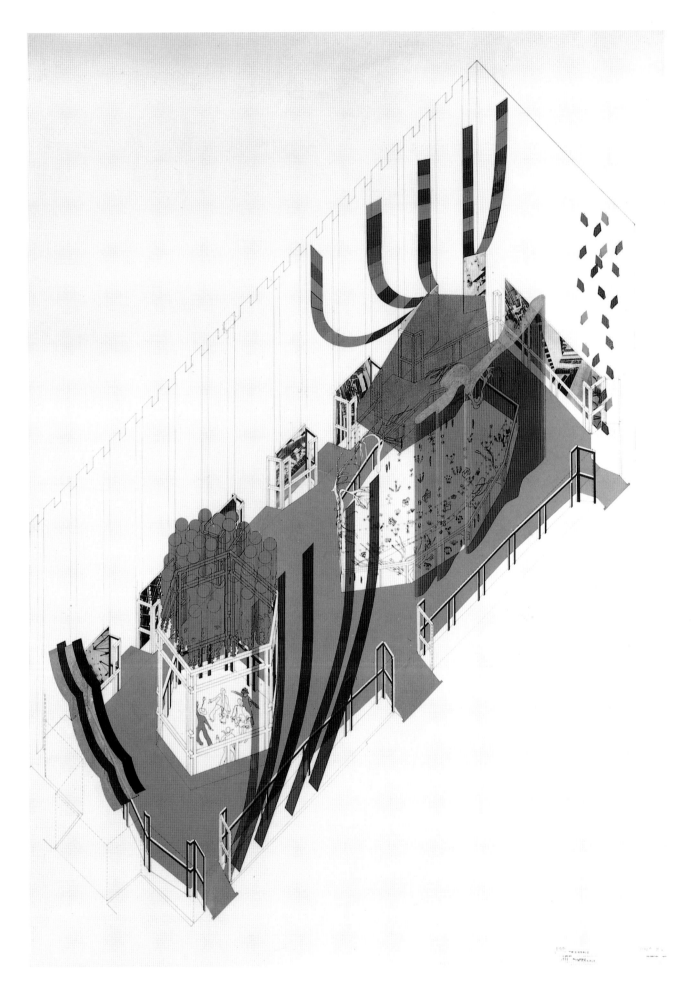

Government Offices, Demonstration Mat-Building,* Kuwait

1970

A+PS

with Ove Arup and Partners

The argument for the urban-form and for much of its resolution in Kuwait can be found in *The Charged Void: Urbanism*.

It is difficult to pull apart the urban-form idea from its architectural resolution, particularly so when both are so dictated by the fierce Gulf and desert-fringe climate of Kuwait.

The architectural language of the demonstration mat-building is one of protection; at the ground level of providing an 'oasis' of shade in the city.

This 'oasis' of shade, with its fringe of shaded car parks, allows an interplay between the most modern handling equipment and the nomad, who can walk in any direction as if he had just come from his tent. Above this level—and serviced from it—are the government offices, unbelievably spacious as an offering to the citizens of the full possibilities for the enjoyment of the traditional pleasures of 'waiting on the administration'.

The protective layering on the faces of the mat-building is a direct response to aspect, changing its form on each facade. The faces to the 'gallerias' which split the mat can have glass walls that are self-shaded and cooled by transverse air movement because of the 'galleria' shaping; the faces on the 'outside' towards open ground are mostly solid wall with small, adjustable-shaded windows. Both speak of the pleasures of air-conditioning within.

If the ground-level pilotis of Kuwait are thought of as a plan drawn through the regularity of the trunks in a grove of date palms, a higher cut in the grove might be a plan of the later Pahlavi National Library, where solar protective domes glint as exotic fruit amidst protective fronds.

* See *The Charged Void: Urbanism*.

Oblique aerial view from the south. Note shine on gilded towers. PS, 1970.

Ideogram of the galleria as a linear, identifying 'fix' in the urban fabric. At each end of each galleria is an existing mosque. AS, 1970.

Perspective view of galleria, looking toward Al Fleij Mosque. William Harrison, AS.

Low-level view from the south over Soor Street (rampart garages). The government office towers are colour-coded as to the ministry occupying the mat-offices below. Model by Jeremy Dixon. Ove Arup and Partners, 1970.

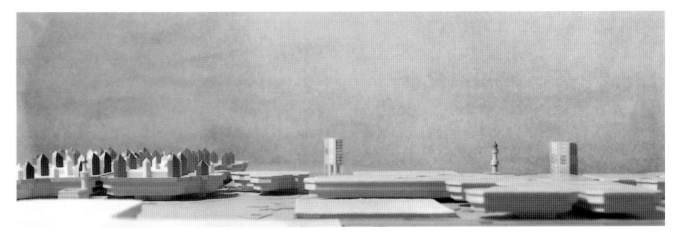

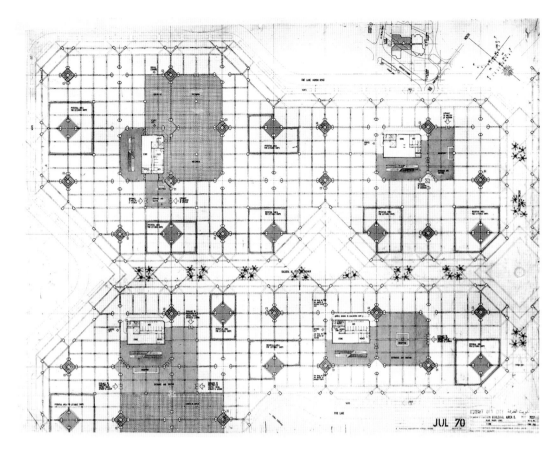

Piloti-level plan: The galleria is marked by the planting of palm trees. The crossing is at the overlay of the east-west galleria, located by two off-site mosques, and the north-south galleria, located by two on-site mosques: Al Fleij to the north and Al Kasman to the south.

Level-one plan, showing typical circulation pattern within offices.

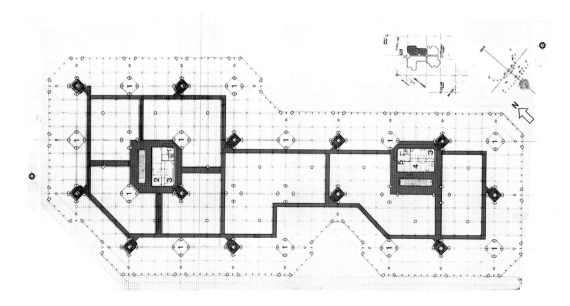

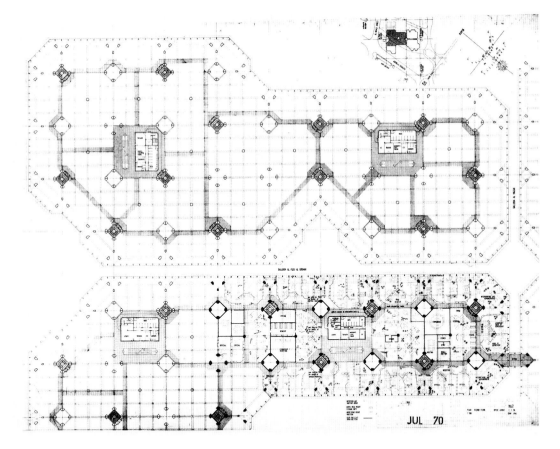

Level-two plan, showing mix of conference rooms, records, and open-office areas.

Roof-level plan, showing ministerial penthouse suites.

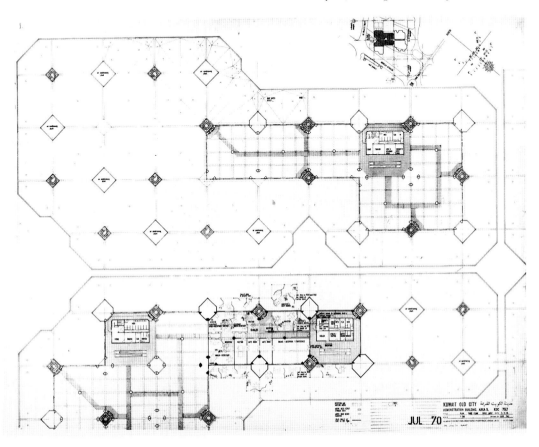

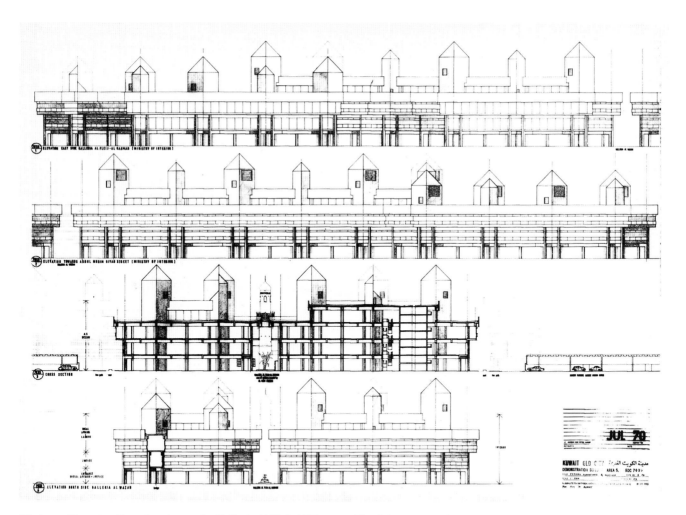

Ministry of Interior: East elevation or the Galleria Al Fleij–Al Kasman side of the ministry (top; large towers hold services; small towers hold escape stairs; large windows facing the galleria are in constant shade throughout the day); elevation towards Abdul Munim Riyad Street (second from top); cross section through Galleria Al Fleij–Al Kasman, terminated by Al Fleij Mosque (third from top); north elevation or the Galleria Al Wazan side (bottom).

View across Al Hilali to Al Fleij Mosque. William Harrison.

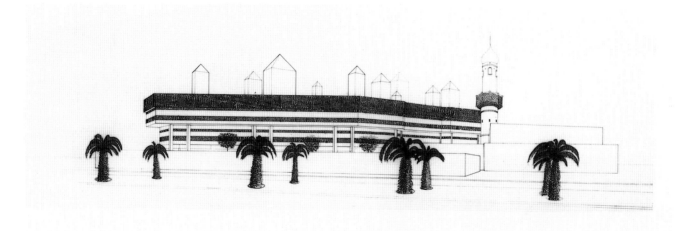

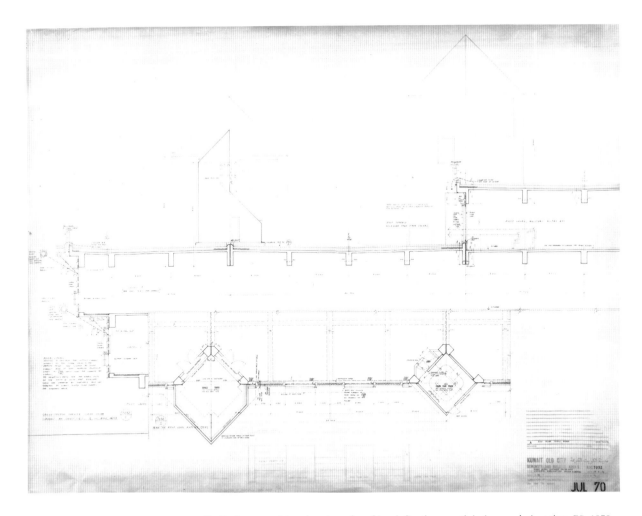

Preliminary working drawing of roof level: Section, partial plan, and elevation. PS, 1970.

Two images developed for the 'Climate Register' exhibition at the Architectural Association, 1994. LW, 1993.

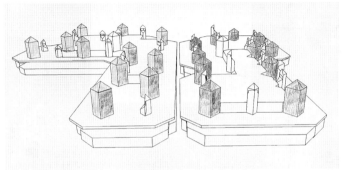

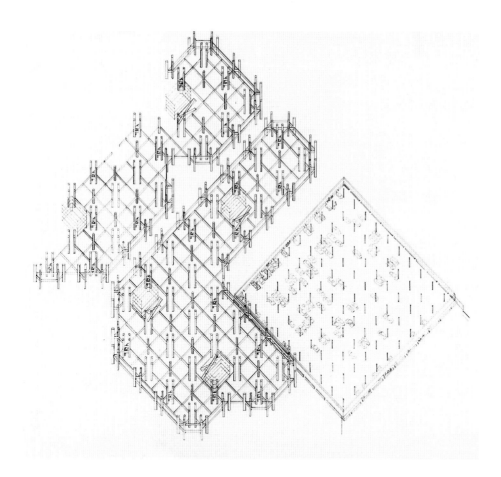

Axonometric of first level over pilotis with access stations. AS, 1980.

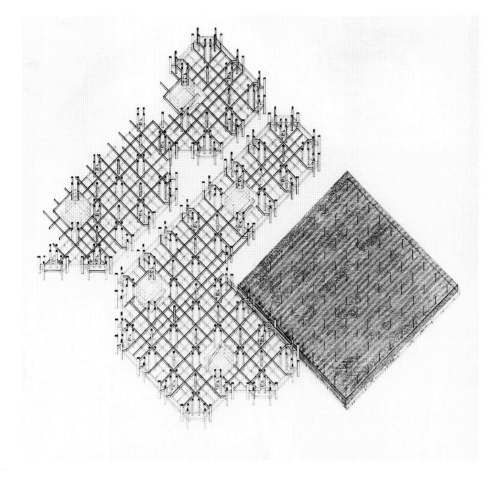

Axonometric showing true structure of first level, which is also the shade-roof level over the garage. AS, 1980.

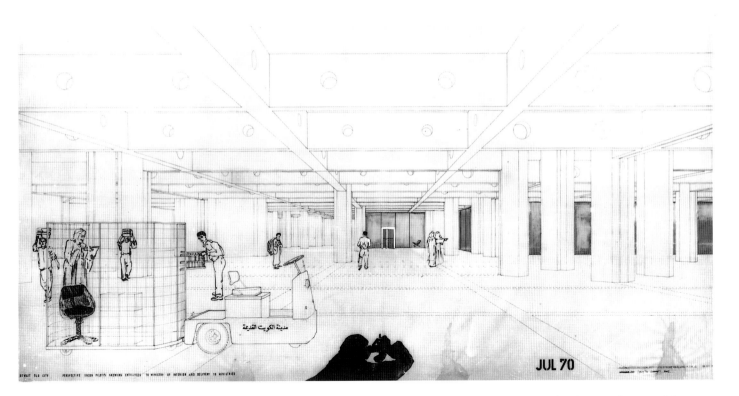

Perspective of piloti space under the Ministry of Interior building, used as a servicing area.

Interior view of open-plan mat-building in use as a government ministry.

Close-up view of structure and cladding. Ove Arup and Partners, 1970.

Structural arrangement at exterior corner. Ove Arup and Partners, 1970.

Detail of cladding panels and grille facias. Ove Arup and Partners.

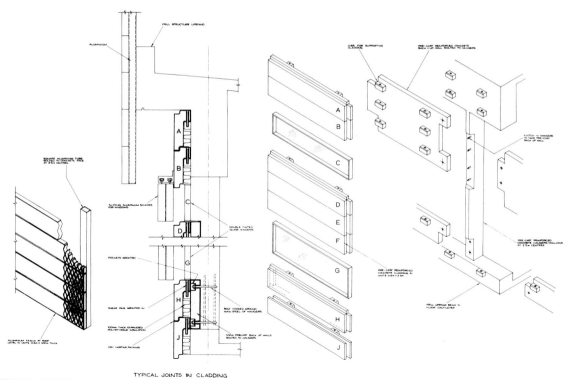

TYPICAL JOINTS IN CLADDING

KUWAIT OLD CITY   MINISTRY BUILDING   OVE ARUP & PARTNERS   SCALES: 1:20
CONCRETE CLADDING DETAILS   CONSULTING ENGINEERS   DATE: JUNE 1970
LONDON   DRAWING NO: 3632/8

View of the entrance to the galleria. Protected from the sun, the building's form encourages the movement of air currents during the day and night. Model by Ove Arup and Partners, Simon Ellar.

The inward-looking face of the mat-building: Elevation to galleria.

New Model House

Another try at a replacement for the 'popular' house.

Plot layout and house plans. PS, 1971.

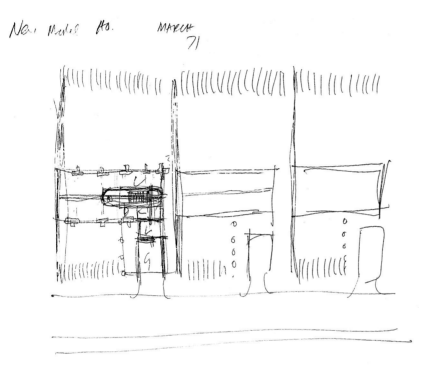

Working detail. PS, 1971.

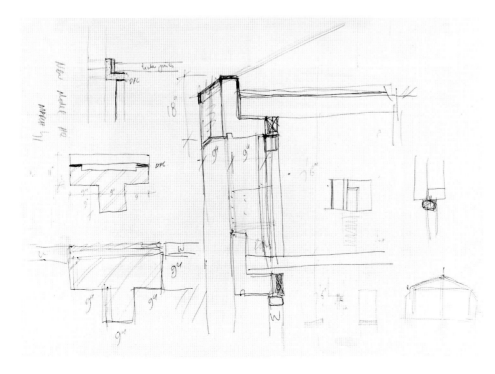

Married Graduate Flats and Squash Courts, Queen's College, Iffley Road, Oxford

Planning requirement for ten car-parking places, our own desire for best orientation, and a wish to give occupants some protection from the traffic on the Iffley Road made too many constrictions on a tight site.

Site plan.

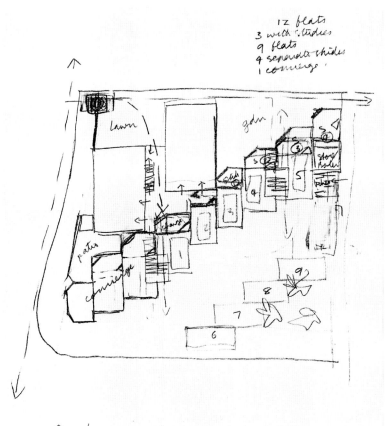

Gilston Road, South Kensington

In 1971 we moved twenty-five metres across Priory Walk into an Italianate urban villa from 1851 . . . built the same year as the Great Exhibition. With streets on three sides, this house could be reorganised to give access for family and work separately, with workrooms on the two lower floors and family rooms on the upper two floors. Internally, storage and insulation are set as a new layer within the old fabric . . . as each preceding generation had added its layers.

The new porch to the old house. PS, 1979.

below: Birthday swag for Samantha Smithson on the new porch. PS, 1978.
bottom: PS's reading room with fabrics from North Africa.

Cherry Garden Pier

Four different architects make a collective offering: the sort of interaction that the renewal of many city sites requires.

In the part we worked on, the first scheme had a chevron or 'kipper' plan where the window orientation was an outcome of the river views on this bend in the Thames* . . . downstream to Greenwich Reach . . . upstream to Tower Bridge.

The skin-layering evolved in this first scheme is weather- and water-conscious, a traditional interplay of terrace-balcony and French windows—an open layer outside an openable but tightly closable layer— such as is recorded in Whistler's etchings of this stretch of the Thames' waterfront.

In the second scheme, called for by site conditions, floors diminish as they go up, to help daylight penetrate to the platform on which they stand. This diminishing offers a variety of accommodation and reduces the floor-loading on the reused pile foundations.

The skin language of the first scheme becomes extended in the second over a range of urban domestic scales:

. . . upper apartments;
. . . cottages that fringe the platform with terrace-balconies;
. . . platform studio-maisonettes.

* See *The Charged Void: Urbanism*.

AS working on Cherry Garden Pier, 1972.

Platform-level studios are at left and ahead, cottages at right. Gordon Cullen.

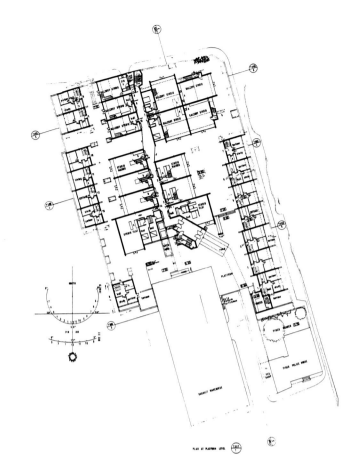

Plan at platform level. North point gives orientation and sun penetration at the equinox.

Third-floor plan.

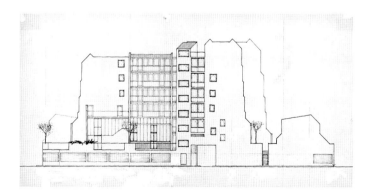

Elevation to the narrow Bermondsey Wall.

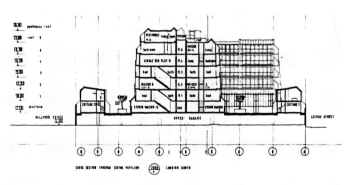

Cross section looking north through centre pavilion and mews cottages on either side.

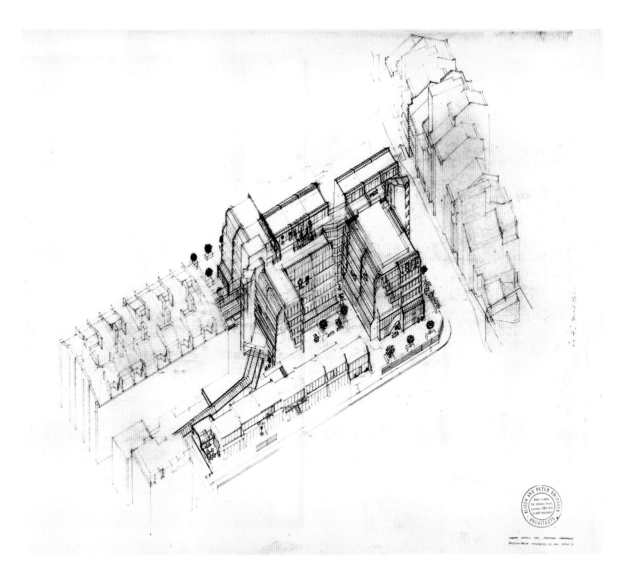

Axonometric. AS, 1973.

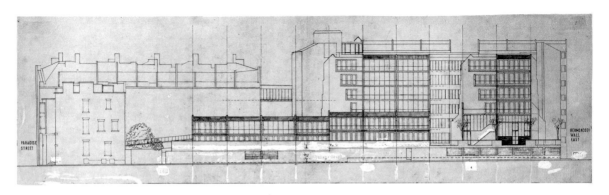

East elevation to Cathay Street and open space beyond.

Battlebridge Basin, Office Collective, New Wharf Road, Islington

1972 – 1974*

A+PS

Battlebridge Basin is a disused piece of water off a hardly used canal.[†]

The building's position on the basin's edge procures a smooth continuum of wall-screen into mirror-image in the water. The stillness and darkness of the basin mean that upwards reflections of sunlight are flat, not dappled; the building responds to this calmness of untroubled repose by presenting a single skin of stainless steel and glass; the layered dimension of the sky and the buildings opposite are ever changing, responding to season, weather, and time.

The theme that begins here—a building's extension by its reflections—is later taken up in Millbank.

[*] A group of architects and engineers formed to build their own offices and apartments in 1967. The first scheme by finders of the site was rejected by the group; the second scheme by A+PS, as originators of the idea of group, went to appeal in 1972. Appeal succeeded in 1976, by which date the economic crisis and need to purchase part of the basin upset funding.

[†] See *The Charged Void: Urbanism*.

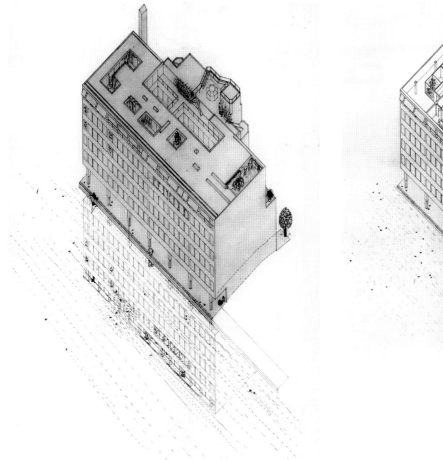
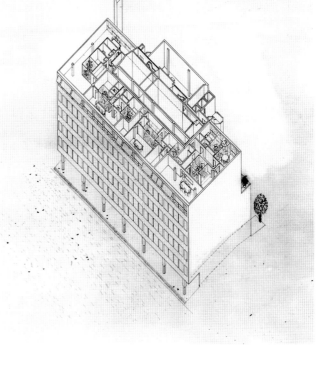

Axonometric with reflection in basin, seen from the south-west. AS.

Axonometric with top-floor flats revealed. AS; amended by Lida Papadopoulou, 1980.

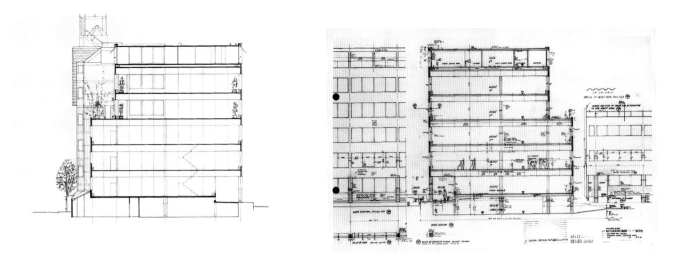

Three stages of development explained in section.

above and above right: Stage 1 section looking south; Stage 2 section looking north.
below: Stage 3 section with internal light well, basin, and road elevations.

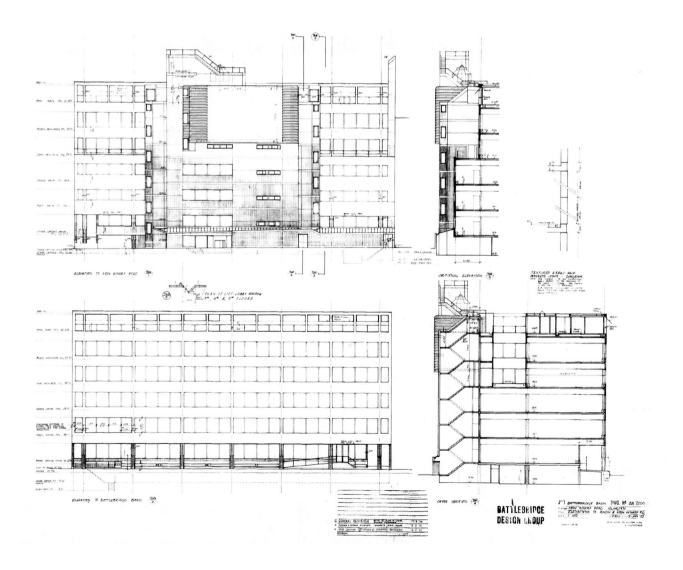

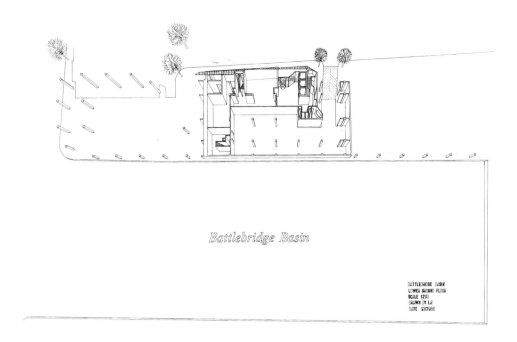

Aerial perspective of lower ground floor, showing the garage for cars and bikes, print room, boiler, electrical substation.
AS; amended by Lida Papadopoulou, 1980.

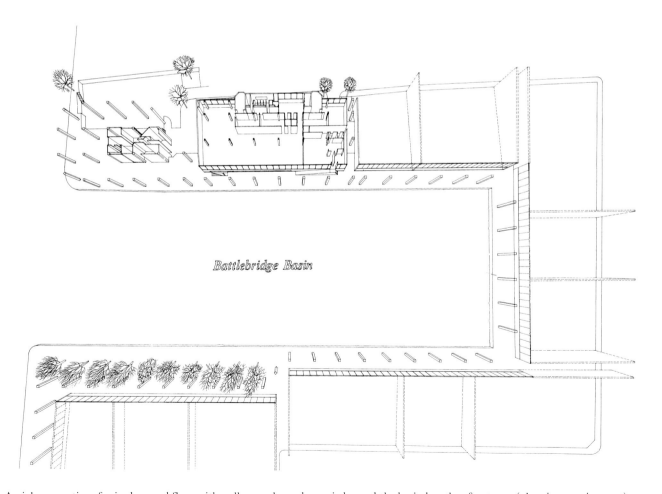

Aerial perspective of raised ground floor, with walkway colonnade carried round the basin by other frontages (planning requirement).

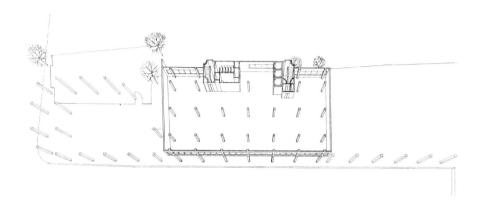

Aerial perspective of first floor. Lida Papadopoulou, 1980.

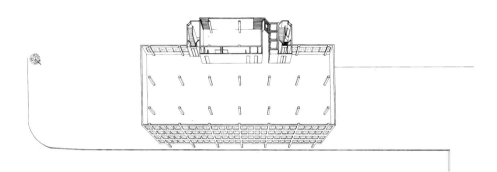

Aerial perspective of fourth floor. Lida Papadopoulou, 1980.

Two explorations of imbuing
a waterside building
with reflective qualities.

right: Perspective from an
acute-angle viewpoint on
the canal. PS.
far right: Perspective from an
oblique-angle viewpoint on
the canal. PS.

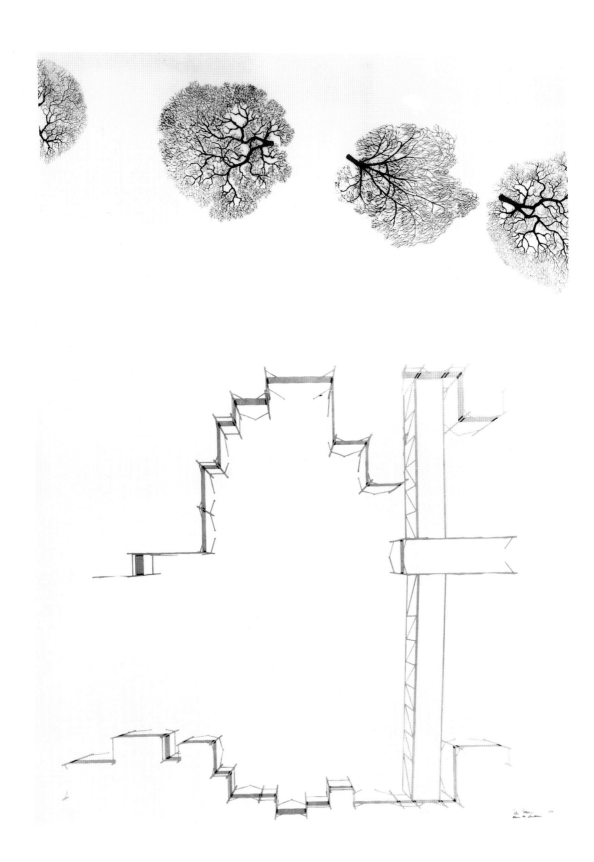

Lucas Headquarters. Bare bones of idea: The interplay between the built and the grown. LW; trees by AS.

8 The Treillage'd Space

something of a return to our first interest in the steel structure . . . the wood structure, the built grove, the grown line of trees . . .

Lucas Headquarters *(1973–74)* 380

'A Line of Trees . . . A Steel Structure' Exhibition *(1975, 1976)* 386

Magdalen College, Oxford *(1974)* 388

Adalbergstrasse *(1975)* 392

'Sticks and Stones' Exhibition *(1976)* 393

The Yellow House at an Intersection *(1976)* 394

Solar-Energy-Collecting Pyramid, Giza *(1976)* 396

Landwehrkanal *(1976)* 397

Riverside Apartments, Millbank *(1976–77)* 398

Anil Avenue Commercial Offices, Khartoum *(1976–77)* 402

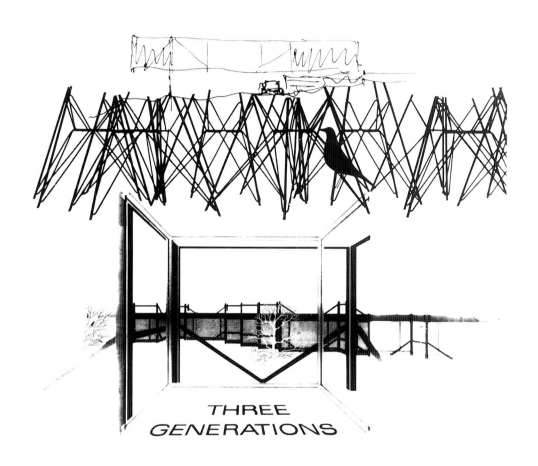

'Three Generations' image: As first generation, Mies van der Rohe's House on a Hillside, 1934 (top); as second generation, Charles and Ray Eames' wire chair legs, 1951 (middle); as third generation, A+PS's 'A Line of Trees . . . A Steel Structure' Exhibition, 1975, 1976 (bottom). LW, AS, 1980.

In retrospect, one can detect no special reason why, beginning with the timber lattices of St. Hilda's College, we should be occupied for fifteen years with the exploration of 'treillage'd' spaces. In St. Hilda's the timber lattice of the skin was structurally redundant; it was to lead to a conscious deployment of bracings and interlacings that disregard strict structural logic.

One can only say perhaps that our generation can see other meanings, other deployments, in the language of modern architecture, including that part of it we had developed ourselves in the 1950s. Certainly there is a clear line of exploration: St. Hilda's leading to the New Gothics at Magdalen College; the Lucas Headquarters (our most ambitious and most fruitful design to date?) which, being unbuilt, meant that the exploration of its devices continued, and continues, in later designs and exhibitions . . . for example, in the exhibition in Kettle's Yard in Cambridge called 'Twenty-Four Doors to Christmas', in 'Sticks and Stones' at the Venice Biennale . . . in the design for the Yellow House's interlaced lattices, in the laced lookouts of Kingsbury, in the bridge over the Verbindungskanal, and in the Yellow Lookout.

A parallel line in corner-braced steel treillage grows directly out of Lucas . . . the Khartoum shipped-in-by-train steel office building, the steel upper floor of the Amenity Building in Bath. Both 'cages' in the sense of those white-wire show-off bird cages of Tunisia . . . light-touch, far from escape-proof, capturing the air not the bird: so Melbourne's Magic Mountains' 'cage' version.

In a peasant building, the tight package that attracts is a coming to terms with what is available; a fitness for purpose raised to a poetic level. This 'coming into being' now re-emerges, changed in manner. A relaxation of pressure turns over the inherent skills of people—from the provision of their basic life supports amidst the grind of labour—into dressing their situation; building a sense of reciprocity with others as they put together their own identity of place within the treillage'd space.

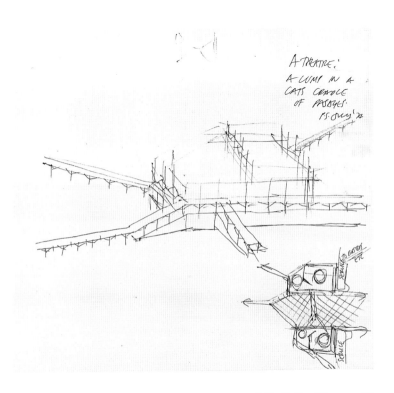

Ideogram: The cat's cradle of walkways. PS, 1974.

Lucas Headquarters, Shirley

November 1973 – January 1974

A+PS

Layers of latticed structure, the inclusion of a layer of trees, a layering of levels: all speak in turn of connection and separation. The building steps forwards, steps back, performs as it were a stately dance with the trees that lace the site on the lines of the old hedgerows; thus, the building form utilises that sense of connection to place that the interpenetrations of existing trees can transmit. The stepping in and out of the building to receive the penetration, or allow the tree line to pass by, offers to the occupants a variety of serrated edge places. In this way the outdoor spaces are possessed differently by each limb of the building. In a landscape that is fringe to city, facing the green-belt, the roof lattices become a bridging element rising into the air between city and countryside.*

* See 'Art Net' exhibition in A+PS, *The Shift* (London: Academy Editions, 1982).

'Layers of latticed structure'. William Harrison, 1974.

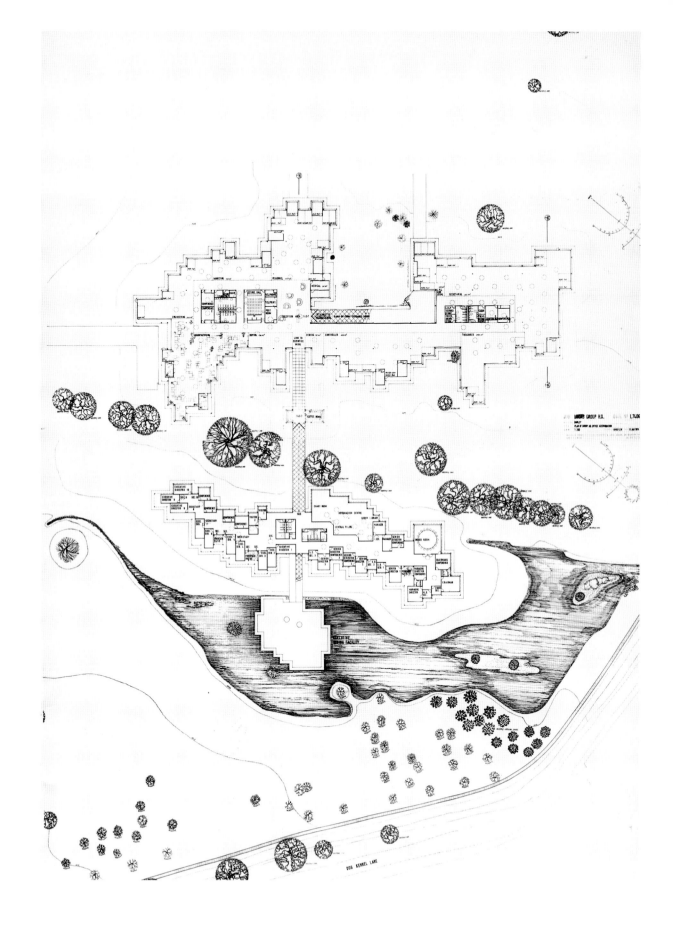

Composite plan showing line of trees.

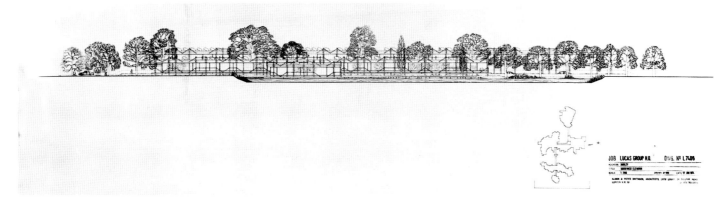

South-west elevation. William Harrison, 1974.

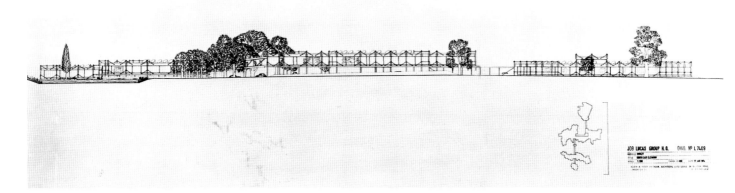

South-east elevation. William Harrison, 1974.

Aerial photograph of model. Lines of trees lace
the building into the landscape and are used as
'remembrances' of the historic agricultural land
pattern. Model by David Armstrong. PS.

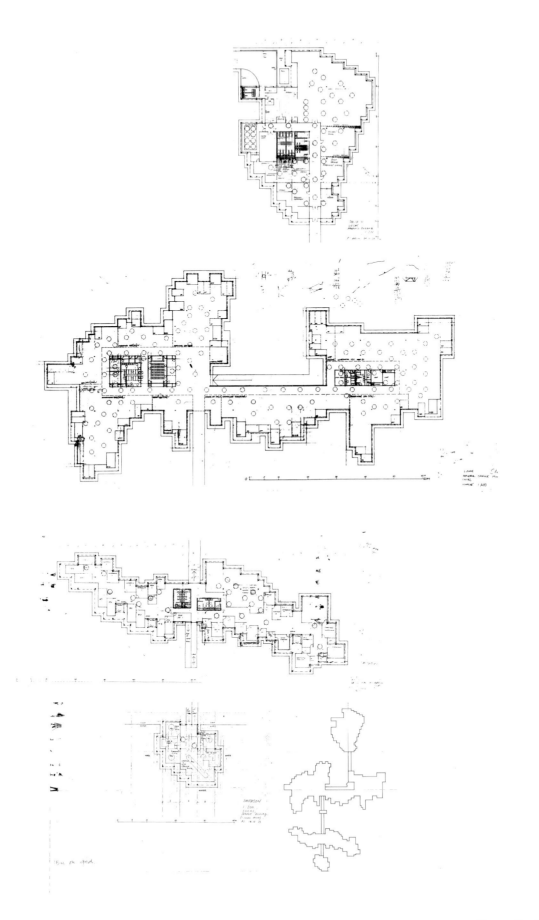

Composite plan in outline.

Three drawings on the space between the main office and the executive wing.

Trees only. AS.

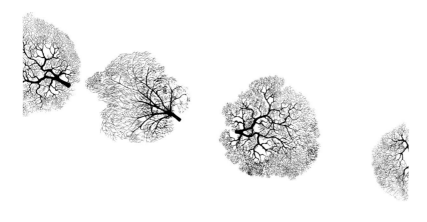

Structure only. LW.

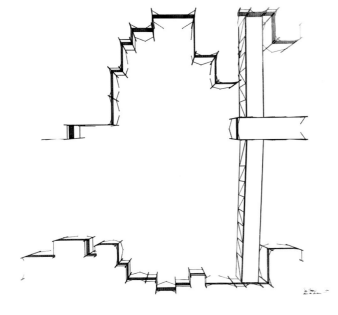

Lawn only. LW.

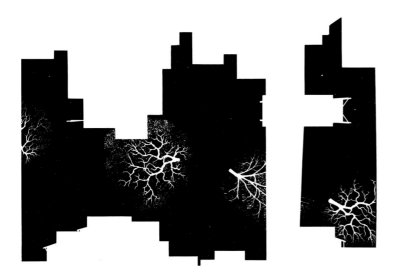

Aerial axonometric of the space between the buildings. William Harrison, LW; trees, AS.

In this exhibition fourteen transparent
panels with coloured latticed images of the
Lucas Headquarters project were arranged
in space so that many images overlapped to
make a simulacrum of the effect aimed at
in the real space of a built project.

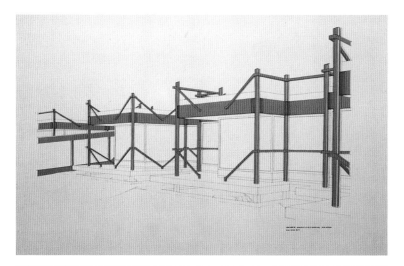

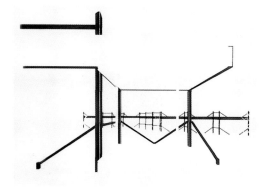

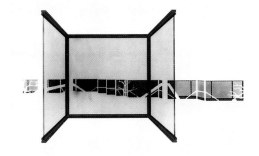

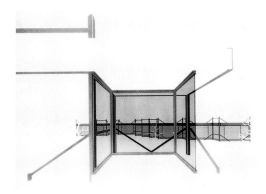

Set of three perspectives looking out from
the interior.
top: Structure only. LW.
second from top: Glass and trees only. LW.
above: Structure, glass, and trees. LW.

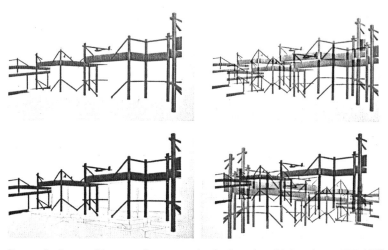

Composite 'extract' images of structure, in single and multiple colours. LW, 1975.

Arrangement in gallery. LW.

'Art Net' exhibition opening. Dennis Crompton.

AS at opening. Dennis Crompton.

Magdalen College, Oxford

"This 'Improvement of Magdalen College' is one of a series of designs exploring external braced framing and lattices."

In February 1978, PS wrote: *"In the old buildings at Magdalen College there are two space-traditions. The first and most obvious is that established by the cloister and detached bell tower of the time of the college's foundation: this space-tradition is very open and Renaissance-seeming in spite of it being Gothic in style. (The feeling that the cloister is post-mediaeval is of course accentuated by the regularisation and simplification that has accompanied the many re-buildings.) The second, more secretive, space-tradition is found in the area around the even earlier hospital and St. John's Chapel. It is this second space-tradition, with everything wrapped up in everything else, which the 'Improvement to Magdalen College' shown in the drawings continues. The outside of the college remains as it is at present except along the riverbank and south cloister, and the slopes of the gables and dormers of the old fabric are reciprocated in all the angles and counter-angles of the new braced-oak-frame galleries.*

Most of the materials of the 'Improvement' are found in the old fabric . . . there is, for example, a lead roof on the cloister and there is untreated exposed oak framing on the rear gables of the kitchen staircase and in the dormers along the High. Only the slightly reflective tinted glass is new. This glass in the long gallery over the south cloister reflects dimly the other side of the cloister. And across the River Cherwell, an observer would see reflected the branches of the trees amongst which he stands as if they were a screen layered behind the structural timbered tracery he faces: a magical encapsuling of the natural within the new. In both, the layered aesthetic is a play between new glass and the old battlements; for the battlements are retained even in the areas that are being most changed."

below: Elevation to River Cherwell, glazed with tinted glass and showing reflections of opposing trees. PS, LW, 1974.
opposite: Perspective of New Gothics gallery on the River Cherwell. Gordon Cullen, 1974.

ELEVATION TO RIVER

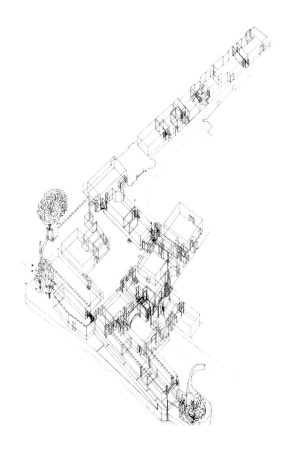

A pair of axonometric studies of existing volumes.

Upper-level volumes of existing buildings to be considered in relation to extension. AS.

Superimposition of upper-level on ground-level volumes. AS.

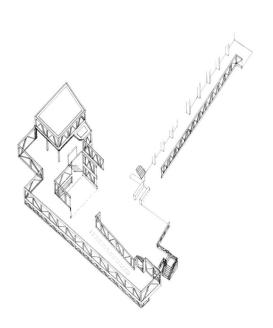

A pair of axonometric studies of additions to existing volumes.

New works, upper levels. AS, 1980.

New works in their setting, with trees. AS, 1980.

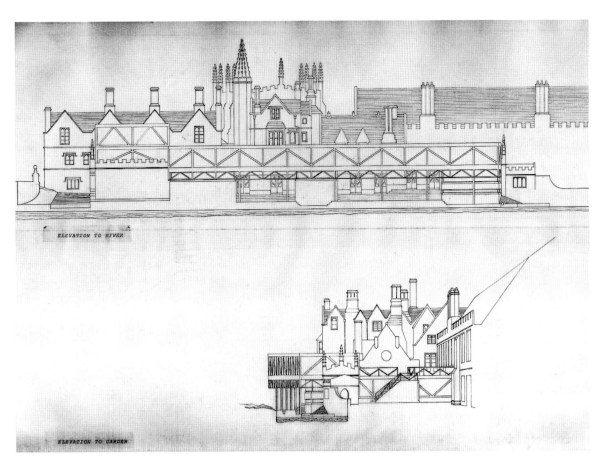

Elevations to the River Cherwell (top); to the garden of New Gothics showing the gable of the mediaeval kitchen (bottom). PS, LW, 1974.

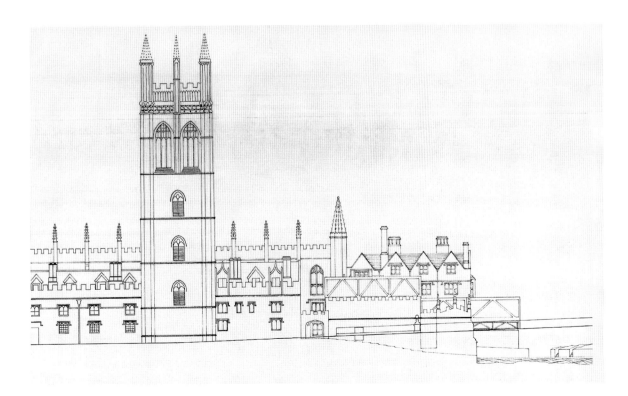

Elevation to the high street: New kitchen block and free-flow servery behind existing wall. PS, LW, 1974.

Adalbergstrasse, Kreuzberg

October 1975

Internationales Design Zentrum, Berlin, studio: AS

The interest of this study* lies in the use of timber framing on the facade—the taking up again of a language not used for many centuries because of the fire hazard. Timber framing is used as urban screens concerned with both transmission and transition: from one state to the next; from one historic context to the present; from the public domain of Kreuzberg outside to the private domain inside. The trick of transition which without disrupting the old allows the new translates from the historic language of the street to the language of the present occupation; the screen allows the intervention of the individual while it re-energises the old Berlin facade as side of city block.

* For urban context, see *The Charged Void: Urbanism*.

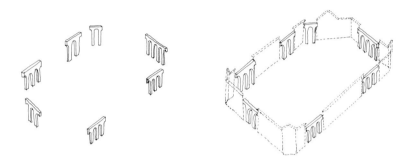

Metaphors for anonymous, running screen: two-part ideogram for continuously running infill. AS.

Viaduct, obviously of a different period, used as a metaphor for a unifying layer.

Infill proposal of timber-framed inner skin behind 'ruined' original stucco skin: Speaking of the need for a buffer layer of protection between the inhabitant and the way the city is now used.

A building under assembly is a ruin in reverse; at certain phases of a building's construction, the anticipatory pleasure of ruins is made manifest:* these pleasures are only enjoyed by those who are part of the process of assembly, and even by them rarely, for making a building is mostly worry. Very many photographs of buildings under construction are taken when the day's work is over, or when the construction site closes at the weekend; under these conditions, a quiet that recalls the loneliness of the deserted ancient site takes over, so that for a moment we do not see worry but the silent marvels of promise.

The quality of place that is about to be is designed into the bones of the construction. Were the 'sticks and stones' to be left lying about from the fabric becoming a ruin, the visitor would be informed of the nature of what the 'sticks and stones' once in their togetherness made. Informed by the fragments alone of all the original idealism, the effort of mind to make fabric out of dreams . . . and knowledge of this, or the scholar's triumph at recognition of purpose, would still energise.

To introduce the exhibition, we wrote: *"For us, an architecture which is palpably built is the most pleasurable of all. An architecture thought out in terms of its actual materials, its actual processes of fabrication, and its means of assembly. In such an architecture one can sense an ordering from its 'Sticks and Stones'. From such an architecture one can get many pleasures; from the child's pleasure of feeling able to put together to the grown-up pleasures of consistency of profile . . . the eloquence of fixings . . . the re-enjoying of how-a-thing-must-have-been . . . lifted up and sweetly come together.*

In Greek and Roman buildings in ruin, the exposure of the neat holes and slots for cramps and dowels adds understanding to the sense of quality, of security, of permeating order, that we get from buildings when whole. For the seeing of the means of assembly and the practical reasons for the size of the blocks or beams, the proportioning of part with part within the formal language, adds to our enjoyment of an architecture that has been made in the mind first, then carried out with all possible attention."

* See A+PS, 'Anthology of Classical Sites' (unpublished).

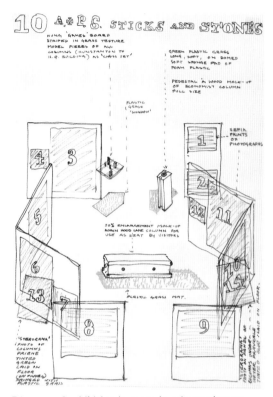

Diagram of exhibition in space in salt warehouses.

AS with Robin Hood Gardens. PS, 1976.

AS holding 'chess board' of all sectional building portions shown on exhibition in full-size mock-up or in photographic enlargements. Photograph of Hunstanton under construction in background.

The Yellow House at an Intersection

July 1976

PS

In the original submission, PS stated: *"The site is in a temperate country in the northern hemisphere in a typical old inner suburb where the original rather spacious layout dates from the turn of this century and thus before the time of many cars. This design is intended to give a greater degree of protection to the private domain so as to restore quiet and privacy; yet to give more to the public domain. People tend to congregate on corners: children to meet their friends, visitors to look for street names or wave for taxis, residents to chat; this design gives a tree-shaded spot for doing these things. A spot with a seat and with tree roots bursting out of the surface of a grassy mound.**

Yet the meetings and scrabblings disturb the house little. The house still commands the corner, not the corner the house. The Yellow House has its back to a thick protective wall, and its rooms face the track of the sun. Its layout puts the noisy elements of the plan—stairs, kitchen, bathrooms—on the wall side as further protection and distancing. The wall acts as a wind-break and as a solar collector. Any really noisy machine and its ductwork would be contained within the wall, well away from the house.

The house, although it has much glass, has heavy floors and roof to store solar heat in winter, with insulation below floor, above roof to contain it and double glass against condensation and heat loss. Silvered curtains internally reflect back body heat at night. By day the silvered curtains and trees to the west would control late afternoon summer sun. There is an upper-level eastern morning terrace, whose roof is tilted to let sun in. And a western evening terrace to drink in the last sun of the day.

The frame is hollow rolled sections rust proofed and lacquered gamboge yellow, as are the window frames inside and out and the handrail of the staircase. The floors to be whitish without strong lines. Clothes storage and domestic equipment to be loose: their choosing and arrangement is to be the responsibility of the occupier.

The trees in the private garden are acacia whose light leafage filters the sun in summer and blows away as golden pennies early in winter."

* See A+PS, *The Shift* (London: Academy Editions, 1982).

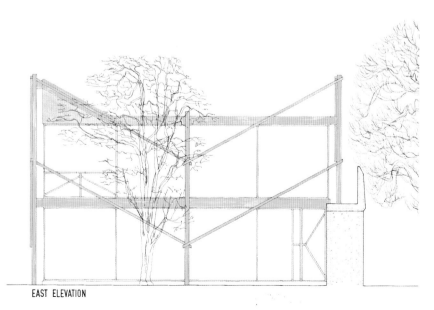

EAST ELEVATION

left: East elevation showing tilt over the south-east bedroom balcony to catch the morning light. A+PS, LW, 1976.
opposite top: Site plan, ground-floor plan, section, elevation to street. A+PS, LW, 1976.
opposite bottom: West, south, east elevations; first-floor plan; perspective with trees. A+PS, LW, 1976.

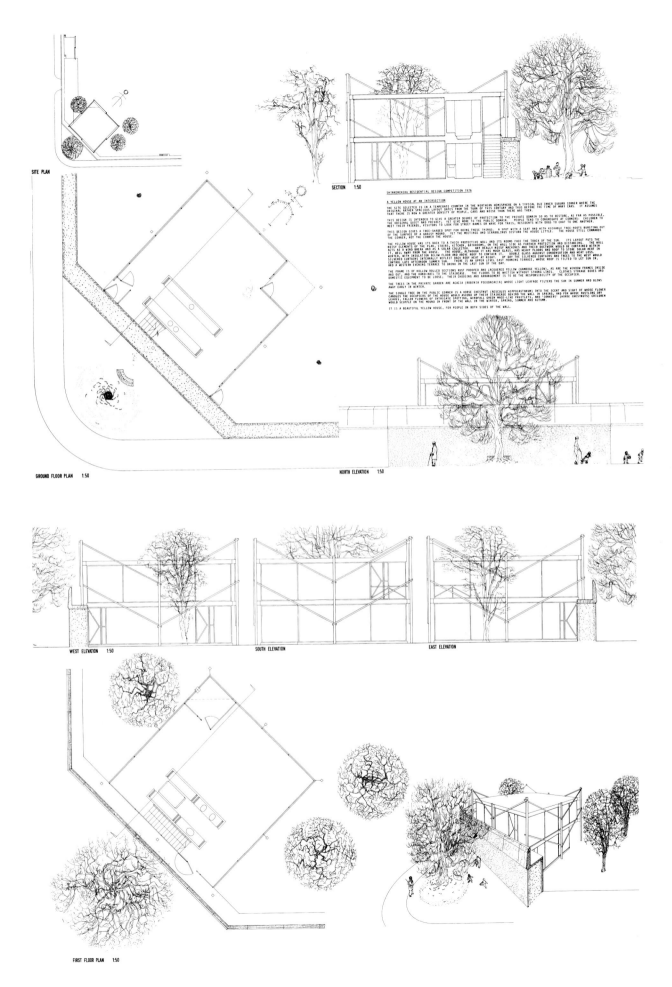

SITE PLAN

GROUND FLOOR PLAN   1:50

SECTION   1:50

SHINKENCHIKU RESIDENTIAL DESIGN COMPETITION 1976

A YELLOW HOUSE AT AN INTERSECTION

THE SITE SELECTED IS IN A TEMPERATE COUNTRY IN THE NORTHERN HEMISPHERE ON A TYPICAL OLD INNER SUBURB CORNER WHERE THE ORIGINAL, RATHER SPACIOUS, LAYOUT DATES FROM THE TURN OF THIS CENTURY AND THUS BEFORE THE TIME OF MANY CARS. IT ASSUMES THAT THERE IS NOW A GREATER DENSITY OF PEOPLE, CARS AND NOISE THAN THERE WAS THEM.

THIS DESIGN IS INTENDED TO GIVE A GREATER DEGREE OF PROTECTION TO THE PRIVATE DOMAIN SO AS TO RESTORE, AS FAR AS POSSIBLE, THE ORIGINAL QUIET AND PRIVACY.   YET GIVE MORE TO THE PUBLIC DOMAIN.   PEOPLE TEND TO CONGREGATE AT CORNERS.   CHILDREN TO MEET THEIR FRIENDS, VISITORS TO LOOK FOR STREET NAMES OR WAVE FOR TAXIS, RESIDENTS WITH DOGS TO CHAT TO ONE ANOTHER.

THIS DESIGN GIVES A TREE-SHADED SPOT FOR DOING THESE THINGS.   A SPOT WITH A SEAT AND WITH KICKABLE TREE-ROOTS BURSTLING OUT OF THE SURFACE OF A GRASSY MOUND.   YET THE MEETINGS AND SCRABBLINGS DISTURB THE HOUSE LITTLE.   THE HOUSE STILL COMMANDS THE CORNER, NOT THE CORNER THE HOUSE.

THE YELLOW HOUSE HAS ITS BACK TO A THICK PROTECTIVE WALL AND ITS ROOMS FACE THE TRACK OF THE SUN.   ITS LAYOUT PUTS THE NOISY ELEMENTS OF THE PLAN, STAIRS, KITCHEN, BATHROOMS, ON THE WALL SIDE AS FURTHER PROTECTION AND DISTANCING.   THE WALL ACTS AS A WIND BREAK AND AS A SOLAR COLLECTOR.   ANY REALLY NOISY MACHINES AND THEIR DUCTWORK WOULD BE CONTAINED WITHIN IT, WELL AWAY FROM THE HOUSE.   THE HOUSE, ALTHOUGH IT HAS MUCH GLASS, HAS HEAVY FLOORS AND ROOF TO STORE SOLAR HEAT IN WINTER, WITH INSULATION BELOW FLOOR AND ABOVE ROOF TO CONTAIN IT.   DOUBLE GLASS AGAINST CONDENSATION AND HEAT LOSS. SILVERED CURTAINS INTERNALLY REFLECT BACK BODY HEAT AT NIGHT.   BY DAY THE SILVERED CURTAINS AND TREES TO THE WEST WOULD CONTROL LATE AFTERNOON SUMMER SUN.   THERE IS AN UPPER LEVEL EAST MORNING TERRACE, WHOSE ROOF IS TILTED TO LET SUN IN, AND A WESTERN EVENING TERRACE TO DRINK IN THE LAST SUN OF THE DAY.

THE FRAME IS OF HOLLOW ROLLED SECTIONS RUST PROOFED AND LACQUERED YELLOW (GAMBOGE YELLOW), AS ARE THE WINDOW FRAMES INSIDE AND OUT, AND THE HAND-RAIL TO THE STAIRCASE.   THE FLOORS TO BE WHITISH WITHOUT STRONG LINES.   CLOTHES STORAGE BOXES AND DOMESTIC EQUIPMENT TO BE LOOSE, THEIR CHOOSING AND ARRANGEMENT IS TO BE THE RESPONSIBILITY OF THE OCCUPIER.

THE TREES IN THE PRIVATE GARDEN ARE ACACIA (ROBINIA PSEUDACACIA) WHOSE LIGHT LEAFAGE FILTERS THE SUN IN SUMMER AND BLOWS AWAY EARLY IN WINTER.

THE SINGLE TREE ON THE PUBLIC CORNER IS A HORSE CHESTNUT (AESCULUS HIPPOCASTANUM) INTO THE SCENT AND SIGHT OF WHOSE FLOWER CANDLES THE OCCUPIERS OF THE HOUSE WOULD ASCEND UP THEIR STAIRCASE BEHIND THE WALL IN SPRING, AND FOR WHOSE RUSTLING DRY LEAVES, FALLEN FLOWERS OF INTRICATE SPOTTING, WINDFALL GREEN MACE-LIKE FRUITLETS, AND 'CONKERS' (HORSE CHESTNUTS) CHILDREN WOULD SCUFFLE ON THE MOUND IN FRONT OF THE WALL IN THE WINTER, SPRING, SUMMER AND AUTUMN.

IT IS A BEAUTIFUL YELLOW HOUSE, FOR PEOPLE ON BOTH SIDES OF THE WALL.

NORTH ELEVATION   1:50

WEST ELEVATION   1:50

SOUTH ELEVATION

EAST ELEVATION

FIRST FLOOR PLAN   1:50

The Yellow House at an Intersection *(1976)*   395

Solar-Energy-Collecting Pyramid, Giza, Egypt

Summer 1976
AS
Japan Architect Central Glass Competition:
Modern Architecture in an Historical Environment

The question asked: What is appropriate to add to an 'Environment of Historical Significance'? The environment chosen is Giza. What is deemed appropriate—at a distance commensurate with the scale of the environment—is something that could create a man-made equivalent in 'fertility' to the Nile's historic fertile strip.

This is the insertion of the first of a series of energy collectors for the development of the western desert, in the wadis beyond the horizon visible at Giza. The series of glazed pyramidal collectors—whose side angles would be determined by the optimum collection—would ultimately echo the line of brick and stone pyramids that fringe the western desert between Medum in the south and Abu Roach in the north.

Section and photomontage.

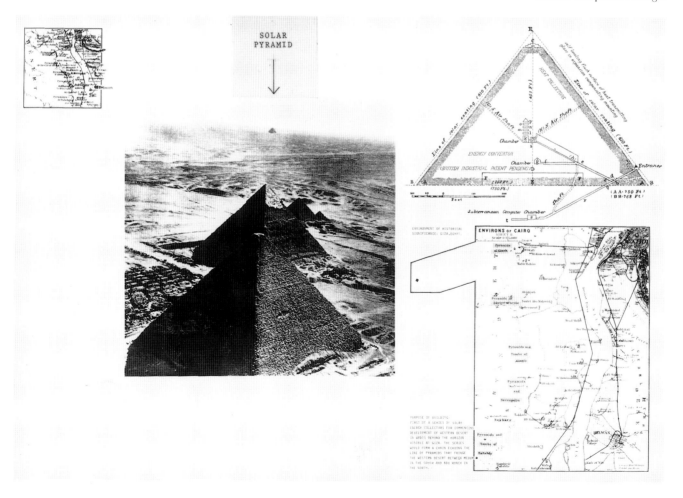

Landwehrkanal, Tiergartenviertel

October 1976

Internationales Design Zentrum, Berlin, studio: PS

The consideration given to this site* became the underpinning to Lützowstrasse, 1980. Here can be seen the growth of a language . . . architectural connection between the Yellow House and the House with Two Gantries. For not only are the facades treillage'd, but also the apartment at the top lets in light from the sky by enlarging the top floor to admit a small courtyard. Thus, somehow the section organisation, widening at the top, as the plan organisation of the Unité at Marseilles by widening at the south end, lets in the sun.

* See *The Charged Void: Urbanism* for layout.

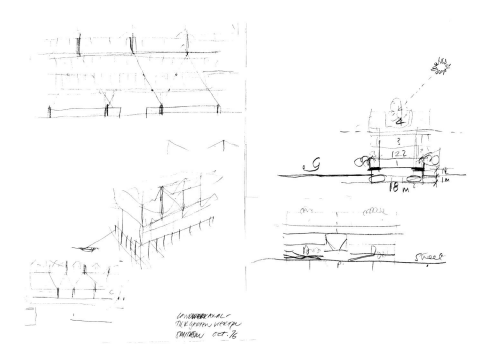

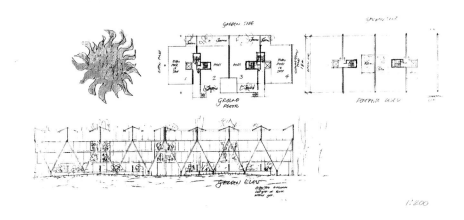

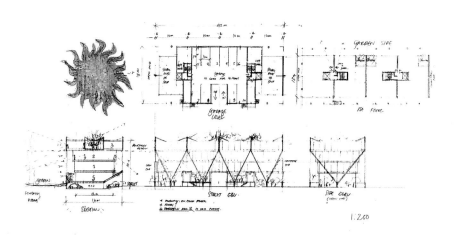

top right: Pair of sheets of first sketches. PS, 1976.
above right: Ground- and penthouse-level plans; elevation to garden. PS, 1976.
right: Garage and first-floor plans, elevation to street, section. PS, 1976.

Riverside Apartments, Millbank

Winter 1976 – January 1977, Autumn 1977

PS with Ronald Simpson

The general description of the competition submission states: *"The fundamental decision is to bring the apartments right to the water's edge so as to make it possible to look vertically down from the balconies directly into the water.*

The apartments follow the water's edge until the site narrows, when they turn to face upstream, into the sun and the finest view.

The balconies onto the river—when the weather is good—can be open; in bad weather the shutting of the sliding glass on their outer face permits the balconies to be used as ancillary spaces openable into the rooms . . . the slatted screens below balustrade level are removable.

The road facade, in contrast, has been made as solid as possible, with high-silled double windows and external sliding shutters for additional night-time noise protection; with natural ventilation by means of an acoustic shunt.

The river facade and the road facade are intended to be profoundly different . . . ideally the apartment plans should become obviously more dense, more excluding, as they approach the noisy side of the building.

On the roof are six penthouse turrets, turned on the diagonal to face up and down river, continuing the successful turreted tradition of the Palace of Westminster and Whitehall Court.

To repossess the water's edge for all, the apartments are cantilevered out over the river walk. The tedium of an overlong covered walk is relieved by a boat-hard; by the building's fretted facade allowing the sun to strike an irregular pattern on the floor of the walk; and by the mid-point portico whose height allows late evening light, morning light, onto the river walk. From Grosvenor Road the noise-protecting screen is formed by the rehabilitated warehouses, continued by a new acoustic wall."

On the axonometric drawings the text stated: *"These drawings are intended to convey the moonviewing, river-struck aspects . . . that its aesthetic is essentially one of many 'skins' . . . many layers of meaning.*

Layers, layering, screening: the dressing of the seasons . . . the decorating by the event . . . lattices . . . degrees of self-chosen exposure . . . some of our oldest themes."

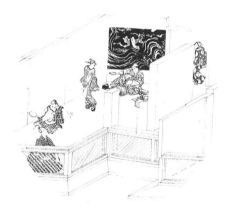 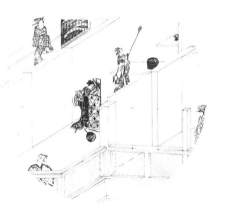

Two 'Japanese' images as plates. PS; tinting AS.

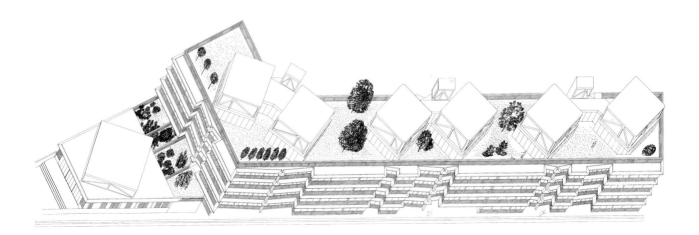

Aerial axonometric. R. T. Simpson, AS.

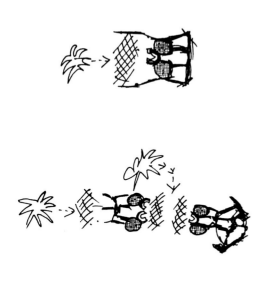

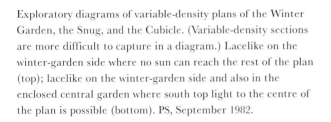

Exploratory diagrams of variable-density plans of the Winter Garden, the Snug, and the Cubicle. (Variable-density sections are more difficult to capture in a diagram.) Lacelike on the winter-garden side where no sun can reach the rest of the plan (top); lacelike on the winter-garden side and also in the enclosed central garden where south top light to the centre of the plan is possible (bottom). PS, September 1982.

Diagram of plan reworked as a put-away version, keeping to the principle of the variable-density plan. PS, 1993–94.

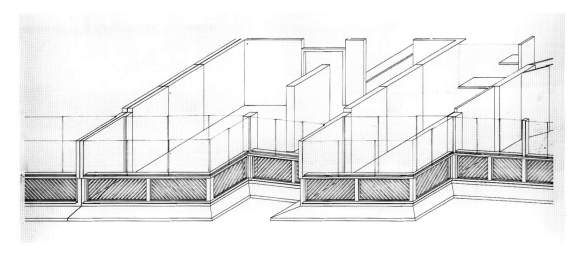

Series of five 'Japanese'
axonometrics demonstrat-
ing the responsive side,
openable to the river. PS.

Base drawing:
uninhabited state.

Delicate inhabitation.

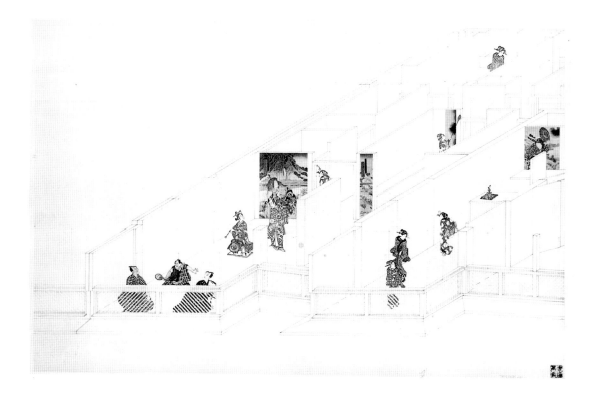

Inhabitation at dusk.

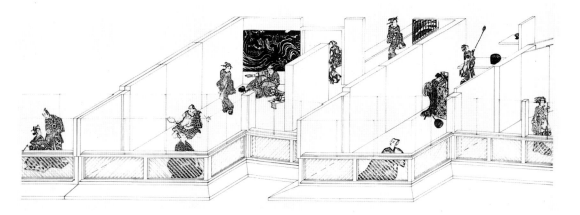

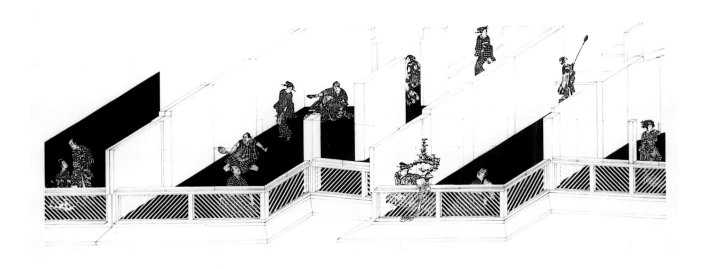

Black floor.

Deep axonometric.

Anil Avenue Commercial Offices, Khartoum, Sudan

1976 – 1977

plans: AS; elevations: PS

In the report to the developer we wrote: *"To satisfy the demand for a short construction period, the superstructure is in structural steelwork, to be used in a special way, combining economy with a radical method of resisting the extreme temperatures in Khartoum. The insulating fire-resisting walls enclosing the air-conditioned commercial space are set inside the line of the outer steel columns and beams so that the outer steelwork can be left without fire-cladding and can act as the support for open-grid steel catwalks as sun-screens. The exposed steel framing goes right over the roof, carrying a light metal shading membrane on which are solar collectors.*

At the latitude of Khartoum (15°36′N), the best orientation is north; on this site that is towards the Nile. Accordingly the largest areas of office floors face in this direction. Each side of the building has a slightly different arrangement of its sun protection; the enclosing wall being set farthest inside the steel frame on the south and least on the north; east and west are each set back the same distance.

Sun-screens vary in height and the density of catwalk open-grids vary. They are arranged so that people have a clear view out from a desk position and can also, even deep in the offices, see the blue sky through the high-level screened windows. The east sun-screening allows a little winter sun into the building as a morning warm-up.

The exposed external steel frame is white and the sun-screens left in natural aluminium. The inner insulating wall is light so as to keep down glare and present a fresh public face. The perforated sun-screening will give the restful dappled effect that leaves cast on light buildings. The sun-screening at the mezzanine level, on a grander scale, can support advertising and illuminated signs."

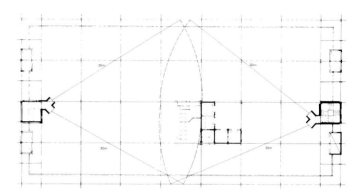

Plan showing typical office floor.

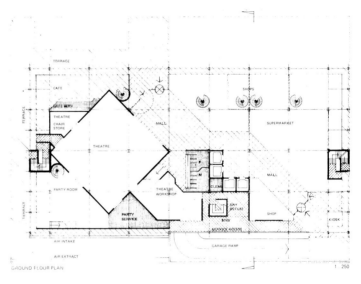

Ground-floor plan: Contribution to the pattern of use of Khartoum. A mall connects Assayid Ali Street with Anil Avenue, giving direct public access to the core while separating the supermarket from the small theatre.

View from the Nile. Victoria Browne.

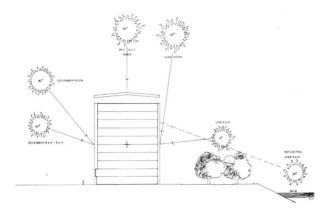

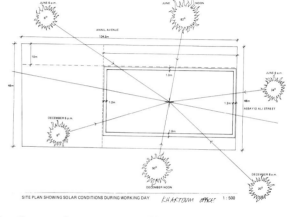

Section diagram of sun movements. What is special on this site is the reflected sun off the Nile on the north side. PS, 1977.

Plan diagram of sun movements. PS, 1976.

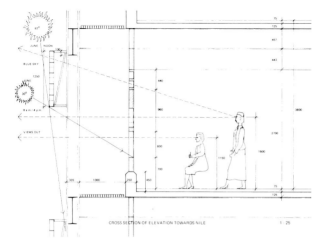

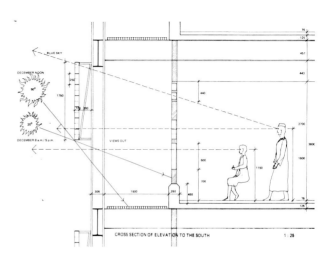

Detail cross section through north facade facing the Nile. Shading devices are designed to protect the occupants from the sun without obscuring the view of the Nile. PS, 1977.

Detail cross section through south facade, where the wall is set in the farthest. The treillage is arranged so that there is a clear view out from sitting position. PS, 1977.

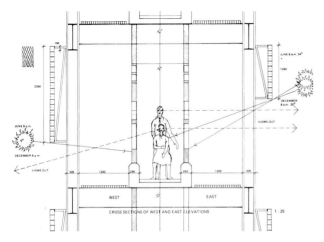

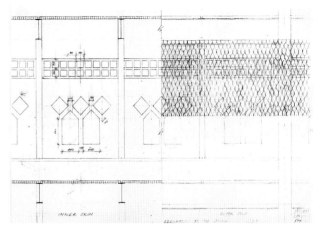

Detail cross section through east and west facades. The enclosing wall is set in the same distance on both sides, but the treillage is different. PS, 1977.

South elevation in detail. PS, 1977.

AS in the 1970s. Dennis Crompton.

9 Variable-Density Plans, Variable-Density Sections

were it achievable, a radical break with the all-over density inherited from the Heroic period . . .

Cubitt Houses *(1977)* 408

Llangennith Cluster Housing *(1977)* 409

Landscape into Art *(1977)*: 410

Swinging Elland 411

Kingsbury Lookouts 412

Tees Pudding 414

The Slaggie Eleven of the Spenymoor Slag Heaps 415

Skateboard Junction 416

Kelvingrove Art Gallery and Museum Approach 417

Leafy Arbours over the Verbindungskanal *(1977)* 418

Cookies' Nook *(1977)* 419

A House with Two Gantries *(1977)* 420

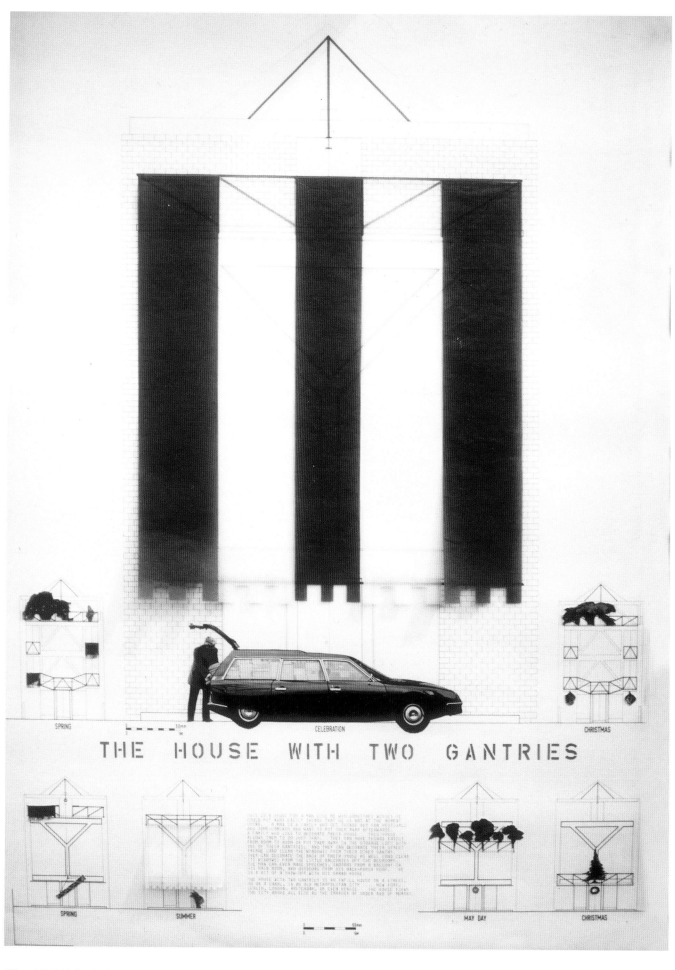

THE HOUSE WITH TWO GANTRIES

This overall variation of density, were it achievable, would be a radical break with the all-over equality of density inherited from the Heroic period. The theme is consciously explored in the development of the format and the language of Lützowstrasse and reaches a very pure state of expression in the Twenty-First-Century Tenement at Maryhill, Glasgow. A realisation—starting with Millbank's opening-up to the river and closing-down towards the road on the noisy landward side—that these opposing needs were not only a question of skin design but also could be organic within the plan, spaces open and structure light on one side, spaces tight and structure thick on the other; by extension, the section also.

opposite: House with Two Gantries: Elevation of street face with celebratory and seasonal decorations. PS, LW, 1977.

Cubitt Houses: Hot, Dry Climate Houses

Speculative houses whose grouping characteristics recall those of the encampment around the oasis and the micro-climate created by the foliage 'tent' over the hair tents. The oasis is here created by the accretion of the double-skin roofs of the family houses, by the open courts that encourage air movement past plants and water, and by the mesh 'foliage' cover above all the open courtyards.

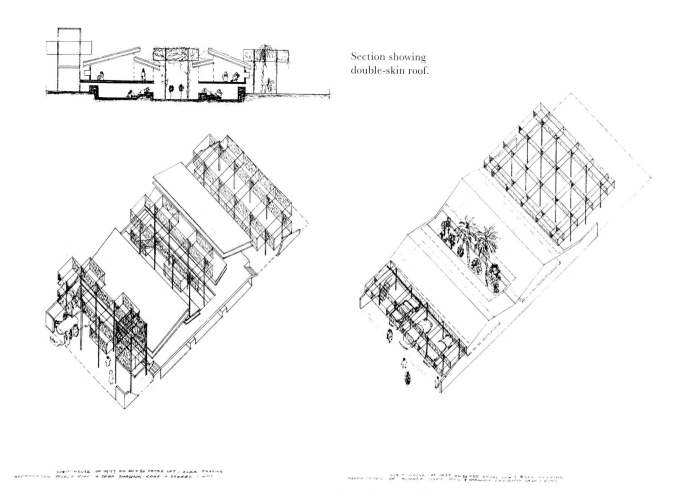

Section showing
double-skin roof.

Two axonometrics of developer's standard lot houses for Gulf states.

House with double-skin roof, shaded central and rear outdoor areas, and gazebo in which to entertain male visitors. AS, 1977.

House with double-skin roof, narrow central shaded court, and larger shaded rear area: Contributing a sense of commu-nality—an oasis space—to an expatriate group. AS, 1977.

"... In a region of scenic beauty ...

The cluster formed of five or so houses could be integrated into villages. The house types required different areas of garden, appropriate roof slopes, contributing to each cluster's unique identity.

The cluster will tolerate porches and small extensions, is capable of accommodating both local people and incomers, is able to integrate the elderly with a variety of neighbours.

In this Llangennith Cluster the roofs rise towards the view; the upstairs parlour* assumes that incomers want the fullest possible experience of the rural location."

* Once a traditional arrangement.

 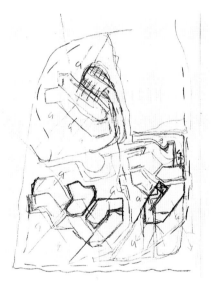 

Ideogram of clusters on-site. AS.

Sketch plan of clusters before adjustment by contour economics. AS.

Site plan of three clusters placed most economically with regard to road access and sitting well on contours. AS.

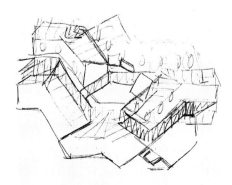 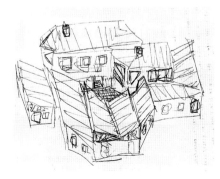

far left: Sketch axonometric of an early cluster arrangement of mixed-area houses for both locals and weekenders. AS.
left: Sketch axonometric of later cluster formation. AS.

A swathe of studies for 'places to go' in the Landscape into Art series of projects.

A line to swing . . . Elland Bridge.

A place to swing as well as to climb to different levels and from these vantage points enjoy the view . . . Kingsbury.

Indications of where not to go as essential as indications of places to go; the use of indigenous vegetation—vandal-proof by its being prickly—that also has a capacity for seasonal renewal through its sweet-smelling yellow flowers; paths to climb confined within banks of gorse that are places not to go . . . Tees Pudding.

The sites were all in debilitated areas; therefore, the stress is on the adventurous, for the fly-wheel effect.

"A pleasance of nature whose planned balance will virtually maintain itself. Where people can go to stand by the river. A natural place, a dalliance in which there are swings capable of carrying adults.

Some Lombardy poplars echo the accents of the old factory chimneys. The initial planting of seven mature trees would set up the relationship with the existing chimneys.

There is even an enclosure made of materials found on site making a pets' memorial ground. Double-walling provides a top width of earth on which ivy and wall flowers and ferns can become established. Steel trowelled rendering on the internal walls would be a surface on which children—and adults—could write up memorials to their pets, the enclosed ground a place to set memorials.

[The site] is an island left by retreating industry and traffic. A place apart regained for nature, comprising trees and shrubs, and indigenous plants through which paths get chosen and trodden; a habitat of birds and butterflies. A place sufficiently pleasant to attract to its landward edge a public house with a sitting-out area, a restaurant with a terrace, a tea room with a lawn."

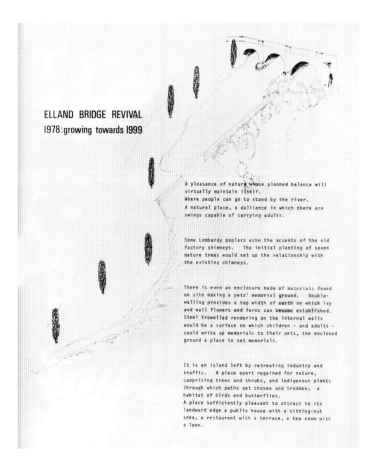

Site 'marked' with Lombardy poplars. AS.   Landscaped site with swings.

"Coinciding with the effect in Warwickshire of Dutch elm disease, the scheme proposes to use the resultant 'bonanza' of timber lavishly in large sections to make viewing structures that allow visitors to view the water park from various levels.

The Name Fence: to climb on and look through.

The Swing Hut: to provide a moving view under a reed-thatched pavilion; its timbers are sturdy enough to take adults swinging on a knotted rope.

Marsh Platform: a platform able to take a crowd; accessible up an easy ramp to the disabled, cyclists, children in push-chairs, it overlooks a bird-marsh.

Straight-Climb Lookout: a small platform under an open roof.

Flag Tower: a platform three flights above ground; its central cage contains a rung-ladder to a 'crows nest'.

Heron's Lookout: four flights above the ground; on its enclosing parapet-seat people can sit sheltered by a reed-thatch roof, to picnic in inclement weather.

In all structures, the use of brightly, differently coloured wood preservative stresses that the timber structures are for people's enjoyment."

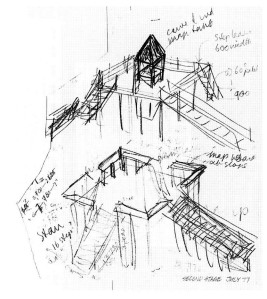

First sketches of Marsh Platform: Accessible to bicyclists and the disabled. AS.

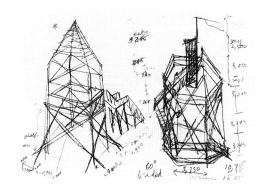

First sketches of Straight-Climb Lookout and Flag Tower, realised for Tecta in Lauenförde, Germany, in 1991. AS.

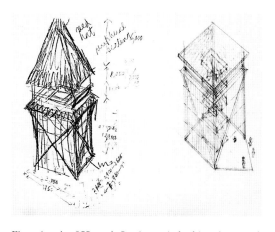

First sketch of Heron's Lookout: A double scissor-stair gives access to the large, seat-encircled platform. AS.

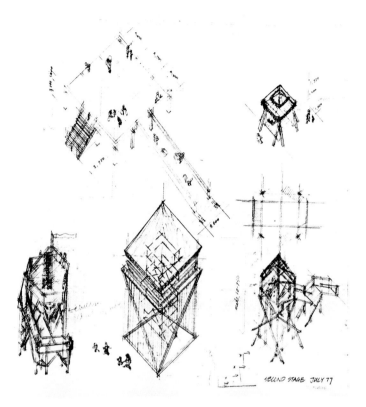

Sketch of the ideas for the viewing structures. AS.

Overview axonometric of the viewing structures. AS.

Model of Straight-Climb Lookout.

Model of Heron's Lookout.

Tees Pudding, Middlesborough, Spring 1977, PS

"*The site is on a striking bend in the River Tees. The proposal is to make an existing low mound of slag dramatically higher so it becomes as steep as Castle Hill at Bishopton.*

As gorse flowers all the year round, planted with gorse this pudding-shaped mound is yellow.

Two paths spiral between fences of railway sleepers to the summit's viewing circle.

From here, on the Ironmasters site which dates back to the railway terminal chosen by Joseph Peas in 1828, there would be a considerable view as the terrain is flat: the industrial wonders of Teesside, the Transporter Bridge, as well as Roseberry Topping and Captain Cook's Monument."

Side view of model.
Ronald Simpson, 1977.

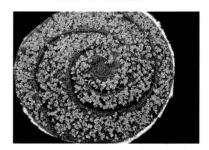

TEES PUDDING

Perspective drawing looking downstream to the pudding-shaped, gorse-covered mound and the riverside walk. Ronald Simpson, 1977.

Four representations of the mound in different seasons.

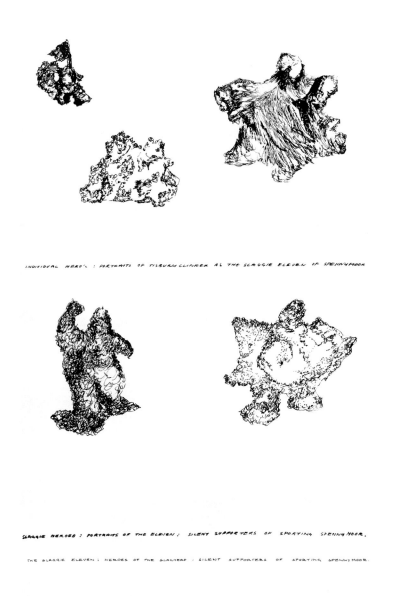

INDIVIDUAL HERO'S : PORTRAITS OF TISBURY CLINKER AS THE SLAGGIE ELEVEN OF SPENNYMOOR

SLAGGIE HEROES : PORTRAITS OF THE ELEVEN : SILENT SUPPORTERS OF SPORTING SPENNY MOOR.

THE SLAGGIE ELEVEN : HEROES OF THE SLAGHEAP : SILENT SUPPORTERS OF SPORTING SPENNYMOOR.

"The Slaggie Eleven: the Heroes of Spenymoor Slag Heaps and Silent Supporters of Sporting Spenymoor are formed of up-ended conglomerates of slag, painted in bright stripes, the colours of local teams, amateur and professional:

Spenymoor: black, vertical white stripes;
Crook Town: amber, black;
Willington: blue, white vertical stripes;
West Auckland: white, amber;
Durham City: amber, blue;
Stanley: red, white vertical stripes, black;
Hartlepool United: blue, white.

The Slaggie Heroes are randomly positioned on the crestline of the bowl which naturally provides a protected pitch. The encircling surfaces are graded for ease of maintenance and will be seeded with grass. Certain hollows elsewhere on the heaps will be planted with biting stonecrop to flower with yellow stars in May to June."

First drawing of slag heaps:
Slaggie Eleven in elevation. AS.

Three sketches of up-ended conglomerates of slag as members of the
Slaggie Eleven. AS.

Oblique view of model. AS.

Skateboard Junction, Stockton on Tees, Spring 1977, AS

"Skateboard Junction is a place to go to; skateboarders' activity providing a spectacle in a hard-surfaced hollow, immediately visible from the curve in the main Durham Road.

Beyond this, paths emphasise the extent of the territory by being partially lined with the traditional fences of wooden railway sleepers, set vertically to form wind-breaks.

The crossing path has a 'soft' surface of sleepers laid flat; it is a 'right of way' that leads to the long footbridge, over the old shunting yard, and is lined with poplar trees; the lattice of branches will extend the sense of the footbridge's lattice across the site. The site's connections with railway history are further maintained by antique rolling stock once used in local yards, parked as pavilion-sculptures."

Sketch overview. AS.

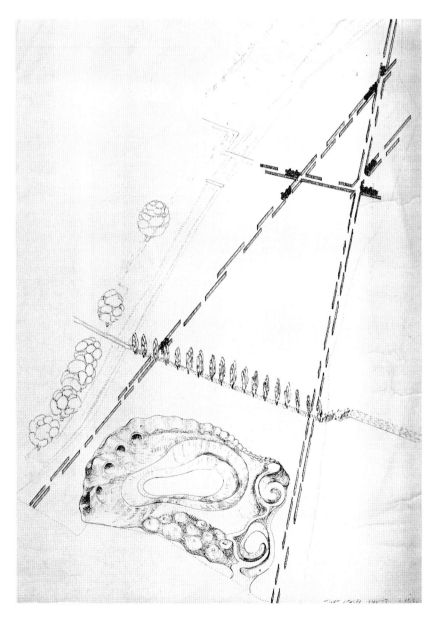

"This is one of the most impressively sited buildings in Europe. Passing on Argyle Street, the great building is seen clear across the open green.

The aim of the present proposal is to simplify the arrangement of the approach still further and yet increase the possibilities for use.

From the main grass area all the trees are transplanted elsewhere except the two elms, and the paths and beds are removed. The turf is then lifted, the area prepared anew all over to ensure even-ness of colour, and the turf put back with matching make-up strips taken from the area outside the main Roman Circus shape. The grass outside this shape area is allowed to be colonized by other grasses to create the two green tones shown on the drawing.

The holly hedges are retained to reinforce the feeling for the Circus shape.

The asphalt surface of the main approach is removed and replaced in stone paving as is the terrace section of the main carriageway (wheeled traffic being deflected to other entrances). This South facing terrace is now able to be used during the times the grass is wet (as it often is in Glasgow) for exterior displays and for sitting out when the sun shines and reflects back from the stonework of the building onto the terrace. From the terrace one can descend by the existing steps down to the main grass area. Here could be displayed, in the manner of Battersea Park, large objects and sculpture temporarily moved out from the museum."

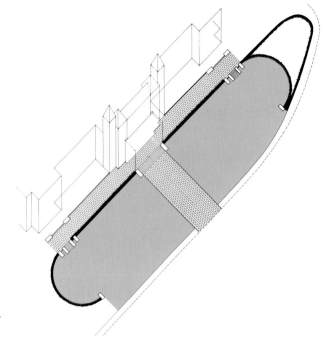

Axonometric of 'changing the approach'. LW, 1977.

Slogan of the *Glasgow Herald* (the graphics relate to the approach geometry). PS, 1977.

Leafy Arbours over the Verbindungskanal, Berlin

This is an urban connection*
as well as a place to stay
a while lingering amongst
the lattices.

* See *The Charged Void: Urbanism.*

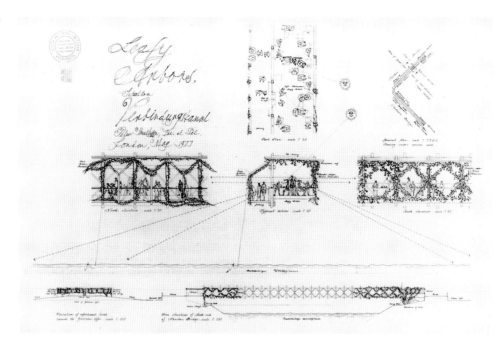

The general arrangements. A+PS, 1977.

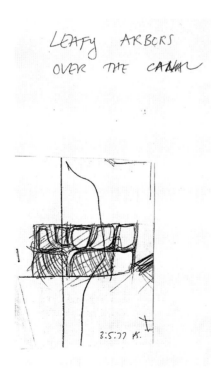

Ideogram of lattice idea:
The arbour and the crossing. PS, 1977.

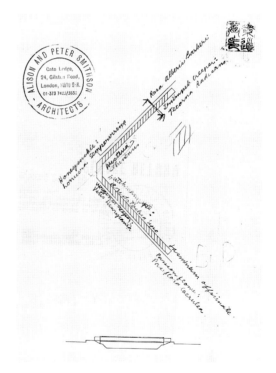

Plan with annotations for suitable climbing plants to
reach across the framework from either bank. PS, 1977.

Cookies' Nook

AS continues, from Kreuzberg, the line of enquiry about what is now needed to be inserted in cities: *"This quality 'pad' is an appliance apartment for the commuting man; so that he is able to find, in each city, the identical arrangement of switches, telephones, machines for servicing himself and his professional life. Yet each time the 'pad' is angled to face that best aspect/prospect the host city can provide."*

The lightness-of-touch aesthetic allows a dressing that responds to the moment, to the needs of a particular individual or interest group.

Model of spiralling 'silver tins' to provide balconies for eating and sitting areas of apartments.

Model of warped 'zeppelin'-type structure.

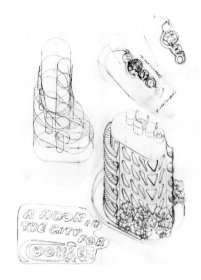

Line axonometric. AS.

Sketches of plan alternatives: The travelling man's 'pad-from-home'. AS.

Series of axonometrics of spiralling stack; photomontage of Nook located in a German city. AS.

A House with Two Gantries

"This house is in a series of explorations on the theme of 'layering' in which it is the intention to offer a fabric which suggests to its occupiers that they should see to its care, its cleaning, and its 'decoration'. A fabric with which people can make a 'connection'; engaging their affection and giving them possibilities for tuning it to the seasons and to the events of the families' or of societies' life:

. . . a building which can be dressed;

. . . a building which builds its meaning in time;

. . . a building which makes many people active.

This particular house is intended for a man like myself who sometimes wishes to put things away that he is not at the moment using. A man in a family who get things out for festivals and home-comings and want to put them away afterwards.

This house allows them to do just that . . . move things easily from room to room or into the storage loft with one of their gantries; and they can decorate their street facade, and clean their windows, from their other gantry. They can decorate the back of their house as well—and clean its windows—from the little balconies off the bedrooms.

The man can even make speeches, indoors from a balcony in his main room and outdoors from his back-porch roof (he is a bit of a show-off with his grand house). The house with two gantries is an infill house on a street, or a canal in an old metropolitan city . . . Berlin, London, Amsterdam, or even Venice."

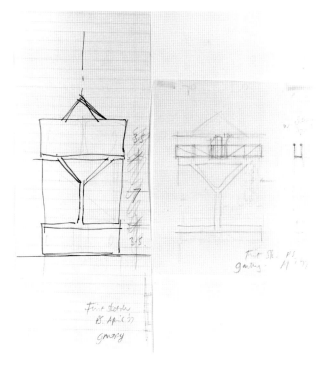

First sketch of elevation; first sketch of gantry. PS, 1977.

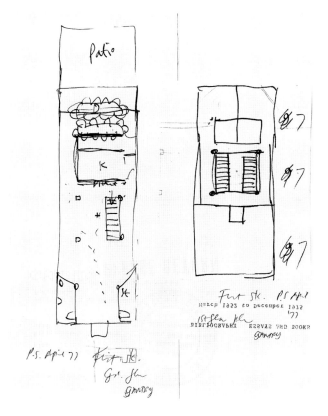

First sketch of ground- and first-floor plans. PS, 1977.

Plans, sections, elevations.

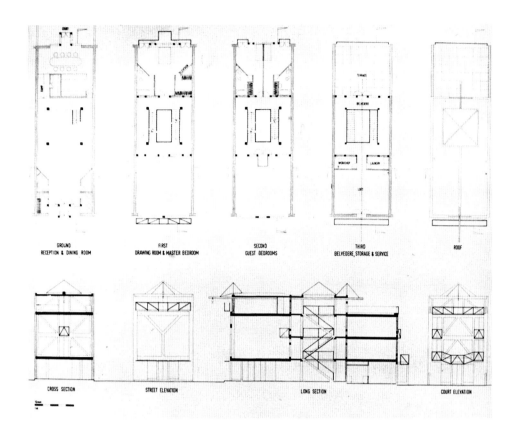

Sectional perspective.
Base drawing, LW.

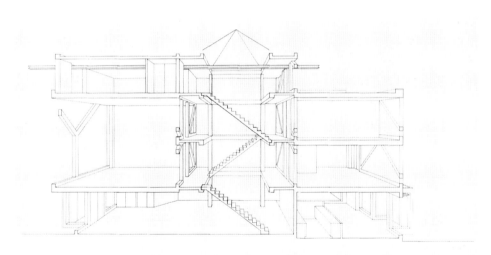

Sectional perspective, inhabited.
Although special to the supposed
occupier, this house's open
invitation to make the place one's
own says something to everyone
in a society with an amount of
leisure. PS, 1977.

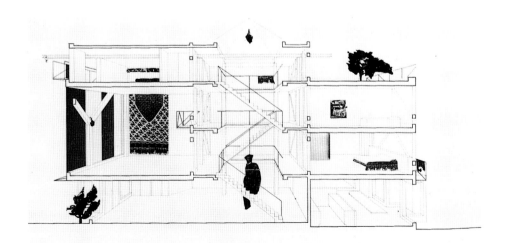

Pahlavi National Library: Report cover with a real peacock tail feather sealed into plastic. AS, Simon Smithson, 1977.

10 The Harnessing of Light

the visits most people make to places of hot sun and shadow have, over thirty years, changed attitudes to light, to reflective qualities . . . maybe ultimately to the pleasures of the underlit . . .

Pahlavi National Library *(1977–78)*   426

Walk in the Dry Passages and New West End to Worcester Cathedral *(1977–78)*   432

Colleges' Gate, Colleges' Path, and Distance Stones, Urbino *(1979–83)*   436

Amenity Building, University of Bath *(1978–80, 1984–85)*   438

Melbourne's Magic Mountains *(1979–80)*   444

Damascus Gate *(1979–81)*   446

'Twenty-Four Doors to Christmas' Exhibition *(1979)*   448

Light pouring into the dwelling, to lift the spirit towards hope; Mackintosh introduced, the Modern movement celebrated. Mackintosh harnessed light inside white rooms; delineated the enlivened space by black ladders, pewter lines; accented with pink or mauve petals, and so on: a sparing use of colour as punctuation in his language.

White became the liberating medium, allowing Modern architects to stand off colour, discover colour, begin again to think in terms of colour.

Ever since the House of the Future we have been thinking in colour: before this—for example in the undercroft of Coventry—there was a conscious colour choice, a decision: books on architecture in the 1950s—apart from certain interwar cahiers—were still in black and white. Thinking in colour appropriate to use gave the monotones of Langside, the rainbow of Wokingham . . . this rainbow touched the various deck levels of Robin Hood Gardens. Countries that traditionally used the tiles of Turkey, Iraq, and Iran can appropriate a palette of iridescent colours: this we used in the Green Belt Gardens and the Dune Gardens, Kuwait.* In the Pahlavi National Library, traditional colours were introduced into the translucent covering over the channelled routes to the various departments.

The quality of light of the domes at Pahlavi as it enters the eyes is controlled by visors, tracking with their protective backs to the sun, gathering the quality from reflection to let this live light pour down the inner surfaces of the domes. This descending, changing quality of light—indication of time of day, season of year—is taken up in the colour mutation of the internal fittings.

* See *The Charged Void: Urbanism*.

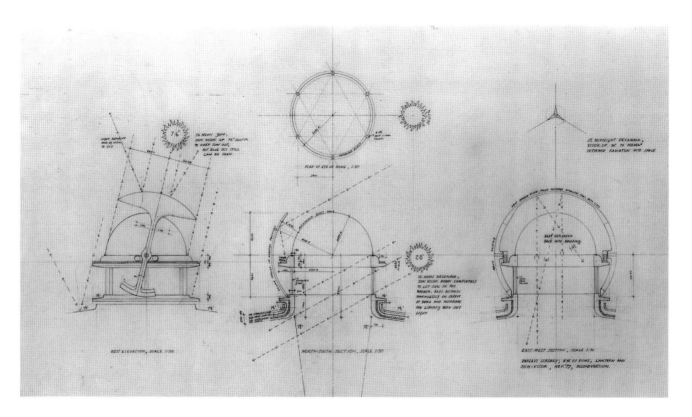

The power of light acting on white, reflective qualities that Le Corbusier probably discovered in El Oued, North Africa, we discovered in Greece in summer 1951.

But the dynamic of reflected light was observed under a storm sky in Mykonos at Easter time, 1958; the paving and steps of the alleyways freshly whitened so that the power garnered by the bounced-around light made it seem as if sunlight was shining from the underworld upwards past the white walls into the air as an aura to the town under the lowering skies. This ordinary everyday truth could be experienced in London by the 1970s . . . paintwork had been renewed in gloss paint, reflective as previously only had been ships.

Certainly since Piero della Francesca light has been consciously observed. Piero's *Flagellation* with its two light sources—the divine and the everyday—celebrates that observation.

From the Modern movement in architecture we inherited the idea of light as a 're-newer' . . . of society . . . of physical body-health . . . and as our aid to the portrayal of industrialisation as a sacred force. The 1920s as a generation turned to light as a source of both form and format for building.*

The harnessing of light in the 1980s and 1990s serves different ends. Natural light is seen as part of a slowly-being-relearned respect for the cycles of natural events . . . their endless wonders: that the carelessness that is part of our natural optimism as changers of things need not, as we grow richer, be so thoughtlessly damaging.

In architecture light can be thought about so that we can live more easily with things; see them in many moods, let them change us; not pin everything down as butterflies in a drawer.

* See A+PS, *The Heroic Period of Modern Architecture* (Milan: Idea Editions; London: Thames and Hudson; New York: Rizzoli, 1981).

opposite: Pahlavi National Library: Diagram of eye of dome, lantern, sun visor. PS, November 1977.
right: Photograph of Priory Walk tiled bench with display.

Pahlavi National Library, Tehran

Winter 1977 – 1978

A+PS

Chief assistant: LW; Assistants: Simon Smithson, John Hare

with Ove Arup and Partners

One is as timid about domes as one is about using colouring. Domes, or funny glass sheds with bits of board or rag over their 'eyes', are common enough throughout Islam, but in our Western world, the power, the fixity, of the Pantheon's geometry is terrifying.

Our domes for the Pahlavi National Library are intended to be 'unfixed' from the Pantheon image by the solar-shield devices and by the lack of emphasis on the domes' seating. Our domes are as veined puff-pastry, the bottom layers held level by the weight of those above, the top layers swelling up into soft air-blobs of various sizes; in the Islamic tradition, low domes of this inner-need sort are much used in secular and near-secular buildings and in passages: they are common in haans, madrassas, and souks; and on the island of Djerba they are used also in farms and houses. A dome on a drum always means a mosque and would be in no way right for a library.

There has been published a preliminary section by Le Corbusier for the great hall for the Geneva competition . . . a Pantheon-type dome with an eye . . . it must have terrified him, too.

All the domes of the Pahlavi National Library are protected from the sun; although, naturally, the setting-out geometry adjusts as the domes diminish in size. Through the eye of the dome can be seen the clear blue sky . . . through the eye the sun in its benign aspects can irradiate the interior with light and warmth . . . at noon in midwinter the sun's rays at twenty-eight degrees above the horizon would reflect from the soffit of the dome over the whole reading room.

When the sun climbs to higher angles as the summer approaches, the sun visor rises to shield the eye. In midsummer the visors rise to seventy-six degrees above the horizon against the sun at its zenith. The sun visors' tilting and rotating mechanism is group-locked onto a solar-tracker, but each individual visor can be taken out of lock and tuned from within the space to give a specific light quality. For this tuning there is an enormous range of possibilities, as the underside of the visor is also reflective and, therefore, can scoop light in as well as hold it out.

View of model from east side. Model: Ove Arup and Partners, C. Wade.

On winter evenings the visor can be raised to the full vertical night sky to limit heat emissions. Thus controlled, the eyes to the domes maximise the use of the sun's energy for both light and heat within the biggest volumes in the building.

"These shields, glittering in the sun, would be immensely popular, for they seem both space-age and as ageless as the hand over the eyes."

Before Pahlavi, a statement by AS at Ramsar: *"A culture starts with the invention of the spirit of the programme . . . as an example— that of the mosque . . . Creswell tells us that the practices and the format that identify the mosque to any observer were invented within something like forty years. The most basic materials can be imbued with the spirit of this programme. Invention looks both ways, outwards to signal there is still life in a culture, inwards to specific place that signals consistency and energy within it.*

Pahlavi uses size, level, and nearness to axis of symmetry . . . for these devices of language have been commonly used in Iran in the past—both in ancient Persian architecture and the Sufi tradition—and are therefore likely to be understood today.

[The library pursues the] Sufi spatial and constructional tradition so that Iranian architecture can continue, as Mies ingested Prussian Classicism into 'Modern' and thus European architecture continues."

During the evolution of the facades—in working outwards from the needs of the reader carrels, the book galleries, and so on—a resolving geometry suggested itself, based on that already chosen for the glass canopies of the circulation routes, a geometry strikingly like that of a peacock tail feather.

From this 'resolving geometry' the principles of the facade patterning and its colouring have been extended over the whole building. This has produced some tremors, as the colouring emphasises the building's unsought nineteenth-century feeling.

View of model from the south, montaged on site's backdrop, against which the domes, lanterns, and sun visors would glitter.
Model by Ove Arup and Partners, C. Wade.

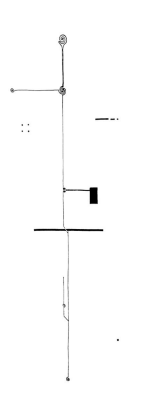

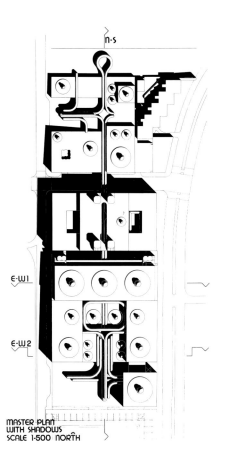

Plan of water channel and pool system that runs down all the public ways, contributing to the internal climate balance.

Roof plan with shadows at 10 a.m., New Year's Day, 21 March. Tom Hennigan.

Aerial view of model. Model by Ove Arup and Partners, C. Wade.

Diagram of use areas.

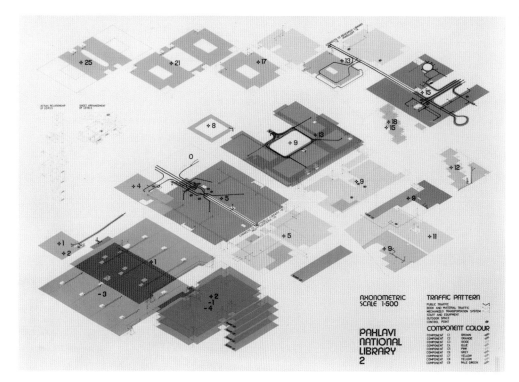

Axonometric of domes with circular
eye at apex, semi-spherical glass lantern,
and solar shield. Tom Hennigan.

General system of public circulation
tubes running through the library mat.
Tom Hennigan.

Detail axonometric of public circulation
tubes at the entrance. Wally Banks.

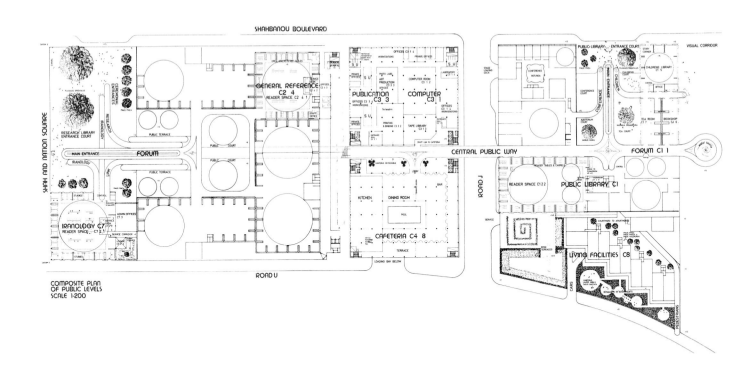

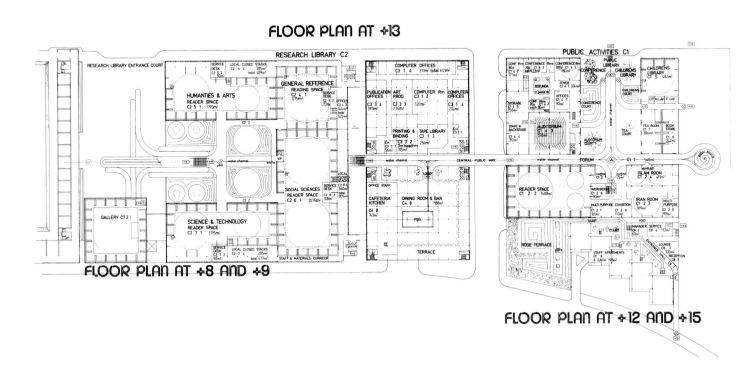

FLOOR PLAN AT +13

FLOOR PLAN AT +8 AND +9

FLOOR PLAN AT +12 AND +15

Two versions of composite plan of public levels. LW.

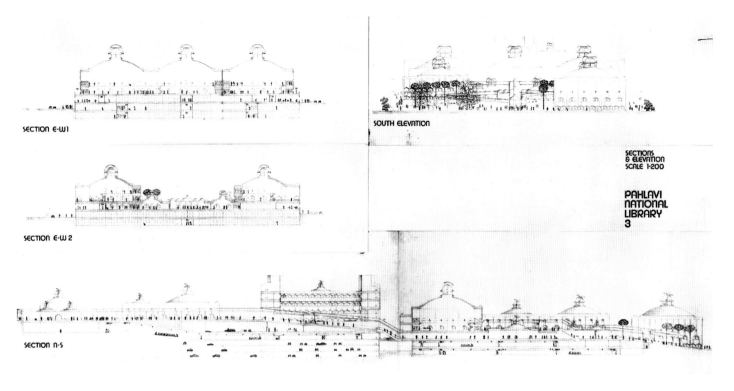

SECTION E-W1

SOUTH ELEVATION

SECTIONS
& ELEVATION
SCALE 1:200

PAHLAVI
NATIONAL
LIBRARY
3

SECTION E-W 2

SECTION N-S

Elevations and sections: South elevation (top right); two east-west cross sections (top left); north-south long section with the top-most layer puffing up into domes whose sun visors, all pointing in the same direction, indicate their sun-responsive control (bottom).

Detail of bay of external skin and plan of carrel inside library: This bay starts the geometry for the building's skin with the 'ideal' window for the carrel. PS.

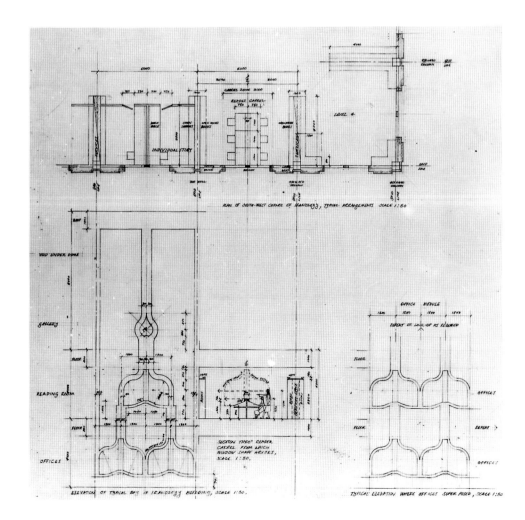

Walk in the Dry Passages and New West End to Worcester Cathedral, Worcester*

December 1977 – 1978

AS; cathedral platform: PS

Two contributions towards the repair of Worcester 'holed by planners'.

In the first contribution, extension of existing and new passages opens possibilities for fresh uses that are yet to be found for places in disuse, the need to magic a change from abrasion by movement to new pleasures of movement . . . full of remembrances and respects and no obliterations. The easily maintainable enclosure of ways, used by us in Pahlavi, is perhaps insufficiently changed in these thoughts on Worcester.

* See *The Charged Void: Urbanism* for study of Worcester's urban grain.

Location and nature of infill fabric to patch the hole in the historic city. AS.

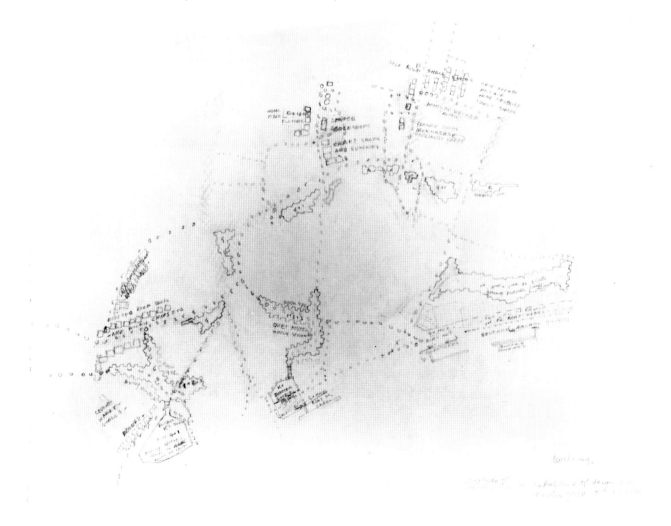

Axonometric of passages.
Raun Thorp, 1985.

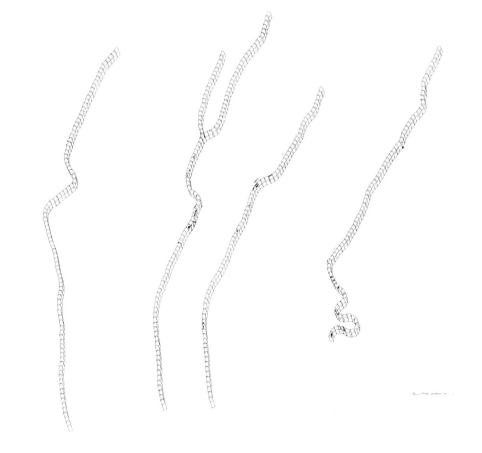

Axonometric of passages in context,
with miniature shop huts attached.
Raun Thorp, 1985.

In the second contribution, the new west end of the cathedral is a response to tourist pressure: *"The platform, riding just below the tree-tops along the river, is at a level one metre lower than the floor at the west end of the cathedral, so that one always looks upwards to the great west door—that is, upwards from the open platform as well as from the enclosed tourist pavilions under it. The platform and the arms reaching out to it are supported on timber trestles in elm, impregnated with purple preservative. The floor is open oak slats so the rain falls through—the tourist pavilions under being roofed with shallow lead falls, set under the slatted floor (as are the service rooms beneath the wing board-walks of Thomas Jefferson's house at Monticello set above the trees of his small mountain)."*

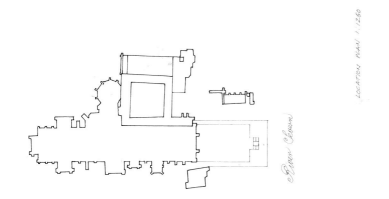

Plan of observation platform extending out from the 'dead' west end of the cathedral. PS.

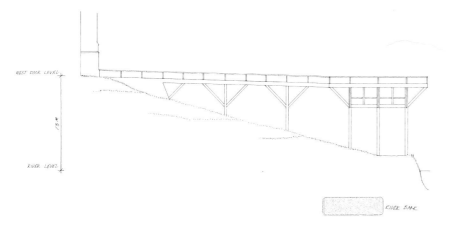

Side elevation of timber platform. PS.

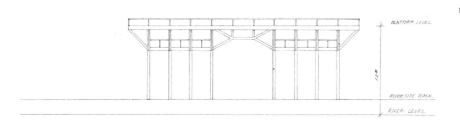

Elevation facing over treetops and river towards Worcester cricket ground. PS.

Pair of axonometrics looking upwards
from the Severn bank path.

Timber structure of platform. AS.

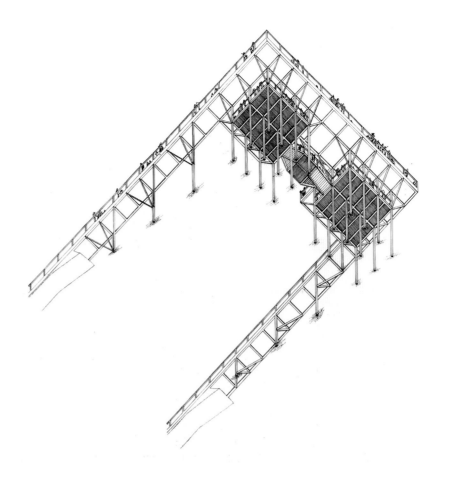

Platform with existing trees. AS.

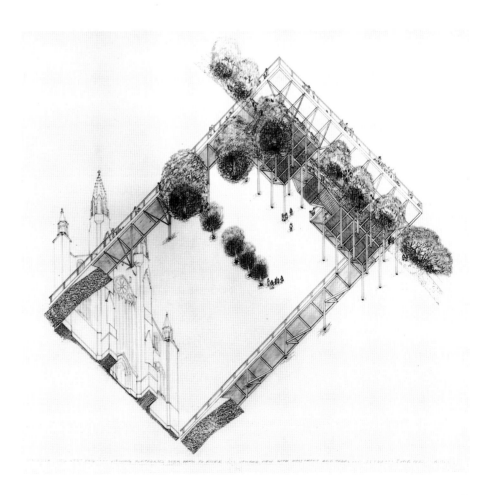

Colleges' Gate, Colleges' Path, and Distance Stones,* Urbino Autumn 1979 – 1983

PS

Every visitor to Urbino sees in his first minute, from the usual point of arrival in the Mercatale, the Porta Valbona.

From the Porta Valbona runs a road without footways to new colleges on the south flank of the Cappucini Hill. It is from here that one sets out to find a new route from the colleges to the city that could be for walking only, locates it, marks the distances with stones, and explores the form of entry through the city's wall.

* See *The Charged Void: Urbanism* for urban context.

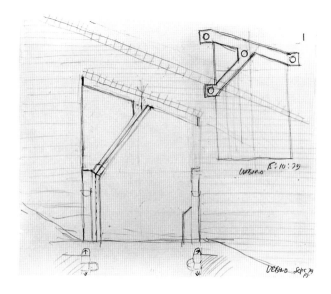

Sketch for Colleges' Gate. PS, September 1979, with overlay 15 October.

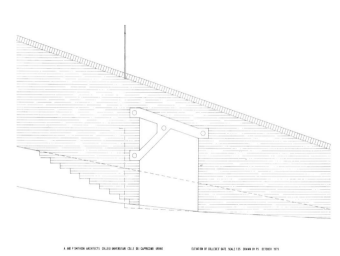

Elevation. PS, 1979.

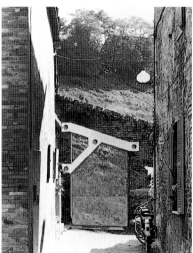

Photomontages.
PS, 1981.

far left: Looking in.
left: Looking out.

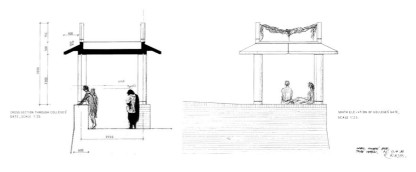

left: Colleges' Gate, third version: View over the rampart path over the Porta Valbona, with AS and Samantha Smithson in foreground. PS, 1983.
above: Third version: Cross section and south elevation. PS, 1983.

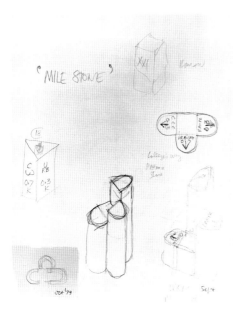

Colleges' Path, distance stones.
Initiatory sketch. PS, 1979.

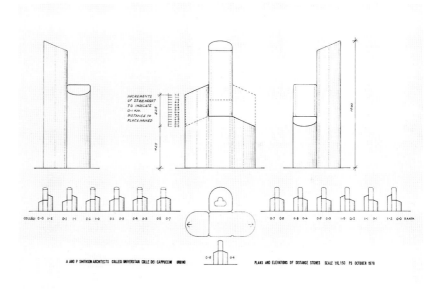

System of distance stones. PS, 1979.

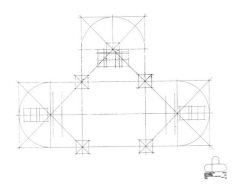

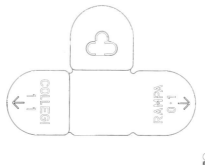

far left: Setting-out for plan of distance stones. PS, 1979.
left: Plan of the distance stone nearest to the Rampart. PS, 1979.

Amenity Building, University of Bath

The building has to meet the social needs of the non-academic staff in very much the same way as a junior common room serves undergraduates.

Its entrance lies at the nexus of paths from all parts of the university's grounds, and to take advantage of the views that lie before it, the principal floor is placed high up with two terraces that on the east side look down to the lake and along the south side look outwards to the south-west over the crest of the university's land, towards the wooded horizon above Widcombe.

The building was built in two phases. The first phase is a heavy-construction supporting box; in the second phase, a light-framed pavilion is set on top of it.

Temporary work in the first phase was identified: woodwork that would later be removed was stained green (to read as 'gardening'); knock-out panels were clearly not bonded-in; ledges that were weather-mouldings in the first phase were floor slab-supports later; outside walls became internal walls thought-out so as to retain their 'outside' characteristics when inside.

A light steel 'cage' sitting on a solid basement-like box was first envisaged for the Bates' Burrows Lea Farm, thirty years earlier.

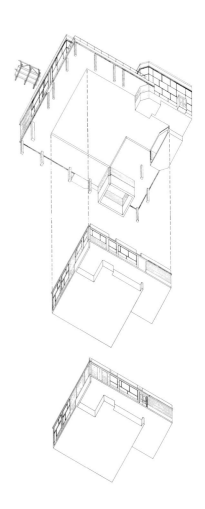

Photomontage of first proposal: View of the roof from the vice chancellor's room as first envisaged. LW.

above: Worm's-eye phasing diagram of original design, showing how the building is assembled: Phase II is placed over a modified Phase I. LW, 1980.
below: View from the south-west. PS, December 1989.

View of south-east corner. Ascent to main floor is on right. PS, 1985.

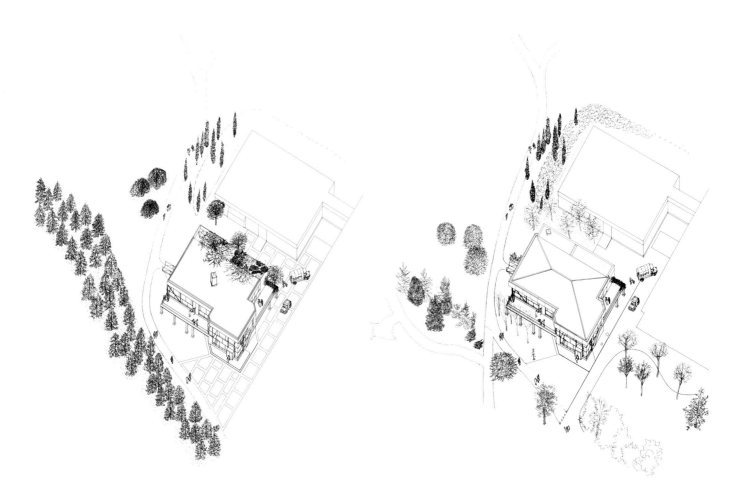

Axonometric of first proposal. LW, AS.

Axonometric as-built. LW, AS; updated 1988.

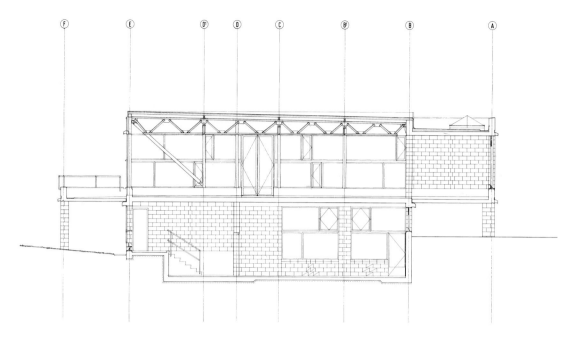

Cross section as first projected, with monopitch roof covered with bituminous felt.
No eaves overhang on balcony front. K. Hayashi, 1979.

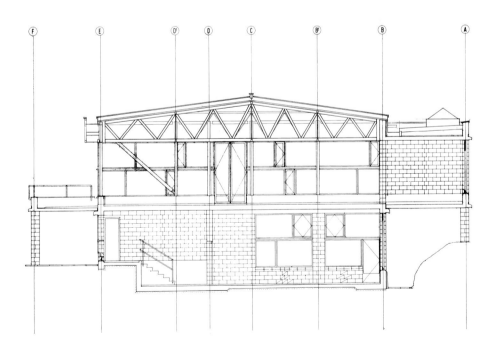

Cross section as built, with double-pitched roof covered in stainless-steel sheeting.
Wide gutter forms eaves overhanging on balcony front. LW, 1979.

opposite top: View of the terrace from the south-east. PS, 1985.
opposite bottom: View of the bridge to the picnic grounds from the west. PS, 1985.
above: South-west corner of main room, looking towards Bath. Here the 'bracing' is inside the weather-skin whereas in Lucas Headquarters it was outside. PS, 1985.

Melbourne's Magic Mountains

'Places to go', a theme explored in the Kuwait Rampart Gardens*
and in the Landscape into Art projects: the place to go offered to
Melbourne is a couple of Magic Mountains . . . to 'travel up' to . . .
from which to experience the spectacular view of the city spread on
its slope, reaching down to the bay . . . high enough to keep to themselves some effects of the coloured clouds they put out at weekends
and on festival days.

Melbourne's Magic Mountains explore the world of lattices laced
with tube routes, a system accessed by aerial cable cars: pleasures we
discovered in Rio . . . perhaps for this reason—the sugar loaf connection—the first sketches still hold the most promise.

* See *The Charged Void: Urbanism.*

Original idea of partly planted hollow mountain, with cable cars
entering and exiting. AS, 1979.

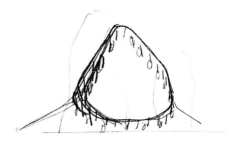

Ideogram of cable-car movement
on mountain. AS.

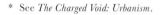

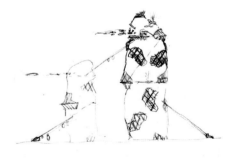

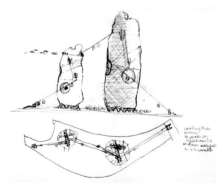

Three sketches: Pair of Chinese mountains
joined by cable cars, as sugar loafs in Rio.
Caves for entrance and exit of cable cars,
with structural close lattice exposed in parts
to light giant internal voids. AS.

As a framed structure.
First sketches of structure. PS, 1979.

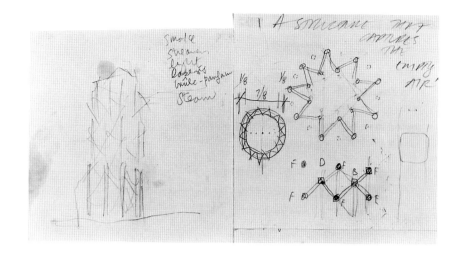

Fireworks on opening night. AS.

Damascus Gate, Departments of City Hall, Jerusalem

The urban-form study for Damascus Gate can be found in *The Charged Void: Urbanism*; the study was deliberately never advanced so as to remain a healing dream.

In the first study, the grain of the 'lining of hole in city' ran with its hinterland. In the second study, all the grain turns to face the sun at noon. It has been assumed that Israeli research on the use of the sun's energy to 'cool' buildings can be applied; the roof slope carries solar panels; the clerestory windows face northwards. An arcade, as in the first study, still fringes the 'lining' of the space in front of the Damascus Gate; its depth, as before, varying with its aspect.

The Hadrianic level of Damascus Gate is still open to serve the souk; the pedestrian route from Mersherim still crosses the open space; rocks break the paving surface; olive trees—which the Israelis seem to successfully replant— grow in crevices as they traditionally did in this valley until the late 1930s. However, the paving has not been resolved . . . this would need the realism of the valley excavated of its rubbish, the real programme, before a Pikionis-type study could be made.

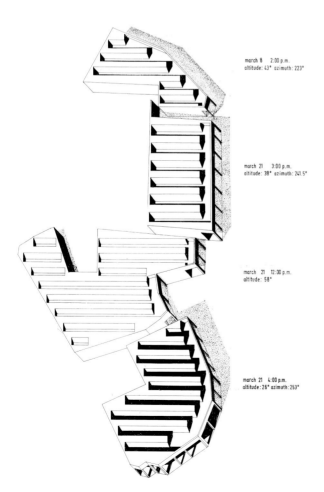

march 8   2:00 p.m.
altitude: 43° azimuth: 223°

march 21   3:00 p.m.
altitude: 38° azimuth: 241.5°

march 21   12:00 p.m.
altitude: 58°

march 21   4:00 p.m.
altitude: 26° azimuth: 253°

Second study axonometric showing shadow periodicity at the spring equinox. AS, Sumirya Bardowil, 1981.

Second study perspective
looking towards Damascus
Gate and Jerusalem's
northern wall. AS.

Second study perspective
looking north up
Tyropean Valley. AS.

'Twenty-Four Doors to Christmas' Exhibition, Kettle's Yard, Cambridge

As the name implies, the exhibition borrows from the advent calender the invitation to children to open doors to discover aspects of Christmas.

Behind each door, the box compartment contains a display related to twenty-four aspects of Christmas; those that seemed most evident in the development of the English Christmas:

Photograph of model. Model, Simon Smithson, 1979.

1. *The Nativity Stall* or *Christmas Market Stall:* This possibly unconscious cross-reference in European painting being represented by an Italian painting of the Nativity depicted in an open timber stall.
2. *Carols:* Bells, sounds of outdoor celebration; going the round of the community.
3. *Spirits:* An influence brought by our Viking invaders.
4. *Saturnalia:* Our share in Roman influence.
5. *Season:* The physical presence of difference, snow, frost, the renewal of the outdoors and the decoration of nature by the season.
6. *Influence:* The fire festival of the turning of the year, renewed by Irish/American influence.
7. *Feasting:* Re-energising at the lowest point of the year.
8. *Mumming:* The visit of the strangers of the night who enact a ritual of cleansing, renewing the domestic fire.
9. *Light:* The coming of the light of the world, a happening of renewal of hope at the darkest time of the year.
10. *The Bible:* Its first English translation and printing.
11. *Contrived seasonal noise:* Wassailing, crackers, gunfire: protection and fertility of the orchards.
12. *Decoration:* Evergreen and paper: the influence of Poland through the Baltic; our turning from the use of 'messy' greenery to 'clean' paper as the means of the temporary change of the domestic environment.
13. *The Figure of Christian Charity:* Santa Claus, the change of name from Father Christmas, in response to the inexpensively printed magazine and book.

Box 5, 'Season'. AS, 1979.

Box 9, 'Light'. AS, 1979.

* Fabrication team: Simon Smithson, Caroline Pitt, John Hare. Installation team: students of the Department of Architecture & Building Engineering, University of Bath.

View past Box 7, 'Feasting,' and Box 8, 'Mumming'. Wall trees to the right. Sam Lambert.

14. *Christ's Bread* or *Christmas Bread:* The regional variations of this remembrance of fertility rites and survival through the winter.

15. *The Family Celebration:* The introduction of the Christmas tree into the home: the contribution of the Reformation, a practice attributed to Melanthion and Luther.

16. *Nativité, Égalité, Fraternité:* The French contribution towards the spread of social freedoms and the secularisation of the celebration.

17. *Glad Tidings:* Exchange of greetings: its most recent wave of popularity coinciding with the creation of the postage stamp.

18. *The Christmas Pantomime:* The wondrous spectacle; the Italian influence.

19. *The Plenty:* The nature of Christmas changed by the Industrial Revolution; giving becomes a fashionable habit and the object, bought.

20. *Charity:* The formalisation of charity within institutions as the population increases.

21. *Personage of Christmas:* The Kristkind, the knave, Ruprecht, Swartpiet, the sweep, Jültomte, etc., as the mysterious visitor.

22. *Expectancy:* The letter to Father Christmas, the contribution of the child.

23. *Twelfth Night:* The Northern celebration of Epiphany and the end of Christmas for the year.

24. *The Renewal of Christmas:* The reinvention of a tree decoration, the swaddled tree.

The bright red structure of the exhibition 'Twenty-Four Doors to Christmas', with its green bracing plates, was itself celebration of the 1979 Christmas season.

The exhibition touches several of our oldest themes . . . 'the stuff and decoration of the urban scene' . . . 'signs of occupancy' . . . the collective achievement of quality of place through the quality of the patterns of use. We hope the sense of renewal, enacted through the individual contribution of 'decoration' at Christmas time, will spill over into the rest of the year.

Father and child open a door. PS, 1979.

Three girls open a door. PS, 1979.

Rosemary swag. AS, 1979.

The temporary red framework. *Architect's Journal*.

A+PS with students in Lisbon, 1981.

to do with rightful spheres of influence, space for each to be its own thing . . . ultimately the sense of territory, respect for another's sense of territory, which is not only the ground but also spatial, to do with sense of overlooking, of unbreathed air, blocking of sunlight, and so, shade and shadow . . .

Second Arts Building, University of Bath *(1979–81)*   456

Der Berlinerbaum *(1980)*   468

Christmas ✗ Hogmanay *(1980–81)*   471

Sealink poster. AS.

Interval is to do with our deepest feelings . . . those concerning territory. Without interval, our sense of self gets lost; we lack the space to mark out what is still ourself, our territory. Those tiny physical marks of pawprint, smell, known noises, known light patterns, known safe places, known places of enjoyable risk.

In those places for specialised human behaviour—for example, music making (Arts Barn), absorbing the flavour of the meaning of pictures (National Gallery), the wish to consciously enjoy a sense of 'rus in urbe' (Lützowstrasse, La Villette)—the more critical the control of interval becomes. Is it not so that the closer music comes to reaching our deepest levels of feeling, the more precise its notation of interval?

The Second Arts Building is a new piece woven onto the edge of an existing mat-building . . . the first of a series of tassels that are going to be needed to make that mat's terminating fringe . . . so it can lie there, on its gently sloping green hillside, seemingly complete.

The pattern of planting in the small triangular courts helps stitch this new tassel onto the old mat.

"[Built] a decade later than Robin Hood Gardens, it has the same belief in the efficacy of connective forms, but by means of a more obvious sun-receiving, sun-excluding plan it responds to the changed sensibility of the 1980s with regard to both the conservation of energy and the welcomed presence of varied functions within the built form."

In their structuring by 'ways', these additions—extending the 'ways' of the existing fabric—relate directly to the Sheffield University project of 1953.

Aerial photograph of 'fringe' buildings.

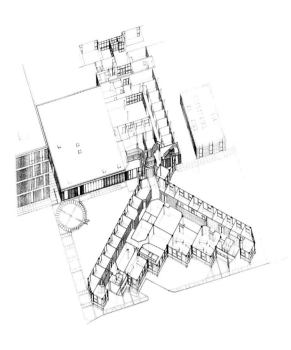

Axonometric of ground floor, showing connection to the ways within the existing buildings. Luiz Neto Breda, Roberto Melai, Amanda Marshall, I.W.

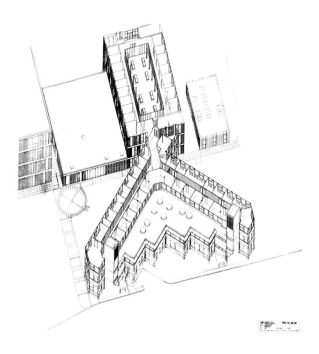

Axonometric of second floor, showing connection to the ways within the existing buildings. Luiz Neto Breda, Amanda Marshall.

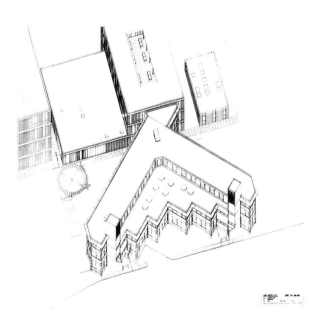

Axonometric view of completed building from the north. Luiz Neto Breda, Roberto Melai.

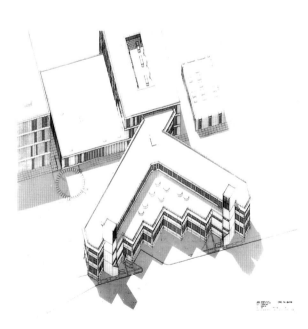

Axonometric of building showing pattern of shadows during the equinox at 11 a.m. Luiz Neto Breda, Roberto Melai.

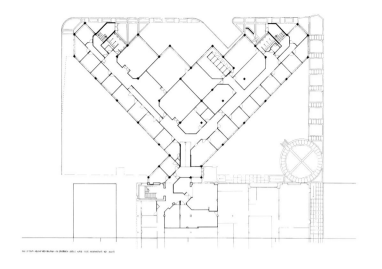

Ground-floor plan. LW, August 1982.

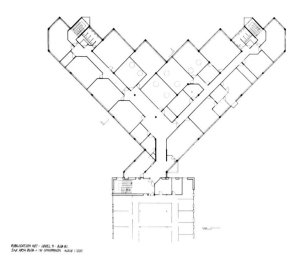

First-floor plan. LW, August 1982.

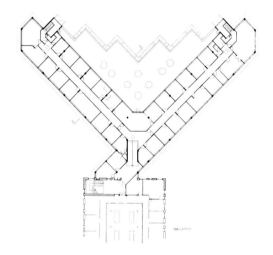

Second-floor plan. LW, August 1982.

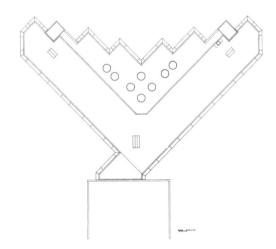

Roof plan. LW.

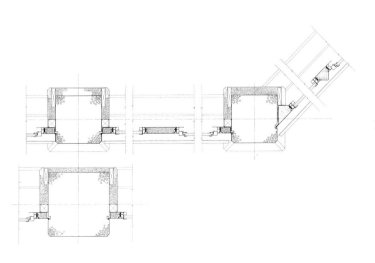

Detail plan of columns and windows. LW, 1981.

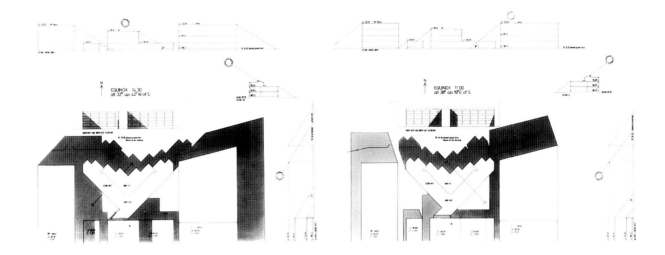

Sun diagrams during the equinox at 11 a.m. and 2:30 p.m.

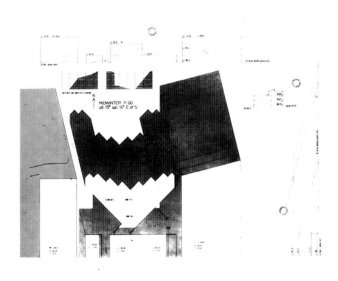

Sun diagram during midwinter at 11 a.m.

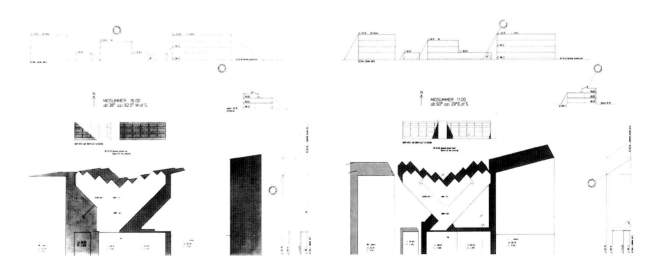

Sun diagrams during midsummer at 11 a.m. and 4 p.m. Amanda Marshall, May 1979.

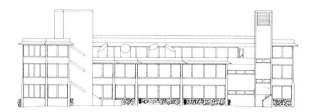

North-east 'true' elevation.

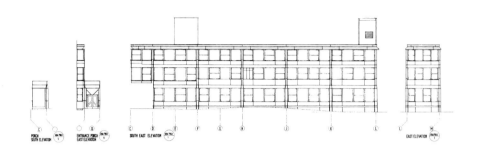

Porch elevations,
south-east and east elevations.
Peter Salter, 1979.

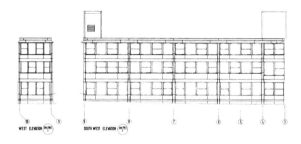

West and south-west elevations.
Peter Salter, 1979.

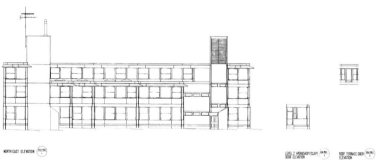

North-east elevations.
Peter Salter, 1979.

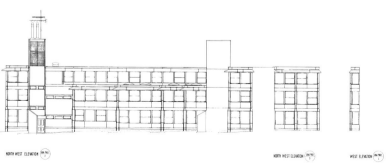

North-west elevations.
Peter Salter, 1979.

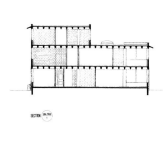  

Three sections.

 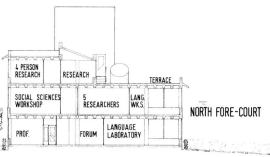

Typical cross section looking north-west.

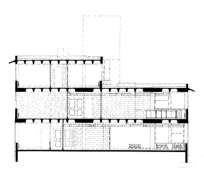

Section through north-west wing looking north-west. LW, August 1982.

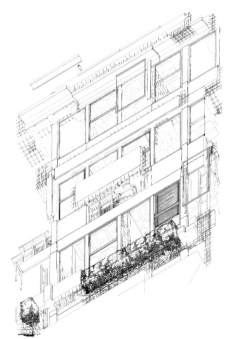

Axonometric of facade assembly. Peter Salter, March 1982.

page 462: North-east entrance. Haig Beck, 1982.
page 463: North-east entrance tower. Haig Beck, 1982.
pages 464–65: North facade.

opposite: North-east corner with services tower. PS, May 1982.

right: General view from the north-west. Haig Beck, 1982.

View from the east.
PS, September 1989.

View from north along axis of fire lane.
PS, July 1982.

Der Berlinerbaum

Summer 1980

AS with Ira Fagin and David Tomlinson of Ove Arup*

The text of August 1980 states: *"When we first went to Berlin—1957—the Tiergarten was a thin growth of self-planted trees . . . over the years we have known it, the trees have gradually grown, but in overall effect they are still quite small, bushy: a shrubbery in the city.*

The Bear is the emblem of Berlin. What would this Bear like to live in? A decent-sized forest tree? . . . Surely it must wish for such a home.

So we make a Berlinerbaum.

What do we know about 'built' trees?

Der Berlinerbaum should be foliate with spray: against days when water-foliage may not be visible we can colour the water. To foliage in light such a gigantic tree, we can use lasers shining up glass fibres. Appropriate to the tree's scale, we can, at branch knuckles, have machines to produce coloured smoke to wreathe the tree in a foliage of self-produced 'clouds'.

By the tree, a ruin . . . (The Aedes Gallery's idea is to celebrate the self-destruction of the Kongress Halle.)

A ruin: what is a ruin? It has to be serene in the quiet of early morning, by moonlight. Its emptiness has to commune with the stars, with the Great Bear of the night sky.

The Kongress Halle was a let-down in the 1950s: without stamina, lacking language potential; not 'man enough' for a Europe whose deep-rooted intellect, honed in its recent war, had been forced to consider the morality of its position. Therefore in this place, the Tiergarten, why not a 'romantic' ruin of our Coventry Cathedral of 1950–51?

A ruin worthy of being overshadowed by a tree.

A place in which the Bear can bury its heart."

* Drawings by Ira Fagin for the Aedes Gallery exhibition.

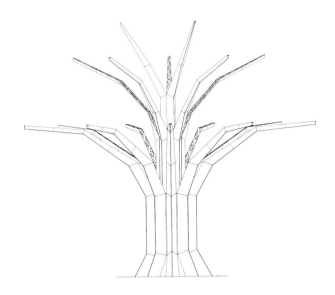

Side elevation and plan. Ira Fagin, summer 1980.

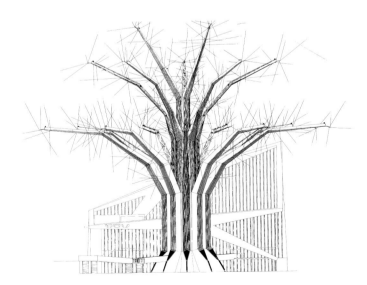

Daytime elevation with lasers, with Cor-Ten 'ruin' behind. (Elevation as if the poor quality Kongress Halle had never existed, and instead, the structurally sound frame of the anti-clastic shell of Coventry had been constructed.) Ira Fagin, summer 1980.

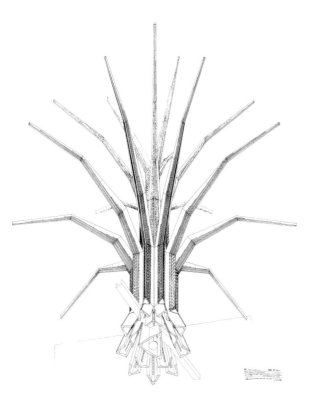

Upwards axonometric. Ira Fagin, summer 1980.

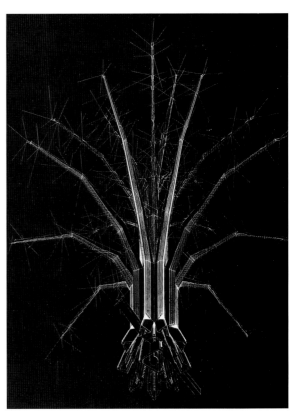

Nighttime upwards axonometric with Cor-Ten laser casings. Ira Fagin, summer 1980.

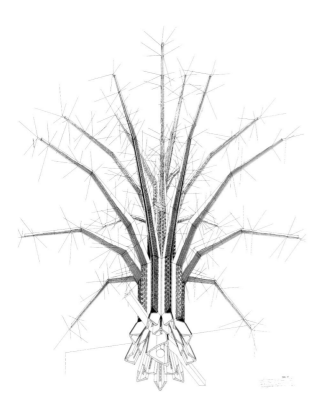

Daytime upwards axonometric with laser beams and Cor-Ten casings. Ira Fagin, summer 1980.

Nighttime upwards axonometric with laser beams and water spray. Ira Fagin, summer 1980.

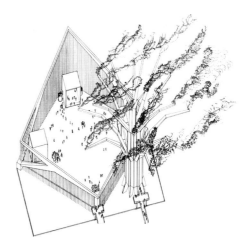

Axonometric of Berlinerbaum, looking north from the Tiergarten, in its setting on the edge of the Spree, with Spree extended into a water-containing tank. Ira Fagin, summer 1980; axonometric of cathedral by Amanda Marshall; floor and trees by AS, September 1980.

Axonometric of Berlinerbaum, with coloured smoke streamers. Ira Fagin; axonometric of cathedral by Amanda Marshall; artificial clouds by AS, 1980.

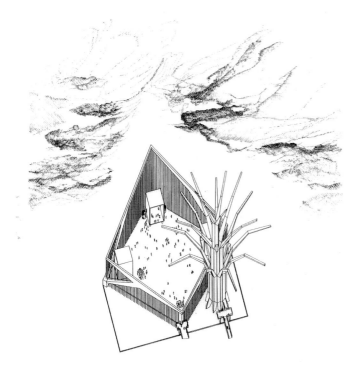

Axonometric of Berlinerbaum with clouds created by its cloud jets. Ira Fagin; axonometric of cathedral by Amanda Marshall; effects by AS, 1980.

Axonometric of artificial rain falling from the Berlinerbaum. Ira Fagin; axonometric of cathedral by Amanda Marshall; effects by AS, 1980.

Christmas ✗ Hogmanay,
Fruit Market Gallery, Edinburgh

"Shimmering silver lattices evoke the magic of expectancy . . . the decoration of nature by frost . . . northern rain in moonlight . . . Scotch mist.

White lattices evoke the countryside clothed in a garb of snow. Black lattice, night, the turn of the year which heralds the great renewal of life.

Among the layers of lattices are displays of the items that traditionally dressed the Scottish Christmas ✗ Hogmanay celebration . . . the purification of the home; the byre, the field, the sea; the assuaging of the spirits and the greetings to absent friends across the water; hospitality and the careful preparation of the food offered; competitive games re-affirming local identity; charitable activities so that no one should 'want' at this season. The architecture of lattices makes a place with a 'lighter touch', even one with a romantic flavour such as we find in gardens of make-believe, the outdoors that makes indoors more inviting.

In the layering of spaces—for the eye penetrates the lattices—we build another sort of place—a receptive place which the visitors are invited to decorate by being there: responsibility is returned to them for quality of use, for style of occupancy. Families become part of the exhibition's celebration."

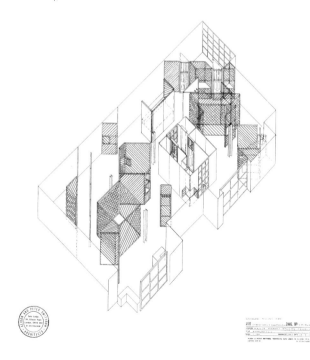

Axonometric of lattices. AS, 24 July 1980.

Photographs of lattices under construction.

top: View of the Guisers cage. Sean Hudson, December 1980.
second from top: View of the white Nature lattice through the black Byre lattice.
AS, December 1980.
above: View through the black Guisers cage beside the white postbox wall. AS, 1980.

A+PS at Cato Lodge, Kensington. Otto Daas, 1981.

12 Sun Acceptance/Energy Containment

and the signals of response . . .

Arts Barn, University of Bath *(1980–81, 1990)*   476

Lützowstrasse Housing *(1980)*   484

Lützowstrasse Apartments for the Elderly *(1980)*   490

Lützowstrasse Youth Centre *(1980)*   491

Lützowstrasse Child-Care Centre *(1980)*   492

National Gallery *(1982)*   496

Parc de la Villette *(1982)*   502

Jubilee sign, Battersea Park: A 'replenishment' image. A+PS, 1977.

Jubilee sign, Battersea Park: Fragments of the 'replenishment' image. A+PS, 1977.

Both sun acceptance and energy containment as themes in our work had early forebears in the Fold Houses of the 'Valley Section'.

In the 'Solar' Pavilion at Upper Lawn, the energy containment is in the 'as found'. Again in the Losey House, the energy containment is in the existing stone structure; the sun acceptance wholly new, opening to the view, like the new butterfly. The Cliff House also is a response to what the site has to offer; being there as base to outdoor activities. Both the Losey and the Cliff houses are the quickly-opened-up/as-easily-closed-down second home. Llangennith Cluster Housing, for a mixture of permanent and transient residents, is an interweaving of houses that have gardens and those whose windowed spaces are disposed to snatch the essence of place in fleeting visits.

In Llangennith, energy containment took the lead over sun acceptance. The style of energy containment requires more of a creative effort than sun acceptance because nothing exists in the language of the Heroic period of Modern architecture; the second generation made little if any contribution to extending the language towards this containment; the language remains largely to be invented. In our work since the 1950s the stress is on the need for immediacy of response and reaction to the changeable weather of England; the almost constant need for full or partial weather protection from one quarter or another, a need that can change several times throughout an afternoon. This ability to snatch enjoyment runs on through the Thames-side apartments: Cherry Garden and Millbank.

The Jubilee signs attempt to graphically announce this phase in which data and even some equipment is readily available to us. Pahlavi selects qualities of the sun to enhance the reading rooms by means of the solar cupolas that are the visored eyes of the domes. Between Pahlavi and Lützowstrasse, the response to the sun theme recedes.

The National Gallery also chose reflected sunlight, weather-live light, in which to view the pictures. Northern Europe involves us inevitably in sun acceptance and energy containment, amelioration of climate, and above all, exclusion of rain.

The Winter Garden, the Snug, and the Cubicle: Exploratory diagrams of variable-density plans. PS, September 1982.

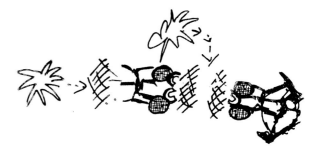

Arts Barn, University of Bath

First scheme: 1980 – May 1981

Shell of auditorium completed May 1990

AS

with Harris and Sunderland

This is an incremental building, a 'scatter' that can be constructed in any order. The Arts Barn accommodation waits on donors since it is a student leisure facility, not a faculty of the university. Its forebears in thinking are the foci to Steilshoop, Hamburg (1961). The functions overlay one another; patterns of use interlace; routes at present in use as paths become covered and part of the building; changes are inevitable. The existing buildings were converted from farm buildings; the Arts Barn project connects them and reaches out to the mound of the 'ski slope' to bury and so protect its rehearsal studio and to hold in the sound volume of pop groups. Existing trees are included, the green is enfolded, and outdoors becomes part of the scatter.

Early drawing showing the scatter plan at ground level of the completed scheme. AS, 1983.

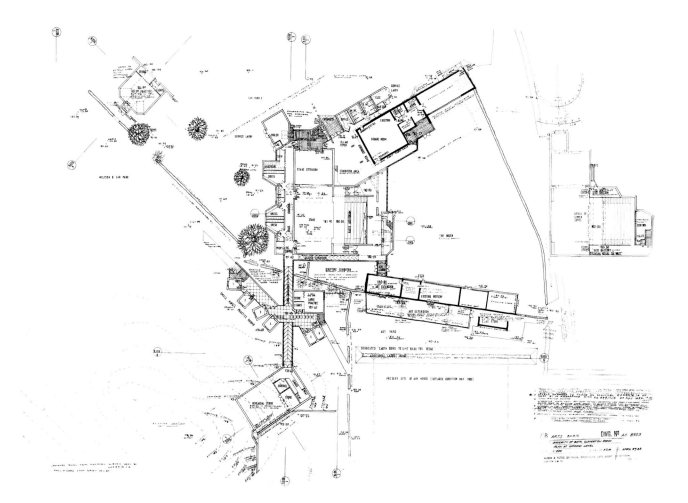

Elevation looking from the green. LW, Suha Bekki, December 1990.

Sections looking south and east.
Ulrika Gynnerstedt, 1990.

Upper and lower floor plans.
Ulrika Gynnerstedt, 1990.

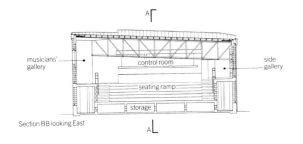

musicians' gallery
control room
side gallery
seating ramp
storage

Section BB looking East

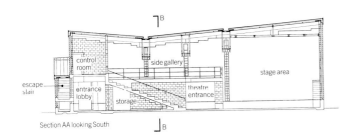

control room
escape stair
entrance lobby
side gallery
storage
theatre entrance
stage area

Section AA looking South

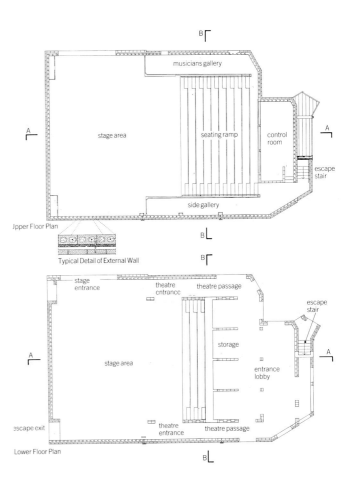

musicians gallery
stage area
seating ramp
control room
escape stair
side gallery

Upper Floor Plan

Typical Detail of External Wall

stage entrance
theatre entrance
theatre passage
escape stair
stage area
storage
entrance lobby
escape exit
theatre entrance
theatre passage

Lower Floor Plan

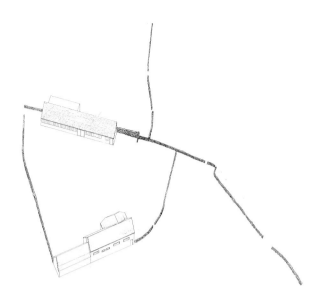

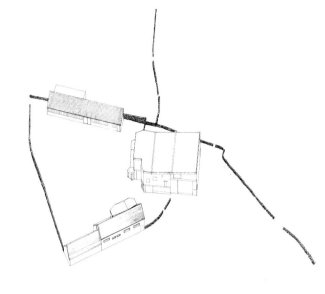

this page and opposite: Series of six axonometrics.

Axonometric drawing of existing buildings.
LW, AS, December 1990.

Axonometric drawing of Phase I with walls.
LW, AS, December 1990.

Axonometric drawing of Phase I: 'The addition of the shell of the
auditorium has an extraordinary effect on the space in front of
Building 6 East . . . it has suddenly the character of a market-place'.
LW on base drawing by others.

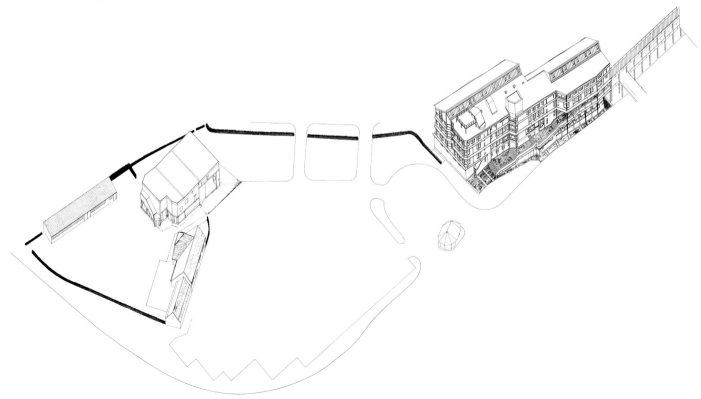

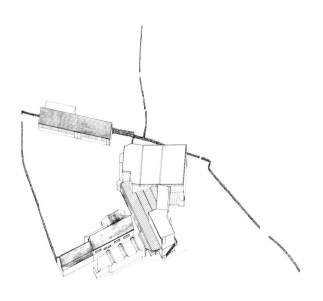

Axonometric drawing of Phases I and II with walls.
LW, AS, December 1990.

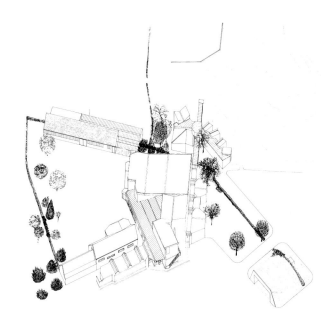

Axonometric drawing of the project upon completion.
LW, AS, December 1990.

Axonometric at fund-raising stage: Identification of new roofs.
AS, 12 October 1983.

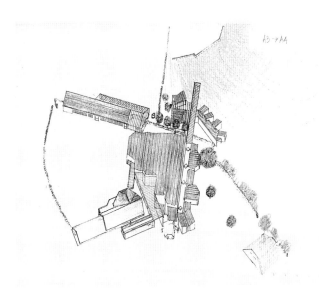

below: The shell of the auditorium seen over the green from the east. PS, April 1991.
opposite top: The auditorium under construction, with the School of Architecture and Building Engineering in the background. Martin Charles, 1990.
opposite bottom: Roof of the Arts Barn with the School of Architecture and Building Engineering behind. PS, March 1990.

Exterior of auditorium, with detail of fixing pads and flashings for the foyer yet to be built. Martin Charles, 1990.

Interior of auditorium, looking west along the side gallery showing the twin-truss lighting gantries. Martin Charles, 1990.

opposite top: Interior of auditorium, showing the twin-truss lighting gantries arranged to also support the roof. Martin Charles, 1990.

opposite bottom: Interior of auditorium, looking south to side gallery with control room at left. Martin Charles, 1990.

Lützowstrasse Housing, Berlin

October – December 1980

AS, assisted by LW

Our apartments along Lützowstrasse are invented in the spirit of Berlin as a garden island. We take up the romantic ideal of Berlin's response to the nature of its site—pines, sand, water.

As the site is just south of the Landwehrkanal, the nearer the buildings approach the canal, the more garden-pavilion in character they become.

To Lützowstrasse, the long, site-protective apartment building has a south-facing 'energy-skin-space' or 'energy-collecting-skin'; to the Landwehrkanal is a north-facing 'energy-conserving-skin'. This is an adventurous extra to the basic, official space requirements.

The cocoon of the apartment bursts open into the south-facing 'energy-skin-space' when spring comes, by the glass doors being folded open; shrinking back when winter returns and the doors are closed.

The south-facing 'energy-skin-space' also acts as protection against street noise from Lützowstrasse. The children's bedrooms rest on the quieter north side facing towards the Tiergarten, their windows openable to where the air is somewhat freer from traffic pollution. On this thick, north-facing 'energy-conserving-skin', external shutters—coloured both sides—can cover all windows at night.

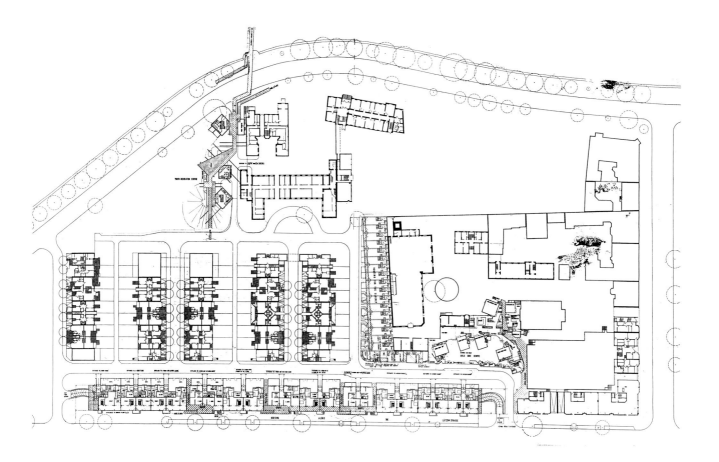

Aerial axonometric in situ of housing for the elderly, with the youth and child-care centres behind, and apartments along Lützowstrasse in front. AS, August 1985.

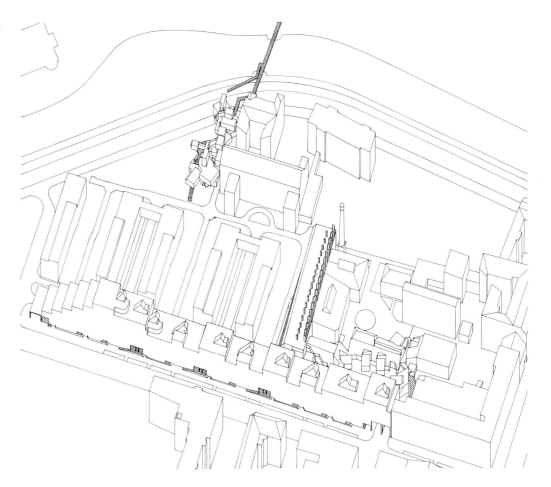

opposite: Site plan. LW, Peter Salter, Amanda Marshall, AS; collaged by PS, 1980.
right: Aerial axonometric showing project buildings only.

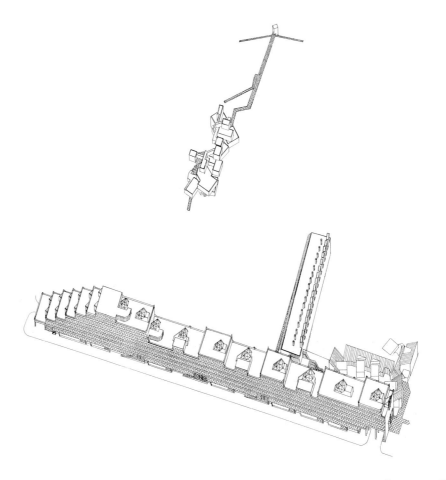

As we consider that a sense of the weather is vital in north-facing rooms, the reveals of all north windows are reflective mirror finish to catch east and west light and bounce it into the rooms; some windows are angled and, where possible, turn corners . . .

The long, narrow site lends itself to the exploration of apartments without lifts . . . a way of progressing up the levels so that the stair and the mechanical means of ascent—the funicular platform—run companionably together; at all times completely surveillable—at a glance—from any point on them. This companionability produces a very special section—not to say structure—and a different ordering to the facades. Roof snorkels beam sunlight down the means of access, apartment doors are close to landings, and within the surveillance path, ample side landings, particular to a pair of apartments, allow space for prams, large toys, and small children's play, which is audible because the landings are on the quiet side towards the Tiergarten.

Axonometric view of apartment from the north showing all
the projecting, light-catching bay windows. Movable insulating
shutters add life to a face much in shade. AS, 1987.

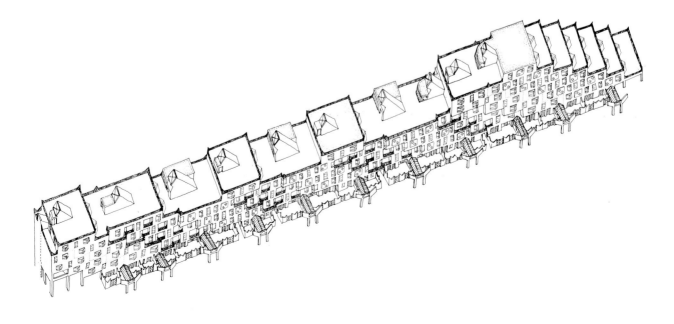

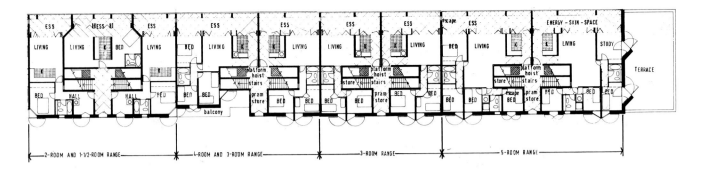

First-floor plans of four townhouse types (compare with diagram of Riverside Apartments, Millbank). LW, 1980.

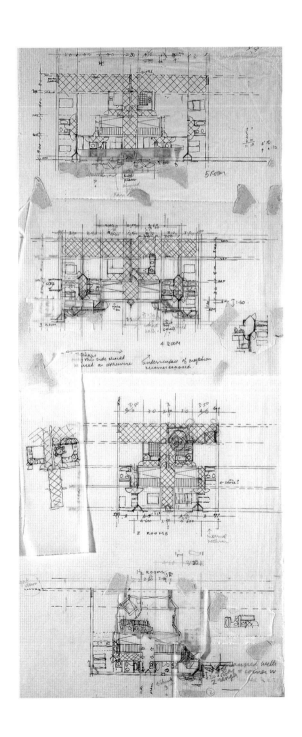

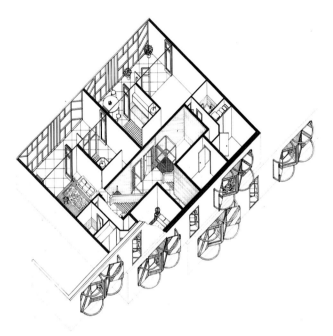

Axonometric of a pair of two-bedroom apartments with facade below and above (partial) to show stacking. The floor and walls have reflective tiles to bounce winter light into the apartments. The north-facing energy-conserving-skin has light-reflecting, coloured, graphic-decorated shutters. AS, summer 1985.

Plans of flat types in formation. AS, 1980.

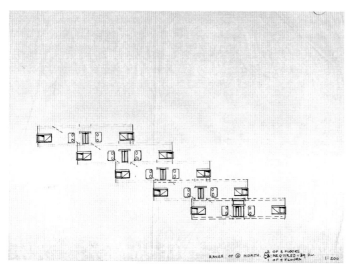

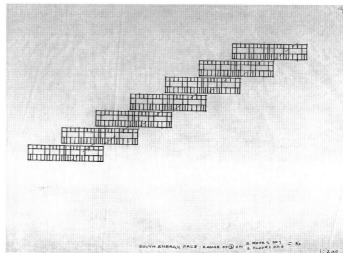

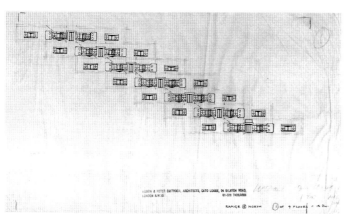

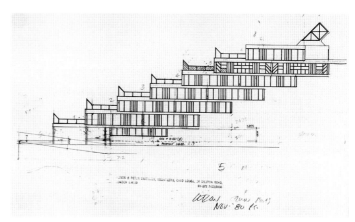

Five section and elevation diagrams exploring slipped stacking of apartment types.

above: Two studies of the north elevation. AS, November 1980.
right: Three studies of the south-facing energy-collecting-skin. PS, November 1980.

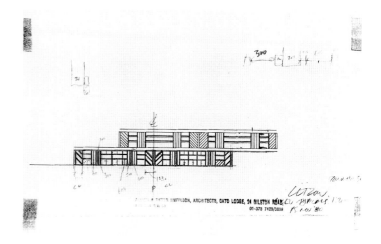

Long section looking
north. AS, LW.

North elevation:
Energy-conserving-skin.

South elevation:
Sun-accepting
energy-collecting-skin.

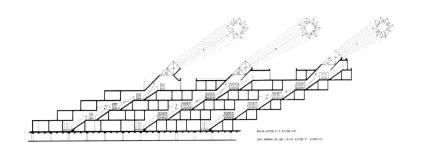

Section showing sunlight
penetration into
surveillance path.

Pulled apart south
elevation, long section,
and north elevation to
show diagonal stacking of
apartment types.

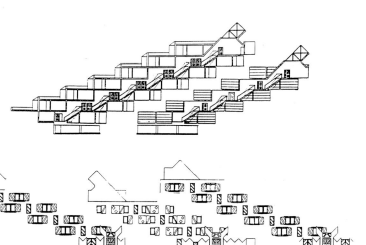

Lützowstrasse Apartments for the Elderly, Berlin

The energy-skin-space and mechanical platform access of the apartments along Lützowstrasse re-occur here. The apartments are half up, half down; close to the ground on first and lower ground floor. Over these apartments for the elderly are separately accessed studios with mezzanine bedrooms. As in the apartments along Lützowstrasse, the western sun is reflected through roof snorkels into the interior; here, to light bathrooms, rear lobbies, and access ways (the programme requirement was to build against the wall of the conserved pumping station).

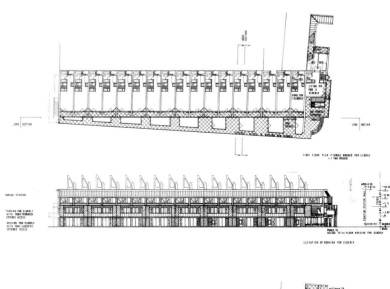

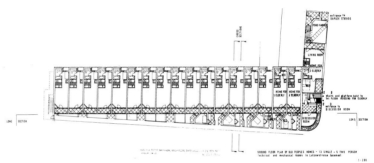

First-floor plan, elevation of foreterrace covered access, ground-floor plan. AS.

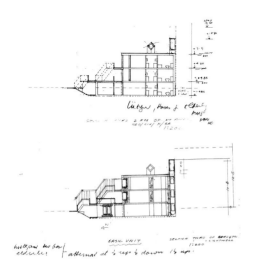

Preliminary sections through two rooms and at access; through light well of basic unit. AS, November 1980.

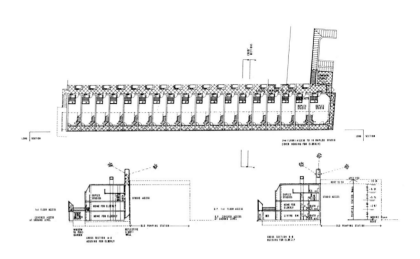

Second-floor plan, cross section through foregarden and light well, cross section through foreterrace covered access.

Lützowstrasse Youth Centre, Berlin

AS, assisted by Amanda Marshall

A cluster of cabins raised in the air with the public walkway through them raised to the level at which the way can 'jump' the traffic route and the canal to connect with the canal-side paths and the south Tiergarten.

The cabin construction is in the manner of the German building industry's site cabins: highly insulated and independently heated on instant demand, as befits this youth centre's pattern of use. Cabin isolation obviates sound transmission; the artificial mound raising the walkway 'contains' the greatest noise source.

Sketch axonometric. Amanda Marshall, November 1980.

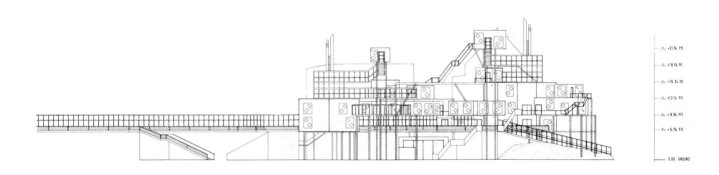

West elevation. Amanda Marshall.

Lützowstrasse Child-Care Centre, Berlin

AS, assisted by Peter Salter

Sheltered from urban noise on its south side by the apartments along Lützowstrasse, the outdoor play area nevertheless receives day-long sun, maintained throughout the winter day by reflection. Each age group finds its own house and ancillary territory under the canopy of the lean-to glazed roof, much as if the houses were separate wood-cutters' cabins under the forest's canopy. The public way passes through the city block within sight of the children's activities, but they remain secure, separated by a change of level.

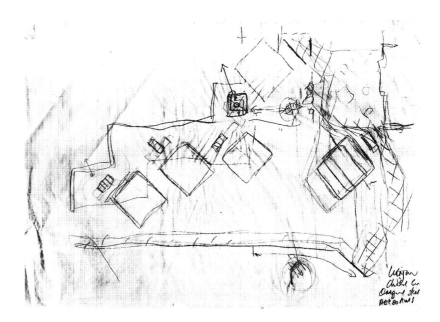

Sketch plan. AS, December 1980.

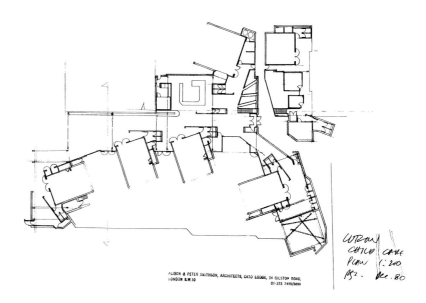

Preliminary plan. Peter Salter, December 1980.

opposite: Roof plan (top right); ground-floor plan (bottom right); sectional elevations (left). Peter Salter.

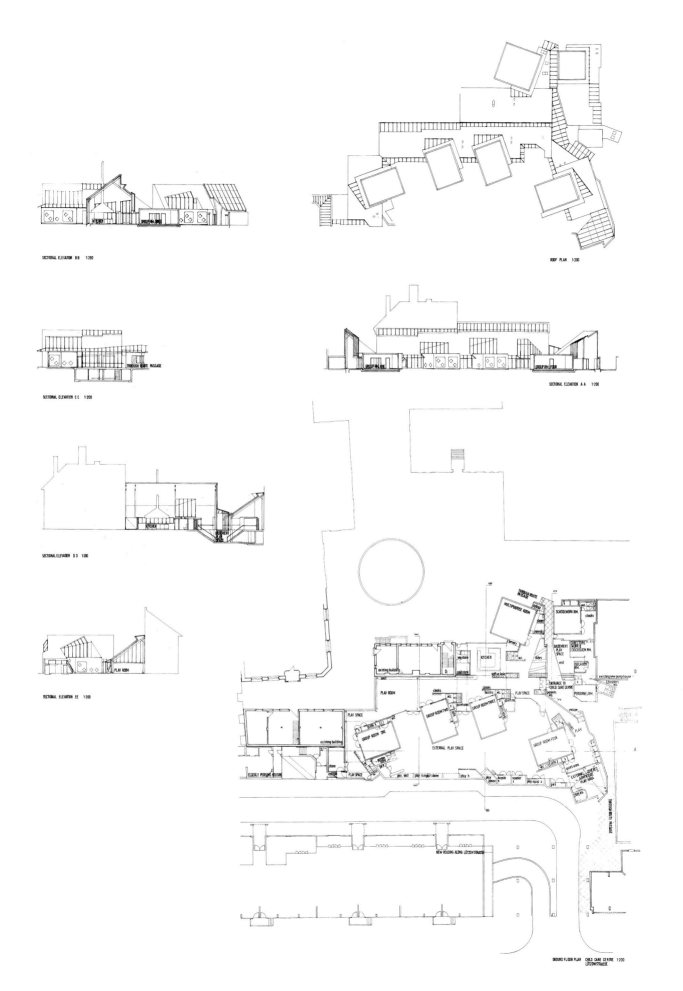

SECTIONAL ELEVATION B B 1:200

ROOF PLAN 1:200

SECTIONAL ELEVATION C C 1:200

SECTIONAL ELEVATION A A 1:200

SECTIONAL ELEVATION D D 1:200

SECTIONAL ELEVATION E E 1:200

GROUND FLOOR PLAN CHILD CARE CENTRE 1:200
LÜTZOWSTRASSE

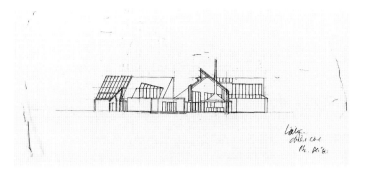

Preliminary elevation. Peter Salter, December 1980.

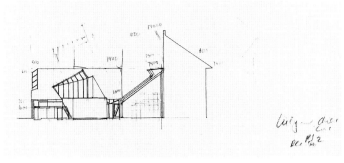

Preliminary section. Peter Salter, December 1980.

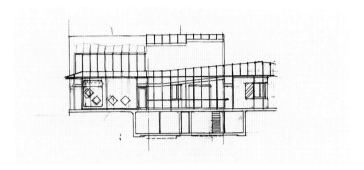

Preliminary section. Peter Salter, December 1980.

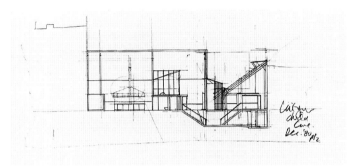

Preliminary section. Peter Salter, December 1980.

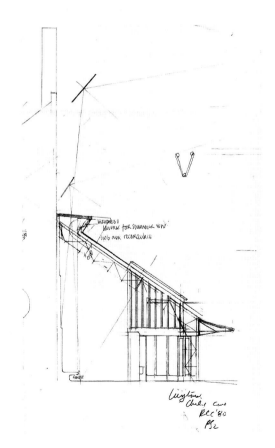

Preliminary section through insulated louvers for
summer ventilation. Peter Salter, December 1980.

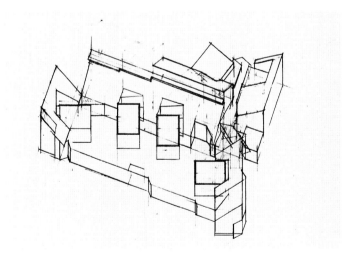

Preliminary axonometric. Peter Salter, December 1980.

Axonometric aerial view of interior spaces and yard.
Pilar Gonzalez Herraiz Ling, December 1985.

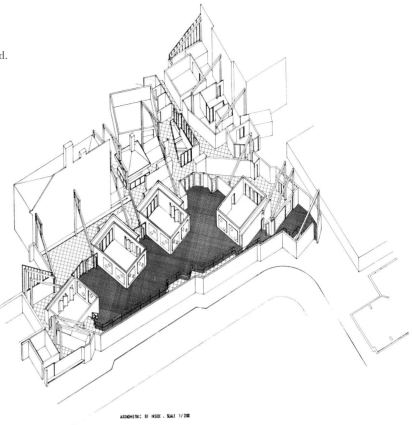

AXONOMETRIC OF INSIDE - SCALE 1/200

Axonometric aerial view of roofs with playground shaded.
Pilar Gonzalez Herraiz Ling, December 1985.

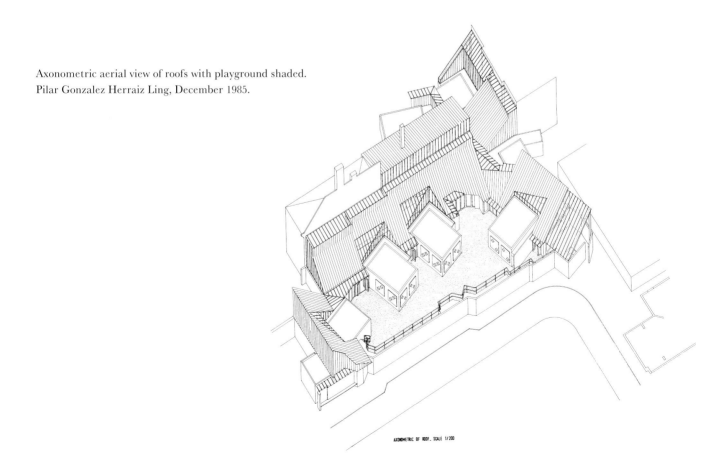

AXONOMETRIC OF ROOF - SCALE 1/200

National Gallery, Pall Mall East, London

January – April 1982

A+PS, assisted by LW

with Ove Arup and Partners

This extension to the National Gallery is for its collection of Renaissance paintings . . . we said at the time: *"A characteristic of Renaissance paintings is that the picture space combines with the real space to include the spectator; in successful galleries, pictures, gallery spaces, views to the outside become a single experience."*

It was, therefore, our intention that visitors be conscious of the outside by the changes of light quality and through glimpses of the sky—without compromising the conservation aspect of light control—and that there should be places off the gallery where they can stretch their eyes and fix their experience with views out over the everyday.

The face of the new extension is kept back from the line of Wilkins' National Gallery. The existing north-to-south pedestrian way, with its lawn and line of trees, acts as the releasant in the design, and its nature is extended under the southern portico of the new gallery.

The new extension is entered by crossing a bridge over this pedestrian path from the old gallery, with views down to the lawn and line of trees, arriving in the naturally lit loggia running the entire length of the new gallery. Access to the light-controlled gallery spaces is from this loggia.

Italian paintings from the 1400s are seen at their best in muted natural light in spaces with white walls and grey stone terminations. Concerning this natural light, the services engineer wrote: *"Natural light will enter the gallery through partially glazed domes; the shape and orientation of the glazed portions will relate to the sun's path in such a way as to prevent direct sunlight from penetrating farther into the gallery than the bottom of the light transfer zone. The natural light entering the gallery space will thus consist of diffuse sky light and reflected sunlight.*

Direct sunlight incident on the walls of the transfer zone will give an indication of external weather conditions.

The level of natural light within the gallery will be maintained at the desired level by adjustment vertically of the conical restrictors within the transfer zone domes."

Exterior perspective: View from Trafalgar Square. Ronald Simpson, 1982.

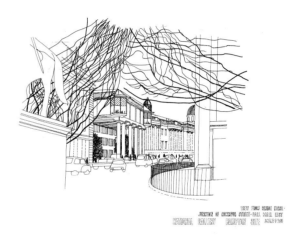

Exterior perspective: View from pedestrian island in Pall Mall East. Ronald Simpson, 1982.

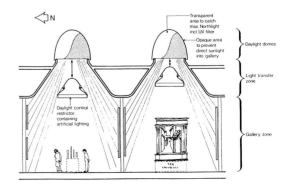

Dome detail showing daylighting control in gallery areas. A+PS with Ove Arup.

Roof shadow plan.
LW, 1982.

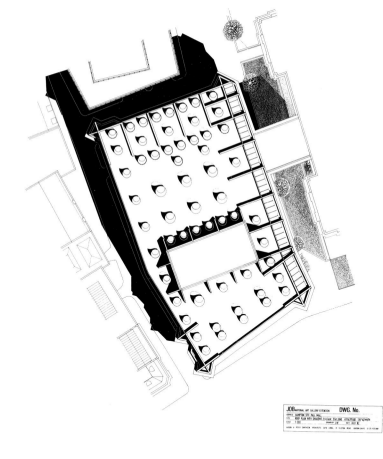

Plans at gallery and roof
level with axonometric
showing hanging of paint-
ings. A+PS, LW, 1982.

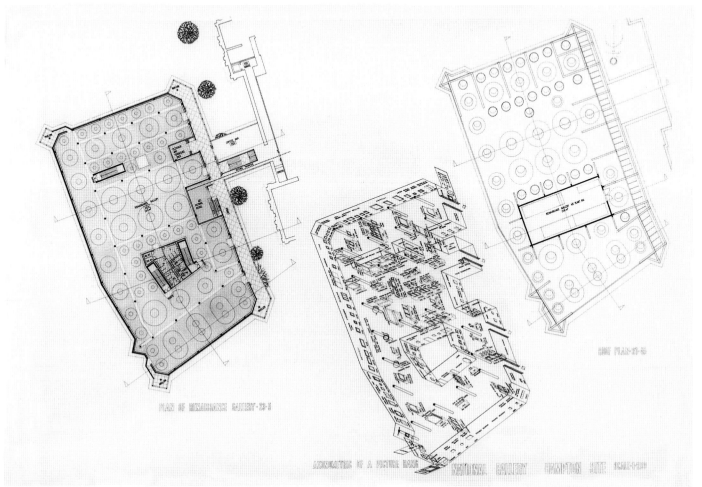

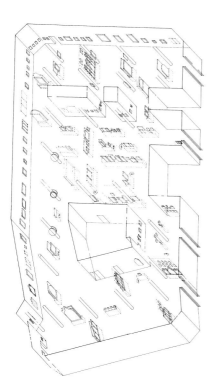

Simplified axonometric showing hanging of paintings. AS, 1982.

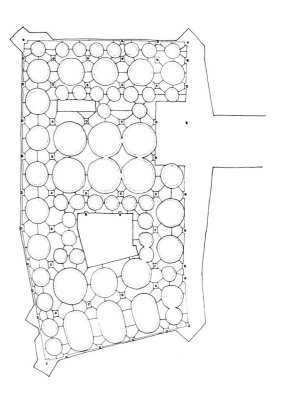

Diagram of possible ceiling-joint plan. Soft edge of light domes shown dotted. (Centre shields to light-diffusing cupolas not shown.) AS, winter 1985–86.

opposite top: Preliminary drawing for interior perspective series. Louisa Hutton, 1984.
opposite bottom: Photomontage of gallery. Louisa Hutton, LW; collage by PS, 1984–89.
right: Axonometric of revised project with roof removed. LW.

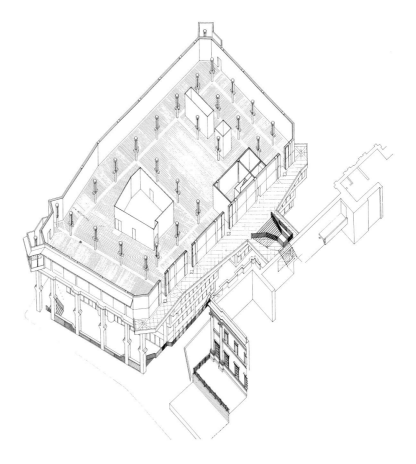

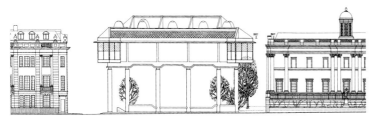

ELEVATION TO PALL MALL EAST

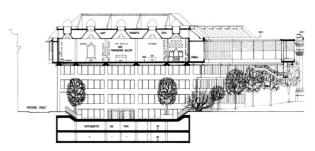

WEST-EAST SECTION THROUGH PORTICO
NATIONAL GALLERY SIDE PEELED AWAY TO SHOW BRIDGE OVER LAWN

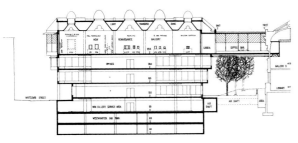

WEST-EAST SECTION THROUGH BRIDGE

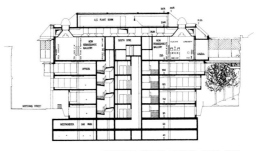

WEST-EAST SECTION THROUGH SOUTH CORE

NATIONAL GALLERY   HAMPTON SITE SCALE 1:200

Front elevation to Pall Mall East (top left); section through entrance portico with recessed elevation (top right); west-east section through gallery (bottom left); west-east section through core (bottom right). A+PS, LW, Laura Grandini, 1982.

Lettered parapet elevation series (idea not submitted in competition, but eventually preferred).

Lettered version elevation to Pall Mall East. AS on base drawing by PS and Laura Grandini, 1982.

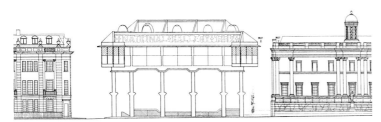

ELEVATION TO PALL MALL EAST

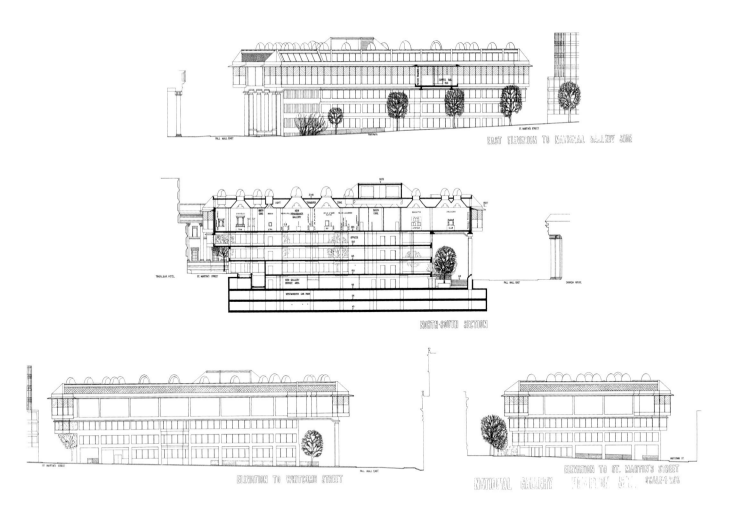

Elevations and section: Elevation to side of National Gallery (top); north-south long section (middle); two elevations to Whitcomb Street and St. Martin's Street (bottom). Materials: Spandrels and columns of roach-bed Portland stone; stairs and loggia floor of shelly whitbed; frames, mullions, balusters, and lattices in metallic-powder-finish aluminium. A+PS, LW, Laura Grandini, 1982.

Lettered version elevation to Whitcomb Street.
AS on base drawing by PS, 1982.

Lettered version elevation to St. Martin's Street.
AS on base drawing by PS, 1982.

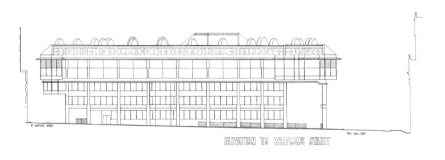

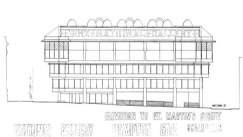

Parc de la Villette, Paris*

Autumn – Winter 1982

AS, advised by Bill Bowen on plants and by
Peter Thoday on greenhouses and grasses

Within the protection of its acoustic shield the park is very much a dense mat; a growing tapestry of planting, with the accommodation for indoor activities withdrawn into the twenty-four-metre-high undercroft of the acoustic shield. The music city is earth-protected under the structures of the artificial Butte de Pantin.

High masts make the north and south gates respectively 'Pines' and 'Palms'.

The enormous park-marker, l'Arbre de la Villette, stands beside the Rond-Point des Caneaux, visible from all nearby quais as framework for fire, light, and water spectacles on festive occasions.

A built hillock raises the plateaus of the picnic islands into the light of early mornings and evenings to attract fishermen. The hillock's southern pooled terraces—Paris Pamukale—are warmed for an extended open-air season of family bathing. The hillock's undercroft, edged by the Grotto Way, with its display of ferns, contains fish tanks for the Discovery of Fish and the trout farm to stock the water around the picnic islands.

* For context see *The Charged Void: Urbanism.*

above: Diagram of the proposed park layout.
left: Claude Monet (1840–1926), *La Grenouillère.* Collection Metropolitan Museum of Art, New York.

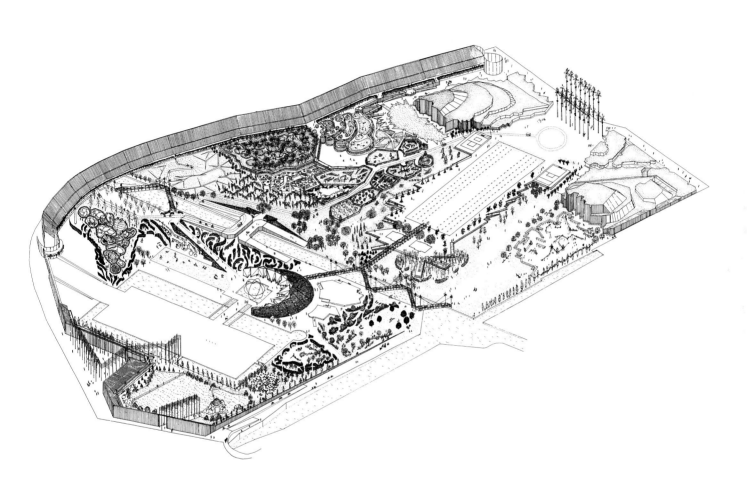

Axonometric view from north-west: Porte des Pins on Avenue Corantin Cariou, looking towards Porte des Palmes on Avenue Jean Jaures with the acoustic shield running along the east flank. LW, AS, 1992–93.

Ten diagrams. AS, 1982.

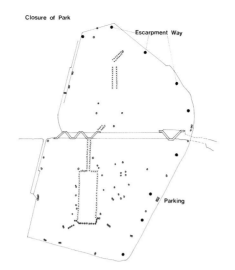

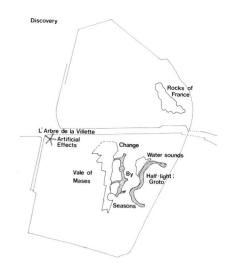

Closure of park.

Discovery.

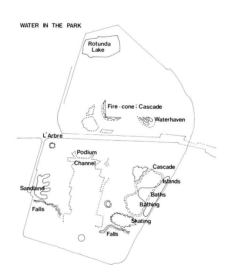

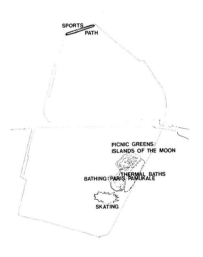

Water in the park.

Picnic greens.

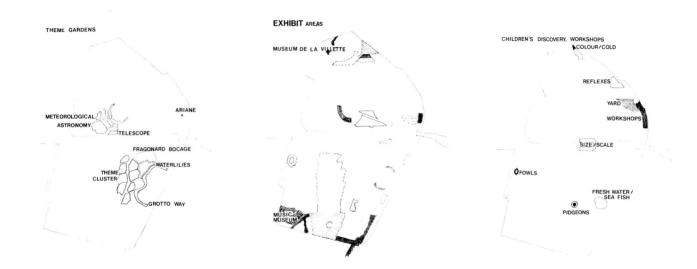

Theme gardens.

Exhibit areas.

Children's Discovery, workshops.

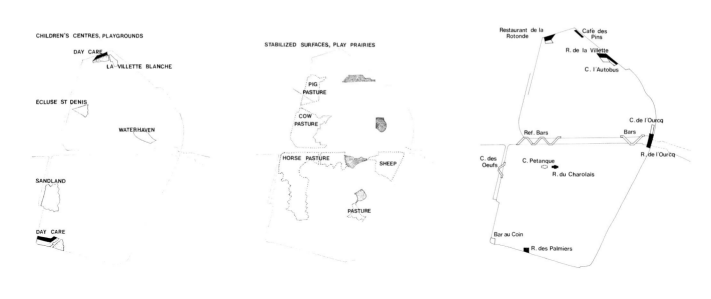

Children's centres, playgrounds.

Stabilised surfaces, play prairies.

Eating places.

Perspective of the western face of the Butte de Pantin whose facets and serrated surface crevices guide falling water. The butte edges the ramp, lined with palm trees, which rises to the Place des Palmiers du Sud. AS, 30 January 1984.

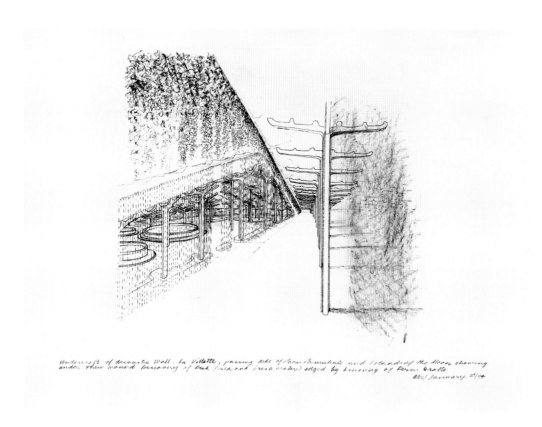

Perspective of the undercroft of the acoustic shield as it passes the side of the Mound of Pools and Islands of the Moon. Occupying the mound's undercroft and seen through falling water is the Discovery of Fish, skirted by the fern grotto, whose tanks are lit by clerestories from above. AS, 25 January 1984.

Grotto of Discovery of Ferns encircling undercroft of Island of the Moon and ...

Perspective of walkway at the grotto of the Discovery of Ferns which encircles the undercroft of the Discovery of Fish and from which the park is seen through water falling from the pools overhead. AS, 18 January 1984.

La Villette.
Islands of the moon picnic grounds under cherry almond, pear, apple blossom of 1982.
AWS, January 1984

Perspective of hillock of pools at the picnic islands. Each island can be rented for picnic groups or for fishing in the gently flowing water. AS, 18 January 1984.

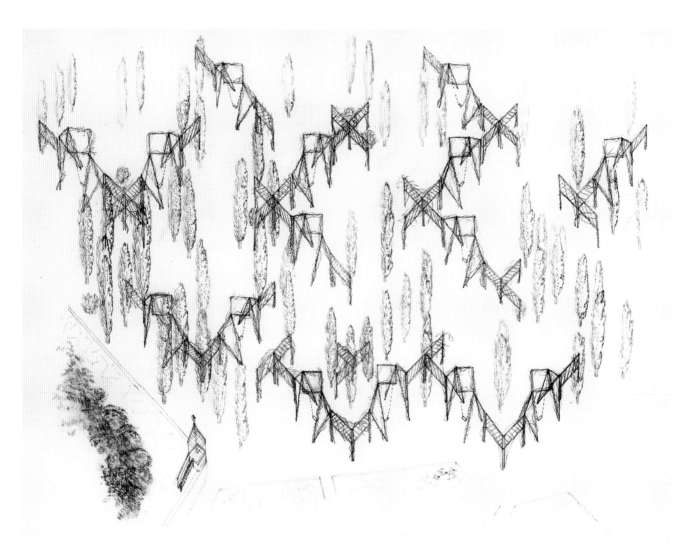

Fragonard Bocage: Axonometric of latticed 'swing frames' supporting climbing plants. Layout punctuated by Lombardy poplars, which also support climbing roses. AS, September 1982.

Fragonard Bocage: Swings and climbing roses on trellis; a broken geometrical layout accented with Lombardy poplars. AS, September 1982.

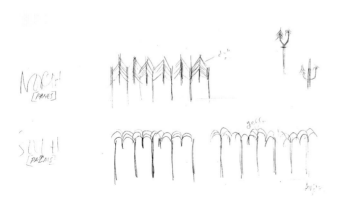

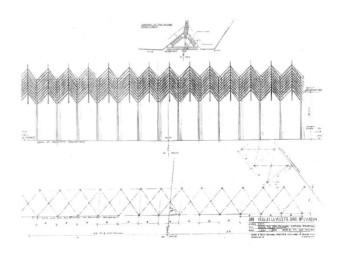

Four ideograms for entrance screens: Pines (north gate), palms (south gate), and park furniture. PS, August 1982.

Porte des Pins: Solution to the northern oblique entrance from the Boulevard Macdonald, where one finds the autobus terminus and metro. PS, 9 October 1982.

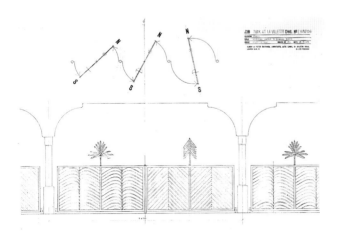

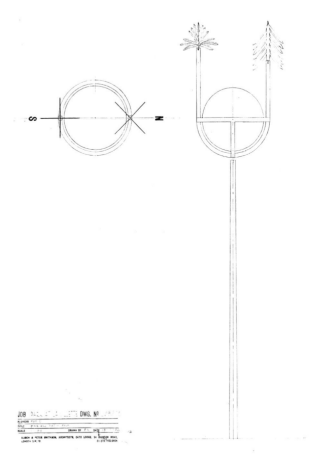

above: Closure gates, with pine and palm motif, in position around the Grande Halle; a part of the park furniture series. PS, 18 September 1982.
right: Pine and palm lamp-post, typical item of park furniture. 'To the visitor, Paris is a city of ironwork'. PS, 18 September 1982.

A+PS against net curtains to French windows of meeting room at Gilston Road. Paul Teverine, August 1984.

13 Sensibility to Car Movement

car movement has changed our inherited view of the landscapes and cities of Europe . . .

Communal Houses on Two Sites, Urban and Rural, Delft *(1982–83)*   514

Second Polytechnic, Hong Kong *(1982)*   516

Porta Camollia, Siena *(1983)*   517

School of Architecture and Building Engineering, University of Bath *(1982–88)*   518

Twenty-First-Century Tenement, Maryhill *(1984)*   536

The car passenger's view of the landscape. AS, from *AS in DS* (Delft: Delft University Press, c. 1983).

In Europe there have been two generations for whom movement by car has been a daily experience for work and for pleasure. Their general sensibility with regard to the fabric of the city and towards the landscape has changed. Now, we begin to make things differently, as well as experience them differently.

The projects we have made to do with 'gates' in Italian towns are a sign of this; made as an intuitive response, rather than the intellectual take on car and pedestrian movement seen at Golden Lane or Berlin Hauptstadt in the 1950s. Colleges' Gate, Colleges' Path, and the Distance Stones are an architect-user's response to many-times-a-day movement between residence outside the walls and work inside the walls. The insights gained in making, then reworking, these designs for a new gate near the Porta Valbona in Urbino over four years gave the start point for the adjustments to the public space just inside the Porta Camollia in Siena.

When one lives within the walls, the passing and re-passing around them by car that the pedestrianisation of a walled city involves allows slow ingestion of its gates.

Communal Houses on Two Sites,
Urban and Rural, Delft

September 1982 – January 1983

AS

Two sites: one in Delft, one outside. In both cases, the Communal House should be honest about its function so that its lifestyle has a chance to evolve.

On the urban site, a new 'wood' is constructed alongside an existing urban wilderness of fully mature trees: by standing tall, no space is removed from Delft; those who habitually pass through from one street to the next can still do so; instead, something of a 'grove' is offered to the community; a place where curiosity in the new 'family' can be pleasantly satisfied. High in the air, the windows have deep sills to protect the surrounding houses from any sense of overlooking; encapsuled in this secret place above Delft, the communal house receives the sun.

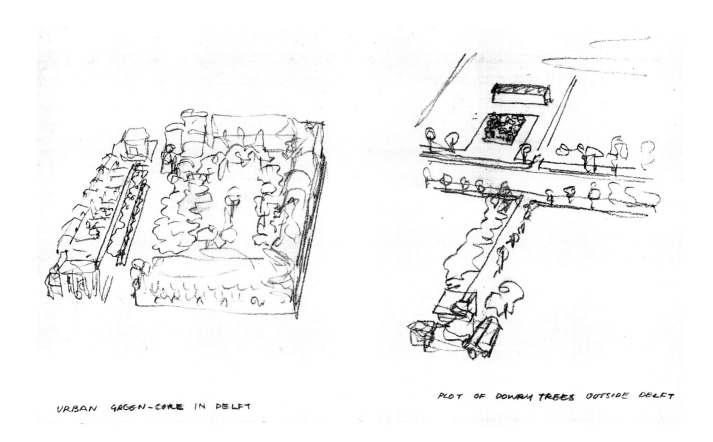

URBAN GREEN-CORE IN DELFT

PLOT OF DOWRM TREES OUTSIDE DELFT

Diagram of two sites in Delft beside a town wood; here, the inhabitants of the Communal House do not seem to be watching the private life in the surrounding houses but looking over and beyond at the roofs of Delft. AS.

The rural site is beside a 'farmed' wood; the Communal House is again a new 'wood'; each cell has a downward-looking window into the water, as well as a view over the farmland through sun-accepting windows.

Personal experience of living in a house and garden overlooked by many houses and many eyes and where one is nevertheless curiously undisturbed leads one to believe that a sense of privacy, or of being robbed of it, is circumstantial, depending on both the arrangement and the customs of inhabitants.

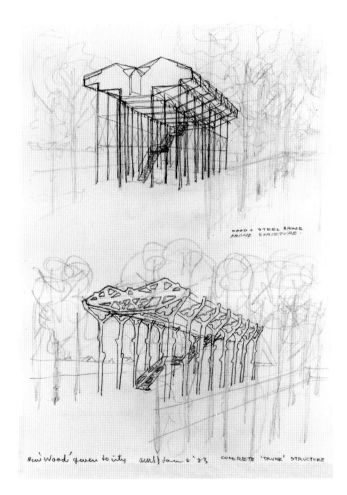

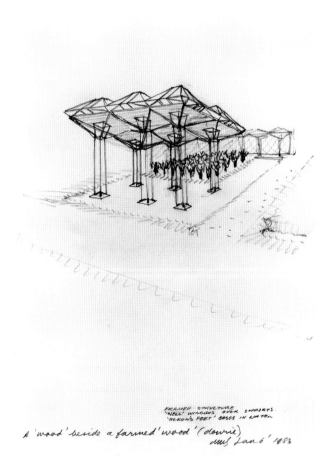

Urban site, old Delft. Wood and steel brace-frame structure and concrete 'trunk' structure, adjacent to a town wood. AS.

Rural site, new Delft. Wood structure at the edge of the greenbelt outside Delft. The Communal House has to tread lightly the margin between the inhabited and the farmed. AS.

A verandah-accessed 'split-mat' building for the appreciation of a ravine. A ravine that is one of the ten remaining open sites in its area on the upper slopes of Hong Kong.

The diagrams indicate a building that respects the ravine's qualities, makes possible enjoyment of its microclimate, its secretness, the accessibility of its rim.

'Split feather' ideogram. (See *The Charged Void: Urbanism* for sketch scheme of insertion without destruction of the valley.) AS.

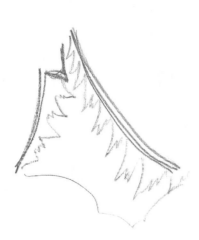

The 'Split feather'
Ideogram of 2nd Polytechnic
Hong Kong

Nov '82
AS

Porta Camollia, Siena

In Siena a small open space at the end of the old main street leading towards Florence—the Via Camollia—seemed to present a typical space-left-over between traffic reorganisation, commune-provided social facilities (here, the market), and the houses and work places of the Contrada (neighbourhood), leaving the citizens of the Contrada of the Istrici (Hedgehogs) with a sense of unease about their territory.*

The intervention decided upon was minimal; focussed on the re-ordering of the space around the small covered market, giving it a full 'community' rather than a neighbourhood feel.

* In the years 1976–81 and 1991–93 in Urbino and 1982–90 in Siena, the International Laboratory of Architecture and Urban Design attempted to identify situations where an architectural intervention could be helpful to the 'fabric'—the fabric being of persons, institutions, and built places.

Axonometric of market. (See *The Charged Void: Urbanism* for urban analysis and other images.) PS.

School of Architecture and Building Engineering, Building 6 East, University of Bath

1982 – 1988

PS

This is a building for many disparate users and uses. Their needs have been resolved by what we are beginning to call a 'conglomerate ordering'—that is, an ordering of the building so that those means of finding one's way, of sensing what lies where, are taken from the old indicators . . . the sense of density of both built fabric and its occupation . . . the position of the sun . . . the way the land falls outside . . . the position of the principal ways inside.

As an example in Building 6 East, the windows in the access ways consciously allow 'fixes' onto features of the landscape outside. These windows span from column to column, from seat height to ceiling, whereas the windows in the enclosed rooms are 'holes in walls'.* Thus, we can also read the running of the internal ways from the outside.

Photographing Building 6 East, one became aware of the likeness of the western gable end to Sugden House.

* We have always believed we were better at column-to-column windows than at hole-in-wall windows.

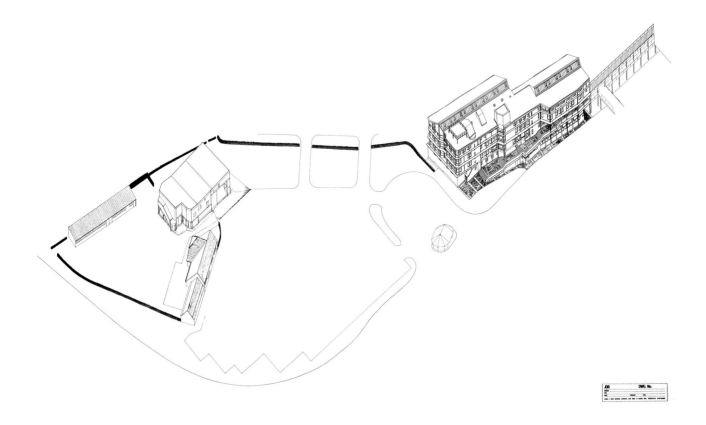

The bus turnaround, car-park, information kiosk, and Arts Barn auditorium shell make a forecourt to Building 6 East and an entry point to the university. IW, 1991.

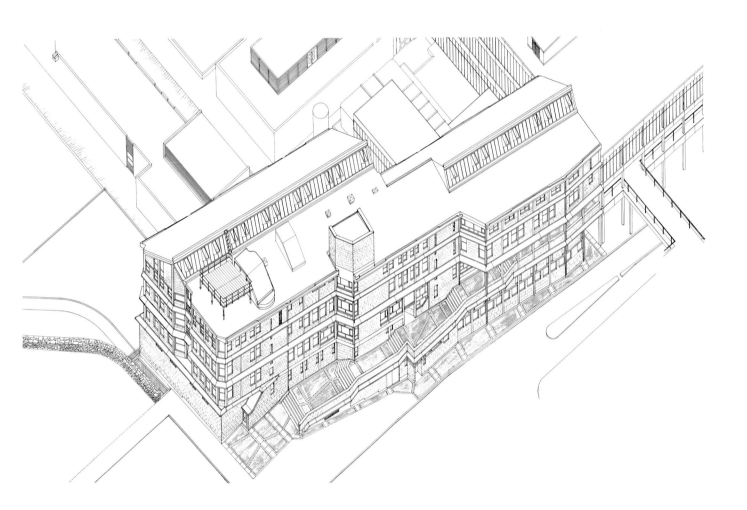

Axonometric of building in context. Various hands; revised August 1988.

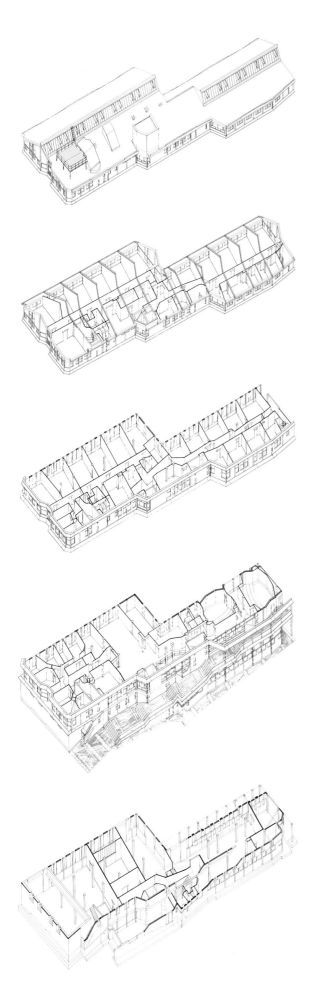

Five axonometrics. Various hands; revised September 1988.

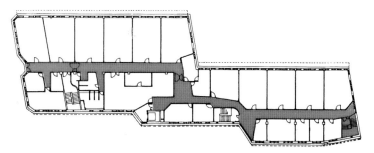

LEVEL 4

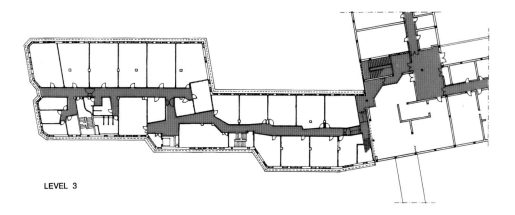

LEVEL 3

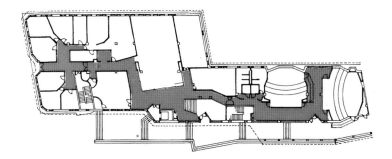

LEVEL 2

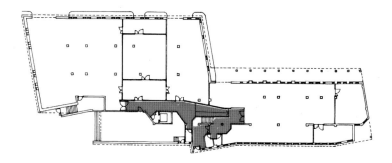

LEVEL 1

Diagrams of all levels with internal perceived pathways shaded. Ulrika Gynnerstedt, 1991.

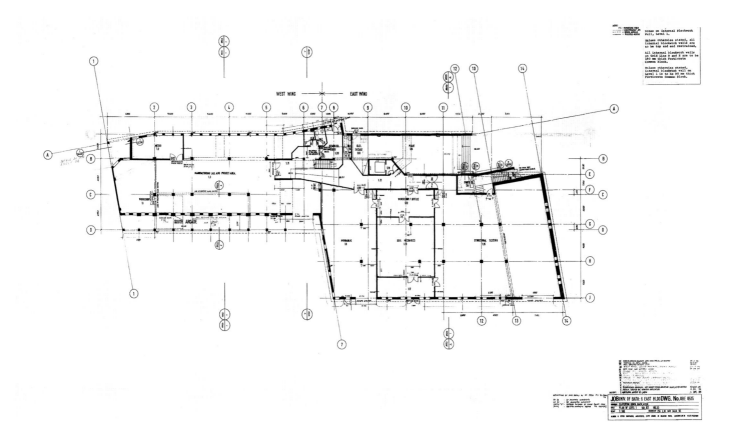

Level 1 plan.

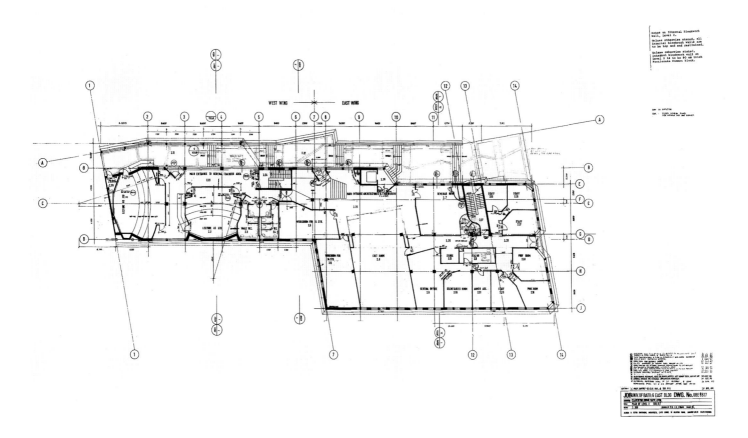

Level 2 plan.

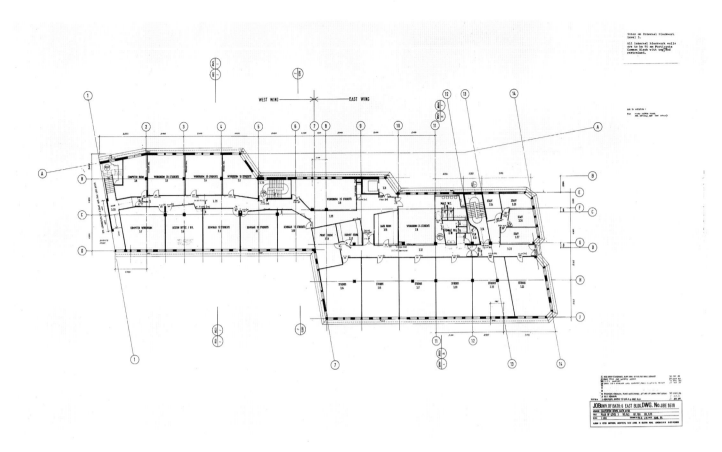

Level 3 plan.

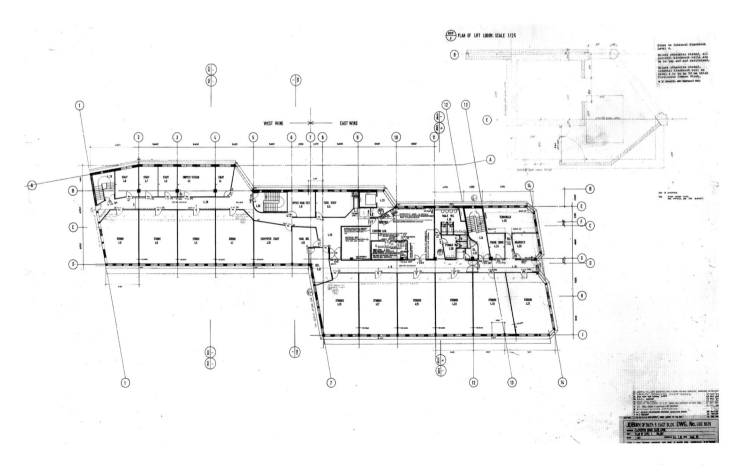

Level 4 plan.

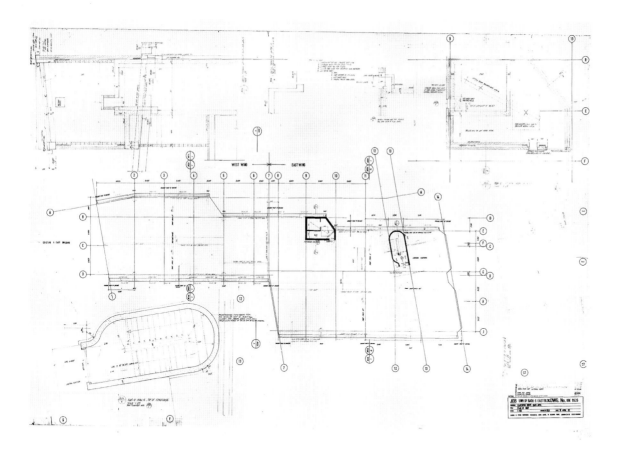

Roof plan.

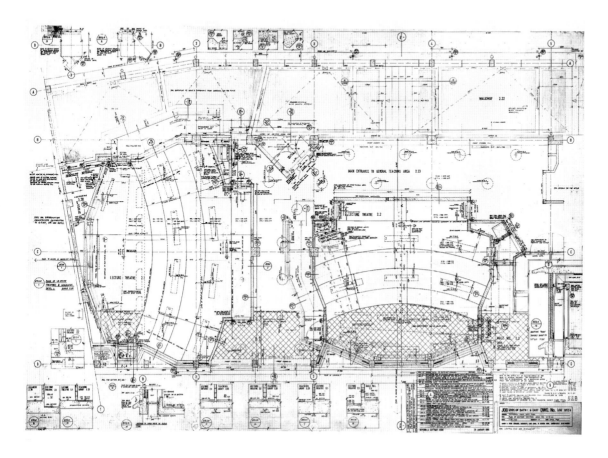

Plans and details of lecture theatres. Louisa Hutton, 1985.

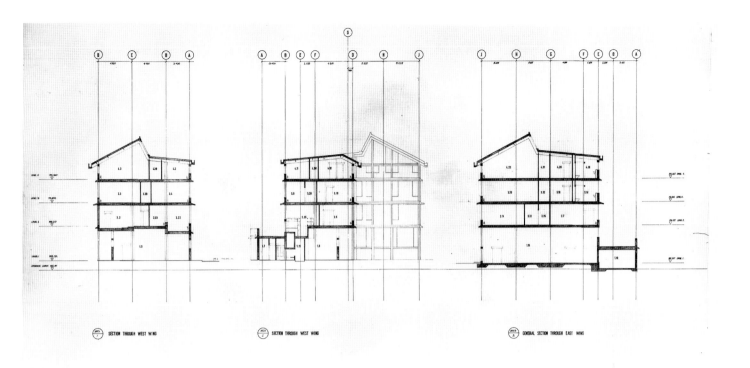

North-south sections.

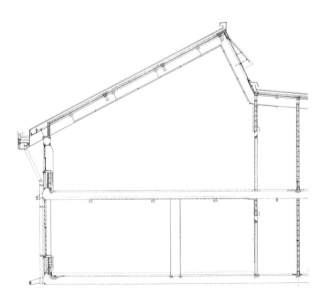

Detail section through Levels 3 and 4 of east wing, looking west.
LW, 1988.

View from Level 4 looking south into the university
grounds. PS, 1988.

page 526: The north facade pushing forwards and opening up
to receive the walkway . . . the forms bound together by the
running cornices and string-courses. Martin Charles, 1988.
page 527: Walkway from the bus-stop up to the campus
main parade. The walkway widens to scoop in the students.
Service areas lie beneath it. Martin Charles, 1988.

opposite: The north face, showing the ascent of the walkway. Martin Charles, 1988.

above: Foot of walkway up to campus main parade level. Martin Charles, 1988.

page 530, top: Walkway from the bus-stop as it passes under the building. Martin Charles, 1988.

page 530, bottom: The 'front door for visitors' . . . the formal entrance to the School of Architecture and Building Engineering . . . one of the many ways in and through that are the natural consequence of existing as part of a mat-building. Martin Charles, 1988.

page 531, top: Level 4 central corridor, showing power, lighting, and telephone wiring. Points of exit and entry from the corridors are understated. Doors are located at a small widening, or at a turn, to mark, but not interrupt, the running of the ways. The main tubes and wires follow along these ways, running, bending, moving up and down, turning, winding with the going. Like the running cornices on the outside, the running tubes and wires on the inside help hold together the conglomerate form. Martin Charles, 1988.

page 531, bottom: Top-floor studio with views down to the landscape. Martin Charles, 1988.

pages 532: South-west corner of the building, level 4 studio. Martin Charles, 1988.

pages 533: South-east corner of the building, level 4 studio. Martin Charles, 1988.

above: Level 4 studio, south-west corner of the building—
all Level 4 studios are opened up to let the sky in.
Martin Charles, 1988.
opposite: The underside of the eaves—the so-called
breathing gutter. Martin Charles, 1988.

Twenty-First-Century Tenement, Maryhill, Glasgow

April – June 1984

AS, assisted by Louisa Hutton

Three 'Glasgow' corners define the territory, acting as terminals to gable ends and extending the traditional urban form of Maryhill.

The bay-windowed, ashlar language of Glasgow is furthered in the energy-containing faces . . . faceted, light reflective. The Glaswegian exterior/interior dialogue between cast-iron balcony openwork and lace-edge window blinds becomes renewed in the language of sun acceptance.

To maintain the dialogue with the air that Glasgow's chimneys began, solar roses turn to face the sun . . . their masts mounted on bearings that can accept torque, each rose motored every fifteen minutes from a controlling clock, so that throughout twenty-four hours, these rose masts signal the twenty-first century.

The programme used to further those fresh attitudes to inhabitation is found in the 'Solar' Pavilion at Upper Lawn and continually explored . . . the Yellow House, Lützowstrasse, Millbank.

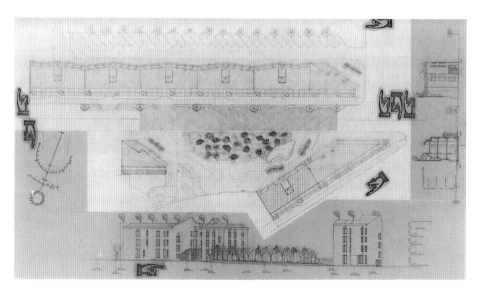

Site plan. AS, LW.

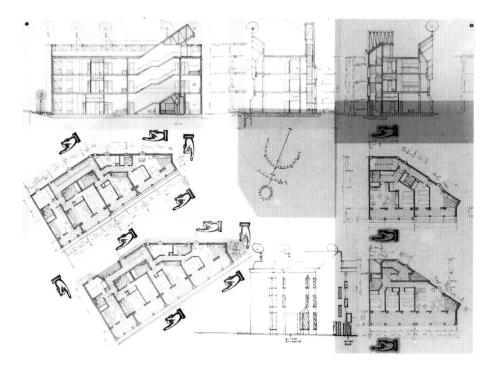

Corner unit: Sections (top), plans (bottom), and energy-conserving north elevation (bottom centre). AS.

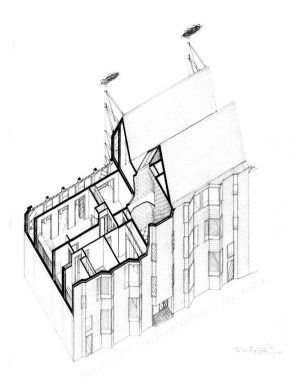

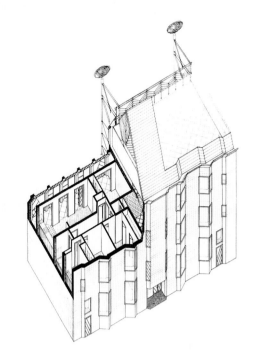

Axonometric of first-floor apartment. Economy version of roof with two parallel pitches. View shows north energy-conserving facade with rear access to car-park and bin stores. Raun Thorp, 1985; roofs, sunflowers by AS.

Axonometric of first-floor apartment, showing snorkel that gathers sun into the stairwell, roof terrace for the close, and signals in the form of solar-rose masts that turn to face the sun on a time clock. Raun Thorp, 1985.

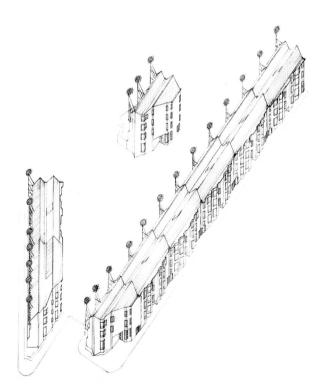

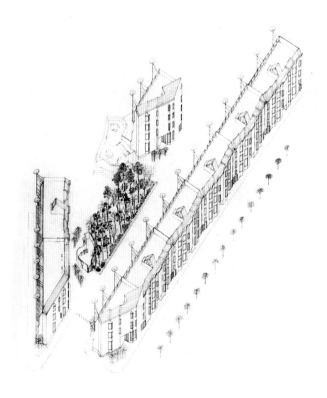

Axonometric with economy-version roofs (possibly carrying solar panels for each apartment) with ordinary skylights. Sunflower signals instead of MacDonald roses. AS, 1985.

Axonometric from Maryhill Road end of site. AS, 1984.

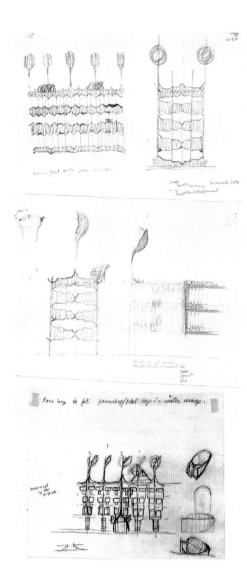

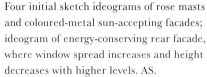

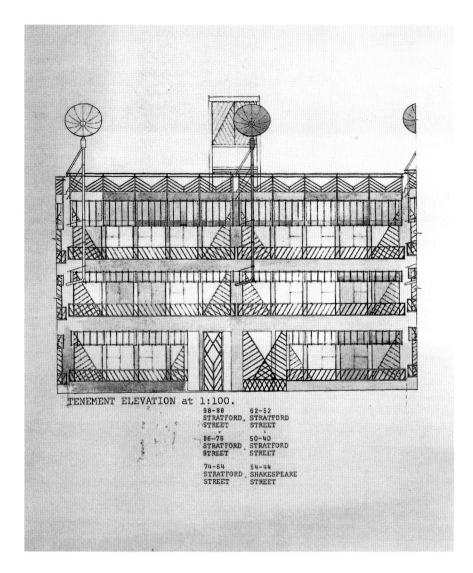

TENEMENT ELEVATION at 1:100.

98-88 STRATFORD STREET	62-52 STRATFORD STREET
86-76 STRATFORD STREET	50-40 STRATFORD STREET
74-64 STRATFORD STREET	54-44 SHAKESPEARE STREET

Four initial sketch ideograms of rose masts and coloured-metal sun-accepting facades; ideogram of energy-conserving rear facade, where window spread increases and height decreases with higher levels. AS.

Elevation of single-tenement-wide detail of sun-accepting facade. Tenements are three-storey walkups, two to a floor, on either side of the stair. An ample entrance hall is provided with communal storage for prams, bicycles, and large toys. Louisa Hutton.

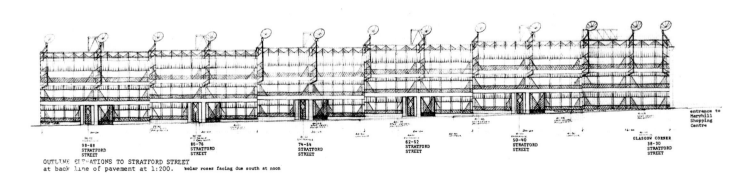

Sun-accepting south elevation to Stratford Street. AS.

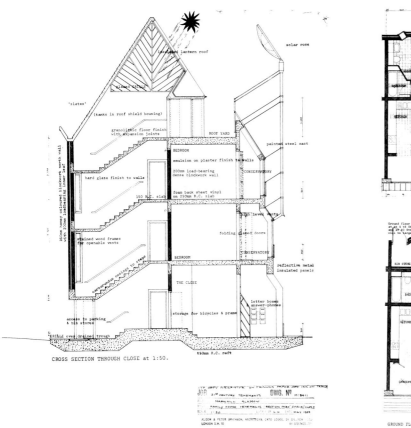

Cross section through stair. Louisa Hutton.

Ground- and first-floor plans of staircase-accessed unit.
Louisa Hutton.

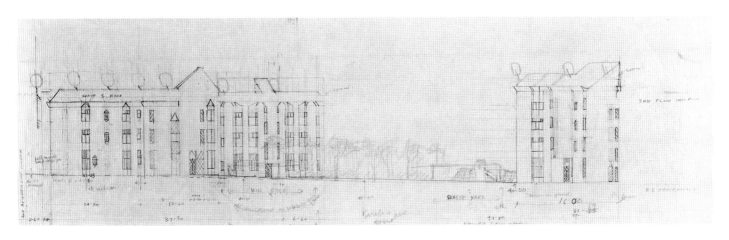

Stratford Street elevation, looking south. AS.

A+PS with Stefan Wewerka at the opening of the Wewerka Pavilion at Tecta, Lauenförde, Germany. 1985.

14 Roofs and Ways

two characteristics of 'conglomerate ordering', a phrase invented in 1983 to describe formulations that were coming into being in our work . . .

Animal House, University of Bath *(1981)*   544

Area di Pré, Genova *(1981)*   545

Come Deck the Hall *(1981)*   546

Porch to University Hall, University of Bath *(1983)*   547

Bath as a Fringed Mat *(1983)*   548

Agitation of Surface, Siena *(1985)*   550

Restoration of Territory, Rackève *(1985)*   551

Axel's Porch *(1986)*   552

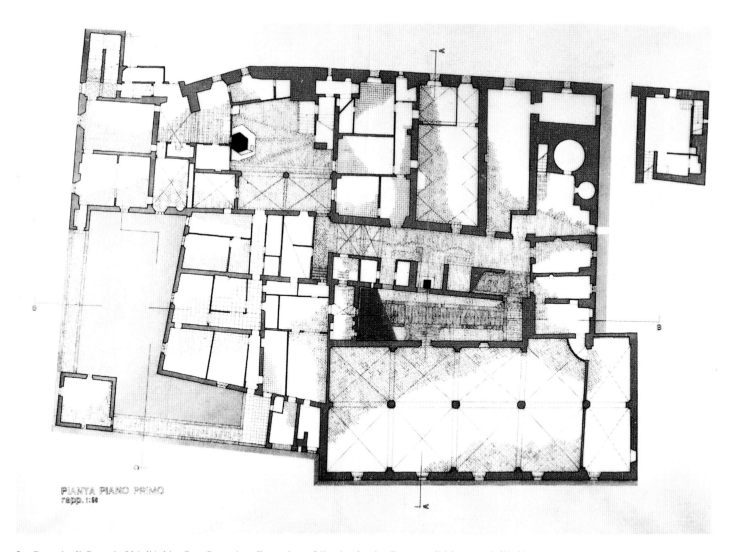

PIANTA PIANO PRIMO
rapp. 1:50

La Grancia di Cuna in Val d'Arbia, first-floor plan. From the publication by the Comune di Monteroni d'Arbia.

From 1983 onwards the characteristics of conglomerate ordering have been slowly identified.

Buildings of a conglomerate ordering have no elevations, they face what confronts them: the roof being also a face.

Buildings of conglomerate ordering use ways as a principal ordering device. Ways that go up and down, bend, widen, and narrow . . . to circumstance.

La Grancia di Cuna in Val d'Arbia, access ramp courtyard. PS, August 1983.

Animal House, University of Bath

1981

PS

A study for a small building on the edge of an existing large building, where the new small building would be mostly seen from above. The roof is, therefore, a 'face'. In the archive file on this study there is a photocopy of a magazine page showing the roof of the Lewerentz Flower Shop at the Malmö Cemetery. That roof in Malmö is certainly a 'face'.

The observation 'mostly seen from above'—obvious, one may say, for a small building alongside bigger ones—was the start point for all the considered-as-equals-to-facades subsequent roofs at the University of Bath . . . and a characteristic of conglomerate ordering.

Sketch elevation showing building seen from above. PS.

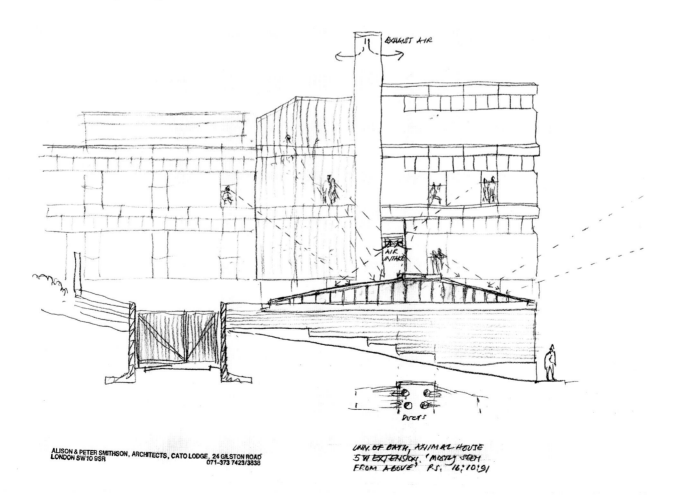

ALISON & PETER SMITHSON, ARCHITECTS, CATO LODGE, 24 GILSTON ROAD
LONDON SW10 9SR
071-373 7423/3838

UNIV. OF BATH, ANIMAL HOUSE
SW EXTENSION. 'MOSTLY SEEN
FROM ABOVE' RS, 16:10:91

544   14: Roofs and Ways

In the narrow Via Pré, arriving off the train in Genova from the north, we first experienced in the late 1940s the Italian gift for light in common commercial signs—bare tube neon, sign behind sign—filling the narrow street.

In this area, the mediaeval, the nineteenth century, and the present century can be read in the nature of their ways.

Sketch plan of street system and modification of insulae. PS.

Come Deck the Hall

As part of a continuing exercise intended to renew the sense of collective responsibility for the look of places, we made three exhibitions in the tradition of people's decoration at Christmas time:

'Signs of Occupancy', Bartlett School (1976–77);
'Twenty-Four Doors to Christmas', Cambridge (1979);
'Christmas 🕆 Hogmanay', Edinburgh (1980–81).

A further event of public participation was planned, where visitors would be invited to bring ephemera—old, bought, newly fabricated—to position or hang in a structural framework. Gradually, the framework would become increasingly decorated, so that by Christmas Eve, this special place would be 'ready', made so by the host community.

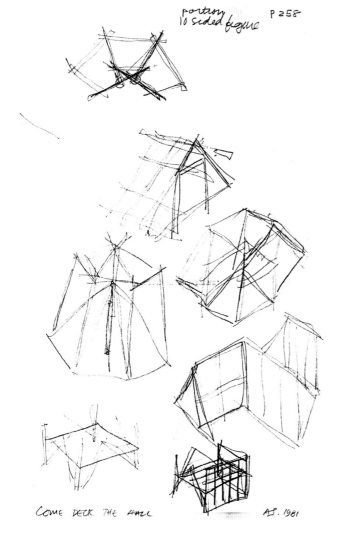

Sketch of a framework to support people's decoration. AS.

A new porch to mark the entrance to
University Hall.

View across pond. PS.

View from inside. PS.

Bath as a Fringed Mat

1983

A+PS

Aerial photograph of 'fringe' buildings at the University of Bath.

At this date, we had studied, started, or completed five buildings 'on the edge' at the University of Bath. That condition of being on the edge could now be observed as a phenomenon.

From the beginning, we had followed the ways of the existing interconnected buildings, discovering the perceived pathways within.

What was now happening was a perception of these edge buildings as terminations, fringes, tassels, as on a carpet.

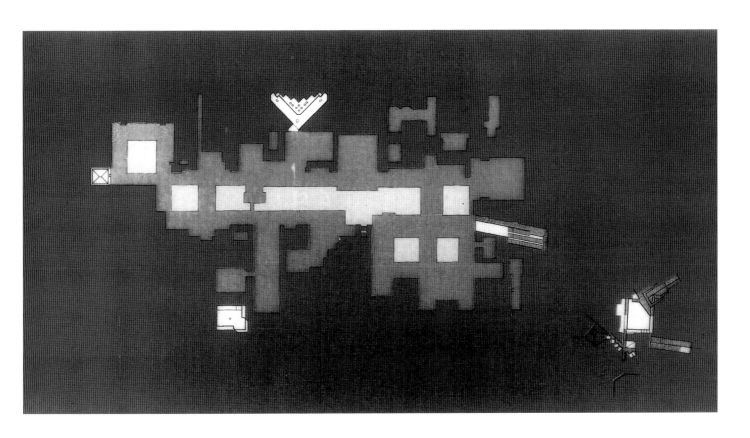

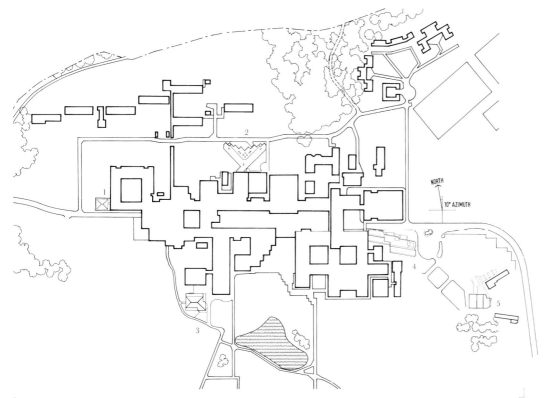

Diagram of the joined-together low campus buildings as a mat with a fringe of tassels. LW.

Site plan of established campus (drawn in heavy line) and fringe buildings by A+PS (drawn in light line):
1. Animal House
2. Second Arts Building
3. Amenity Building
4. School of Architecture and Building Engineering, Building 6 East
5. Arts Barn
Additions to *Architects' Journal* base drawing by LW, 1989.

Agitation of Surface, Piazza del Duomo, Siena

As the Hospital of Santa Maria della Scala gradually transfers its functions to the new hospital on the edge of the city, the lessening of the density of use of the piazza could allow an increase of agitation in the surfaces that define the space: for less human activity allows more gesture in the architecture.

The gesture of this study is an agitation of the surface of a certain strip of piazza to provide a place where the pace is slowed down, a place for tourists, but not disturbing the piazza's use by the citizens of Siena.

Plan showing the area of agitation
with summer morning shade (10:30 a.m.).
PS, 13 August 1985.

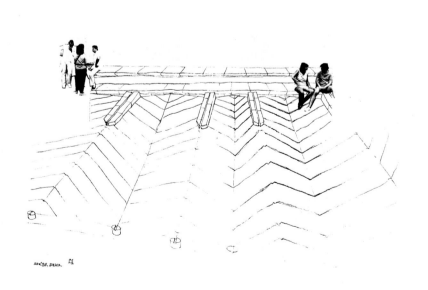

Photomontage of area of agitation with bollards, benches, and dundulations. PS.

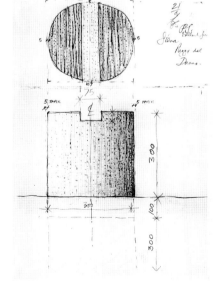

Detail of bollards. PS.

Restoration of Territory, Repair of Territorial Defects, Rackève, Budapest

1985

AS with Charles Polonyi

A study intended to uncover the characteristics of Rackève as a territory with smaller, and smaller yet, overlapping territories within it.

As to Rackève as a whole . . . its first characteristic to a stranger is its evenness, its notation of long green plots and long brown verandah houses set into long lines. These lines converge, and thus limit the 'islands' that are the territories of inhabitation. Rackève's 'drabness' conceals a satisfying variety for the visitor looking over garden walls: until this century, no wall was ever straight, no roofline even, no verandah columns of precise spacing, no road regularly paved, and today . . . no family use, no family celebration is quite the same. Sensibility towards such differences is, we believe, important for the next generation to try to recover.

Then, there is the territory of the river bank; the immensely long, seemingly parallel existence that gives equally to all the town a special riverbank light and the smell of a continent.

Everywhere Rackève is recognisable as a 'village with the rank of a town'.

For us, the basic points of reference are:

. . . every man in touch with the ground directly before him, growing
   things;
. . . having to the street his own gate, his own fence;
. . . a dwelling that, in the oldest types, accepts the sun, turns its back to
   the north.

In the proposals for traffic within Rackève, the existing street network is treated as near as possible as an ideal grid that spreads the traffic distribution in a way that leaves equably habitable 'islands'. This equal sense of a growing, lived-in territory will allow rehabilitation of this place as a gentle urb, a quiet place with its own identity. The maintenance of the size of the island is crucial; therefore, it is important that extra roads are not added to the street network. The recent penetration of the island by roads has eroded their sense of inviolate territory: this diminishing of their 'smell' should be resisted and wherever possible restoration made.

To follow the old long house with verandah and the L-shaped house, Rackève could do with a new house type that would appreciate its own ground.

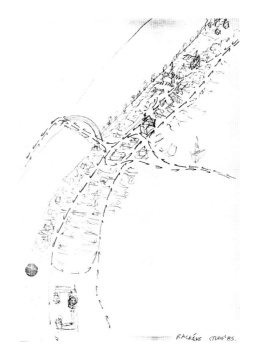

Sketch of one-way traffic-flow system. AS.

Axel's Porch, Hexenhaus, Bad Karlshafen

Bad Karlshafen (with Beverungen and Lauenförde) lies alongside the River Weser some thirty-five kilometres north of Kassel in Germany.

The owners of a 'Hansel and Gretel' house, the Hexenhaus, in a wood near Bad Karlshafen—a man and his cat—felt they were not, when inside their house, appreciating enough of the quality of the wood surrounding the house on the slopes above the River Weser.

At first, they thought they wanted a porch to open fully and give them—like the French windows that they already had—a wide opening into the woods. Then they remembered they never left anything open in summer because of the flies.

So the porch, as built, reuses the two halves of the original French windows and their special weather-sealing ironmongery, this time as single doors on the two desired routes out of the porch, whose frame, supporting the all-around glass, is as a built part of the wood, yielding two built-trees whose branches cannot move with the seasons.

Someone has added a loose corner seat—finding it good, after all, to be sitting there in a raised corner—in place of the corner storage box/seat/base that was in the construction design but not built; someone else has hung a small coloured blind—the architect's offering of tiny portions of coloured Perspex was missed after all. The cat looks down through his window onto the terrace below as intended . . . and the porch does extend outwards the pattern of the lives of man and cat, so that these adhere to the pattern of the seasons in the beloved woods much in the way envisaged: whether trees and porch bare of leaves, or trees and porch patterned with leaves; a bright place in snow, in sun; a connective place in rain, in wind. The architecture of this small porch grew out of paying attention to a man and his cat. The porch can be read as an exemplar of a method by which a small physical change—a layering-over of air adhered to an existing fabric—can bring about a delicate tuning of the relationship of persons with place.

First movable scheme, early sketch of roof. AS.

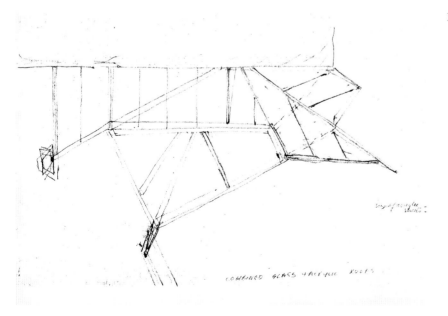

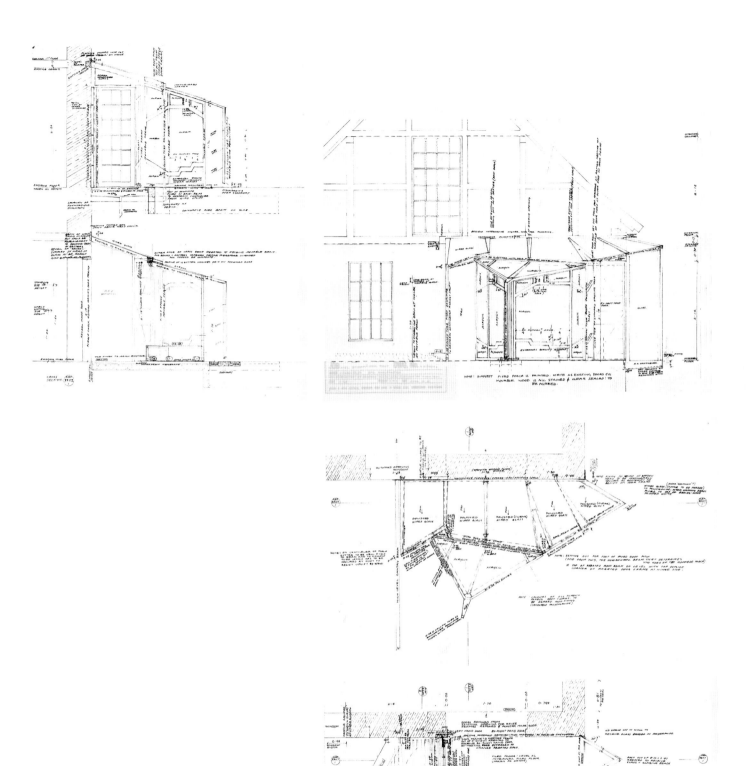

Working drawings of first movable scheme. AS.

top left: Cross section and end elevation.
top right: Elevation against Hexenhaus.
above right: Roof plan.
right: Ground plan.

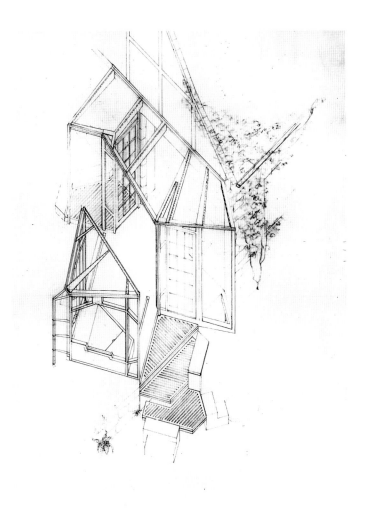

Axonometric of first movable scheme, in open position. AS.

Axonometric as built (i.e., without seat aedicule being movable on diagonal track to edge of revetment). AS.

View out through the built-trees.
AS, April 1988.

View to the River Weser. PS, 1988.

View of porch with door open, with the
River Weser in background. PS, 1988.

A+PS in Stockholm, Sweden, opposite Asplund's library where, unbelievably, a McDonald's has replaced the nannies' tea shop. 1992.

15 Outside Inside

paying attention, outside inside . . .

The Toilet Tree, Tecta *(1986–90)*   560

Triangle Workshop *(1987)*   562

Janus, Siena *(1987)*   563

Bibliotheca Alexandrina *(1989)*   564

Tecta Paths *(1990)*   571

Riverbank Window *(1990)*   572

Hexenhaus Holes *(1990)*   573

Tecta Canteen Porch *(1990)*   574

Acropolis Place *(1990)*   576

Hexenbesenraum *(1990–96)*   584

Beverungen Roof *(1990)*   588

Brodia Road *(1990–95)*   589

Deodar Road *(1991–99)*   590

Tischleindeckdich *(1992–93)*   592

Tecta Yard Gates *(1992)*   594

Porter House *(1993–95)*   595

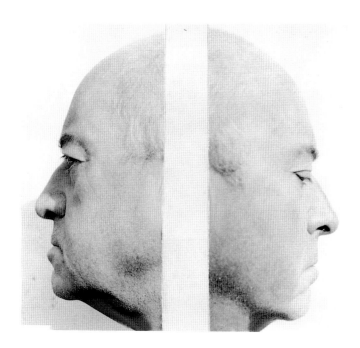

Looking in, looking out: Janus thoughts for Siena. Soraya Smithson, January 1984.

The Heroic period of Modern architecture had as one of its tenets spatial continuity between outside and inside.

This was a critical part of its formal vocabulary, backed for the de Stijl architects by a theory of 'universal space'.

The outside inside of these texts is different, more to do with what is actually seen and felt at a specific place, outside inside and inside outside.

The Toilet Tree, Tecta, Lauenförde

The male and female toilets at the Tecta furniture factory in Lauenförde were re-arranged so that from them, one can look out into the garden court of the factory yet not be seen or have the feeling of being seen.

The materials and the sanitary equipment used are the best available, resulting in remarkable rooms with an astonishing quality in their natural light. It is called the 'Toilet Tree' because the arrangement used an adaptation of the Kitchen Tree* already available from Tecta.

* Kitchen Tree by Stefan Wewerka.

Two photographs of the rooms' 'astonishing quality in their natural light'. PS, August 1992.

Preliminary sketch
of idea. AS, 1986.

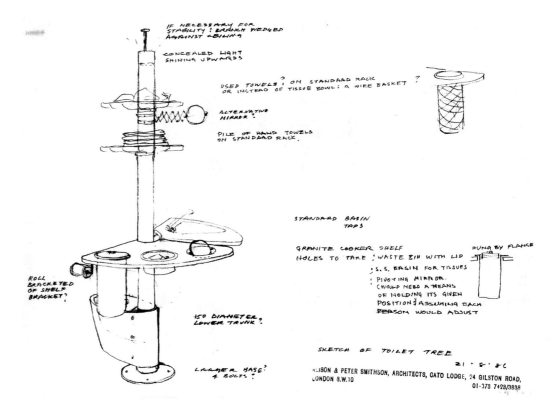

Setting-out plan.
AS, 1992.

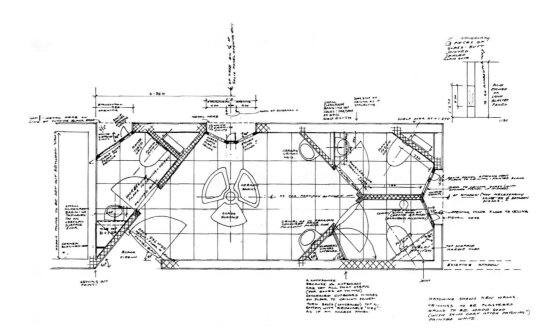

Triangle Workshop, Pine Plains, New York

Triangle Workshop* is an art workshop initiated and run by Anthony Caro, the English sculptor. Our participation marked the first year that architects were included.

Our work team set out to address the sky, by concentrating its effort on the roof of a very early reinforced-concrete dairy from 1906. This abandoned building was once part of a dairy farm that by European standards was huge, and whose buildings—used by Triangle as studios—are still impressive. None more so than the dairy.

The solidity, the size of this building brought from the artists involved a larger-scale effort than any of them had achieved before.

Our role was that of 'enablers', interpreting the dimensional, structural, and spatial possibilities of the dairy's fabric to the sculptors.

We also made two 'devices', a screen in rough shuttering plywood and a mast in steel with a fabric pennant, to act as indicators on visiting day.

* The 'Triangle' is the triangle of English-speaking countries—
England, the old British Dominions, and North America.

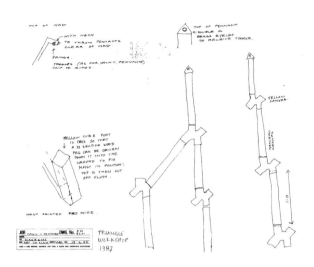

AS's diagram of pennants' jointing.

below left: Photograph of events on the roof of the abandoned dairy, constructed of reinforced concrete in 1906. The roof's strength suggested its use as a work plane for sculptural manifestations. PS, July 1987.
below right: Photograph of welded square-section steel mast with pennant marking entrance space, and behind, a plywood 'tree-screen' that extends the entrance corner of the building into the landscape. PS, July 1987.

Janus, Siena

The outside of the Hospital of Santa Maria della Scala has evolved with two distinctly different faces: one towards the city, the other towards the countryside.

On the inside, the hospital uses have declined, and by 1999 have ceased.

This project considers the appropriate changes to the building's two faces consequent of what lies before them now and the possible changes for new uses.

The countryside is now kept open by planning controls; it is still in agricultural use but is really more of a kind of park.

In this project, therefore, the face of Santa Maria della Scala 'towards the countryside' is treated as the edge of a park, as a kind of park wall; the park being extended up to the back wall of the old hospital by demolition of certain of the hospital annexes.

What lies before the other face, 'towards the city', is at certain times completely dominated by tourists. This face we accept as it is, forming a safe edge to a tourist enclosure.

The roof is to be opened up, as appropriate to new uses, to let in the sun and air to give the feeling of a cleansing of the old fabric after the long centuries of hospital use (and it is opened up below towards the stairs and tunnels of Etruscan times and of the Dark Ages!).

Coin with Janus, god of all doorways. His two faces allowed him to observe both the exterior and the interior of the house.

Janus

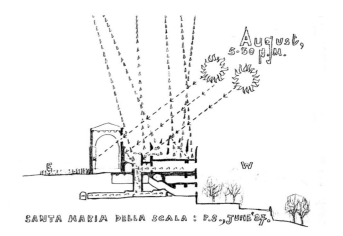

New section for the old hospital of Santa Maria della Scala, which takes account of its Janus situation, facing the countryside on one side and the city on the other. The conglomerate is re-energised by opening the dense building enough to allow the sun to indicate the time of day and the seasons. PS.

Elevation towards the countryside, now a kind of park. PS.

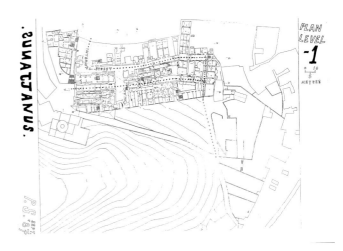

Plan showing the park running up to the back of the hospital, which becomes a kind of park wall. PS.

Bibliotheca Alexandrina

1989

AS

with Buro Happold

What lies outside at the site of the Bibliotheca Alexandrina varies dramatically: on the north side there is the Mediterranean Sea; on the south side the town and the impact of the sun.

The response was to give the library reading rooms on the north side with views of the sea and to close the walls to the south as far as possible. The mass of the building itself is used to self-shade the east-west running internal 'streets' in the Oriental manner.

Because of the configuration of the shoreline at this location on the Corniche of Alexandria, these internal streets acquire a magical characteristic in that the sun setting in the sea at the equinox will radiate for a few minutes horizontally along their length: a dramatic occurrence based on the Islamic foundation of 'filtered light from within' that the shaded internal street gives to the accommodation it serves.

The construction of the library could be said to be Egypto-Roman . . . a solidly built concrete bearing structure with marble slabs attached. The same gentle-on-the-eye striped system clads the whole building, inside and out.

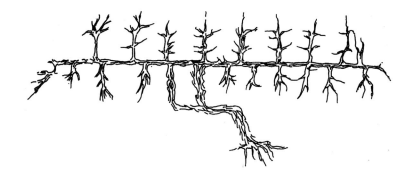

Internal streets ideogram. PS, 1989.

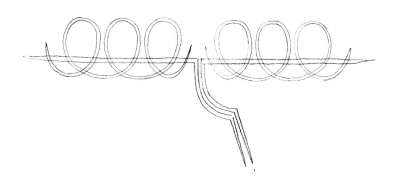

Internal streets ideogram. AS, 1989.

opposite top: Ground-level plan and perspective of entrance. LW; infill by AS.
opposite bottom: Plan showing the impact of the sun on the three parallel ranges and how the setting sun at the equinox runs along the internal streets. Lloyd Rubidge; original by PS.

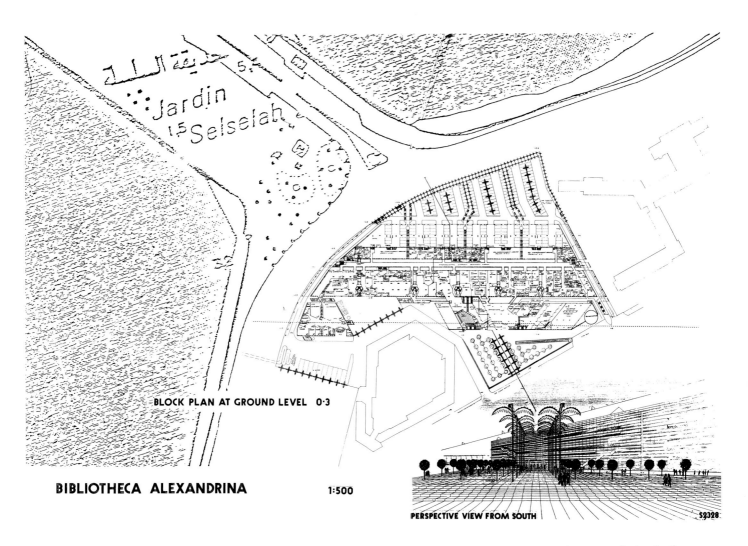

BLOCK PLAN AT GROUND LEVEL 0·3

BIBLIOTHECA ALEXANDRINA

1:500

PERSPECTIVE VIEW FROM SOUTH

S2328

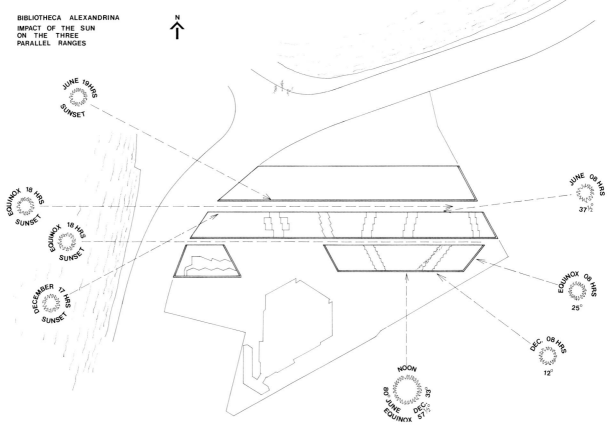

BIBLIOTHECA ALEXANDRINA
IMPACT OF THE SUN
ON THE THREE
PARALLEL RANGES

N

JUNE 19 HRS
SUNSET

EQUINOX 18 HRS
SUNSET

EQUINOX 18 HRS
SUNSET

DECEMBER 17 HRS
SUNSET

JUNE 08 HRS
37½°

EQUINOX 08 HRS
25°

DEC. 08 HRS
12°

NOON
80° JUNE DEC. 33°
EQUINOX 57½°

On the sun-facing facades this marble skin is set well in front of the bearing fabric, the air gap between them carrying off the heat from the outer skin, there being an air-inlet at the bottom—over a trough of water—and an outlet at the top.

To permit views for the readers in south-facing rooms and give a sense of the time of day for those deep in the building, certain slabs of this 'closed' wall's marble skin are, as it were, lifted up to form shades—like an eyelid—for readers to look out, or omitted near ceiling level to let light deep into the building. For the libraries facing north the bearing fabric is columnar, and glass is substituted for marble to give a full view of sea and sky.

In Egypt it seems natural to give the action of the sun a consciously formal role; for example, on the entrance facade at noon in midsummer the vertical face is in full shadow from the projecting window shades, the window shades themselves being in full sun: for a few moments the building's striped nature is highlighted.

Throughout the individual libraries there are devices to bring the sense of the sun, the state of the day, the seasons to the readers and staff; to place the library indisputably on the Corniche of Alexandria.

Theoretically, the thermal gains into the interior spaces during the day will be minimal, and at night the rising cool air will 'draw' the heat from the bearing fabric. During the time of year when heat is needed, the top of the void between the bearing fabric and the outer marble skin can be closed to trap the solar gain, reducing the heat loss from the building.

The second feature of the ventilated air-gap system is that in the event of total failure of power supplies, this by-pass 'free cooling' can be used together with the opening of high-level windows on the north and south facades to encourage air movement across the building, removing the built-up heat from occupants. The 'stack' effect in the air gap on the southern facade will encourage the draw-through of air.

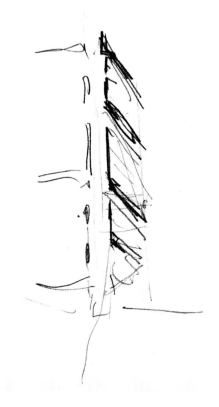

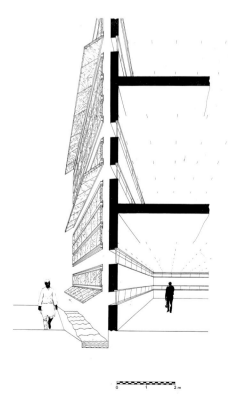

far left: Diagram of the ventilated south skin. AS, March 1990.
left: 'Double-perspective' section through sun-facing facade, showing air gap to carry off heat between bearing structure and marble facing. PS, 1990.

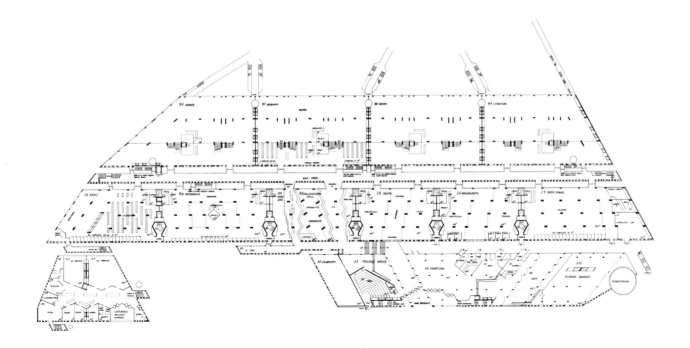

BIBLIOTHECA ALEXANDRINA

**COMPOSITE PLAN OF GROUND LEVEL
AND PIANO NOBILE LEVEL**   **1:250**
TO SHOW THE ROUTE OF THE READER

PIANO NOBILE LEVEL 4·5 + 5·9

GROUND LEVEL 0·3   **S2328**

Composite plan at ground level and piano nobile level. IW.

Connecting links between the north and central ranges across the internal street. Guido Kintrup, 1992.

On the northern facade, maximum use is made of glazing which is thermally lightweight and will respond well to the cool sea breeze—as well as maximising the views to the Mediterranean.

The active systems of air movement rely on wind towers collecting the sea breezes on the north side and the air being drawn to basement level where the mechanical plant 'plugs' into the fresh-air shafts and then delivers the treated air up the building in vertical shafts. At night the mechanical plant can be by-passed, and the vertical shafts will allow the air in them to rise naturally to the zenith, cooling the inner structural masses.

We believe that at certain times of the year, this system, with suitable filtering of the air, could be used successfully in providing a natural environment in spaces where precise control conditions are not essential.

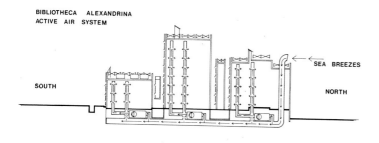

Diagram of active air systems. Lloyd Rubidge; original by Tony McLaughlin, Bruno Happold.

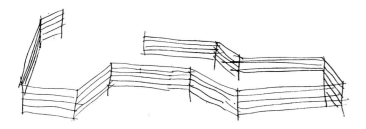

Alexandrina banding. PS, February 1991.

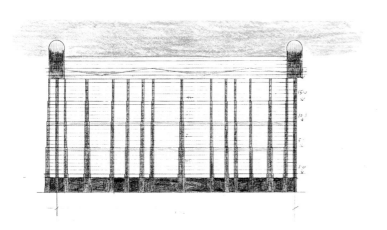

Drawing of one bay of north facade towards the sea, showing turning air-intake in stove-enamelled rainbow colours; stainless-steel-mesh roof shading; all glass to sea view, apart from marble facing to floor slabs; and columns faced with Egyptian purple porphyry. PS; colouring by AS, 1989.

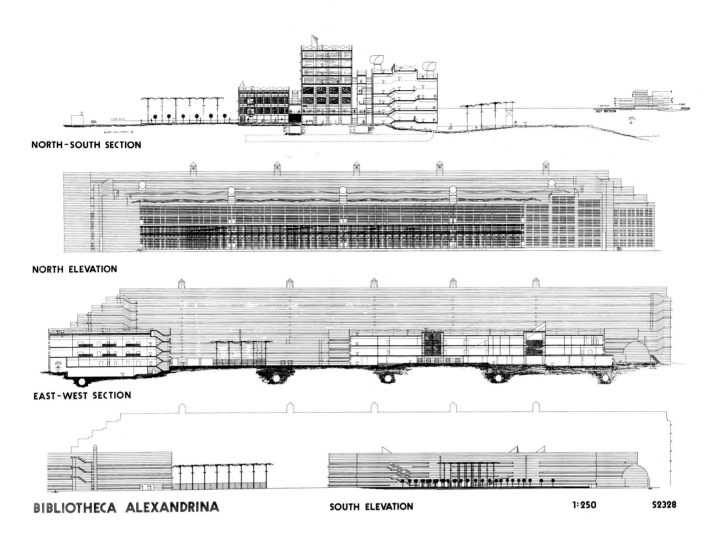

NORTH-SOUTH SECTION

NORTH ELEVATION

EAST-WEST SECTION

BIBLIOTHECA ALEXANDRINA

SOUTH ELEVATION   1:250   S2328

Elevations and sections. PS.

South facade of the south range, showing gentle-on-the-eye colour banding of indigenous Egyptian blue-green and white marbles. PS; colouring by AS, 1989.

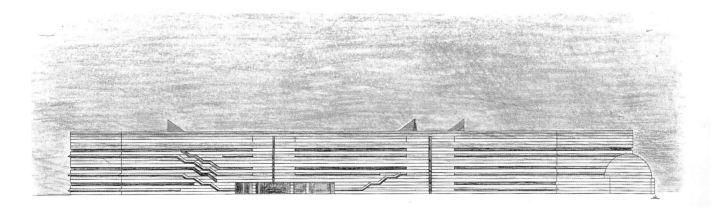

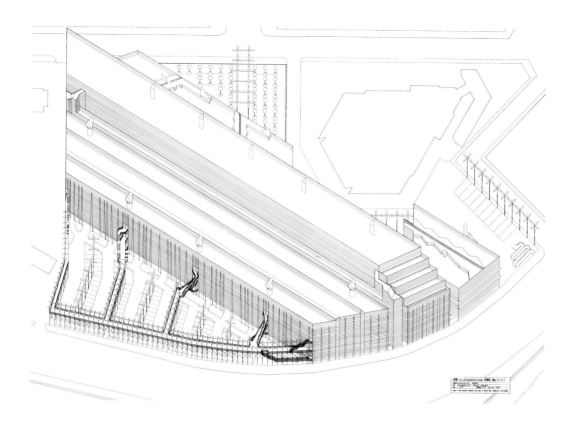

General axonometric from the north. Charles Anderson, 1991.

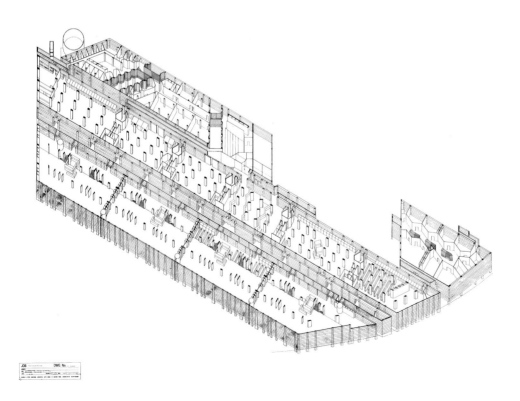

Composite axonometric. AS, Melanie Feldman, Roman Pardon, winter/spring 1989–90.

Tecta Paths, Lauenförde

The forecourt to the Tecta factory serves as a loading bay, car-park for staff and visitors, and as one gets closer to the entrance, an indicator of the nature of Tecta activities.

This modest rearrangement gives a direct path from the forecourt over the grass on stepping stones to the Wewerka Pavilion, where Tecta furniture is displayed, and gives additional protection from overlooking to the closest factory offices.

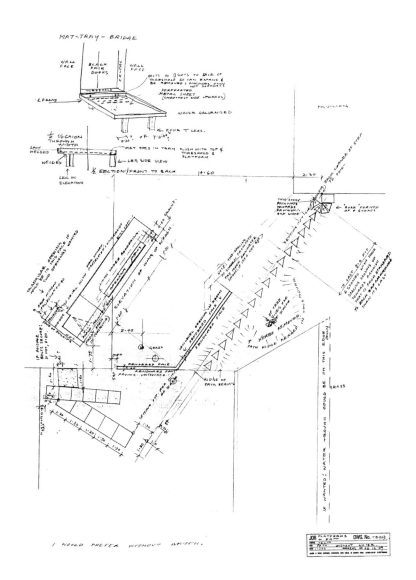

above right: Sketch layout. AS, 26 December 1989.
right: Approach to the main door, looking out. Chair by Stefan Wewerka. PS, April 1995.

Riverbank Window, Hexenhaus, Bad Karlshafen

Downhill from the Hexenhaus slides the River Weser, and the Riverbank Window opens the house to the river . . . outside, inside.

Allowing one to sit on the edge of the floor dangling one's feet 'in the outside'.

As at Axel's Porch here at the Hexenhaus and at the Canteen Porch at the Tecta factory, one is not conscious of the Riverbank Window as a bay window . . . that is, of the line of the wall being bent outwards; rather, there is a further space outside that wall, another layering of space.

It is an extraordinary effect, consequent simply of the side returns being beyond the sightlines seen from inside.

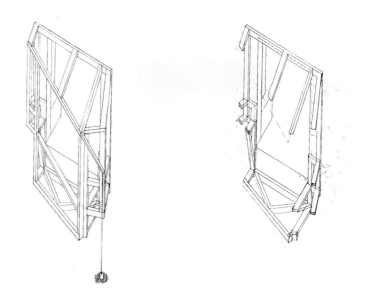

Pair of axonometrics from the outside. AS, November 1989.

View from the outside. PS, May 1992.

View to the River Weser. Axel Bruchhäuser.

Hexenhaus Holes, Bad Karlshafen

Branches of trees grow over the Hexenhaus: holes were made in the roof to let that branchy outside into the inside. The geometric language of these holes is of the same order as that of the earlier Axel's Porch and the Riverbank Window.

One hole is passed through the floor above at the back eaves to open up and light the ground-floor room: the other hole simply passes through the roof at the front eaves into the same room.

Plan of preferred version with three rows of roof tiles removed. AS, 24 May 1990.

Section study of four rows of tiles removed. AS, 24 May 1990.

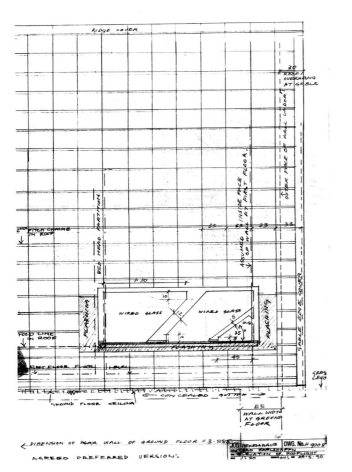

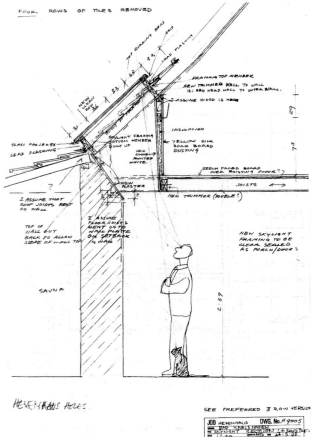

Tecta Canteen Porch, Lauenförde

The Tecta factory has a small room where the workers take coffee. It has a fixed bench along one long wall and a platform at the same level as the bench across the end. The other, window side of the room has the coffee bar. Outside the windows is the garden courtyard.

The idea of the porch is to open the room to that garden courtyard, so coffee could be taken outside on fine days.

The opening in the window wall of the canteen is smaller than the width of the porch, so that, as in Axel's Porch and the Riverbank Window at the Hexenhaus, the effect is of a further latticed space outside; a bridging space between outside and inside.

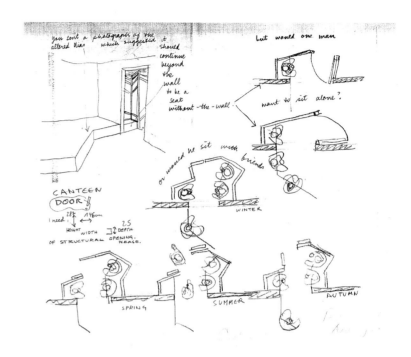

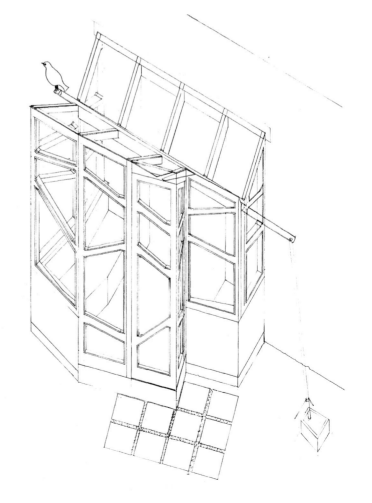

above right: Exploratory sketches. AS.
right: Axonometric from outside. AS.

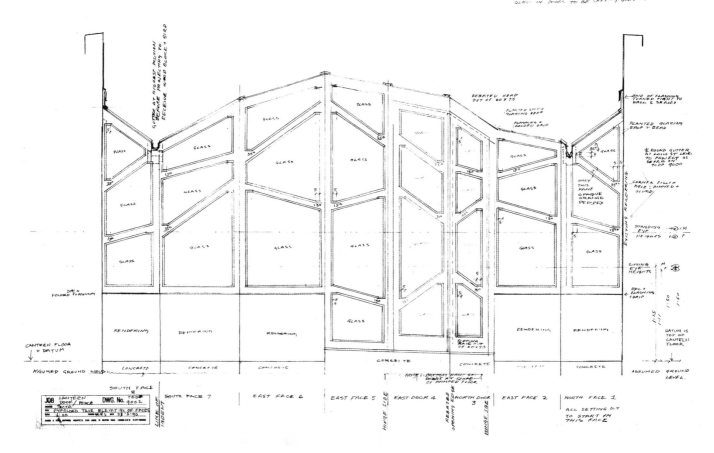

NOTE:
TWO ANGLES ARE USED FOR GLAZING BARS
THAT OF ROOF IN SECTION = 35°
THAT OF WALLS IN PLAN = 15°
ALL WINDOW GLAZING BARS OUT OF 10×10
DOOR GLAZING BARS OUT OF 10×8

GLASS IN DOORS TO BE SAFETY GLASS.

Unfolded elevation of all faces. AS.

View from the outside. Axel Bruchhäuser, 1995.

View with the later stainless-steel fascia. PS, 1997.

Acropolis Place, Athens

1990

AS; roof: PS

with Buro Happold

Three sites were offered by the Greek Ministry of Culture.

The site chosen by us was the Makryianni site, because it lay closest to the Acropolis below the slope on which sits the Theatre of Dionysus. It was a site with a direct relationship to the Rock. Furthermore, the use of this 'town' site would not erode the extent of the established archaeological park.*

Being unwilling to re-imprison the Elgin Marbles and other scattered fragments within the walls of yet another museum, we started with the idea of arranging the fragments of sculpture and building on platforms that could receive the sun in their original relationship one to another and with their original orientation to that sun.

These platforms were sloping and were reached from more steeply sloping ramped ways analogous to the Rock itself.

The fragments on these platforms, such as pediment sculpture, when viewed from the lower level, were at the height they were seen originally.

The whole was arranged under a glass cover-all roof supported on masts and placed to give the minimum interference to the display.

From the northernmost platform, there are views out to the Rock.

The viewing platforms play the role of 'earth'; the alignment maintains the sense of 'temple'; the light of Attica beams down as remembrance of the gods.

* See *The Charged Void: Urbanism*.

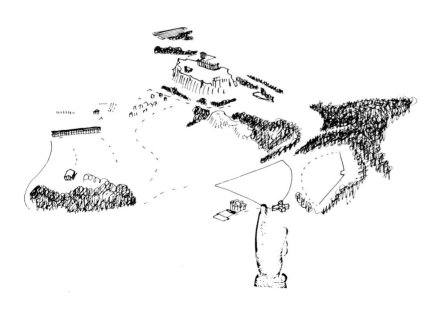

Diagram showing triangular site in Thesion, against Nymphon Hill and below the Pnyx. The site is also known as Pericles' choice for Acropolis Place. AS, December 1989.

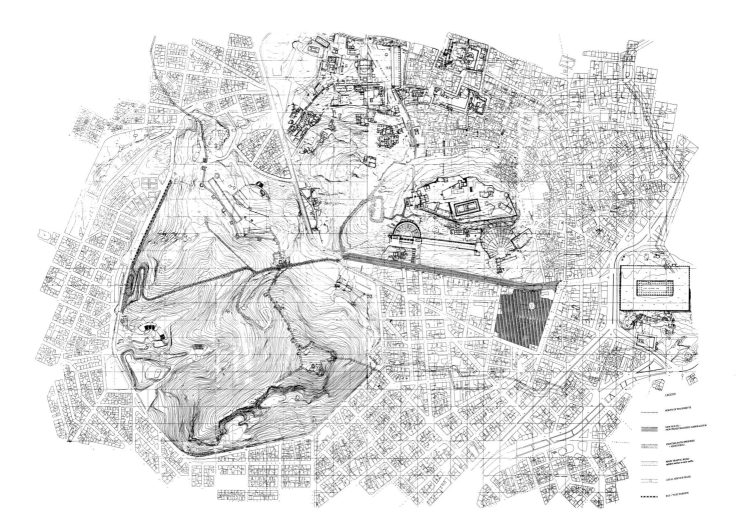

Archaeological Park movement pattern

Plan of Athens Archaeological Park, showing the location of the Acropolis Place Museum and the re-organised and extended pathway system; car- and bus-parks are located along the tangential road on the left edge of the park. AS, Antonio Medina Mercendes, 1990.

Sketch of the view from the 'best-view-track' on the contours behind the Pnyx and above the Koile site, used as a car- and bus-park for the Makryianni site. AS, September 1989.

VIEW ON 'BEST VIEW TRACK' ON CONTOURS ABOVE (N) OF KOILE SITE.

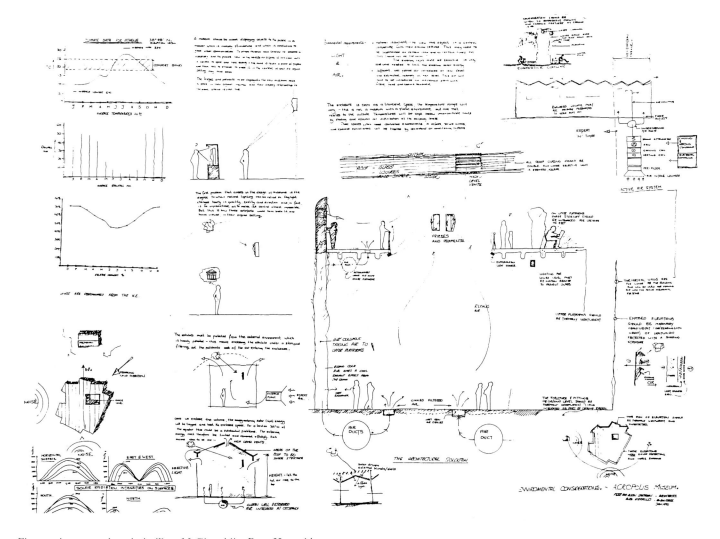

First environmental analysis. Tony McCloughlin, Buro Happold.

Diagram of desired environment.
Tony McCloughlin, Buro Happold.

MAKRYIANNI.
THE 'ACROPOLIS PLACE'

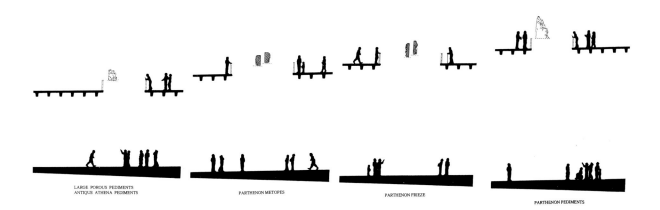

LARGE POROUS PEDIMENTS
ANTIQUE ATHENA PEDIMENTS

PARTHENON METOPES

PARTHENON FRIEZE

PARTHENON PEDIMENTS

Drawing of the viewing of the archaeological fragments: The fragments' display is viewed by the observer on sloping platforms at two levels: the same level for a close view and the lower level for a distant view at which the fragments are at heights above the observer. This drawing was used as the cover of the competition report.

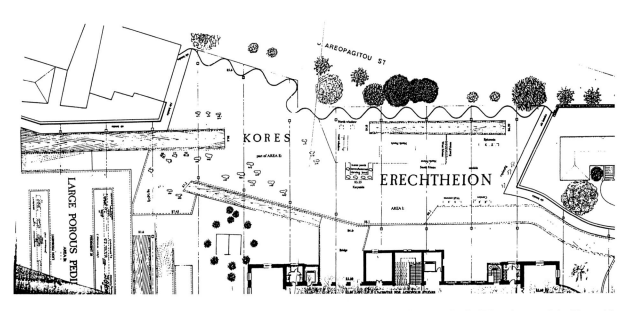

Diagrammatic plan of the northern upper viewing level, the Erechtheion, and the adjoining 'field of Kores' west of the Karyatid Porch. View is northwards, towards the Acropolis. LW, 1991.

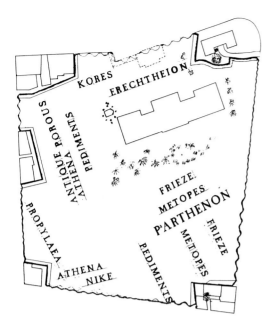

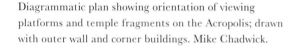

Diagrammatic plan showing orientation of viewing platforms and temple fragments on the Acropolis; drawn with outer wall and corner buildings. Mike Chadwick.

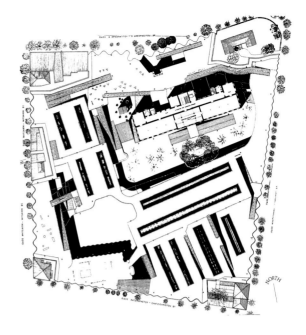

Shadowed plan of viewing platforms within the perimeter enclosure. Shadows of the upper-level platforms are cast onto the lower-level platforms. LW, 1991.

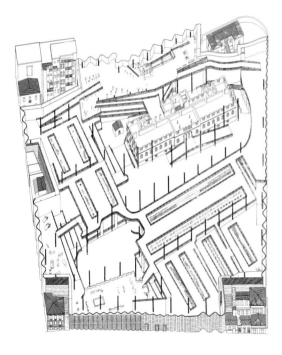

Axonometric of the upper-level viewing platforms, with archaeological fragments. Cornelia Pruecklmaier, LW, AS, 1991.

Axonometric of the lower-level viewing platforms, with archaeological fragments and trees. Alberto Nicolau Corbacao, Tony McCloughlin, LW, AS, 1991.

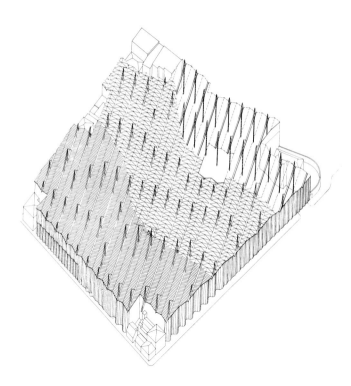

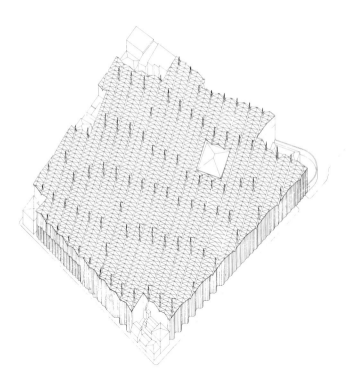

Cut-away axonometric of roof seen from the south-east, showing masts and cable stays supporting primary trusses, triangulated apex arches, and glazed covering. AS, winter 1990; LW, summer 1992.

Axonometric of roof seen from the south-east, showing supporting masts and cable stays with transparent covering. AS, winter 1990; LW, summer 1992.

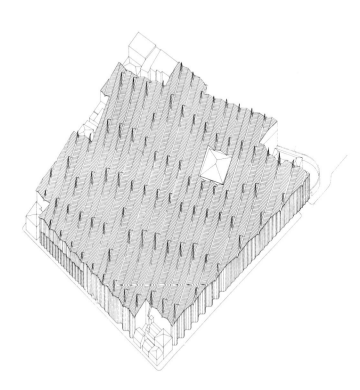

Bird's-eye axonometric view from the south-east of the structure supporting the roof's transparent covering. Primary support trusses run north to south with cable stays connected to masts. Between the primary trusses, triangulated apex arches support the transparent covering. Antonio Medina Mercendes, 1990.

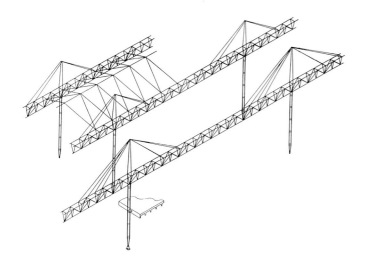

Axonometric of roof structure showing triangulated apex arches connected to primary support trusses supported by cable stays to masts. Buro Happold.

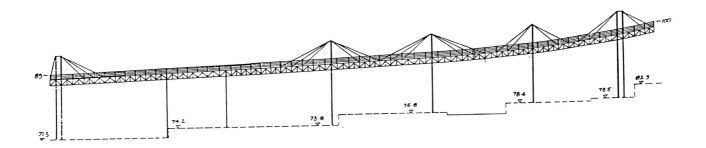

South-north section of roof structure: Primary support truss with cable stays connected to masts. Buro Happold.

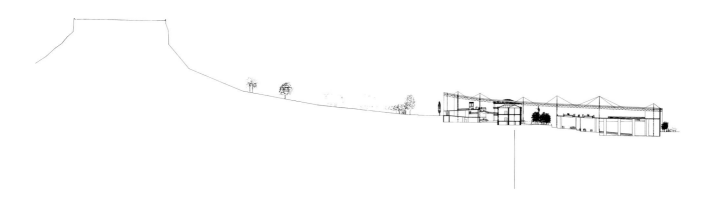

North-south section, extended to pass through south slope of the Acropolis at its east end. PS.

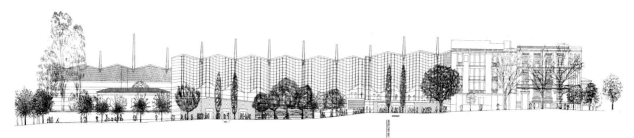

1:200   Elevation to, Entrance on Areopagitou

North elevation of entrance on Areopagitou Street. A+PS, LW, Antonio Medina Mercendes, 1990.

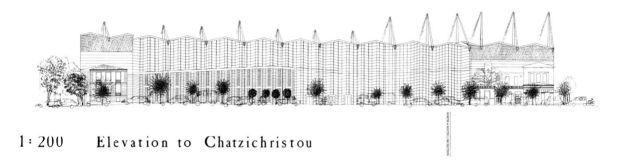

1:200   Elevation to Chatzichristou

South elevation of Chatzichristou Street. A+PS, LW, Antonio Medina Mercendes; mast heights corrected in 1990.

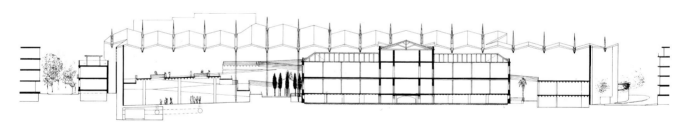

East-west section. A+PS, LW, Antonio Medina Mercendes, 1990.

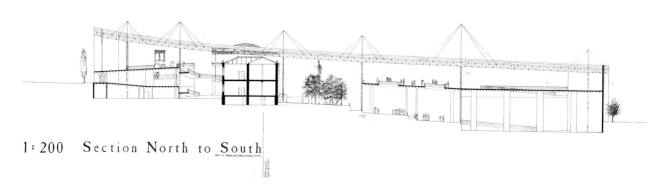

1:200   Section North to South

North-south section. A+PS, LW, Antonio Medina Mercendes; mast heights corrected in 1990.

Hexenbesenraum, Hexenhaus, Bad Karlshafen

1990 – 1996

AS; bridge: PS

with Hermann Koch

The Hexenbesenraum is a tiny pavilion on stilts over the slope down to the River Weser and reached by a bridge from the Hexenhaus.

It is constructed in timber on concrete foundations.

As with all the other changes made to the Hexenhaus, it allows further engagement of the house with its site . . . to view the sun as it slides through the trees over the river.

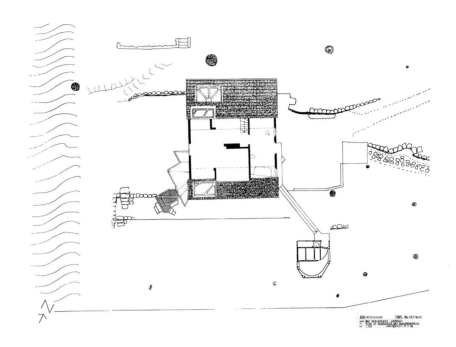

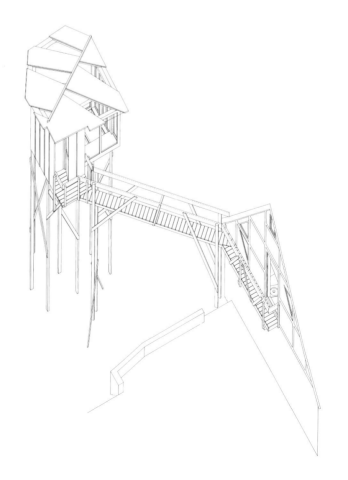

right top: Upper-floor plan of the Hexenhaus, with bridge over to the Hexenbesenraum. Rosa Jackson, PS, 1996.
right: Axonometric. Roger Paez di Blanc, 1996.

Working drawing of the bridge. PS, 1995.

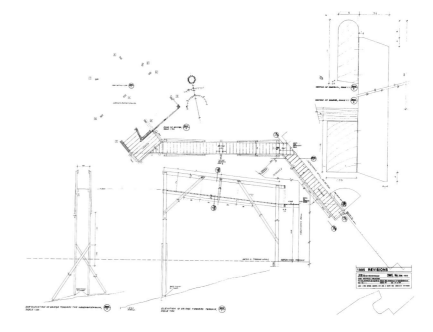

Working drawing at various levels of the
enclosed Hexenbesenraum. AS, 1991.

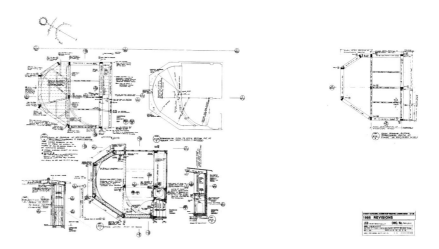

Working drawing of north elevations of the
Hexenbesenraum (left) and the Hexenhaus
(right). A+PS, 1991–95.

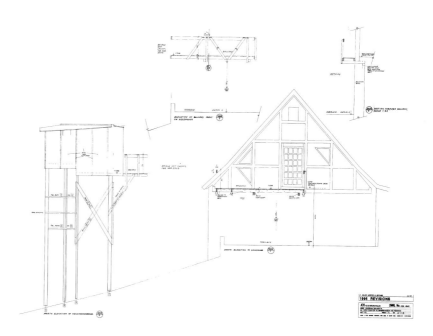

Bridge from the Hexenhaus to the Hexenbesenraum.
Delft Technical University, winter 1996–97.

Snow comes to the Hexenbesenraum.
Alex Bruchhäuser, January 1997.

Bridge from the Hexenbesenraum to the Hexenhaus.
Delft Technical University, winter 1996–97.

Full-height general view with glass floor visible underneath.
PS, October 1996.

Autumn view from the south-west. PS, October 1996.

Interior of the Hexenbesenraum with view to the forest floor, under the sleeping bench and through the floor.

View from the forest floor through the Hexenbesenraum to the leaf-canopy overhead. Delft Technical University, winter 1996–97.

Autumn view looking down from inside to the forest floor. Reflections of the sky through the glass panels in the roof are visible in the glass floor. PS, October 1996.

Beverungen Roof

There is in Beverungen a mediaeval customs tower at the head of the river crossing. This tower has been leased by Tecta to use as a cantilever chair museum and Jean Prouvé archive.

To mark this change of use, it is proposed to put on the ridge of the roof, a line of enlarged cantilever chair frames.

AS wrote of this proposal: *"The most important view of this museum is of the roof when approaching, from a distance, from the higher-level roads of the region, when a visitor would be able to identify the place he was looking for.*

The chair frames as symbol-signs will, because they are of relatively small diameter tube, only 'lightly touch' the solid fabric of the customs tower.

The coloured frames will, seen against the sky from below, be less substantial than, say, five storks.

The order of the frames along the ridge line is as follows:
Stam: white,
Prouvé: silver,
Mies: blue,
Pogo : gold (or yellow),
Wewerka: red.

The frames diminish in size—like the five musicians of Bremen—from the Stam at 170 centimetres high to the Wewerka at 47 centimetres high, 60 wide, 69 deep."

Photomontage of chairs on roof. View of the approach to the tower across the modern bridge, showing the line of enlarged chairs placed along the ridge to mark the tower's change of use to a cantilever chair museum and Prouvé archive. AS.

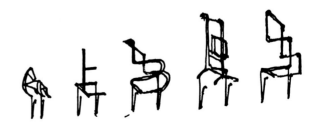

Sketch of chairs for roof. AS, 1990.

Brodia Road, Stoke Newington

Brodia Road is one of those London streets of small terrace houses with ground-floor bay windows to the street, a minute front garden, and a backyard where the coal and the privy once were.

The house has been re-organised to make a single space of that backyard and the ground-floor kitchen by opening up the kitchen so both outside and inside are equally usable by grown-ups and children.

The new sanitary arrangements have been inserted into the core of the house.

below: The street face in an ordinary road. PS, August 1995.
bottom: General view of the kitchen opened up to the garden. PS, August 1995.

below: General view of the kitchen windows from the outside. PS, August 1995.
bottom: General view of the kitchen windows from the outside, all open. PS, August 1995.

Deodar Road, Putney

1991 – 1999

AS with Simon Smithson

Deodar Road is a rare street in London: the gardens run down to the river.

The Art and Crafts period house on this street has been re-organised to give the best possible sense of outside inside.

The storage, service, and sanitary arrangement is tucked into the previously unused volumes, giving the maximum volume to living uses.

The working drawings of both Brodia Road and Deodar Road, when virtually complete in November 1994, show the house in a considerable state of ruin, where much could be observed only after opening up. The drawings are only the base for the works rather than their delineation.

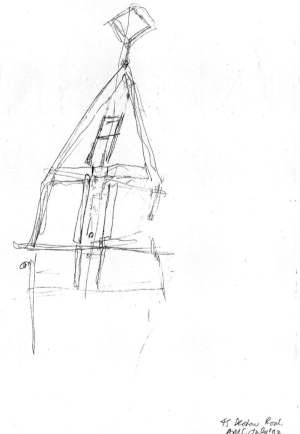

45 Deodar Road.
AMS, July '93

Axonometric of 'Vauban emplacements' as built. LW, June 1999.   Ideogram of 'Vauban emplacements'. AS, July 1993.

Drawings are revised or completely reworked as the works reveal the actual state of the fabric, then the people on site follow their own assessment of what can be achieved.

The result is remarkable, seemingly absolutely under control; but that control has been achieved through a different route . . . a large part being dedicated self-build, together with energetic, young, direct-labour craftsmen.

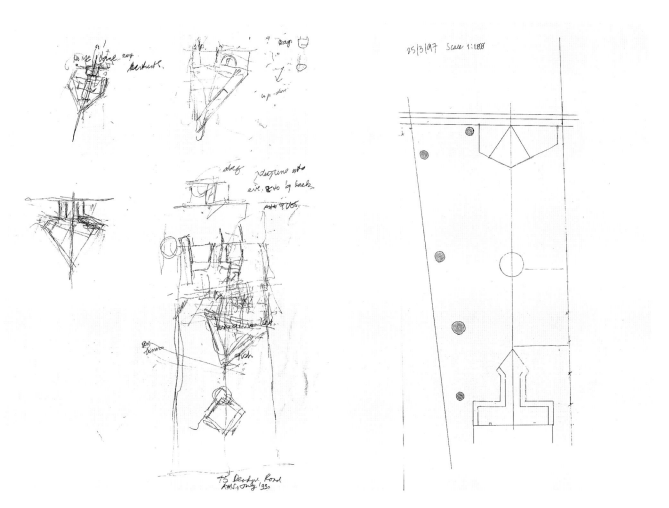

Idea sketches for 'Vauban emplacements' extending the house into the garden. AS, July 1993.

Plan of 'Vauban emplacements' as realised. LW, Diego Varela, 1997.

Tischleindeckdich, Tecta Exhibitions, Cologne and Berlin

It was decided to make a showing of Tecta furniture in two art galleries, the Gallery Mautsch in Cologne and the Aedes Gallery in Berlin.

The pieces chosen for display were predominantly from Mies van der Rohe, Marcel Breuer, Jean Prouvé, and A+PS, and the mechanical Tischlein from Tecta.

Tischleindeckdich . . . a table of ordinary appearance and made of common wood, but say 'table, table, cover thyself', it then laid and covered itself with food and wine, which replaced themselves when consumed. PS said at the first opening in Cologne: *"The text in the catalogue says that the pieces of furniture in the Tischleindeckdich exhibition are 'actors in a staging of the possible' . . . a staging carried by a transformation of the familiar.*

The familiar being those pieces of furniture from the 1920s and 1930s which Axel Bruchhäuser has sought out and reproduced from originals or fragments of originals, or made from original drawings and patent documents.

The transformation of these familiars in this exhibition is effected by paint and by light as in a theatre. All the pieces are painted the same dullish metallic green.

For transformation is a theatrical word . . . we remember from childhood the wonder of the transformation scene where Cinderella is made ready for the ball . . . made ready for a new life. We must ask if the transformation of the familiar pieces in our drama gives indications of how things can act spatially together in a new way . . . can project an 'ensemble' quality, as the catalogue text claims.

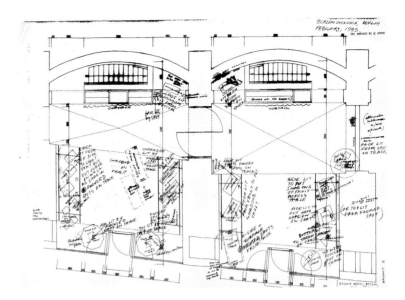

top: Sketch layout of furniture on display at the Aedes Gallery. AS.
above: Children attracted by the movement of the Tischleindeckdich. PS, February 1993.
left: Poster. AS.

*Amongst the familiar old pieces are some new . . .
and of these, certainly, the silk-lanterns in their
habit here of soft green create an ambience . . . they
are no longer quite objects.*

*The Marcel Breuer pieces, painted complete in dull
metallic green without the glitter of nickel or
chrome, are rather like rattan. They remind one
of the real bicycles of the 1920s with their steel
tubes, wheels, and brakes predominantly, even wholly, painted—as one can still see in Holland—the
mythical beginning of tubular steel furniture.*

*The Trundling Turk, upholstered in soft green silk
with a dull metallic green chassis, changes from a
student knockabout piece to something luxurious.*

*The Ironyarn fabric in green seems no longer, as it
were, a tough sailcloth but has, for example on
the Prouvé tabletop, the dustily sacred quality of
the fabric cover of an Islamic prophet's tomb.*

*The Collector's Table, a dull silver in the original,
changes little spatially by being metallic green,
but its cabinet of curiosities character is reduced,
the metallic green tending to consume the objects
placed upon it.*

And so on.

*Like the director of a drama we set up the staging
and shift the actors and the lighting to try to
uncover the mode of our time."*

It was a blind step towards the idea of a
furniture for the 1990s that would make a
room . . . an ensemble.

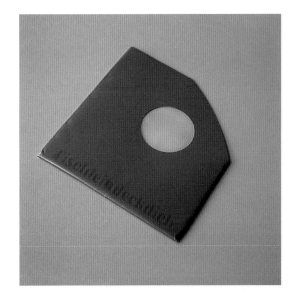

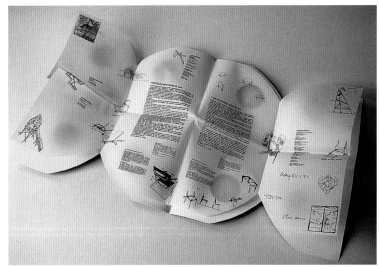

Catalogue for both exhibitions, folded and unfolded.

Tecta Yard Gates, Lauenförde

Axel Bruchhäuser of Tecta is a collector of fragments of metal construction from the French metalworker Jean Prouvé.

In 1992 AS wrote, concerning this gate between the Tecta factory and the adjacent factory to the north, to make clear that what lay beyond was not public territory:

"The gate is perforated . . .

. . . because if wild animals are used to coming through this gap, I do not like to stop them,

. . . the gates must be of the country, not the town; be an indication, not a barrier.

The ring hinges on the posts are the generating idea. The principle of the gate posts is of a core post of steel tube within an outer steel tube that is sliced up according to its allocated function."

Detail of post with Prouvé-inspired side screen. AS, May 1992.

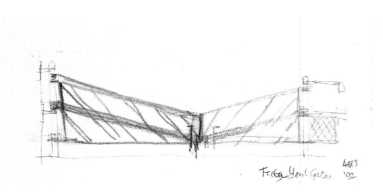

Sketch. AS, 1992.

Two views of Prouvé gate.

Porter House, Rousset-les-Vignes, Drôme

This house is part of an ancient fortified village.

The thick-walled and stone-vaulted 'caves' (cellars) are opened up to the garden with the intention of making a summer kitchen and summer dining room.

The upper levels of the house retain the existing kitchen and dining/living room as winter accommodation.

At a later stage it is intended to add a winter living room, similarly opened up to the garden to admit low winter sun, for there is a channel of space within the village and in the landscape beyond that allows the winter sun at low angles to reach the house.

far left: Rousset-les-Vignes postcard.
left: Axonometric from south-east, material version. Nuria Garcia de Duénas Geli, LW, 1995–96.

far left: Photograph from rue Basse. PS, May 1993.
second from left: Underside of 'caves'; vaults consolidated.
left: Stair down to 'caves' level from upper level.

Attributions

Every image—diagram, drawing, photograph—is dated and attributed to the person who was responsible for that image, not for its evolution.

The attributions are not absolutely complete.

AS, PS, A+PS indicate responsibility for the evolution and for the image.

In the case of drawings, this gives some clue to the persons who worked on the project: necessary as no job-workers list has been kept.

These persons, in any case, are very few.

Many drawings are attributed to Lorenzo Wong, designated as LW throughout this volume. His name is an assumed compound from a childhood in Cuba when the other children gave him the commonest of Spanish names. The name has become himself . . . an architect, a delineator of magical skill.

Follow-up drawings, to explain better or further evolve an unbuilt project, can sometimes be dated forty years after the project's initiation.

—PS, 2000

Index

Acropolis Place *(1990)*, 576

Adalbergstrasse *(1975)*, 392

Agitation of Surface, Siena *(1985)*, 550

Alderbury, House Extension *(1953)*, 102

Amenity Building, University of Bath
  (1978–80, 1984–85), 438

Anil Avenue Commercial Offices, Khartoum
  (1976–77), 402

Animal House, University of Bath *(1981)*, 544

Appliance Houses *(1956–58)*, 190
  Bread House *(1956)*, 193
  Cubicle House or Cupboard House
    (1956–57), 193
  Portico Row and the 'Wareite' or White
    'Formica' House *(1957)*, 194
  Provençal House *(1957)*, 196
  Snowball House *(1956)*, 192
  Strip House, the *(1957–58)*, 195

Area di Pré, Genova *(1981)*, 545

Arts Barn, University of Bath *(1980–81, 1990)*, 476

Axel's Porch *(1986)*, 552

Bark Place Mews *(1954–56)*, 146

Bates' Burrows Lea Farm *(1953–55)*, 124

Bates' Burrows Lea Farm *(1953–55)*, Isolate
  project for 'Housing Appropriate to the
  Valley Section' *(1954–56)*, 131

Bath, University of
  Amenity Building *(1978–80, 1984–85)*, 438
  Animal House *(1981)*, 544
  Arts Barn *(1980–81, 1990)*, 476
  School of Architecture and Building
    Engineering, Building 6 East
    (1982–88), 518
  Porch to University Hall *(1983)*, 547
  Second Arts Building *(1979–81)*, 456

Bath as a Fringed Mat *(1983)*, 548

Battlebridge Basin *(1972–74)*, 372

Bayswater, Wayland Young Pavilion
  (1959–82), 224

Berlin Hauptstadt *(1957)*, 200

Beverungen Roof *(1990)*, 588

Bibliotheca Alexandrina *(1989)*, 564

Brasilia, British Embassy *(1964–68)*, 328

Bread House *(1956)*, project for Appliance
  Houses *(1956–58)*, 193

British Embassy, Brasilia *(1964–68)*, 328

Brodia Road *(1990–95)*, 589

Building 6 East, School of Architecture and
  Building Engineering, University of Bath
  (1982–88), 518

Burleigh Lane Houses *(1965–66)*, 336

Caro House *(1954–91)*, 143

Chance Glass Flat and Mammoth Terrace
  House Conversion/Renewal *(1953–56)*, 140

Cheddar House of Cheese *(1955)*, 104

Cherry Garden Pier *(1972–76, 1983)*, 369

Christmas ⚹ Hogmanay *(1980–81)*, 471

Church Sort of Place, a, and Monument on
  the Goodwin Sands *(1955)*, 148

Churchill College *(1959)*, 230

Cliff House *(1959–61)*, 281

Close Houses *(1955)*, Town project for 'Housing
  Appropriate to the Valley Section'
  (1954–56), 136

Colleges' Gate, Colleges' Path, and Distance
  Stones, Urbino *(1979–83)*, 436

Colville Place *(1952)*, 96

Come Deck the Hall *(1981)*, 546

Communal Houses on Two Sites, Urban and
  Rural, Delft *(1982–83)*, 514

Cookies' Nook *(1977)*, 419

Cordell Studio House *(1957)*, 197

Coventry Cathedral *(1950–51)*, 68

Crematorium at Gosforth Park *(1947)*, 21

Crematorium at Kirkcaldy *(1954)*, 142

Crispin Hall *(1965–66)*, 338

Cubicle House or Cupboard House *(1956–57)*,
  project for Appliance Houses *(1956–58)*, 193

Cubitt Houses *(1977)*, 408

Cupboard House or Cubicle House *(1956–57)*,
  project for Appliance Houses *(1956–58)*, 193

Damascus Gate *(1979–81)*, 446

Delft, Communal Houses on Two Sites, Urban
  and Rural *(1982–83)*, 514

Deodar Road *(1991–99)*, 590

Der Berlinerbaum *(1980)*, 468

Distance Stones, Colleges' Gate, and Colleges'
  Path, Urbino *(1979–83)*, 436

Doha Hospital *(1953)*, 105

Economist Building, the *(1959–64)*, 248

English Climate House *(1957)*, 198

Exhibitions
  'Extensions of Man' *(1962)*, 326
  'Line of Trees . . . A Steel Structure, A'
    (1975, 1976), 386
  'Painting and Sculpture of a Decade,
    1954–1964' *(1963–64)*, 316
  'Parallel of Life and Art' *(1953)*, 118
  'Sticks and Stones' *(1976)*, 393
  'This Is Tomorrow', Patio and Pavilion
    (1956), 178
  'Twenty-Four Doors to Christmas' *(1979)*, 448

'Extensions of Man' Exhibition *(1962)*, 326

Festival of Britain, Vertical Feature and
  Restaurant *(1949)*, 33

Fitzwilliam Museum *(1948–49)*, 28

Fold Houses *(1954)*, Village project for
  'Housing Appropriate to the Valley
  Section' *(1954–56)*, 135

Folly . . . A 'Solar' Pavilion, Upper Lawn
  (1959–82), 238

Galleon Cottages *(1954)*, Hamlet project for
  'Housing Appropriate to the Valley
  Section' *(1954–56)*, 134

Garden Building, St. Hilda's College, Oxford
  (1967–70), 340

Genova, Area di Pré *(1981)*, 545

Gilston Road, South Kensington *(1971–)*, 368

Giza, Solar-Energy-Collecting Pyramid
  (1976), 396

Golden Lane *(1952)*, 86

Government Offices, Kuwait *(1970)*, 356

Hexenbesenraum *(1990–96)*, 584

Hexenhaus Holes *(1990)*, 573

Hong Kong, Second Polytechnic *(1982)*, 516

Hot Springs *(1955)*, 157

House Extension, Alderbury *(1953)*, 102

House of the Future *(1955–56)*, 162

House with Two Gantries, a *(1977)*, 420

'Housing Appropriate to the Valley Section',
  five projects for *(1954–56)*, 130
  City: Terraced Crescent Housing *(1955)*, 138
  Hamlet: Galleon Cottages *(1954)*, 134
  Isolate: Bates' Burrows Lea Farm
    (1953–55), 131
  Town: Close Houses *(1955)*, 136
  Village: Fold Houses *(1954)*, 135

Hunstanton Secondary Modern School
  (1949–54), 40

Iraqi House *(1960–61)*, 284

Janus, Siena *(1987)*, 563

Kampala, Offices for the Electricity Board
  (1952–53), 98

Kelvingrove Art Gallery and Museum
  Approach, project for Landscape into Art
  (1977), 417

Khartoum, Anil Avenue Commercial Offices
  (1976–77), 402

Kingsbury Lookouts, project for Landscape
  into Art *(1977)*, 412

Kuwait, Government Offices *(1970)*, 356

Landscape into Art, six projects for *(1977)*, 410
    Kelvingrove Art Gallery and Museum
        Approach, 417
    Kingsbury Lookouts, 412
    Skateboard Junction, 416
    Slaggie Eleven of the Spenymoor Slag
        Heaps, the, 415
    Swinging Elland, 411
    Tees Pudding, 414
Landwehrkanal *(1976)*, 397
Langside College of Further Education
    (1958), 212
Leafy Arbours over the Verbindungskanal
    (1977), 418
Limerston Street *(1953–61)*, 81
'Line of Trees . . . A Steel Structure, A'
    Exhibition *(1975, 1976)*, 386
Llangennith Cluster Housing *(1977)*, 409
Losey House *(1959–61)*, 280
Lucas Headquarters *(1973–74)*, 380
Lützowstrasse Apartments for the Elderly
    (1980), 490
Lützowstrasse Child-Care Centre *(1980)*, 492
Lützowstrasse Housing *(1980)*, 484
Lützowstrasse Youth Centre *(1980)*, 491

Magdalen College, Oxford *(1974)*, 388
Mammoth Terrace House Conversion/Renewal
    and Chance Glass Flat *(1953–56)*, 140
Married Graduate Flats and Squash Courts,
    Queen's College, Oxford *(1971)*, 367
Maryhill, Twenty-First-Century Tenement
    (1984), 536
Mehringplatz *(1962)*, 292
Melbourne's Magic Mountains *(1979–80)*, 444
Millbank, Riverside Apartments *(1976–77)*, 398
Monument on the Goodwin Sands and a
    Church Sort of Place *(1955)*, 148

National Gallery *(1982)*, 496
New Model House *(1971)*, 366
New West End to Worcester Cathedral and
    Walk in the Dry Passages *(1977–78)*, 432

Occupational Health Clinic *(1962–64)*, 314
Offices for the Electricity Board, Kampala
    (1952–53), 98
One-Thousand-Square-Foot House *(1952–53)*, 103
Oxford
    Garden Building, St. Hilda's College
        (1967–70), 340
    Magdalen College *(1974)*, 388
    Married Graduate Flats and Squash
        Courts, Queen's College *(1971)*, 367

Pahlavi National Library *(1977–78)*, 426
'Painting and Sculpture of a Decade,
    1954–1964' Exhibition *(1963–64)*, 316
Paolozzi Studio House *(1959)*, 216
'Parallel of Life and Art' Exhibition *(1953)*, 118
Parc de la Villette *(1982)*, 502
Patio and Pavilion, 'This Is Tomorrow'
    Exhibition *(1956)*, 178
Pierced Wall Structure *(1955)*, 149
Porch to University Hall, University of Bath
    (1983), 547
Porta Camollia, Siena *(1983)*, 517
Porter House *(1993–95)*, 595
Portico Row and the 'Wareite' or White
    'Formica' House *(1957)*, project for
    Appliance Houses *(1956–58)*, 194
Priory Walk *(1961–71)*, 289
Provençal House *(1957)*, project for Appliance
    Houses *(1956–58)*, 196

Rackève, Restoration of Territory *(1985)*, 551
Redington Road *(1960)*, 282
Restoration of Territory, Rackève *(1985)*, 551
Retirement House *(1959)*, 218
Riverbank Window *(1990)*, 572
Riverside Apartments, Millbank *(1976–77)*, 398
Robin Hood Gardens *(1966–72)*, 296
Royal Academy *(1949)*, 24
Rumble Villa *(1954)*, 144

School of Architecture and Building
    Engineering, Building 6 East,
    University of Bath *(1982–88)*, 518
Seafront Flats *(1960)*, 283
Second Arts Building, University of Bath
    (1979–81), 456
Second Polytechnic, Hong Kong *(1982)*, 516
Sheffield University *(1953)*, 108
Siena
    Agitation of Surface *(1985)*, 550
    Janus *(1987)*, 563
    Porta Camollia *(1983)*, 517
Skateboard Junction, project for Landscape
    into Art *(1977)*, 416
Slaggie Eleven of the Spenymoor Slag Heaps,
    project for Landscape into Art *(1977)*, 415
Snowball House *(1956)*, project for Appliance
    Houses *(1956–58)*, 192
Solar-Energy-Collecting Pyramid, Giza *(1976)*,
    396
'Solar' Pavilion, a, Folly, Upper Lawn
    (1959–82), 238
South Kensington, Gilston Road *(1971–)*, 368

Squash Courts and Married Graduate Flats,
    Queen's College, Oxford *(1971)*, 367
Steilshoop *(1961)*, 288
'Sticks and Stones' Exhibition *(1976)*, 393
Strip House, the *(1957–58)*, project for
    Appliance Houses *(1956–58)*, 195
Sugden House *(1955–56)*, 150
Swinging Elland, project for Landscape into
    Art *(1977)*, 411
Sydney Opera House *(1956)*, 188

Tecta, Toilet Tree, the *(1986–90)*, 560
Tecta Canteen Porch *(1990)*, 574
Tecta Paths *(1990)*, 571
Tecta Yard Gates *(1992)*, 594
Tees Pudding, project for Landscape into Art
    (1977), 414
Terraced Crescent Housing *(1955)*, City project
    for 'Housing Appropriate to the Valley
    Section' *(1954–56)*, 138
'This Is Tomorrow' Exhibition, Patio and
    Pavilion *(1956)*, 178
Tischleindeckdich *(1992–93)*, 592
Toilet Tree, the, Tecta *(1986–90)*, 560
Town Planning Studies *(1946–48)*, 20
Triangle Workshop *(1987)*, 562
Twenty-First-Century Tenement, Maryhill
    (1984), 536
'Twenty-Four Doors to Christmas' Exhibition
    (1979), 448

Upper Lawn, Folly . . . A 'Solar' Pavilion
    (1959–82), 238
Urbino, Colleges' Gate, Colleges' Path, and
    Distance Stones *(1979–83)*, 436

Vertical Feature and Restaurant, Festival of
    Britain *(1949)*, 33

Walk in the Dry Passages and New West End
    to Worcester Cathedral *(1977–78)*, 432
'Wareite' or White 'Formica' House and
    Portico Row *(1957)*, project for Appliance
    Houses *(1956–58)*, 194
Wayland Young Pavilion, Bayswater
    (1959–82), 224
Wedding in the City *(1968)*, 352
Wokingham Infants School *(1958)*, 206

Yellow House at an Intersection, the *(1976)*, 394

AS in the Wewerka Pavilion, Tecta, Lauenförde, Germany, September 1985. PS, September 1985.